MW01285234

AMERICAN GRIDLOCK:

The Legacy of Secular Governance

**Corporate and Evangelical Absolutism
vs.
Women, Labor, and Racial Justice**

Tom McGrath

Table of Contents

Table of Contents, continued

Our Founders' Intent

"Government is instituted for the Common Good, for the protection, safety, prosperity, and happiness of the people; and not for the profit, honor, or private interest of any one man, family, or class of men."

John Adams

From the Author:

Original church-state government was founded on the absolute authority of kings and bishops over all property and men as subjects, revealed as the will of God.

I understand secular civil government was founded on a philosophy of God's natural creation that left men free to self govern the relationship between property, citizens, religion, national defense, and the common good.

The following quotes inform us of our founders' intents for the generations to follow as beneficiaries. It is our duty to keep these goals sustainable!

Thomas Jefferson: On Informed Authority to Govern.

"I know no safe depository of the ultimate powers of society but the people themselves, and if we think them not enlightened enough to exercise their control with discretion, the remedy is not to take it from them, but to inform them by education."

James Madison: On Original Intent and a Christian Nation.

"The Compromise of a Committee has as many original intents as members."

"Government should never be in the position of sorting out what was true and what was heresy."

Alexander Hamilton: On Divided Government.

"Give all the power to the many, they will oppress the few. Give all the power to the few, they will oppress the many."

John Marshall: On Settled Law and Judicial Review.

"Every Right Deserves a Remedy."

Benjamin Franklin: On An Empire of Reason.

"A wise man will desire no more than what he may acquire justly, use soberly, distribute cheerfully, and live upon contentedly."

Introduction

The first organized State Church mechanisms of governance were introduced by the Romans in 325 AD. They included revelation of the will of God and approval of the founding documents: the Nicene Christian Bible and the Nicene Creed. The ever growing knowledge gained over the next thirteen hundred years disproved the coerced belief in the infallibility of the Roman bishop (Pope), and in the process disproved the revealed (will of God) doctrine known in English as the divine right of kings. The sun did not circle the earth at the center of the universe as the Roman bishops claimed; this error was fully proven to be false five hundred years ago on a three year expedition launched in 1519 by the explorer Magellan, the first successful expedition to circumnavigate the earth. This was just six years short of twelve hundred years after Nicaea to close the seventeen hundred year arc of time our nonfictional narration will review.

Since Magellan's Voyage of Discovery, learned men have believed the earth to be a naturally free, ever changing domain of man gifted by the God of creation. In response, men over the past five hundred years have adapted mechanisms of self rule among free men no longer living in constant fear of abuse and death in service to the few men falsely believed to be favored by God to rule over all other men, required by the will of God to live in fear.

The three absolute sources of political gridlock from twenty-first century America we will review are the continued belief from revelation of the absolute rights of property owners as the only beneficiaries of profit, the absolute belief in Christian revealed sin as the definer of secular criminal law, and the belief in absolutism as a right of those who support these two key revealed will of God demands rooted in the modern GOP ideology. The more obvious but less acknowledged factors will be reviewed as unresolved factors of nationalism including the long held hope and growing demand for justice among minority races, religions, and cultures.

The Romans very effectively precluded gridlock by adding a secular commandment I call, thou shall not commit heresy. Heresy was not a sin against God, punishable by loss of salvation; heresy was a crime against the state church teachings, punishable by death. Heresy as a punishable crime ended as a possible crime in America in 1791 with ratification of the establishment clause of the Bill of Rights. It began as a capital crime in Rome in 386, and ended in Spain as a death penalty crime in 1826, an example of what I call a political outcome that does more good than harm. I will use this standard to judge transitional leaders, their policies, and the overall outcomes of their policies of their eras, from Constantine to Reagan.

As a boy I said both the Nicene Creed and the Pledge of Allegiance at my Catholic School every day. It never once crossed my mind that duty to one demanded absolute belief based on revelation, and to the other a pledge of tolerance to different beliefs based on the knowable understanding of nature's God's creation, or how that has plays out in different nations depending on their established authority to govern, and culture based on their nations founding documents' stated intent.

Arguably as the first nation with a duty to tolerance greater than a duty to the absolutism of the king and/or the bishop's beliefs were the U.S. founding documents when finally, fully ratified and legislated in 1791. Revolutionary transitions in beliefs and culture die hard. In the U.S. two hundred and thirty years later our transition is still in full gridlock, in blow back to the meaning and loss of power and absolute rights for men of property and the pulpit.

Between early 1500 AD and early 1600 AD five transitions came together that forced educated European men to rethink governance of both the church, and the state. They include the use of the sextant and the explorers from Iberia proving the Roman church's Pope had revealed Gods creation in error. In the kingdoms that were to become Germany, a theologian supported by his greedy king successfully challenged the Pope's absolute authority which spawned the reformation. Germany contributed a second factor of transition during this century of change, the printing press was invented, and men could then afford to own a Bible and read it printed in their own language.

In England, the source of the governance system our colonies revolted against a little over two hundred years later, King Henry VIII had a great problem, and evangelical Protestantism began as a solution to his problem. Late in the century of change, in 1611 when the King James I Bible was printed in English, the king required his bishops to translate England's authority from Latin "by the will of God" to "by the divine right of kings". The Enlightenment had already begun on the Continent, the English Civil War and the English Enlightenment followed.

The new and factual knowledge of the cosmos as created led to the enlightenment on the continent, and helped pave the way for the reformation of the church, yet kings kept their bishops with a weakened heresy threat. The enlightenment led to a fuller understanding of God's natural world, and helped learned men understand the concept of natural rights, including self government by the consent of free men.

For English philosophers the laws of nature were as old as the Greeks Plato and Cicero; they would become a dilemma for England after their civil war. England ended the absolute monarchy but kept the Christian Bible's (English edition) idea of the Divine Right of Kings as England's authority to govern with the king or queen as head of government. The prime minister became head of government by delegation from the crowned king or queen who since the 1680s only serves as head of state. William Blackstone was author of the *English Common Law Commentaries*, the text book for the study of law at the College of William and Mary, where George Wythe the first professor of law in the Colonies taught Jefferson, Monroe, and John Marshall the Supreme Court Justice who established our principle of judicial review.

Blackstone settled England's post civil war hybrid authority to govern as a democracy at least among the nobility while retaining the revealed rights of property ownership (feudalism lived on for another 200 years), and a state church by keeping the king as head of state but not of government. Jefferson explained they rejected Blackstone's rationale as abusive to subjects (once they became citizens).

After the English civil war, parliament passed The Toleration Act in 1687 and gave a bit of freedom of religion to subjects, including some in the Massachusetts colony, but this was not a significant factor in our founding documents in the 1770s in my reading. The Reformation included translation of the Bible into English and led to increasing schisms. This Act relieved the tensions the English Bible debates created. Philosophy, theology, and discrete ideologies could finally be discussed openly without constant fear.

Thomas Jefferson penned the Declaration of Independence noting both the laws of nature and nature's God. Our founders relied on John Locke who came of age as a philosopher during the settlement of the reformation period in England. The Toleration Act established a role for reason in man-made secular law regarding liberty as well as religion, it allowed men freedom to seek salvation without a state church. Locke was a man of the enlightenment more than the reformation, and the father of what became individual rights for citizens based on observed intent of God, rather than revealed intent.

Jefferson's intent was to modify the abusive English system by eliminating the Nicene Christian Biblical concept of God that revealed God's will granting king and bishop absolute authority over all property and all men as subjects, by establishing our new nation's authority to govern by the consent of the governed.

In 1791 all former subjects in the colonies became citizens of the U.S. regardless of the state they lived in when the revolutionary process was complete. In England men of property had assured themselves continuation of absolute property rights, by establishing a mechanism whereby the king delegated his authority to the Parliament.

In the U.S. Jefferson did not fully forewarn in the Declaration an expectation for the property owners as for the subjects of what the change would mean. In the Constitutional Convention ending thirteen years after the Declaration, common law survived as well as the state church . Established justice for citizens was not addressed in the Constitution; ratification. was only accomplished subject to a Bill of Rights being added, addressing newly to be established rights of the citizens of the United States. The Bill of Rights was ratified and legislated in 1791, still without a defined means of settlement of dissent. Early in the nineteenth century the Marshall court settled the settlement mechanism to be judicial review.

Constitutional law was based on the enlightenment view of the God of nature, a view that acknowledged all men were born free in nature, which allowed for the freedom to self govern, for the common welfare (good), and to establish justice, a new system still in dispute among some factions of the original founding states after ratification of the Bill of Rights, continuing after the Civil War, and continues still today in the modern GOP.

This common law versus the 1791 view where the "this for that" was assured justice from abuse by states and state entities has been as absolutist as the Roman Christian Bible's view of the God of revelation. U.S. secular governance eliminated heresy and the fear thereby of a death sentence, but we do not yet have a sufficient understanding of mutual best self interest among a large enough majority required to govern a democratic republic, i.e., tolerance and compromise.

I will make the case that ideology is the culprit, because common law understanding of authority to govern claimed as States Rights in the south left the rights of property owners, and the establishment of a state church in place after our founding. , and damned be the Constitution.,

This has been used to fight accommodating the intent of the Constitution once the Bill of Rights was ratified, legislated, and found Constitutional by judicial review. Every Supreme Court ruling against a citizen's right versus a corporation has been based on this form of abuse of citizens in America, especially women and blacks.

Our Constitution established that federal laws were to be enacted regarding secular issues with two key goals of the Constitution's Preamble, defined by John Adams as noted in this book's first presidential quote. The first is the general welfare (common good is the term Adams used as will I in the rest of this book), and I include my insight for the second, which is establish justice, among the other Preamble goals. Remember, federal law is superior to state law regarding citizens rights, no one has a passport issued by the state they live in.

In the twenty-first century evangelical pastors and property owner advocates have created a political ideology called economic freedom, reintroducing revelation as a Constitutional tenet in the modern GOP as a founding principle. They cite Blackstone's concept that granted absolute authority based on revelation to the king, and delegated Parliament (in Blackstone's time before our Declaration) to apply it to their unitary president. Justice Anton Scalia, Attorney General William Barr, and Secretary of State Mike Pompeo are leading advocates for the return to this pre Bill of Rights belief system for America in the twenty-first century. That is the core of our twenty-first century gridlock in the Trump era. President Trump allowed his aide Steven Miller to claim he was not to be questioned, ever, in defense of President Trump's first executive order, called the Muslim Travel Ban.

In refusing to allow witnesses to testify in President Trump's impeachment, Mitch McConnell upheld Trump's contempt of Congress. The GOP Senate enabled a presidential end to oversight without a Constitutional Amendment as this book went to print. This year 2020 is a showdown year in American history regarding the rights of the few and the many.

The new understandings based on reason led to first the English civil war, and finally to the American Revolution. Authority to govern in England led to the nobles inflicting what came to be known as the "intolerable acts" in the name of the king on English subjects in the American colonies, locally led by well educated men who at the time enjoyed a limited form of home rule but no representation in the English Parliament that assessed taxes and set all trade conditions.

In response our founders revolted and created our founding documents, the Declaration of Independence, the U.S. Constitution, and the Bill of Rights. These documents led to the separation of civil (secular) government from personal beliefs based on religion, and salvation, based on our new authority to govern. The new authority was known as "by the consent of the governed". Based on our founding as a nation under the knowledge defined in these documents, the American mechanisms of governance we live under were finally fully ratified by the citizens of the United States of America in 1791. Note worthy is that they were ratified by citizens and not by the states. In America, passports are issued only by the

U.S. government, and only to U.S. citizens, regardless of their state of residence.

The balance of the book will lead to three more or less seventy-five year eras in review of American government outcomes, beginning with our founding through the Civil War era including sorting out two different labor and economic systems, followed by the next seventy-five years after the north defeated the south and reunited the union if not the value systems of the two regions, in the middle era of industrialization, segregation, boom and bust speculative capitalism, early regulation of business and banking, the economy, ending with the great depression of 1929.

The third and final seventy-five year era is the current one that covers the last two chapters I call the FDR New Deal era, followed by the Ronald Reagan "Starve the Beast" era, bringing us into the Trump presidency in 2020. We will review throughout this 1705 year history the outcomes of the great changes in theology, ideology, philosophy, and policies of our most prominent change agents: emperors, kings, prime ministers, bishops and presidents.

I judge the authority to govern, government founding documents, government leadership, governing ideologies, and enacted political policies simply on outcomes.

At each transition in history did founding document mechanisms and presidential policies do more good than harm in the next era than the one they overturned, or transitioned to, irrespective of the source of the new insights, revelation, reformation, revolt, constitution, or even routine election?

The ten eras we will explore in this book start with the first organized government in history that survived into modern times, and the longest lasting religious belief system so far: the Romans' combination of a state church (Biblical Christianity) and head of state king crowned by the bishop of the state church, instituted to govern an empire of kingdoms based on the economic concept of feudalism.

The state church of Rome established the Roman Republic's authority to govern their Empire. The Roman Pope (bishop of Rome), believed to be infallible, revealed the Roman empire's authority to govern would be by the will of God. It was revealed God granted kings absolute property rights, with an absolute right to subordinate subjects bound to serve the king on his land they were born on; to question God's will was both heresy and treason and meant death by the authority of the king or the bishop depending on the nature of the offense.

I divide eras by each new transitional leadership as they arose from time to time. A new authority or new understanding of continuing authority occurred when a transitional leader assumed power and proceeded to change the major theology, ideology, philosophy, or policies of a nation and thereby, the outcomes for subjects before 1791, and citizens thereafter, for better or worse.

The following is my understanding of the difference between these three belief systems. Philosophy is concerned with reasoned analysis and science including the reasoned belief in the God of nature mentioned in the U.S. Declaration of Independence. It tends to be less absolutist than theology or ideology. Theology is what men believe has been revealed as God's will to key founders of a religious creed such as the "divine right of kings" we revolted against. Ideology is a secular system of shared absolute beliefs among a group regarding the best theories and policies to meet the best outcome for their group regarding economics and governance.

There are three problems with ideology as practiced. First, the possible outcomes are often not reviewed in advance of implementation. Second, effects are not reviewed as they occur, and finally, unanticipated consequences are often ignored in what amounts to a denial process; blame is shifted using spin to cover up intentional blindness regarding negative outcomes. Remember, good is skewed for their group's best interest, not the common good, nor the established justice also defined in the Preamble to the Constitution of the nation.

The longest governance era by far in this book affecting the future United States was the Roman church state era, lasting some fourteen hundred years without successful revolt until the English civil war, but never overturned until our founding. This in spite of military defeat of the republic and the empire and reformation of the church, along with internal reform of the various kingdoms of the original empire. The empire was defeated but the church state and feudal system survived as the key mechanism of governance.

The Roman church state, both Catholic and protestant remained after the reformation, based on Biblical Christianity established at Nicaea, and remained the longest authority to govern anywhere in the world. The Roman system is still nominally in place seventeen hundred years later in our mother country England, although modified by parliament, democracy, and capitalism as key new mechanisms that over time allowed a transition of Englishmen as subjects of the crown to also become citizens of the nation, based on English Common Law that remained our founding state law after 1791.

As I'm not a lawyer I will not try to fully define the difference between constitutional law, statute law, and common law. Suffice it to say until 1789 all of the colonies operated under English Common Law, which I understand to be defined by judges. In 1789 America was founded with each colony becoming a state that retained common law statutes as the law of the state, and federal law became a hybrid with two levels of statute courts, state and federal. Subjects of England became citizens of the United States without defined rights.

In 1791 with ratification of the Bill of Rights the citizens of states were granted federal rights the states were prohibited from violating, or entities the states created under state law. The citizens ratified the Bill of Rights, and the U.S. Government enacted the Bill of Rights into federal law. The Supreme Court went on to adjudicate these statutes. The southern states have never accepted these outcomes, and have fought various realities of this bifurcation of jurisdiction, as the key gridlock of the American experience. This fact will inform almost every dissent we review in this book.

The history of the United States of America and its authority to govern by the consent of the governed with freedom of religion will be reviewed as five major eras. Key transitions include establishment of political parties, the Federalists versus the Democratic-Republicans, followed by post Civil War industrialization, Teddy Roosevelt's progressive GOP eras followed by the Woodrow Wilson progressive

Democratic era, and last two eras make up Chapters 9 and 10, about half of the total book and are paired in contrast. In 2020 our nation is in its two hundred thirty-first year; however, the combined FDR and Reagan eras take up only eighty-seven years, covering more than half of the book, and define the lifetime of nearly everyone alive today in America.

I will make the argument the belief systems in the first half of the book covering just over sixteen hundred years impact nearly every factor of the gridlock we all live with daily in our personal, family, and economic lives, and we are well served to understand how true this is.

The tenth and final chapter begins with the Ronald Reagan presidency beginning in 1981, an era that is all but ensured to last at least until either 2021 or 2025 to the end of the Trump presidency.

The United States practiced compromise and unanimous consent in the first two years from 1789-1791. Gridlock erupted in 1791 with ratification of the Bill of Rights, and the institution of a strong central government with the power to tax, create money, and own a national bank with a mint, with the authority to issue bonds and create debt in an economic system that came to be known as capitalism.

All of my comments in this book about what was the founding bargain relative to authority to govern and ratification of the Bill of Rights, including dual citizenship issues regarding state and nation, personal freedom and rights including liberty and justice, will be considered as later interpretations of the founding intent of the winning side in the partisan battles decided in 1791 and again in 1865 after the Civil War.

A second major factor of gridlock related to nullification, and/or states' rights relative to property rights, and concerned control of labor costs and taxes at a time when slaves were not citizens except as a representation compromise. They were in fact human property, functioning as a labor system, without dignity, rights, or hope.

The third major factor of gridlock concerned regulation of speculative capitalization, banking, and debt, beginning with the creation and growth of industrial wealth which put new demands on both labor and government; neither had a defined right to share in the new wealth, at or near equal to the value they added in the creation of wealth. Speculative capitalism means government did not regulate banking or investment opportunity, too often leading to boom and bust opportunism.

Our current twenty-first century gridlock is between the ideology of the GOP, and the secular policies of the Democratic Party that I see Constitutionally differentiated as follows. The Preamble clearly states three great goals for the federal government: the mutual defense of the nation, the common welfare (good) of the citizens, and to establish justice. The modern Democratic Party fully supports all three goals. The modern GOP fully supports the defense of the nation but it does not fully support the common good or concern itself with established justice, other than support of the common good of property owners and contracts as a national goal; that is the limit of their support of the common good or established justice.

The modern GOP sees no role for the federal government regarding the common good or established justice for citizens, in spite of the authority to govern bargain that assured ratification of the Constitution by adding a Bill of Rights which included ten defined rights as numbered amendments and made the Constitution amendable going forward as a living document..

I have sixteen policy suggestions after Chapter 10 which I believe will lead to better outcomes in the twenty-first century, subject to the final choices of the next generation as the competing models that carried over into the twenty-first century are replaced, amended, or scrapped, hopefully in favor of more good outcomes for more citizens.

Among my hopes for this book is that readers will have an understanding of how the founding of Biblical Christianity still impacts our present era of secular governance in gridlock. I also hope readers will better understand the trade-offs and compromises that were made to reach agreement on a settled U.S. Constitution that changed the Romans' revealed authority for kings to rule absolutely, based on a belief the bishops knew as God's will under a mechanism called revelation. These compromises are in conflict to this day.

Fortunately, the founders also gave us an amendment clause in the Bill of Rights, ending absolutes, a key factor of the old system. I'll make the case that absolutism has been reintroduced into our system as a mechanism of governance since the election of Ronald Reagan.

In some ways it might be easier to research the dates, names, battlefields, outcomes and simply report these facts as history. It is more complicated when adding the sociology, theology, philosophies, and policies in play. We need to better understand the outcome of changes in economic governance authority, defined in founding documents from the emerging eras of governance systems: the Roman, the English we revolted against, and our own.

I hope this work of plain talk narration of historical non-fiction legacies impacting each of these human issues over the centuries is helpful to readers' understanding of the long cultural, economic, religious, and political history of organized government, regarding their own understanding of what they have been taught versus what they understand for themselves about our government and politics as they have lived life as American citizens among our some five generations still alive today, early in the twenty-first century.

This is a full telling of American political reality that I'm attempting to make both interesting and understandable for general readers who find our governance history interesting as well as confusing. I'm not a historian and this is not a text book, history book, nor religious book; to me it is just a book hoping to promote reflection and positive action towards ending our vexing gridlock for voters wishing to be informed, with improved acceptance of mutual tolerance and compromise. Realizing that whatever you or I believe, almost every political bias among our more than three hundred million souls is held by tens or even hundreds of millions of fellow voters on every issue. Absolute agreement is and always will be impossible.

This is a political story of our recent history, as impacted by European colonialism in development of modern American's mix culture. As the result of near lifelong nonfiction reading and thinking about outcomes, I have gathered our founding stories, and have applied what I hope are rational insights and boundaries of the layers of legacies that underlie each. I am attempting to shed light on conflicting reactions of individuals to evolving norms regarding rules of law, as well as outcomes of the interplay of religion, politics, economics, and human nature. My only qualification I believe is a native born analytic ability to make sense of what is really going on. I include my email address at the end of the book, I invite both corrections of misstated facts and interesting insights of readers, to become part of a future web sight if the book becomes widely read, in the mean time I'll respond and leave insightful responses posted.

All of us are trying to understand how we became so conflicted since 1776, and how to get our arms around the past thirty-five or forty years of the current era that cover the lives of the generation about to take over America's future, building off of what we have brought forth both good and bad as America's secular legacy as of 2020.

Thank you for reading this book, a review of our transitional decisions based on the outcomes.

Part I

Introduction to Authority to Govern
"By the Will of God"

Chapter 1 - Rome

The fourth century Biblical revealed knowledge of the Roman church was accepted by Caesar to be infallible. To question this was heresy and treason, the punishment was death; gridlock-free belief was the outcome. The first principle of governance was that this belief was God's will. The rule of the few over the many was absolute.

The Romans' Nicene Christian Bible was the founding document of the Roman Republic's state church. Kings across the Roman Empire ruled per revelation by the will of God once crowned by a bishop of the Roman church. This rule assured absolute control of all property and every subject of each kingdom. This system would survive without challenge in Europe except for the kingdoms of what are now Spain and Portugal (occupied by the Moors for seven hundred years) until the reformation. There would be some reform but the Roman church and its Bible as translated into the local language would survive and is still the founding document of the belief system (Christianity) with the most members in the world.

The king also ruled over the agricultural subsistence labor economy, a manor house system eventually called feudalism. This was an organized system of governance that proved nearly perfect for an empire to rule its kingdoms, without the cost of the former legionaries as an embedded army.

By 285 AD the Roman Empire had grown so large it was no longer reasonable to govern it from Rome, or under the norms of barbarism, i.e., attack and plunder. Emperor Diocletian divided the Empire into halves and suggested it was time for the Roman Republic to become an organized government.

The Eastern Empire was governed from Byzantium, later Constantinople, now called Istanbul. The Western Empire was governed from Rome. Each half was ruled by six Caesars. By 290 AD Diocletia believed it was time to replace myth with organized religion as a department of organized government. Emperor Constantine was on Diocletian's staff; he climbed his way up the ladder, and in 312 AD there were only two Caesars left vying to be the next emperor of all. This would be settled at the Battle of the Milvian Bridge.

Both halves of the Roman Empire worshiped pagan gods at the time. Constantine's mother was a Christian, so he was familiar with her religion. According to his story, the night before battle he heard a voice telling him to replace the symbol of his patron god Sol Invictus with a cross. If he did this he would triumph; he complied, won the battle and became emperor.

Our story begins thirty-five years later, as Constantine fulfills Diocletian's vision at Nicaea in what is now modern Turkey.
Constantine eventually settled in the east in Constantinople. He made Christianity legal throughout the empire. There were differences within branches of Christianity even at the time of its founding, just as there were at the founding of our United States. The Roman church split between east and west; the states of the United States split between north and south culturally, politically, and economically.

One of the biggest belief differences in the time of Constantine was the nature of Jesus relative to God the Father known as the Arius heresy, and what the west called the Holy Spirit (or Holy Ghost in some translations). The Roman branch believes in all three, which they call the Trinity; the Orthodox or Eastern branch does not believe in Savior to God the Father. The Nicene Creed came from this first of seven councils that established the original doctrine's cannon law of the Roman church.

Constantine called the council, inviting all eighteen hundred bishops from across the empire. Three hundred more or less attended, the most important legates of then Pope Sylvester I. It is believed the council was presided over by Hosius of Cordoba in what is modern Spain. A few details were cleared up such as settling the Easter question, and as noted below the split between east and west relating to the relationship of God the Father to the Son.

Of note, the founding apostles had not settled on an organized system of governance for the early Christian church. Constantine offered as an inducement to the bishops the same authority over the sacred interest of the Roman Republic and Empire in what were to be called dioceses, as Roman governors exercised over organized secular government for the Republic and the Empire. They also were given a meaningful annual income, which Pope Sylvester I accepted by agreeing to send his bishops.

Constantine established both the sacred and secular authority to govern the Roman Republic and Empire to be declared by the Pope based on revelation as by the will of God. In 380 the Roman Church became a department of Rome by Emperor Theodosius. For a more informed overview of this period of Roman and Church history I recommend the writings of Will Durant.

Europe had long had strong men controlling large agricultural manor houses, but the raiding, warring, plunder, pillage, killing, raping, and enslaving that terrorized the villages and work sites of the peasants who worked the land had remained barbaric for centuries. Constantine did not lessen the coercion or workload nor improve the living conditions of the peasants. He did lessen the cost of controlling them, as well as their masters and kings. Legionaries were costly, as were idle fields due to peasants being killed at the hands of the legionnaires.

Constantine did not invent the idea of masters and vassals, as kings and peasants were known. He did set up a total governance system including an authority source (the revealed will of God) that survived beyond the Roman Empire. In the Roman system feudalism became a self funding labor and military system, and the leaders were established as a noble class of manor house place holders operating in the name of the king as lords and masters.

I have never read a good biography per se explaining how Constantine conceived the final norms of the Roman feudal system, a method used to govern so many diverse nations with an economic system that sustained itself without major disruption from about 325

AD until 1791. We can only speculate about the insights that led him to his conclusions.

This system, based on the Bible as the source document for the absolute rights of kings and the absolute duties of subjects to serve with their only reward promised after death, survived even as the Roman Empire fell a little more than a century later in 476 AD to an obscure little remembered Germanic warrior king named Odoacer in what are called the Goth Wars. The last Emperor of the Empire was named Romulus Augustus. The Roman Republic and the empire ended; Constantine's church state system survived.

What we do know is that in the year 325 AD, Constantine called for a council of bishops who followed the teachings of Jesus from across the empire to meet at Nicaea (now Iznik in western Turkey). Constantine ordered this council to create the first fifty Bibles.

The Roman Catholic Church and all European Christian Protestant Churches that have survived into our American twenty-first century have their roots in what we will refer to in this book as Biblical Christianity. I will expose my bias throughout this book in favor of consent government, including both English Common Law property rights, and justice for citizens as an individual right deserving of a remedy when violated, in compromise, versus absolute political war without compromise or tolerance, and locked as American is in gridlock.

There is never gridlock in revelation based governments; however due to absolute authority to abuse as a means of conformance, without elections or a legal right to appeal, the outcome is always an absence of freedom and justice. The supreme leader can be a secular or a religious autocrat, or most often a leader with control of the army, the economy, and the treasury. Even the military dictator keeps his nation's bishop or imam as examples of a religious man who speaks for God in control of the many, fearing for salvation after death.

The supporting nobles and churchmen lived in luxury such as it was at the time, and the laborers who became the soldiers in times of war lived at a subsistence level. All of the wealth of the nation was at the disposal of the king.

In a democratic republic the roles remain, but the incumbents, the limits on coercion, and assured freedoms with a means of appeal for justice are defined and enforced to maintain a consent to govern bargain; those who govern must face periodic elections. However, the role of the religious leader ends regarding governance; his role pertains only to salvation for those who choose to belong, and his civil role is replaced by a supreme legal system of settlement of what the civil law means as long as the law is respected as just by both the few and the many.

The bishops also had a sacred duty regarding salvation that included police power to guard against heresy. That side of their jurisdiction is only part of our story until our founding. In modern secular (not related to religion) civil states such as America and most European nations, police powers have been relegated to the state court system, and secular government does not adjudicate heresy, as freedom of religion is a basic principle. In societies of free men there is no such crime as heresy, so no more burning at the stake, or drawing and quartering for a heretical idea about religion or what is or is not pleasing to God or hurtful to Jesus.

Constantine had one other major effect on the governance of Europe that lasted into our founding era. In the years of war before Constantine gained full control of the empire, turmoil caused people to become displaced. Many fled when their home territory was disrupted by war. This often resulted in inadequate grain production because the farmers left their fields as noted above. The Empire depended on this grain to feed those under its jurisdiction. Bringing a stable food supply to the Empire assured sustainability. Constantine tied peasants to the land by heredity, if I understand how historians have parsed Constantine's decisions. Peasants were no longer allowed to flee from where they lived. This became the key enforcement basis of the feudal system as it spread to all kingdoms of the Empire.

The bishop was the moral authority for the salvation of all, and the enforcer of the king's rules as law. It was an almost perfect system as long as most people were uneducated, lived in mortal fear of the king for their life, and in spiritual fear for their soul under the bishop. In the centuries before our founding, kings beheaded and bishops burned subjects at the stake for treason or heresy even if only verbal.

In England and its colonies the state church's role in government as translated was by the divine right of kings and lasted into the American Revolution when our founders formed a new nation based on a new set of source documents: the Declaration of Independence, the U.S. Constitution, and the Bill of Rights.

In the newly formed United States, the authority for the right to govern became "We the People" defined as "by the consent of the governed". As noted this ended any official duties of the bishop in governing, while retaining his right to lead folks on the path to salvation as he taught whatever religion he led.

Individuals had the right to choose religion or not. State funding of the clerics' salary also ended, although the church did later gain exemption from taxes on church properties. No test of religion remained to be eligible to hold civil office in the United States.

Remnants of this governance system, i.e., a crowned king as head of state and a bishop as head of a state church performing the coronation, remains in England our mother country and other countries to this day, in an all but ceremonial role only, but still officially head of state. The right to govern resides in an elected parliament, and the people indirectly elect a prime minister as head of government. Each citizen votes for their political party representative from their district, and the leader of the winning party with the most elected members is asked by the queen or king to form a coalition government to create a majority block, as most often the winning party does not have a fifty-one percent majority; this leader of the coalition then becomes the prime minister.

The former state church of Rome, today's Roman Catholic church and its many reformed protestant successors, are all based on the Biblical form of Christianity Constantine imposed on the Roman Empire in 325 AD. It has two billion adherents in the twenty-first century, some sixteen hundred years after the end of the Empire in the fifth century.

As a note of clarification, this book only refers to the Bible in regard to its civil (state church) role in the Roman feudal system of government during and following the era of Constantine. Nothing in this book is intended by the author to deal with or question the life, purpose, or teachings of Jesus, including salvation (my understanding of the primary purpose of Jesus' time on earth).

The Old Testament (the Jewish Tanakh) was made a part of the Roman Nicene Bible. In my study the Jews established monotheism (one God), revelation, a book of the laws, and established the leader as a dynastic king. All of this worked as a basis for establishing Constantine's new system.

I believe most Christian secular folks, those who are practicing Christians but only apply their religious beliefs to their own salvation concerns, would not insist the Constitution agree with the Bible regarding what is a sin for non Christians. Going back to John Kennedy's answer to Baptist leaders in 1960, Kennedy advised he would resign the presidency if he found a teaching of his pope would cause him to have to chose. In modern America, at a minimum I believe most Christians would agree that feudal abuse enforced in support of agricultural necessity has never seemed to have been God's intent in sending his son Jesus to die on the cross.

It was Constantine's intent to subjugate laborers politically and economically to a life of subsistence duty (a form of slavery); neither freedom nor justice was ever a concern of the Roman system of civil, economic, or religious governance. The Christian kings and Russian czars never once, between the publication of the first Bibles until our Declaration of Independence, ever saw or attempted any reform of the abuse of peasants across Europe or around the world in any nations of their empires. Greed, abuse, and self interest were taught to princes in their youth, and to a man they believed and demanded the only entity they owed any oversight rights to was God in judgment after death. They and their subjects both believed this absolutely.

Modern birth control is considered a modern sin by some American evangelicals and is so taught by the Roman Catholic Church. However, it is a right of all American women to chose for themselves, as modern birth control has only been medically possible since the

1960s. For an evangelical or Catholic to demand that it is a sin and that it should not be legal for any American of any faith or of no faith was resolved in 1791. No office holder or judge sworn to uphold the Constitution should be tolerated if they do not agree with John Kennedy's view noted above. It is not for government to chose among heresies as Madison stated, or for pastors to call for nullification of the Constitution or the judicial review system of judicial settlement in America. Yet this is a factor of gridlock today in America which will be part of our contrast of GOP ideology and Democratic Policy making.

From the fifth chapter on, our story will focus on the more than three hundred million Americans who enjoy what are acknowledged today to be natural individual human rights intended by the God of creation, which are guarantied by a secular state that includes constitutional freedom of religion as a civil right understood by our founders when they formed a constitutional government under God, as explained in Chapter 4, titled the Enlightenment.

Secular rights versus sacred duty has been confusing for many Americans including my father regarding my upbringing. Individual rights only became understood as a norm for all Americans beyond freedom from abuse in the twentieth century, when the concept of latent Constitutional rights were defined as settled by our Supreme Court.

I hope it is understandable that we need to compare the changes in governance that have taken place over the many eras covered in this book to understand how we got to where we are today. Too many legacies of Constantine's capture of Christianity and feudalism co-opted the message of Jesus and the agricultural system his legionaries ravaged, into a method to coerce subjects as labor and military slaves in service to the few, as they are still in GOP ideology concerning absolute property rights.

In the end we will compare legacies from each era that have informed and have made the norms of each ensuing era more complex for those who rely on reason as a guide for their lives as well as for those who rely on faith, and like my dad, those who believe they are fully committed to both secular patriotism, and sacred duty to God. It is this third of our nation that seem to find tolerance and compromise the most difficult to reconcile with natural greed and sacred duty.

The Roman system physically punished subjects for violating any of the king's laws. Subjects were also punished for any violation of what the bishops referred to as sin. On the other hand, America created a secular Constitution, including the Bill of Rights, without input from any clergy of any religion regarding the concept of sin against God.

In America, the government can only prosecute a citizen for violation of a civil law. Sin is a theological belief only, and is only punishable by God, affecting one's personal salvation. The only authority the bishop or pastor retained is to excommunicate unrepentant sinners from their defined religion. The church's corporal power to punish ended.

This is one of the two most significant parts of the gridlock problem among those who find these legacies of the concept of sin such as birth control for some Christians, who as citizens have a secular right to practice birth control. The second great factor of gridlock is the church state view of God's will being absolute regarding property rights over subjects in their role as wage laborers, a view still held under the ideology of the modern GOP as if laborers were still subjects and not citizens. The secular Democratic Party view of labor rights relates to the right of laboring citizens to associate and negotiate for their value added portion of modern wealth creation.

When we review the Hobby Lobby case in depth readers will likely be surprised by how many citizen's rights were in conflict. Politicians deal with changes in society, such as when new medical, scientific, and financial products and procedures become commercial; large minority negative cultural beliefs often in place remain personal norms for much longer after the new option becomes a majority societal choice.

Judicial review by our constitutionally secular Supreme Court in the past century has often found faith-based sin to be a legally protected individual activity. This means that people who don't believe an activity is a sin have a legal right to engage in that activity without abuse, as long as it does not harm any other citizens' constitutional rights. As of 2020 a majority of Evangelical leaders have refused to tolerate this American legal right of U.S. citizens, even claiming is a war on Christianity.

From the prehistoric era to the time when people consistently progressed beyond being nomadic hunter-gatherers, warfare meant the winners could keep no prisoners. Almost all captured opponents were killed. This was a fact of warfare at least until the rise in growth of agriculture. The rise of agriculture meant a new dependence on cheap labor, leading most societies to change from the slaughter of prisoners as the norm, to an acceptance of keeping prisoners as slaves as a practical labor source. Over time, slavery became the new norm, which Constantine kept as an optional labor practice.

For post Roman Empire Europe, slavery was not a major factor of life until the colonial period, when manning the large plantations in the colonies required masses of cheap slave labor. Africa became the source. In Africa, the strongest tribes did not need the number of slaves they could acquire in combat, but they always needed money. Thus began the exchange of defeated enemies for money and trade goods. This became the reason for constant warring, and the labor manning system of choice for the sailing nations that owned colonies for some plus three hundred years, starting in the fifteenth century. As slavery became profitable, African slaves became an export commodity; at least eleven million were exported to South America and at least four million to North America.

In addition to serfs and slaves, certain skills were practiced and appreciated by the king, nobles, church men, and armies, such as tanning, stone masonry, and blacksmithing, especially regarding armament. These trade folks worked for wages, were not tied to the land, and formed into groups called guilds.

Guilds were associations of craftsmen or merchants who oversaw the practice of their craft in a particular town or region. Most of Europe's rulers adopted Constantine's systems and operated under the norms from the early Roman Church State system of practices until our revolution fourteen hundred years later. It is not a meaningful factor in the early days of our tale except to begin to spell out the evolution of wage labor issues in conflict yet today.

Let's get back to earlier times before we move on to the Dark Ages. After Constantine, the western half of the empire ruled all of Europe that bordered the Mediterranean Sea, as far west as Britain, for only another hundred years or so. We will discuss the demise of the Roman Empire, even as Constantine's system survived those who conquered Rome, in Chapter 2.

I will occasionally use the story of the Middle East and its eighth century conversion to Islam in the southern half of its Arab territories in contrast to what happened in Europe. A new eastern empire arose that became Muslim, the religion of the captured peoples from the Arab territories of the Byzantine Empire. Europe and the Middle East both evolved from the Roman Empire, with similar economic governance, including serfs in Russia, and the Fellaheen in the Arab lands.

The east has never had a successful political revolution freeing individuals from abuse by the state and/or the church, as has happened in the west. However, over the past two hundred plus years, beginning with Napoleon's time in Egypt, some modernization did take place, particularly in Cairo, but never to the extent that it ended clerical power joined to strongman rule. There was and is no right of appeal for individuals who find themselves abused by their government. Strongmen in the Middle East share oil revenues with religious leaders for support of the economic and political leaders in Islamic countries just as they do in Christian nations. Even Russia, since the fall of the USSR, after Boris Yeltsin put Putin in charge in 1999, has shared oil revenue with Orthodox bishops in exchange for their political support.

As the sole emperor, Constantine wished to make Rome's many nations, states, tribes, religions, languages, and cultures more connected, as well as easier and less costly to administer. So, how well did Constantine's efforts to unite all of Europe into one governable entity turn out? Other than they all became Christians and adopted his feudal system, I'd say not so well as life was horrid for ordinary subjects.

There are many traits that can unite a people, such as language, culture, religion, or form of governance, even common enemies. They all evolve into "widely held societal views" known as norms.

During the peak of the Roman Empire, for hundreds of years, the Roman republic had three branches of government. These were the legislative (the Senate), the executive (two co-consuls, elected annually), and the judicial (judges, elected yearly). These officials all came from the patrician class, somewhat like our elite educated class of specialized leaders beholden to the modern one percent of our wealthiest citizens.

The Roman army was made up of men from the lower class, much like our own non-commissioned officers and enlisted men today. Rome itself always remained a local republic; they defeated those who attacked them, starting with a group called the Latins. Eventually, peoples across southern Europe were conquered by the legionaries and became part of the Roman Empire. Local men were seduced into becoming legionaries and priests. By the time of the fall of Rome, the legionaries and priests in the kingdoms seem very likely to have been as loyal as or even more loyal to their local kingdom than to the Roman Republic or Empire. The church leader was the same for both, so not quite the conflict for religious leaders as civil.

At the local government level, governors ruled jurisdictions, and judges heard criminal complaints against the civil laws of the empire. Herod, the handpicked Roman king of greater Syria, is well known to modern Christians, as is Pontius Pilate, the local judge during the life of Jesus. Following the adoption of Christianity by Constantine in the fourth century, kings and bishops for the most part replaced governors and judges.

Beyond the Bible and the state religion of Rome as a legacy, we still have Roman built roads, viaducts, bridges, and arenas. The Romans constructed long lasting structures all across Europe, wherever they established their system. As modern tourists, we see that every major city has a palace and a cathedral, a testament to the absolute authority and power of the king and his bishop during the period between the fall of Rome and the Enlightenment (about 500-1600 AD). The Romans left written records by the thousands still studied by modern scholars.

The ability of these rulers to amass the vast labor pools and wealth needed for such magnificent displays of power attest to the harsh life and poverty of the common folks, and the absolute authority kings and bishops were granted in the feudal era. This was an era of limited productivity (before industrialization) and unlimited greed of kings and bishops as autocrats.

In the fifth century people began to seriously attack from the north and east. Others crossed the Mediterranean Sea to invade from the south. First the Visigoths, and then various hordes spread across the lands of southern Europe. This was the beginning of the end of the Roman Republic and its conquered kingdoms in the west, meaning Europe.

The Eastern Roman Empire fell and split into many small kingdoms. However, it was not the end of the feudal system nor the state churches, including the mother church located in the former capital city Rome. The Roman church, with its bishops and pope, maintained powers equal to the kings in Catholic nations; after the reformation the protestant nations ordained their own priests and the king appoint his own bishop. Authority remained over over all subjects, even the king in Catholic nations as members of what was called the Body of Christ.

Those who conquered the Romans from the north became Christians, and absorbed the Roman way rather than imposing their own less developed mechanism's (systems. The Constantine system was also carried into areas of northern Europe which had not been conquered by Rome. As Rome fell, the Bibles were not all burned; most of the bridges and viaducts were not destroyed. This era is an interesting study for anyone interested in more historical information. Few folks were literate outside of Rome or the monasteries of its church in this period, so much of the record was pieced together later, rather than reported at the time.

The masters of the peasants were selected by each king as his sub or assistant masters. It was believed that in addition to the king they also served by God's will. The nobles were part of a class known as the aristocracy.   Aristocracy granted an expansive title with land ownership arrangements which transferred to eldest male heirs as birthrights. As the only beneficiaries of the feudal system, the nobles had few complaints and risked the ire of the king if they were to air them. Emperors, kings, czars, cardinals, popes, also generals and governors were all masters, regardless of their titles, especially those church and military leaders who controlled large estates as a personal resource.

Subjects lived out their lives at a subsistence level. In most countries, they also owed a duty to their masters as foot solders in times when the king declared war, or if the king's lands were invaded. The attrition of males under war-waging monarchs such as Napoleon much later, often led to a shortage of peasants, making the value of the survivors even greater to the master.

For peasants the reward for faithful service to God and their masters would be eternal life in the hereafter or next life, still a sacred belief of Biblical Christians, known as salvation. As a boy, I was taught these principles in my church history classes as the resurrection of the body and the final judgment as a baptized Catholic member of the Church of Rome. The Roman's Nicene Creed survived the fall of Rome as a belief statement of all Christians, and still does.

Prior to Industrial Age mechanization, productivity was very low per peasant or slave. As a result, life remained the same for feudal system labor for over fifteen hundred years. Peasants were illiterate, lived at the edge of hunger, in the dark and cold, poorly clothed, with the reward of the hereafter promised by the state church and Bible stories their only succor. They were subjected to various forms of fear; they seldom raised a complaint let alone confronted a master. Masters held life and death powers over subjects, with coercion, fear, hunger, and the threat of death as day-to-day motivation.

Jews lived outside this system of master/subject. Over time in Christian majority Europe, an economic role was found for Jews in most western countries. Christians could not charge interest per the rules of Biblical Christianity, based on their interpretation of the Bible requiring Christians "to earn their bread by the sweat of their brow". Jews had no such restrictions, so they were tolerated by kings and allowed to exist as bankers. We will see further impact of this dogma later, when Jews were abused as greedy scapegoats in reaction to wasteful kings when a king ran up debt in poorly planned losing wars.

Kings and landowners needed banking from time to time, especially to fund wars. If the war was lost, this usually meant ruin for the loser and reparations owed to the victors. Meanwhile, the war debt was still owed to the bankers. This debt became viewed as owed to the Jews, which caused resentment. War reparations sowed the seeds of ensuing war in the next generation. This was a vicious cycle not broken in Europe until after WWII in the twentieth century. Tensions that led to WWII itself were to a large part fed by resentment of reparations imposed on the Germans at the end of WWI.

We are reviewing eras, and also relationships across the centuries as systems grew, solidified, and changed; knowledge was gained, understood, and accommodated. Each norm was subject to change due to new realities, and then just as now caused disruption. This created friction, as change always does in human societies. In modern democracies, including America, cultural differences within a nation often lead to reluctance to fund the less successful cultures equitably. In America I believe our most insolvable cultural disparity is based on cultural differences originating from the legacies of the American slave era.

In my school years, the nuns taught us some world history and some European history, some American history, but mostly Church history, written by theologians for students being trained to still accept the pope's knowledge as infallible, even after the enlightenment regarding faith and morals.

Writers who have written about the fall of Rome usually claim the Barbarians overthrew the Roman Empire; this is hardly my insight in understanding what really happened. First the Roman Empire in the east continued for another thousand years, until it was overthrown in the Middle East by the Ottomans.

In the West, the Roman Republic in Italy was overthrown in the fifth century. The Roman Catholic Church and the European kingdoms of the Empire continued and survive even today, much altered but still structured based on Constantine's basic state and church absolute authority to rule by God's will, introduced at Nicaea along with Biblical Christianity. What was really overthrown was the Roman Republic located in the middle of what is now Italy.

The absolute kings and bishops of the European kingdoms were to my mind the second of the seven great authorities in the history of western organized governance to oversee religious and secular governance that had become widespread and sustainable for many centuries over the past seventeen hundred years, and forms much of our U.S. history of governance legacies, in conflict and gridlock.

I'm noting these seven great authorities: The Greek Republic, the Roman Empire, the Holy Roman Empire after the Dark and Middle Ages of feudal state church rule with a pope but without a Roman civil head, the Enlightenment in revolt against clerical error based on Biblical revelation and supposed inerrant Roman popes in matters of the nature of God's creation, the Reformation in revolt against the absolute belief system of the bishops, the English Civil War in revolt against the absolute authority of the king, and the American Revolution against the absolute authority of the divine right of kings and bishops to abuse the economy and the subjects in the colonies that at the time was delegated to the Parliament by the king after the English civil war.

So let's move on to the overthrow of the Roman republic, and the raiding and/or infiltrating if not full conquest of the various kingdoms of the empire by what were called at the time Barbarians. History of this era is somewhat scarce, as the Barbarians were for the most part illiterate, and the monks of the Church who did record most of what history we have, were not fully concerned with preserving the struggles for secular/civil dominance. Whoever captured or was adopted to be king by the nobles was crowned to be an absolute king by a bishop by the revealed will of God as an act of preservation of their own best interest which in turn became the pope's best interest for the short term.

I'm pretty sure people emerge from a modern American education without a working understanding of secular/civic lawmaking as enacted or adjudicated by our government. I also believe too many people do not understand how individual citizen's rights found in the Constitution might be in conflict with the beliefs of their faith, let alone options on how to reconcile these conflicts. Fallibly claiming the United States to be a Christian nation is not dealing with the conflict, it is adding to the gridlock. Churchmen who advance this argument of near riot inducing rhetoric need to be confronted by members of their flock who actually understand and appreciate what the establishment clause does and what it assures for whatever interpretation a congregation is free to practice; because there is no absolute state church in America, we are a heresy free zone one might say.

In a theocracy system of government the law is based on revelations from God; there can be no amendment clause in such nation's founding legal documents. There can be local civil law, but it must be approved by the national religious powers to ensure no deviation from the law of God. Islam's Shari a Qur'an law is an example. I am not sure how those in America who advocate for the United States to become a true Christian nation would square this reality if it came down to a meaningful national debate over what is believed today among American Biblical Christians as to what is or is not heresy.

It is not my intent to judge the truth of, nor the correct interpretation of, the Old or New Testament. I simply submit they are the key documents of the system of government that formed the Roman and English state church economic governance system that oversaw the nation's property, individual, and religious rights as legal systems, all combined in one system called feudalism.

As you read this book and look back, hopefully you will see the scope of how Constantine's state church, and feudal system of economic governance evolved until our founders revolted. They sought a new understanding of God, His creation, and man's role and rights within that creation. They thought about the authority to govern. They did not attempt to deny the universe was created by God, only to admit the church did not have an infallible Biblical answer to the nature of that universe or man's place therein.

They did want to undo how men (over the centuries with the absolute power of kings and bishops) had perverted Biblical Christianity from the intent of Jesus as He preached, to the intent of the Roman Emperor Constantine as he governed. It is obvious to me, Constantine began by ignoring the advice of Jesus regarding rendering unto Caesar what is Caesar's, and rendering unto God what is God's.

It is not surprising how easily crowned men ruling by the will of God became tyrants, enamored of the favor they believed God held them in. These tyrants abused millions of God's children over the centuries, for their own aggrandizement. What is undeniable in my opinion is that the Bible was and is misused by men, allowing state church bishops to control our political economic prehistory from 325 until 1791, and allowing unconscionable abuse of individuals for too long and too harshly. The Spanish Inquisition is a perfect if extreme example of a state church abusing ordinary subjects with the cooperation of the Roman Church.

In Chapter 2 we move to a period history calls the Dark Ages, the time after the Barbarians primarily from the north invaded and defeated the Roman Empire. This period of little change between the fifth and ninth century that leads into what historian's call the Middle Ages is combined with the Dark Ages in Chapter 2; they seem to me very different from any history book I read on my own or as a school assignment.

We'll continue on in Chapter 2 as the Holy Roman Empire of Biblical Christianity and feudal kingdoms are reestablished as the pope again has power, led by a warrior king of Gaul whose influence as well as the pope's was directly felt between 800 and 1492 AD across Europe.

Chapter 2

The Dark Ages and the Middle Ages

Barbarians invade, Feudal System and Biblical Christianity survives and then thrives, while kingdoms consolidate for their own benefit.

Europe invaded by the Visigoths from the North, Mongols from the Far East and south from Africa by the Muslim Moors, followed by the rise of the navigators which portends the beginning of the end of absolutism, and the onset of secular reasoning, based on and recognized as scientific knowledge among non-churchmen of learning.

This is the shortest, least written about, and the longest period of little change in organized government and religion of all the eras of European history that I found in my quest to understand how European history informed as well as misinformed our modern society of self governed free men as we came to be governed into the twenty-first century.

There are great histories of the Turkish people, the Persians, the people of the Steppes, of India, and China. It took the Vikings and the British centuries of destructive warfare to become empires, but the Barbarians came, saw, conquered, and settled. They did not destroy anywhere close to the rate I would have expected. But then I was taught the term Barbarians had a very negative meaning, while at the time comparatively it just meant unorganized raiders.

While they were not Christians, they had already adopted, at least in many of the Germanic States and in Gaul, a manor house relationship between the aristocrats and the peasants. Their term for it, feudalism was adapted to the Constantine system of each king's authority as it applied to the economic system of the kingdoms of the former Roman Empire.

In the North, the Germanic Visigoths invaded across the western end of Europe into Iberia which became Portugal, Spain, and part of

France along the northern Mediterranean Sea. In the south, Vandals from Carthage now today's Tunisia invaded what is now Italy, and up the east side of the Adriatic sea to what is now Croatia. Further west in mid and northern Europe the Franks invaded Gaul which became France, Belgium, and the Low Countries. The Saxons of Normandy, a part of Roman Gaul and now modern France, over time conquered what is now England after fighting off the Danes, as Europe moved towards the end of the Middle Ages.

Constantine's system was recognized by almost all of the invaders as efficient. They retained it as their own system of governance and made Nicene Biblical Christianity their own religion across Europe. We will see almost a thousand years later England revolted against the pope, not as the first protestants or for the same reason as Martin Luther, but still as part of what came to be known as the reformation. This revolt, mostly across northern Europe beginning in what is today protestant Germany with the exception of Poland, Hungary, and Austria, left the pope as bishop of the Roman Church. His bishops remained the state church's bishops in most of southern Europe including Italy, France, and what became the Austrian-Hungarian Empire known as the Hapsburg's kingdom.

England's king also kept the Roman feudal system and its Nicene Bible after it was translated into English by King James I about sixty years after the death of King Henry XIII. James I's bishops with the king's authority translated the will of God as the absolute divine right of kings! All of this turmoil had little direct impact on our founders other than the fact that the idea of absolute rule under king and bishop over property rights and citizens (as if still subjects without rights), was still in place as a norm at the end of this period and continued into the first scientific age to follow. The main impact of this era was that kings, popes, Bibles, manor houses and the feudal system survived this thirteen hundred year transition. A little over three hundred fifty years later England will have a civil war and introduce English Common Law to administer property rights among other newly secular laws. This common law will be brought to America, and will be the mechanism of governance at the state level that introduces property rights administered at the state level into our Constitution, based on Blackstone's commentaries noted above.

It is easy to understand how much kings liked having absolute authority, and how much nobles and bishops and their priests liked having key subordinate authority from the king to control land, labor, and wealth on large manors across the kingdom. A comment is heard from time to time "it is good to be king" and it was true. Even after the Roman Empire, Constantine's system had staying power. He had tapped into four of the most compelling attributes of human nature; a quest for power, adulation, abuse of power, and hereditary dynastic wealth accumulation, each a mechanism of greed; perhaps the most compelling reality was an absence of censure by any mortal during the life of a European king.

The largest upset to the basic Roman system of economic governance between Constantine era norms and our revolution-introduced capitalism did not begin until the sixteenth century as we shall see during the age of sailing and the establishment of colonial empires. It was a credit system for control of the profits of trade in empires, called mercantilism. However, the Roman system of feudalism remained the only economic system of Europe on the home continent throughout the Dark and Middle Ages.

In the west the so called Barbaric tribes we mentioned came over the Alps and up from the Balkans, across the sea, and down from the north, defeating the Roman legions after sacking Rome, as there were garrisoned legions in all the kingdoms of the old Empire. Many or most of these were made up of nationals of the kingdom in which they enforced Roman rule. Wise kings invited these native sons to become the king's own military protectors. As such I'm sure they often played a role in keeping the invaders from full conquest, meaning the locals accepted the new leadership and the new leadership needed the old peasants to continue working the land.

These invaders were still living with what southern Europe saw as barbaric and pagan values. This invasion plunged Europe into a stagnation known historically as the Dark Ages through the ninth century. Regional kingdoms had emerged but no overall state king or Caesar-like king became emperor as in the time of the Roman Empire.

To state clearly, none of these tribes significantly changed the governance, nor the religion that the Romans had introduced. To govern their new territories they recognized Rome had a better system of governance than theirs. They left the pope in place at a price as we shall see, as well as the Roman religion but with reduced influence and without a civil counterpart as king of the Holy Roman Empire. However, one will arise and his dynasty will co-rule with the popes for the ensuing four hundred years. The invading armies stayed, the men married, and the leaders assumed roles in the new kingdoms.

One interesting fact I've read is these Barbarians were often more considerate of women and children than the Romans, especially the Franks. However, like England the country of our origin, they always enforced absolute property rights over individual or even family rights.

For the most part in these early European times family property actually meant property of the king awarded to a family for service to the king (a fief) to live on, manage and tax, keeping a portion of the tax themselves. Actually this was a tax on the crops of the serfs who were attached to the land, for as long as the head of the hereditary family was in favor with the king. There was a hierarchy of titles, depending on the size of the estate, for all advisers and supporters of the king in war and peace.

When a father died who had a married daughter but no son (male heir), the estate was left to the daughter's husband; if the daughter's husband died, she did not inherit the estate, her brother-in-law inherited it, and he could literally put her and the children off the land of her birth without recourse, condemning them to a life of poverty. The brother-in-law did not even owe her a portion of his agricultural income as a stipend to live on.

Mohammad resolved this male dominance practice that caused women to resist having their husbands fight for his king due to her risk. Mohammad's simple solution was to require the brother-in-law to marry his sister-in-law as an additional wife, and to assume protection and provisioning for the widowed woman and her children. I have never read a discussion of why the same God of Abraham would reveal two different solutions for land distribution in the case of widowhood. I do not understand nor can I explain thousands of years of religious dogma disparity.

In England our Germanic heirs who ruled England over the long period until the Normans, made no bones about the primacy of property laws over family law. The Normans later conquered England, with little change in English property rights. Normandy, now part of France, was an independent kingdom at the time of its conquest of England.

Like every age, the Dark Ages only died as knowledge expanded. Until the Industrial Age, ages often lasted five hundred to a thousand years. In the ages of Discovery and the Enlightenment, once knowledge was ascending and free of the limits of church controlled knowledge believed to be infallible, things changed fast enough that new ages occurred in about two hundred year increments, but never until the nineteenth century did the basic realities end for peasants trapped in the feudal system. Today, eras often last hardly more than fifty years, that is how fast knowledge and understanding progress once reason has been allowed to adapt to new realities.

The Visigoths, etc. were followed by the Huns, who invaded Europe from the east after the turmoil from the fall of Rome settled. The Huns were led by a Mongol Khan named Attila, like the Visigoths all the way across Europe, into the Iberian Peninsula, and into what is today modern Spain.

Meanwhile in the Eastern Roman Empire in Constantinople a sixteen feet thick wall was built around the city. They paid tribute to Attila, and survived. In Rome the pope who remained the leader of the state church paid tribute, and Rome was also spared from pillage by the Huns.

The pope in Rome however did feel diminished in influence, especially by the Huns' invasion. The pope was looking for a defender of the faith to reaffirm the old Roman granted power of the pope to play a dominant role in the granting of power to kings as masters of their realm, and to re-enforce acceptance by the servant or peasant class of their role, bound to the land in allegiance to their masters, and the Roman Church, whose bishops crowned their kings.

There were more invasions of Europe to mention. At about the same time the Danes were ravishing England. The Moors who were Islamic warriors (Islam of the Sword) from Northern Africa captured southern Spain. They would hold Spain for about seven hundred years. We will address the end of their time in Europe in our chapter at the beginning of the Age of Discovery, Chapter 4.

Late in the ninth century a warrior king of Gaul (today's France), known as Charlemagne was crowned by the pope as the king of the Holy Roman Empire, and Defender of the Faith. Charlemagne united the Germanic tribes, the old Roman territory of Gaul (modern France, and Belgium), and what is now northern Italy. Over time most of Eastern Europe joined the Holy Roman Empire and became part of the Hapsburg Empire that eventually ruled most of the Eastern half of Europe for four hundred years or so until the end of WWI.

A bit of modern northern Spain also fell under the influence of Charlemagne, and later his heirs. Modern continental Europe entered the Middle Ages, and would never be successfully invaded by outsiders again, until D-Day in 1944 when American troops as allies of England came ashore in western France in WWII to defeat Nazi Germany.

There was troop replacement in the last year of WWI by the Americans, but more in relief of French and English troops than as an invading force. The Ottomans and Eastern Europe remained in conflict until WWI, and returned to a new level of conflict under the thumbs of Britain and France until the end of WWII. We will readdress the Middle East in Chapter 9 in the age of American dependence on imported oil.

Wars among the Europeans themselves however continued for about eleven hundred years until 1945. Harry Truman and the WWII Allies formed NATO after the war, with all of the old European countries allied against the outside threat of communism to unite Europe, another factor of governance we will review in Chapter 9.

I am unaware of any remnants of the Holy Roman Empire in Europe today other than Vatican City. We will review how today the pope is the head of an independent state within the city of Rome, primarily to accommodate the Catholic church's massive banking operations around the world in the twenty-first century.

Of note is the staying power of the cultural norm of the old Roman masters and servants as a state church continued in both the Orthodox Catholic eastern part of Europe, and the progressively changing protestant portion of Europe including our former mother country England until the nineteenth century for the servant or serf class, and the twentieth century for the masters (nobility).

The pope held on to much of what today is central Italy as the Papal States, which made the pope a sovereign for the first time, and gave him a personal source of income. During later upheavals the pope lost control of the Papal States, and was in dire straits until rescued by Hitler and Mussolini with a small city state, and a one hundred million dollar a year income in the 1930s, which also gave "Vatican City, the pope's modern kingdom" access to the global banking system. The gift to the pope in the 1930s was in return for the pope's recognition of the Fascist States, another story worthy of a more in-depth read.

There were a couple of stepping stones in this period. First, a few hundred years after Charlemagne at the end of the Magna Carta settlement in England, the English king granted the English nobles a foothold in what amounted to a narrow crack in the idea of a say in the absolute authority of the king, which the kings all but ignored for another six hundred years, but it was the first introduction of the concept "by the consent of the governed" to enter the minds of men, and to be heard by an absolute king.

Christians were exhorted in the Roman Bible to convert the peoples of all nations. Muslims were exhorted to conquer all lands, and convert the people, or collect a higher rate of tax and demand submission once a territory became an Islamic State. This is the concept in the Qur'an that leads to Jihad in its extreme interpretation. People who do not convert or submit and pay the fees are legally eligible for the sword.

It is worth noting that Islam was founded as a potentially violent religion. Mohamed divided the world into two parts; Dar al Islam (the house of Islam) and Dar al Harb (the house of war). How the Qur'an is interpreted today has much to do with how violent a sect is, based on eighth century Muslim norms. Fundamentalist Islam was founded in the Dark Ages, and to a large extent remains unreformed, particularly in the nations still ruled by an autocrat.

Capture and conversion was to be at the point of the sword. Not all Muslims resorted to the sword, but that is the religious law (Sharia in Arabic), a return to this relationship with non-Muslim nations that is longed for by today's fundamentalists. It is often tolerated for political support by the less fundamental but power hungry leadership class among the wealthy, i.e., the generals and tribal leaders who court the support of the clerics as they all share control of the nation's wealth. This is a common enough arrangement of political interest in the history of the world.

Today Islam is mostly of interest to us as an external threat, or an oil resource. However, in today's America the concept of freedom of religion, a U.S. Constitutional right, is in political tension over the issue of sorting Jihad terrorists from non-violent Muslims, as an interesting political issue, but an impossibility for a religious Muslim. So far at least Turkey is established as a modern democracy, yet the concept of a secular (civil laws with freedom of religion) government is less than fully settled. A key insight in this book is that our own secular Constitution is still not fully settled in at least fifteen or twenty of America's states in the twenty-first century.

During the six hundred years of little progress in human productivity continuing in the next two chapters the feudal system remained the way of life for most of the European population, as well as in the Eastern (Orthodox) Roman Empire.

The thirteen hundred years between the fall of Rome, and the rise of the enlightenment were relatively uneventful as far as our modern history goes other than as noted above, and other than the invention of sailing instruments that led to the natural understanding of the universe, leading to the enlightenment.

The sextant, the telescope, and the printing press all helped to break the role of the Church as the only source of knowledge in Christian

Europe, especially regarding the defining the nature of the universe and man's role in it; not as bishops claimed to know from revelation, but as God's intent for all of His creation to naturally occur in the freedom of the universe became known, based on the free relationship God created among all aspects of his natural creation. Note: The understanding of the "nature" of God (monotheism) began about 700 BC with Moses, was accepted by Constantine in 325 AD, and our founders in 1776.

As a Catholic I was discouraged from reading the Bible; to this day the Roman church still is the source of knowledge for Roman Catholics, at least in regard to questions of faith and morals (salvation), a reluctant concession of the pope to scientific proof of modern knowledge only amended in the nineteenth century.

Salvation remains faith based in the United States' among the majority religion at our founding as church dogma, and the Constitution was adapted into an individual citizen's right if a religious believer, as long as it does not infringe on the individual right that all other religion's citizens are free to believe in or not.

One last factor about the invaders is the lack of interest the tribal invading hordes had in maintaining the written record of what the Romans had printed by hand in the monasteries, including Bibles. To a large extent we owe that printing to the Byzantines in the eastern Roman Empire, and also to some extent to the monasteries in Ireland that were of lesser interest to the invaders, especially in the rugged west of Ireland. With renewed interest in learning, along with the invention of movable type, the old manuscripts of the East and Ireland were valued once again.

We are spending only a few pages on the Dark Ages, to understand the continuity that made it meaningful as a place-holding period until the Age of Discovery that led to the settling of America and the Age of Enlightenment. The Enlightenment led to the philosophies that underpinned the changes in governance introduced in forming our new government, after our founders revolted against England and Constantine's old Bible-based Roman church state system, ending absolute authority by the will of God.

These first two chapters have introduced organized government. The upcoming two chapters will describe how our founders' understanding of the creation changed our relationship to God and the role Constantine introduced regarding sin and salvation.

Washington, Franklin, and Jefferson, who were at least interested in deism, believed in a God of creation, which became the understanding of the nature of God America was founded under. They did not ever profess an absolute belief in Biblical Christianity, the concept of sin or salvation, and made none of these three factors the concern or business of the U.S. Constitution, or a department of our government.

Leaving the Dark and Middle Ages behind, the first changes called by many the Age of Discovery allowed the minds of the men of science to expand knowledge, first about the nature of the universe and then to rethink the limited economic and governance roles allotted to individual men as subjects under feudal economics, and revealed the fallibility of Biblical Christianity's system of Roman governance, especially God's believed will regarding subjects' absolute and total duty to God, without any rights of their own as men in their own right.

In brief what I have defined here are three factors of human nature from the time of Constantine that are still frustrating America's stated ideals defined in our founding documents.

1.   The need of men driven by greed to absolutely control all wealth.

2.   The need of men of God to absolutely control the lives of all of the free citizens of modern nations as if they are still subjects of absolute kings.

3.   The need of politicians to absolutely control the dominant culture in subjugation of the peoples of all minority cultures even in democratic nation, also noting how happy dominant culture members are to have all other cultures subservient to their own leaders.

The only four outcomes for politicians and pastors who are absolutely committed to coercing a society of free men are war, gridlock, failure, or compromise. To choose compromise is to abandon an absolute control ideology that favors one group over another. To use guile and spin to hide a minority's ideology goals is to abandon compromise. To choose autocracy and tyranny which do ensure absolute control of all three is to abandon a society of self-governed free men. America cannot remain a free nation under such ideology as we shall review in Chapter 10.

I for one still honor our founders' ideal, a society of self-governed freemen, tolerant of each others rights as the only means to ensure our own rights to equal opportunity to pursue life, liberty, and the pursuit of happiness as we each chose, without infringing on each other's rights, in a nation where the purpose of government is the established justice, common good, as well as mutual defense, and where we each have freedom of religion or not as we each chose.

Based on proof of the nature of the earth to the sun, key factors of revelation were finally recognized as false. Men of reason observing the natural world God created including natural man, rejected the intent of the first organized government and religion introduced by the Roman Empire seventeen hundred years ago, with the introduction of Biblical Christianity, that avowed the intent of government was service to God and his chosen king as God's will.

Chapter 3

The Age of Discovery

Christopher Columbus introduced the Age of Discovery in 1492 with the first attempted voyage to the far east from the western most edge of Europe based on his and others' heretical theory the earth was in fact round. Discovery under the flag of the Queen of Spain led not only to the new world, but also to the invention of colonial governance and mercantilism as a new economic system by four sailing nations with trained navigators: Spain, Britain, The Netherlands, and Portugal.

Columbus's first voyage to the west seemed to prove the bishops were wrong about the nature of the universe and therefore the nature of creation of His universe, and man. This exposed Biblical Christian theology based on revelation by the Roman church as the will of God to be false.

Columbus proved the world was not flat. Twenty-seven years later Spain sent the Magellan Expedition to discover a western route to the Spice Islands. It took three years; over two hundred sailors in five ships left Seville, but only one ship, the Victoria, returned three years later. They named the Pacific Ocean, and put the final nails in the infallible revelation coffin. The natural world was not as the Roman Pope revealed it to be. It was free, wild, and vast as God obviously intended His creation to be.

Spain had finally driven the Moors (Arab Muslims from west Africa, and part of the Ottoman Empire who occupied Spain from 711-1492) out of their country. Queen Isabella scapegoated Spain's Jews to escape debt borrowed to fund the conquest of the Moors; the Queen was broke and needed a new source of wealth. Columbus provided a possibility and thereby a bargain was struck. Columbus was an Italian, married into a minor royal of Portugal from the island of Madeira, a nation where Isabella's mother had married into the family of the king. Columbus set sail with a crew of mostly Basque fishermen without a homeland who occupied the northern region of Portugal, Spain and the very south of Atlantic France.

The knowledge of the Basque whalers of Spain who knew the Atlantic and its currents conquered the fears of both theology and the unknown during Columbus' four voyages, which opened the continents and islands of the Americas to European exploitation.

The methods of inflicting fear and pain that kings, queens, and bishops used to achieve their goals and to enforce both their economic system and loyalty demands, were well perfected between church and state at this point in European history when the Spanish queen and the pope agreed to impose the regimen of horrors, called the Inquisition, on those to be eliminated. It survived in the New World until 1811, and the office still exists in the Roman Church.

The inquisition terror was never exceeded until the Nazis inflicted horrors once again on the Jews in the 1940s, again in repudiation of debt and cleansing of the culture of the nation. If such cruelty were not still part of human nature I would consider the concerns of this book less urgent, for the America of the twenty-first century is becoming fearful of an end to white Christian America rule and that white protestant culture will becoming a minority culture if our nation remains a democracy.

The open ocean had always been feared by the men of Europe, yet they were driven to overcome their natural fear and they dared to sail beyond the safety of their known Mediterranean Sea. Trade routes had long been established between Europe and the Orient. The major route was the nearly four thousand mile ancient land route across the Middle East, the steppes of Russia, into India and China called the Silk Road.

The Silk Road included lands conquered by Alexander the Great before the Roman era. These lands were reintroduced to European curiosity by Marco Polo in the thirteenth century. The Arabs and Persians had known the lands and the route long before Europeans.

Spices from India improved the taste and quality of food in Europe. Silk from Persia and China, and cotton from what is now Uzbekistan and India lowered the cost of garment making. Europe's climate precluded local cultivation of spice, silk and cotton, and later tea, so a natural trade partnership was born, but it has been difficult for me to really solve the mystery of what equal value goods the west sent to the east.

Carpets, camels, and horses are mentioned, gold and diamonds are also mentioned, but the amount of spice, silk, and tea is hard to fathom. It is easier to understand how in later centuries the British forced Indians to grow poppies used to trade opium for China's goods and tea to make great profits while destroying the local economy of both Asian nations, and devastating the peoples of both cultures.

Goods traveled slowly by land however, and people longed for a faster route by sea. No major culture in Europe really knew what existed in the open sea beyond Gibraltar. The Roman Empire and others had used both sailing ships and slave powered barges to travel the Mediterranean Sea, but the open sea was virtually unexplored other than by illiterate minority groups of open sea fishermen in large, mostly open ships. When the Huns' (Tatars) invasion of Europe from the east disrupted the Silk Road, it forced Europeans to seek a sea route to the Orient around Africa, or even by sailing west which Magellan did by sailing south and around what today is Argentina.

By the time of the first voyage of the Age of Discovery in the late the 1400s, at least four countries had mastered the art of navigation using the compass, charts, and astrological means noted above. With these tools the Portuguese set sail on voyages south along the west coast of Africa using skills taught by the great Portuguese teacher Henry the Navigator.

Christopher Columbus was from Genoa which was often in dispute between France and Italy. Columbus went to sea at a young age and traveled west, finally sailing with the Portuguese down the coast of Africa and the Portuguese islands of the mid Atlantic. The Portuguese were looking for a sea route around Africa to Asia.

Columbus however believed the earth was an orb. Henry knew a degree of latitude was just less than sixty miles, but Columbus had also sailed north with the Basque whalers from what is now Spain, and had an understanding of currents and winds in the open Atlantic. He also knew the Basques built ships more sea worthy for the open ocean. In the end his captains and ships were better said to be Basque than the generic Spanish.

Other countries were only minor players in this naval exploration. In Italy the Hapsburgs were a sea power only in the Adriatic Ocean. The Russians and Swedes were a sea power only in the Baltic Sea. Beginning in the late nineteenth century and early twentieth century, the Russians also became powerful in the Pacific Ocean in eastern Asia, after Peter the Great developed an avid interest in sailing which led to Russia's development of a navy and a need for ice-free ports. For the most part the Black Sea was controlled by the Turks.

However, at the end of the fifteenth century many in Europe knew that if a sea route was found to Asia vast wealth would be available to those who discovered it. As noted above, one of the navigators who believed the earth to be round and that Asia could be reached by sailing west was, as all American school children learn, Christopher Columbus.

Columbus had not followed his father's trade as a weaver; instead he had gone to sea as a young man. He married the daughter of the Duke of Viseu of Portugal who was of Portuguese royal blood, and Spain's Queen Isabella's mother had married into the Portuguese royal family. This facilitated the connection that allowed Columbus to seek support for an expedition west to the Indies, funded by the Spanish queen. It was only with the encouragement of her husband Ferdinand that the first voyage was approved.

Let's review a little history of Queen Isabella. After defeating the Moors she was the strongest Catholic monarch in Europe. In the late fifteenth century she united one of the first areas of Europe into a nation, partly by marriage and partly by war financed with debt owed to the Jews. Her marriage to Ferdinand II of Aragon united the Christian kingdoms of Castile and Aragon. After her marriage, she defeated and mostly expelled the Moors, Muslims from Africa who had ruled parts of Spain for centuries. Then she reinstated the Roman state church, and made adherence to Catholicism required by law.

As queen she forced all of the remaining descendants from prior invaders, including Jews and Moors, to convert to Roman Catholicism. Non-converts were subject to conversion or expulsion. Eventually the so-called conversos were compelled by the Inquisition (cleric-managed torture on behalf of the state and the pope to force absolute allegiance to the pope and the Queen) to prove they were Catholics; they were often tortured to death in the process. A convenient if unstated outcome of expulsion or death was cancellation of debt and/or confiscation of all property and other forms of wealth.

Queen Isabella had a hard time funding Columbus's voyages. There was little money as such at the end of the Middle Ages, even for monarchs. What they had or could borrow was usually allocated to war or castle building, along with the cost of funding the lavish lives of the court nobility. However, she agreed to fund Columbus's famous 1492 voyage and later voyages as well, with the goal of finding a sailing route to Asia around the globe.

Instead, Columbus found the Caribbean Islands and the continent of South America. The reason he landed in these areas is that Atlantic Ocean currents were not well known even by the Basques at the onset of open ocean travel. When Columbus left Spain in southern Europe, the winds and currents brought him to the mid and southern areas of the Americas. This caused them to be explored, or better said exploited, first.

Columbus negotiated a ten percent share of all wealth found for Spain for life, as well as the governorship of all lands claimed for the crown. The stories of the four voyages of Columbus are well known, and for more in-depth information there are many good histories. The results were the early interplay and eradication of the natives by the Conquistadors as his forces were known.

The natives died from disease, swords and guns, and by exhaustion from forced labor. Perhaps less well known is the fact that the good padres brought the Inquisition with them when they accompanied the conquistadors to the new world. While the natives were suffering and dying the padres hoped to convert them to Catholicism.

Spain collected billions of dollars of wealth in today's dollars from Central and South American, as well as Caribbean Island colonies over the next four hundred years. The native populations were decimated. However, after four voyages and a decade of poor administration, Columbus was deemed unfit to administer the Spanish system of governance. He was displaced and his contract was retracted. He died out of favor leaving two sons, one legitimate, the other acknowledged. They and their descendants contested his estate for almost two hundred years in the Spanish courts. Today the legacy of Columbus is mixed at best.

I've read that his place of burial was moved six times. Today it is in the Cathedral in Seville, Spain. This Cathedral is about a mile from the Tower de Oro (tower of gold) where the billions (in today's dollars) of wealth from Mexico, Central America, and Peru that landed in Spain were stored. This wealth was collected in Cartagena, Colombia for escorted transport to Seville via Cuba.

Spain, South America, and Columbus himself play only a minor role in the story of the founding of the United States, other than the fact that our young country acquired Florida from Spain for five million dollars as part of a negotiated settlement. This settlement occurred after Andrew Jackson, while still a general, had invaded and ousted the Spaniards from Florida. He did this while on Indian removal patrol duty.

North America was not discovered by Europeans for settlement until later at the beginning of the sixteenth century (except for early explorations by the Vikings in the eleventh century).

First the English, then the Dutch, and finally the French landed on the northern continent. Over time England became the major player in North America. The English ousted the French in Canada, and made a land swap to remove the Dutch government from North America. The Dutch had settled an area from what is now New York south to what is now Wilmington Delaware.

Exploration and colonization was not limited to the Americas. After the death of Portuguese Henry the Navigator, his students continued the exploration and mapping of the African coast all the way to the

Cape of Good Hope. Then Vasco da Gama found a sea route to India across the Indian Ocean less than ten years after Columbus' first voyage. As a result of these explorations Portugal founded and maintained colonies in Asia, such as Goa in India, and Macao in China, which were held until the end of the twentieth century. Spain eventually captured the Philippines. Portugal never colonized any part of North America but it did colonize the most eastern portion of South America, now Brazil, the largest nation in South America.

All of the above explorations are part of the Age of Discovery and colonization. During this time the pope and his bishops still maintained a lock on knowledge. However, the minds of bright men continued to analyze, test, and propose theories and/or proofs of the facts of nature. These were often counter to the teachings of the church and its interpretation of God's design and intent for the universe and the men he created to live thereon, still believed by about two billion people in the world today.

The church taught and supported as infallible, knowledge regarding God's creation, such as the relationship of the earth to the sun. Church theologians taught the sun rotated around the earth (geocentrism). Less than a decade into open ocean navigation, navigators all but proved the world was not flat; more importantly they had also established that the earth revolved around the sun.

To disagree with church teaching at the time was heresy; to ignore science was madness for increasingly inquiring minds such as Galileo and Copernicus.

Galileo, the inventor of the telescope, was tried by the Roman Catholic inquisition for insisting that the earth revolved around the sun. He was found guilty of all charges, without any counter proofs by the church. He was excommunicated and silenced for life.

Almost one hundred fifty years after the Age of Discovery began, a man of science, Isaac Newton, proved the theories of Renaissance thinkers including Galileo and Copernicus. However, Galileo's conviction was not re-thought by the Roman Church, nor was his excommunication retracted for another three hundred years.

Following the Age of Discovery, the late fifteenth, all of the sixteenth and part of the seventeenth centuries brought the Age of Enlightenment philosophies, ideas, and scientific proofs from Europe to the Americas. The Enlightenment included a variety of ideas, all centered on science and philosophy, both referred to as reason, as the primary source of legitimacy and authority, as opposed to Biblical Christian concept of infallibility and state church enforced belief in revelation.

Once the church had been proven fallible about the nature of the universe, their revelations regarding the nature of man, his place in the universe, and God's intended lot for man all such knowledge came under increasing proofs from science regarding the true nature of God's creation. The Enlightenment embraced and advanced ideas and ideals like republicanism, liberty and freedom, individual citizen rights, secular law, judicial review, as well as constitutional government, the separation of powers within government, re-establishment of democracy, and finally separation of church and state.

Movable type and the printing press made publication of discoveries and philosophical ideas quickly, broadly, and inexpensively available to readers. At this point in history for the most part the only people who were educated and could read were men born into noble families. Science replaced theology regarding the natural world and man's place in it. Philosophy replaced fear and abuse as the controlling rationale between those who governed and those they governed.

During the Enlightenment scientists proved that Biblically sanctioned infallibility regarding the universe was unsustainable. This enabled later philosophers of the Enlightenment to shine a light on church doctrinal errors regarding creation, finding natural rights for man who for centuries had been taught that one was born into one's class, meaning a peasant was meant to be a peasant by God's will.

Science was used to prove that the Biblical role assigned to man by Constantine's Roman Nicene Biblical church had been formed in ignorance at best. At worst it had been intentionally adapted to rationalize the Roman support for feudalism, which benefited the Roman Empire, as opportunism corrupted some of the bishops, or perhaps better said, those priests who were willing to be corrupted were preferred by the kings and popes for elevation to bishop. The most famous of such men to compare in the English reformation's handling of what was called the king's great matter, the annulment of King Henry VIII's marriage, are Sir Thomas More and Sir Thomas Cromwell.

In either case, first the emperor and then the bishops or the kings just as easily accepted the legalization, aggrandizement, and enrichment of the Roman Empire, her state church, and the kingdoms of her empire. All this in return for upholding Constantine's founding myths at best, and intentional errors created as revelation at worst.

National ideologies take on a life of their own as they are bent to conform to all obstacles and/or objections based on ideology or theology which by definition are absolutist beliefs, and always very resistant to new conflicting facts.

The Roman Church's teachings from the time of Constantine kept the minds of the people stalled in awe, ignorance, fear, and obedience. It caused millions upon millions of human beings to meekly accept subjugation and poverty until well into the nineteenth century, almost completely without dissent and always subject to a life of abuse by church and/or state leaders without appeal. This condition not only changed slowly, it also carried into the twenty-first century for the twenty percent of Americans who are raised today with the poorest educations, or taught from a point of view described by sociologists as motivated reasoning; I call it emotional bias. Its cry today is "I just want my country back".

Knowledgeable assaults on church traditions in the early sixteenth century began to bear fruit. Philosophy based on science began to replace theology based on revelation as the cornerstone of human understanding of the world, as the misconceptions of revelation were confirmed to be in error.

Our founders were all influenced by men of science and philosophy who negotiated their way to not only an independent government among the nations, but also to establish a constitutional system that allowed amendment, insuring the United States became a society of free men able to self govern, which allowed compromise as well as Judicial settlement of Constitutional questions of men in dissent, as new realities begat new understandings and possibilities, especially regarding new forms of wealth creation and property. However, traditional property rights understanding regarding distribution of the fruits of those who labored remained mired in the traditions of rigid class limitations.

I'm making an argument in this book that the modern Supreme Court has made a gross mistake of its duty under our secular system of authority to govern based on the "by the consent" bargain that replaced the English system of authority to govern by divine right. Kings could not be subject to oversight, nor overruled; they could only be judged by God after death.

Our founders in the Declaration noted that our new nation would be authorized to govern by the consent of the governed. This was not defined in the U.S. Constitution, so a number of states ratified the Constitution provisionally, noting that the Constitution was ratified only if a Bill of Rights was added. The Bill of Rights like the Constitution was ratified by the citizens of the United States residing in each of the individual states; this became the authority to govern bargain that the southern states fought from 1791 into the 1960s. Until Supreme Court jurists acknowledge they are to protect citizens' federal rights against abuse by state chartered corporations, and that they are superior to these state common law based property rights, we will not be a nation of assured rights for citizens.

It is important we understand this if we are ever to settle our gridlock over property rights and religious rights that are still argued by the GOP as if they are still authorized by the will of God. In the 2020 impeachment of Donald Trump, the crime was not seen by the GOP rising to a need for impeachment. Their refusing to allow the Congress to review documents or interview Trump's key advisers was to ignore the Constitution, and rule as if by divine right.

One serious look ahead at this point. Between 2017 and 2019 Mitch McConnell and Donald Trump installed more new judges on federal benches than any other three years in history, and they all have this GOP ideology that will make protecting the republic a full time job if we are to keep it as Ben Franklin warned us.

As we review several key twenty-first century Supreme Court five to four decisions, we will see that the GOP Court at this time in history has ignored the intent of the Bill of Rights provision the Constitution remains subject to.

This legacy came about because state laws adopted English Common Law, which was based on the divine right authority. I believe this is the biggest cause of gridlock in all of our national partisan wars.

It became apparent that some prophets must have allowed human error or their king's demands to cloud what was believed to be inerrant knowledge of what God had reveled to them. However, the Bible has never been proven fallible on matters of the life of Jesus because His teachings of the path to salvation were never presented as facts, they were presented to be the intent of God, believed based on faith, so they were not subject to dissent other than non-belief.

An American understanding from the time of our founding of these progressions is discussed in many letters written over the years by founding father Thomas Jefferson, and are still available to read and worth the effort. You may not agree with all Jefferson wrote, but it will better inform your understanding of our founders' intents.

Throughout this book you will find discussion of our founders' intent regarding settlement of dissent that impacts citizens. Almost to a decision the settlements and the discussion of intent will relate to the 1789 Constitution itself. The Bill of Rights was never used to settle a founding intent until the 1930s and then only regarding citizens' rights vs. civil rights.

Only matters related to the proven, natural world regarding God's creation formed the belief system that guided our founders. That explains why even secular folks like myself include "under God" when we pledge allegiance to our flag without objection. The will of God is not denied nor confirmed in the U.S. Constitution, as it does not concern itself with salvation; it grants personal faith as an individual freedom. Secularists do proclaim God created the universe; we do not accept any ideology or theology that denies men were created to be free within that creation as long as no one else is denied their right not to be abused, provided the majority agrees the activity is not harmful to others regardless of their own personal beliefs, even those acts theologians declare are Biblical sins. They are addressing truths that only inform the salvation of believers and is not a factor regarding the civil police powers of the states over free citizens of the United States.

Today in America, and in all free societies, a man's individual rights as a citizen are based on the observable and provable nature of God's universe applied to the extent we have explored and proven what is true about the nature of that universe.

We shall see how this recognition led to discussions of what a non-abusive economic governance system would look like including economic governance with both property and individual citizen rights in non-abusive tension. We will review how this tension was finally addressed in America in our ninth chapter during the FDR New Deal era, and resolved within the concept of latent rights, meaning undefined, but rationally requiring defining if America is to insure economic justice as an outcome of the employment bargain.

Was labor's added value embedded in goods and services sold by property owners to be factored into not only the cost but also the distribution system in the future? Was a return on human knowledge and effort to be added and conveyed just as the system accepted the owners right to a return on their investment?

It was and is a fact that the capitalism system of modern America is a huge success regarding production of wealth; it is just as true that it has no mechanism for valuing or rewarding labor's value added beyond the lowest wage as close to base subsistence as the market will bear.

Philosophers' key questions regarding governance were, what are the individual liberties subjects should have based on these new proven truths, and not yet proven theories of justice based on observable phenomena? How can or should a government make laws to govern men in a free society as citizens with rights, that are self sustaining and accepted with good order? By what authority did an underlying contention at Philadelphia blossom in the ratification process regarding the demand for a Bill of Rights, as the people voiced their contempt for the abuse under which they had been born, reared, and labored as subjects when ruled by the old autocratic authority of the divine right of kings?

Our founders, leading men of the colonial era from the mid-eighteenth century forward, became avid students of the philosophers' ideas and how to best put them into law in balance with these natural truths in contention with obvious fallible revelation; English Common Law regarding property rights remained. The property owners did not revolt against property rights, only the unfair taxation thereof. The idea of God's will, at the heart of Biblical Christianity, was rejected in Philadelphia, as a key abuse in the system we revolted against.

In fact, human rights were recognized as flowing from nature as found in God's natural universe, not from the flawed knowledge of clerics in support of absolute rulers. Modern evangelical teaching in America today lives in denial of this reality politically. The modern GOP has embraced the myth that our civil rights are Bible based instead of a reform of Biblical beliefs enforced with coercion.

The only thing not limited by God in the life of confirmed autocrats was their absolute authority to abuse the individuals they ruled by the will of God including their life and death. In the ratification process the people demanded and the U.S. Congress approved an end to abuse by both state and church leaders alike under the new system that included a embracing preamble incorporating security and opportunity, and an amendable Bill of Rights subject to specifically large majorities in favor thereof among the states in Article Five.

The argument concerning executive authority as the change from Biblical authority to secular authority was made clear by George Washington who rejected the ambitions of the Cincinnati Society and many founders who feared the mob. Washington always rejected seeing himself as anything but a citizen serving as a duty in the interest of the governed and the Constitution. He served under the Constitution in the best interest of the common good of the nation and its citizens, and retired back to his status as a citizen of the United

States who resided in Virginia, as an example of the key role he believed he had played in creating the new norm for the United States and the future of free self governed men.

Property rights and religious rights supporters are now seen by millions of blacks, women, gays, and labor to be demanding an absolute right to continue abuse of these citizens' rights based on their property and/or religious rights being superior to secular (civil) rights of the abused, simply as U.S. citizens. These four formerly abused minorities without rights are still subject to continuing levels of abuse (they and I hope to see ended) in the twenty-first century.

In practice since ratification of the Bill of Rights the key individuals in our society of free men who have demanded and often been granted a lock on absolute abuse of another class of individual citizens, are employers (in twenty-first century GOP America, "the job creators", as if all jobs are created equal). This class of the abused is known in the twenty-first century as hourly wage earners. Over the course of United States history there have been many forms and many names for what is now known as hourly labor. The end of much of the protections enacted by the Democratic Party in the twentieth century were later repealed or impeded by the GOP, and will be addressed in our tenth chapter.

These employers, capitalists as we know them in modern times, perpetually claim the Constitution gave government no authority in what they claim is the private relationship between employers and those employed. I believe government has two roles to play. First, to ensure   sustainability of funding our education, defense, and infrastructure. Second, to assure due process is equally available to capital and labor in the exchange of value added for wages.

Instead of leaving citizens' rights to the federal government as intended by ratification of the Bill of Rights, many states have passed limits on the rights of citizens living in their states, causing them to be subject to state created entities known as corporations with absolute authority over employment issues in such states. These corporate employers (this applies to private employers also, but the vast majority of those so employed work for corporations) are allowed to treat citizens as if they are still subjects when it come to contracts between property owners and free citizens. So called right-to-work states limit the democratic right of American citizens living in those states to associate as a union to sell their labor to their employer, a latent right that the Democrats' Wagner Act addressed, and the GOP's Taft-Hartley Act compromised. I argue the states have been unconstitutionally authorized by the Supreme Court to allow this to continue as an abuse without a remedy. I have suggested a solution at the end of the book where I make suggestions in the hope of finding improved outcomes in compromise for the remainder of the twenty-first century.

Wage abuse is an unjust form of inequality enabled by denial of the right to bargain as free men in association for the sale of their labor as an example. Hunger as a bargaining tool in limiting wages is a form of abuse, just as gerrymandering is an abuse for Democratic Party voters, or as the Hobby Lobby and Lilly Ledbetter Supreme Court cases were for women's due process and equal rights in their right to conduct their family planning rights.

The gridlock over these issues of citizens' rights versus property rights should be seen as a misuse of the federal rights versus states' rights issue that goes back to the drafting and interpretation of the intent of the Bill of Rights, especially in the former slave states which have resisted the rights of labor since our founding.

So first let's look at property rights. Property deeds are registered in the state where the property is located, regardless of where the owner resides. In the Declaration of Independence property rights are not recognized as a natural right bestowed by the God of creation, therefore the founders' natural right theory does not apply to property. Property was a common law issue, and remained so in the Constitution. Private property has no standing regarding rights in federal courts or for sure was not a federal intent at our founding.

Second, what did the Constitution say about "We the People" as citizens in settling the final draft of the U.S. Constitution? At the end of the Convention, there was a Detail Committee and a Style and Arrangement Committee who were charged with the final edit for pre-signing publication. In the final draft the words "We the People" was repeated for each of the enumerated states, for example, "We the

People of New York, We the People of Virginia", etc., which could have made them treated as citizens of the state. However in the final arrangement "We the People" reads "of the United States of America". This clearly announced that individually, all Americans regardless of state of residence, are citizens of the United States. Once the Bill of Rights was ratified, states' rights concerning property rights remained. However, the federal courts have jurisdiction over citizens' dissent when abuse of a federal right is adjudicated. Remember, when a dispute is between a state right and a federal right, the federal right is superior. In 2020, 5-4 settlements hardly reflect this intent.

A fallible belief has too often been resurrected by advocates of property and faith based rights, based on a deceptively attractive ideology, that all profit produced on a man or a group of men's property is by right of equity and justice as well as a fair understanding of his or their freedom, solely his beyond the minimum wage the market demands he pay his employees, no matter how much value added labor provides, or how much they have invested in acquiring the knowledge and skill to provide these benefits and efforts.

Likewise it is alleged that any claim on the increased prosperity that has flowed from any services of government including the better educated workforce, public service sector, consumer economy with a high velocity of money, is a limit on the property owner's freedom and an illegal confiscation of his rightful due if taxed, meaning it is seen as confiscation.

The folly regarding sustainability of such a position should be obvious but we will review it as we go, both from a view towards sustainability as well as a just society of free men, for the millions who toil to produce the output from property aided by the services of the government. I'm calling it value added without just compensation.

How did the Enlightenment and its philosophers feel about Jesus? The key minds of the Enlightenment and our founders never questioned his role, the divinity (except Jefferson), the rationale, nor the message that Jesus taught during his time on earth, nor does this book. Some did not accept it as part of their own belief, but none attacked Jesus for his message, or his believers for their faith.

Our founders supported church men's freedom to continue to advance these beliefs. They totally debunked the errors of the men who claimed to represent infallibility which was not a teaching of Jesus. The myth about God's will or the divine right authority to rule was not a message Jesus taught. Jesus taught a separation of God and Caesar. Jesus told us he came to lead man to salvation, not to form a government, let alone an autocratic one.

I accept the promise of salvation as the key message of Jesus. He requested his followers to spread this message. This was the only worldly role Jesus requested for the church. I will interject here that he did ask us to love one another and to do unto others, as well as to address the needs of the sick, poor, and afflicted. I take it to mean he believed his father expected us to be tolerant of each other, as a fellow creation of God, whom he loves, the same sole duty of tolerance Madison assigned, if we hope to keep our own rights respected by our fellow citizens.

I will spend less time questioning motives, other than obvious greed and ego, and focus more on the outcome of policy decisions and actions of men as we get further into this book. I'm not teaching or debating Sunday school lessons, yet the political role evangelical pastors have been happy to step into in the twenty-first century is a factor in our gridlock, so we need to understand from the early history of our fore bearers how and why that role was ended.

Funny, as kings saw the pope was fallible and confiscated the pope's property, the English Parliament saw the king was abusive and usurped his absolute property rights. However, no king or parliament ever suggested the pope or the bishops were fallible about the concept of the divine rights of kings, and all continued to abuse citizens who labored, or kept house and bore and raised children.

Let's meet the thinkers our founders became first students of, then admirers of, and who finally became the first men to implement the philosophies of the Enlightenment into a self governing experiment as a society of free men.

If the narrative so far seems heavily dominated by questions of

Biblical Christian belief, it is. Our system of government was a reform of abusive state church theology. Our Supreme Court should reflect this fact in its remedies.

Chapter 4

The Enlightenment

New scientific truths discovered by the voyages of discovery in the 1490s into the early 1500s proved that the revealed truths of the church about creation taught since 325 A.D. were false. This led the men we call philosophers to re-imagine the natural role God intended for the men He created, to govern themselves upon his creation, and led learned men to first challenge the infallible knowledge and absolute authority of the pope.

This enabled kings to support local churchmen in challenging the pope, beginning what came to be known as the Reformation, led first by Martin Luther in what is now Germany. Luther was protected in his revolt by his local king who benefited by confiscating the local wealth of the Roman church for himself.

The early reformers of both church and state beginning early in the sixteenth century had little effect on the realities of life for peasants for another two hundred and fifty years, but these early reformers are owed our thanks for their reasoning for the rights we Americans enjoy even in tension in twenty-first century America.

Note: The concept of philosophy was introduced seven hundred years before Constantine introduced Biblical Christian state church feudalism, by Plato in his dialogues in his *Republic*. Most of the terms the sixteenth to eighteenth century philosophers debated and defined were based on early Greek words for justice, constitution, democracy, and happiness, all conceptual words that made it into our founding documents.

This chapter is the turning point for enabling subjects to remake themselves into citizens, to worship God as faith led them without fear of punishment for heresy, and the pursuit of life, liberty, and happiness as their own nature led them, in mutual toleration of each other's rights, and in keeping with the laws established by representatives of the majority without abuse of the minority, at least in America. However it was not without a fight by those who prefer absolute control of some or all aspects of the life of the many. They allowed themselves to claim they are worthy of their beliefs being imposed on the many without recourse.

We are in such a time again early in the twenty-first century when a minority feels that way about the religious, cultural and racial life, and the economic life of American citizens, that have our divisions of government among the two major political parties in gridlock, too often with contempt for the American ideals stated in the Preamble to the Constitution. From this chapter on we will review how our American values were built, and how our impasse has evolved, out of the eras of the fourth to sixteenth centuries we have just reviewed in our first three chapters.

The first three chapters introduced the establishment of organized government and religion in Europe, which endured through eleven hundred and sixty-five years of turmoil. Only in the beginning of the sixteenth century was the authority of the pope successfully reformed, first in Germany by Martin Luther and his king and then in England by Thomas Cromwell. In the following century at Westphalia in 1648 a treaty was signed granting kings the authority to select a religion for their kingdom, Roman or reformed, and for the nations to agree on defined borders. At this point there were few major nations; there were several peoples, Germanic, Normans, Turks, Brits and so on.

One hundred twenty years later having won our Revolutionary War our founders looked to and relied on enlightenment philosophies to establish for our nation a new authority to govern that ended absolute roles and rights, creating representative government as individual citizens were no longer to be viewed as subjects without rights, but as citizens with rights and recourse for the first time in the history of organized government, and/or religion. If the GOP ever acknowledges this transition, especially GOP Supreme Court Jurists, gridlock in America can finally begin to subside. This is not because the Democrats are superior, but because secular belief is more open to compromise than absolute religious belief, or absolute property rights based on a revealed religious belief that God chooses winners and losers, as President Trump might state it.

I like Emmanuel Kant's quote on what is meant by Enlightenment: "the freedom to use reason publicly in all matters".

The new truths led to a new understanding of God's creation, and man's role and rights as part of the natural freedom of God's creation, seen not as God's will but as God's allowance.

In 1517 a German monk and professor of theology named Martin Luther, supported at the time by his temporal elector (king), announced a challenge to the pope based on his self serving stewardship primarily regarding the selling of indulgences. Over the next eight years Luther and his king separated about half of the future German church and nation from the pope and the Holy Roman Emperor. This led to the onset of what came to be called the Reformation. Luther and the king established a new state church where the king would be head of both the nation and the church. The king would still be crowned by the state bishop, and thereby would still be an absolute ruler of all property and subjects by the will of God. Luther was a true man of the Bible; he rejected reason as not leading to God or salvation.

Within twenty years, based on a question regarding the English king's marriage status, Thomas Cromwell, the king's chief councilor, guided his king to also challenge the pope. This challenge led to the same outcome in our mother country England as Martin Luther effected. In Germany the new Lutheran church clergy retained the right to interpret the Bible for the laity; they became known as Lutherans.

In England the king founded the Church of England; the laity were allowed to read the Bible in English themselves. This church form became known as evangelical. In both countries the feudal economic system continued for more than two hundred years. In Germany the peasants rioted during the transition from the pope. Luther supported the king's crackdown on the rioters, and he re-established church leadership in support of the government over the peasants. Luther accepted he was leading men to salvation and not to freedom from the king's absolute rights. Luther never questioned the king's right to abuse the laboring peasantry, a property right churchmen defend still into the twenty-first century; it continued to be accepted that "the poor would always be with us".

During the next one hundred fifty years the key question among the men known as philosophers was, if the pope no longer had absolute authority over the king, then did the king still have absolute authority over his subjects and property owners? The philosophers developed new ideas concerning freedom, justice, law, and the concept of secular governance no longer based on faith alone, but on the right to reason based on provable science, and consent.

The question stemmed from the radical idea that God did not intend for any man to fear another, or to be subject to abuse from one man to another for life, to be accepted as God intended for life on the earth He created. The Philosophers did not question the idea of salvation related to governance. They saw that God's intent was actually an absence of abuse in a society of self governed free men.

We will soon review these men and their ideas. However, to pre-examine the outcome, in the 1680s during the English Civil War a settlement was reached that created another new relationship between king and parliament, based on the ideas this time not of the reformation, but of the enlightenment philosophers. As a result the king became only head of state and church but not of government. This introduced ideas such as the king no longer had authority over the economy or the treasury of the nation; Parliament now had the authority. England went a step further than Luther, adding reason to the secular side of governance, yet retaining absolute revelation as the only path to salvation.

In England, the king was no longer the absolute law maker; Parliament became the law maker. One house of Parliament was the House of Commons whose members were elected by those allowed to vote, the other remained the Lords who only had veto power over the laws enacted by the Commons side of Parliament.

This change made Parliament representative and political. It was political in that a member of the Commons side was now to be elected prime minister by his fellow members, still ruling based on divine right now delegated to the Parliament by the king. The country's constitution would be whatever English Common Law said it was, as established by Parliament. The authority to govern remained by divine right as the state church bishop continues to this day to crown the king as the head of the state in England.

The reformation was the first turning point in this structure; the English Civil War was the second. Our revolt would be the third. Each advancement from absolute rule by pope and king, to "by the consent of the governed" without a return to military rule has led to blow back, and a resurrection of legacy beliefs that would allow a "true church" to define culture. Each step has taken centuries to transition, and then always less than fully. Our current gridlock is just another example of this continuing phenomenon although it is happening more quickly. Remember, the U.S. Bill of Rights ended the concept of a true church, ending the possibility of heresy.

Our founders relied on these rational philosophers' insights to create a constitution equal to the task of governing a complex society of free men, assured of justice, and in return for authority to govern by consent, to rule a large independent nation among the many hostile nations of the world.

The task was how to reconcile economic and civil justice between men who own property and govern, and men who labor and are governed, while leaving each free man's individual religious quest for a personal religious creed to live by and to seek salvation or not, without government coercion. This dilemma is where I believe modern American evangelicals and their GOP bedfellows are gridlocked. Religious intolerance and the believed absolute rights of property owners are hostile to the democratic process in a society of free men. How to reconcile this without destroying America is my only goal. Before we wade into the key philosophies, let me remind readers that the only path our founders saw was tolerance of differences and compromise.

To our founders, justice meant an absence of government abuse, ending an accepted norm of Biblical Christian church state governance passed down from Roman and English history dating from the fourth century.

It was not a teaching of Jesus that abuse of peasants was his Father's intent; however, under Constantine the fourth century leaders of the Jesus movement known as Christianity accepted an absence of

individual subject's rights permitting government authority to coerce and abuse uneducated laborers as God's will. In the United States Evangelical Christians continue to demand their followers continue this belief, today in service to corporations in place of kings.

To replace the absolute lack of individual freedom and justice with assured freedom and justice for all became the great task, as revolt led to independence in our colonies at the end of the eighteenth century.

The twenty-first century task of corporations and evangelical pastors is to solve this dilemma they and their GOP political party still advocate. We will see much evidence that the blindness regarding abuse is too often held hostage to cultural issues such as gender, race, and nationality. This is the task for all of us, but the keystone is corporate and evangelical ideology.

The quest of this book is rational acceptance of the fact our founders understood the natural contention between property owners' rights, advocated in the twenty-first century by the GOP as Economic Freedom, and the individual rights of free citizens advocated in the twenty-first century by the Democratic Party as Economic Justice. The founders intentionally granted free men the freedom to seek salvation and happiness without coercion by secular or religious authority.

We will begin with a short review of what prompted our founders to utilize these philosophical writings as they created first state constitutions, and finally a federal constitution. These constitutions not only defined the intent of the new government for the few men of property but also for the many common citizens who usually toiled for subsistence or tightly limited wages, often without property ownership, a voice, or a vote, at the beginning of our national experiment in governing that was to become a continental society of free men.

One late Enlightenment writer at the time of our founding was a pamphleteer named Thomas Paine. He explained our founding ideas in a manner that was understandable to educated subjects voting to ratify the transition to citizenship. He wrote that free men were entitled to free thought and speech, democracy and justice, assured by those they entrusted with governance. These are also some of the principles that our founders found in the writings of the men of science and/or reason in the Age of Enlightenment. Jefferson was a fan of the Enlightenment writers, and he alone held special esteem for men who were not only philosophers but also scientists such as Isaac Newton and John Locke.

Of the many philosophers writing during the Enlightenment period the three key philosophers we will meet in this chapter are the men behind the ideas that formed our Declaration of Independence and our Constitution, including the Bill of Rights and our government's system of checks and balances, and our judicial system of settlement of dissents under the law.

Our founders' insights made several key and unanimous changes in governance and its mechanisms, which came out of debating to compromise the ideas of the philosophers into a workable government without a single absolute sovereign not subject to oversight, review, or removal for cause.

Instead of a full review of the history of the Enlightenment, we are listing below the intent of our founders, and featuring the writers who most influenced the final founding documents that are still the intent of our Declaration of Independence, followed by our Constitution, and finally our Bill of Rights that balanced citizens' rights with property rights at the state level, that our modern leaders swear to uphold.

The following goals were agreed to in the first meetings to form a confederation of the colonies that would review their status and options, as resentment of the king and Parliament grew between about 1760 and 1776 when they finally declared their intent to become a new state among the nations of the world.

The following list of our founders' goals were each advocated by one of the three key philosophers who influenced our founding principles. The philosopher is noted for each. We will follow the list with a further introduction to each of these three key men of science and reason.

In no particular order, first our Constitution allowed for the creation of a government established and operable under law with oversight, and a national economic system, without a state church. Our founders chose to introduce Scottish economic philosopher Adam Smith's system of capitalism to govern labor, property, money, credit, productivity, trade, contracts, and settlement of the mechanisms of exchange between the parties engaged in exchange of goods and services.

The United States became the first nation to adopt Smith's system as our economic system that came to be called capitalism, introduced legislatively into law in George Washington's first term. Capitalism replaced mercantilism except for an exemption in select southern states for continuation of a slave based export crop mercantile system with one customer, England, already in place without an expiration date certain for the labor or the economic settlement systems.

Second, we opted for freedom of religion in lieu of the state church, under the Establishment Clause of the First Amendment of our Bill of Rights. This was a concept advocated by John Locke, an English philosopher who was the clearest philosopher I've read regarding the concept of the God of creation who set in motion a natural world and everything in it, with all destined to exist naturally free in God's natural world, and to unfold as God willed it at the beginning of time.

Third, the founders retained absolute property rights at the state level, not at the federal level to maintain control of the economic interest of each state based on English Common Law that arose not as a philosophical idea but as the result of the laws of Parliament being a natural constitution in the English system.

It has always been difficult to monetize property values without defining the added value of labor; now in modern times we call this value added. However, wage labor was not a large factor of national life in the eighteenth century; labor rights, like voting rights, were not addressed at our founding in the Bill of Rights. Fortunately the Bill of Rights is amendable, and the U.S. legislature has the power to make law as we will see as our narrative progresses.

Fourth, the authority to govern changed per revelation from the Christian Bible "by the will of God" to the secular concept of "by the consent of the governed" as noted above, another idea adopted from the writings of John Locke.

Fifth, we established a democratic divided republican form of government that included an elected executive subject to terms, neither hereditary nor monarchical for life, and a two house legislature, one elected by the people to represent U.S. citizens and one of an equal number of representatives (two) from each state regardless of size, population or wealth, to represent each individual state.

The philosopher and father of the idea of divided government was a Frenchman names Charles-Louis Montesquieu, the third key philosopher our founders turned to for inspiration as they set out to first declare independence, and then to established a Constitution and a Bill of Rights.

Sixth, a new concept of a supreme judicial branch that established a concept of judicial review to settle constitutional dissent between the government branches, as well as between the federal or central government and the individual or collective states, and finally between individual citizens alone or as associated legal entities and actions of a state or a legal authority established by state government. This new third branch of government that in effect replaced the role of the bishops interpreting the laws of the church as well as the state, also came from the mind and pen of Montesquieu.

To not understand or to deny the reality of this chapter is to not understand the nature of gridlock in America today, between our political parties and the judges they support for the Supreme Court as they exercise judicial review in settlement of the question of standing regarding dissent in our legal process.

So let's meet the three gentlemen who profoundly influenced the thinking of our founders in dissent: the Englishman John Locke, the Scotsman Adam Smith, the Frenchman Montesquieu.

Most agree that John Locke was the key man of reason behind our decision to opt for a new form of government. We chose to seek a form of government compatible with Locke's understanding of the natural universe God created free to pursue equally what is understood by each citizen as his hoped for happiness in life. Locke was a medical man, a scientist who also became a philosopher. He created a role for those who govern, wherein men of means agree to govern all individuals in society without abuse, meaning justly.

Adam Smith was another of the influential philosophers. We adopted Smith's views regarding the *Wealth of Nations* in forming our new economic system. Locke and Smith philosophies overlapped regarding property rights. Locke rejected the idea that massive accumulated wealth was in the nation's interest especially when much of it was tied up in unproductive property. Both men saw it was an injustice to poor men if property under the absolute control kings or dynastic families was allowed to lay fallow. Both saw governments should be formed by free men for the common good as a compact. A compact like a contract is moot without utility; there is no utility to wealth without use, especially if exempt to taxation for the benefit of the established justice and common good.

The whole point was civil order and common good sustainability for a nation so governed. All citizens' rights were need based on mutual tolerance of each other's equality of rights. Under this philosophy producing goods and distributing the fruits of property including the added value of labor, must also include adequate rewards for the investor, the laborer, and the government that provides the infrastructure, the safety and the order. Locke and Smith understood the reality of the future; neither claimed to believe it would evolve as a natural process, as each understood the reality of greed, authority, and power.

Locke wrote on the rights of man, what some call natural law. Thomas Jefferson relied to a large extent on the mind and writings of Locke when writing the Declaration of Independence. Jefferson formulated the reasoning or the justification for the revolution primarily based on Locke's writings. This document was the United American colonies' announcement to the English and to the world. The Declaration expressed their desire to take their place among the independent nations of the world.

The Christian Bible, the Roman Empire, the English government before and after the English civil war, the U.S. Constitution, even the U.S. government never addressed the lack of wealth distribution concerning the value added of labor, the dignity of work, or the fact that starvation wages were cruel, even after mechanization in the mid nineteenth century increased not only wealth production, but also the danger and weariness of hourly toil. As property owners grew richer, new demands on labor and government continued without property owner acknowledgment. These new demands became increasingly unjust, even as return on investment grew and made sustainability affordable, but the wealthy, the king, and the bishop all stuck to the old understanding of God's will granting all wealth solely intended by God to accrue to the few. This remains the view of the corporate and evangelical wings of the GOP in the twenty-first century.

It was not until after the American Civil War that increased productivity due to industrialization produced enough wealth to create an obvious level of cruelty by continuing to limit labor to a subsistence existence, although Adam Smith had predicted growing productivity would lead to growing demands being imposed on labor.

Adam Smith was the father of the new economic order of free labor, free markets at home, and free trade among nations. Smith defined the efficiency of free markets. He created the idea of capitalism (although that word would not be used until the mid 1800s) without defined regulations. However, he did see the need for future regulation of capitalism. As experienced men of law, property, and commerce, Smith and our founders understood well the woes of unfettered greed, speculation, risk, fraud, opportunism, and intentional blindness. Smith admonished that to ensure sustainability, regulations would be needed regarding labor as well as taxes on income regarding government.

In 1760 Smith could already see that mechanization and mass assembly would lead to ever greater wealth creation due to the productivity, which would enhance the value of the investor's future returns, and increase the burdens on laborers' efforts. Adam Smith did not become a key influence in our founding until after the Constitution was ratified and the first president and legislature were sworn in, with a Constitutional mandate to form a government destined to become a continental nation supporting a sustainable military.

However, in the end the most influential among our founders in writing our legal enabling document (the Constitution) regarding our new form of government was Montesquieu, a noble with the title of Baron. He was like a modern rock star in the time of the enlightenment.

Montesquieu introduced the concept of freedom from fear of abuse by the government. He wanted the branches of government to be in tension so no one was above the law. His most famous quote was **"No man should live in fear of another"**. This idea led to his developing the philosophy of divided government which became the idea behind our authority to govern bargain, and the Bill of Rights that changed the Biblical "by the will of God" to "by the consent of the governed", which in the end enabled just governance of men of unequal gifts and contribution. This is the idea that made America a secular nation, and this is the fact that causes modern Biblical evangelical Christians in the United States to have contempt for U.S. Secular government, and believe it is the government being unfair to them, instead of recognizing how unfair they are to the majority for refusing to grant tolerance of any belief system but their own, regarding the establishment of crimes based on Biblical concepts of sin.

In the twenty-first century the president, who is most embraced by those who have contempt of the secular nature of our government designed to govern a society of free men, is Donald Trump. Based on Montesquieu's philosophy I fear Donald Trump, and for the first time in American history a majority of Americans fear an American president. Evangelicals, nationalists, and segregationists feared the first black President Barack Obama, but they are a minority and often overlap in a culture referred to as white supremacy.

Montesquieu did define the need for settled laws, as well as dissent against unjust laws. He is the father of our system of judicial review and is the father of the Supreme Court, our third branch of government. Our Supreme Court replaced the state church as the judge of breach of laws against heresy no longer a civil offense, or treason, becoming a much different threshold of offense in a nation that extends free speech to its citizens.

Settled law decisions were to be decided by the new court, instead of the leader of the king's approved church. Montesquieu also created the settled meaning of federal law as a concept in a democratic republic. In Chapter 6 Chief Justice John Marshal settles the question of how the Supreme Court settles law in the United States, as well as the rationale required by our Constitution, that being "to uphold the Constitution".

According to James Madison, Montesquieu was the single most quoted and cited individual thinker and writer of all of the philosophers of the Enlightenment era. Our founders depended on Montesquieu for insight in establishing a founding document for an independent nation to govern a society of free men at the Constitutional Convention, required to be ratified by the people to be governed, subject to the addition of a Bill of Rights in the 1789 ratification, which was added by ratification in 1791, the documentation we live under today in the twenty-first century.

Madison became known as the Father of the U.S. Constitution. He was our fourth president and a key advocate for ratification of the Constitution as the second most prolific contributor to the Federalist Papers written to support ratification, a key insight to this day for most members of the U.S. Supreme Court by their own acknowledgment.

The new Constitution (in its final form with the added Bill of Rights including a right of amendment) established authority to govern by the consent of we the people. The role of the government and the court is to uphold the Constitution. Montesquieu knew that new discoveries would change societal realities, and that a democratic government would need a mechanism for settlement of new laws and rights, since there would be no state church to have the final word. He knew we would need an independent court to sit in review. This is one of the ideas behind our founding document being a living document, i.e., an amendable (Bill of Rights) Constitution.

Two key founders at the Constitutional Convention were students of Montesquieu: Benjamin Franklin and James Madison, the lead author at the proceedings. They made sure we had settled law as an aspect of the Constitution (judicial review) for our government system. To this day judicial review is the means of settling secular law in nations without a state church.

John Marshall was the founder who was the primary implementer of judicial review as a method of settling what federal law means, and the final definer later as Chief Justice. John Marshall did not represent his home colony of Virginia at the Constitutional Convention, but he was the key supporter of the concept at Virginia's Constitutional Ratification Convention. Marshall was the one who won the nullification debate with Patrick Henry who argued for a state right of nullification of any federal law a state wished to not be subject to, regarding the rights of citizens who resided in that state.

Nullification lost in the Constitutional Convention ratification process, and was John Calhoun's key rationale in leading his home state of South Carolina to secede and start our Civil War. Nullification was again defeated in the U.S. Civil War. Today evangelicals do not suggest secession, but they do suggest an end to judicial review, which would amount to much the same thing, chaos and abuse again of the many by the few.

Marshall's side won and if it hadn't, federal law would be meaningless as a protection of individual rights since any state could opt out of any federal law at any time.

What would our government be like without Montesquieu's inspired Supreme Court? An example of how lack of a secular form of settlement of laws can be found today, is in a Muslim country with an absolute leader of the state and a Muslim leader under one supreme authority (Allah). Citizens as subjects have no defined rights, and no appeal process. Their equivalent of a king always rules for the state and its church. There isn't even a right to express dissent. The law is always whatever the messenger of God revealed the will of God to be without appeal.

Imagine if you could be arrested and sentenced without a fair court hearing, and without appeal, what our Bill of Rights calls due process. Such abuse is what happens when one of our children, a journalist, or combatant is captured in a Muslim country like Iran, Syria, or Saudi Arabia. Whatever the Qur'an defined as an offense toward God twelve hundred years ago as interpreted by a modern Imam, is the absolute law, leading even to the death of a child for doing his job or on a youthful adventure.

Policy has outcomes; a policy of limiting judicial review regarding fourth century Christian concepts of sin looms as a present danger for those of us who fully uphold the U.S. Constitution and its civil (meaning secular) intent.

Advances in agriculture and manufacturing productivity had not changed much in the thirteen hundred years from the end of the Roman Empire to the American Revolution. Some inventions, such as Watt's steam engine, the spinning jenny, and the steel plow were precursors to the introduction of ever increasing productivity in the nineteenth century. Rapid technological inventions meant that philosophical theories needed to allow for political and economic progress. All governance and economic systems needed to be able to address changing economic realities, as wealth creation expanded beyond any previously known norms.

Norms encoded in English Common Law which the former colonies retained as states after 1791 were not adequate to address these ever more complex governance dilemmas, and people were often inflexible regarding changing a norm that was not only comfortable, but had also been seen as kind to their type or tribe, especially men of property who supported revolt against unjust taxation yet have since fought to limit individual citizen rights. They refused to consider any taxes beyond the cost of protecting their property and defense of the national borders; they saw all other taxes as confiscation.

As eighteenth century thinkers, neither Smith nor Locke had much insight or knowledge concerning improvement of the labor system at the time. The only instance is a common sense story Smith tells in *The Wealth of Nations* which defined improved systematized manufacture of pins. This story is similar to the insight of Henry Ford some one hundred sixty years later, when he used standardization and a moving assembly line in Highland Park Michigan to manufacture Model T Fords.

Ford priced the cars at a cost that allowed improved income for his laborers as well as lower prices for his customers, made possible as a share of his lower cost. Almost magically his sales and profits improved, creating ever growing wealth for all tiers of American society as this system was slowly adopted by others, at least before the crash in the Depression of 1929.

Of the major philosophers, only Smith foresaw that productivity would impact governance in the many ways it has. Smith conceived a rationale for a role for government that would be in the best interest of all. His solution was sustainable levels of taxation for government, and a sustainable living wage for labor. The one time in U.S. history this was tried was the longest, largest, and most sustainable period of growth in U.S. history, from the end of WWII until the onset of the Ronald Reagan era in 1981. This period is called the FDR New Deal era and the mechanisms and outcomes make up most of Chapter 9.

John Stuart Mills, a nineteenth century philosopher similar to Locke in his thinking, saw that Smith was correct within one hundred years of his publishing *The Wealth of Nations*. Mills wrote about the poverty among the working poor, which happened in spite of the never-ending improvement in total wealth output called gross domestic product (GDP) of the national economy. As individual productivity continued to improve, this phenomenon of divergent outcomes is known as the wealth gap.

Each generation improved the tools and methods of productivity which improved the output and profits, but not laborers' standard of living, nor the tax income of the nation. Almost all of this new wealth accrued to the owner class. Visit Newport Rhode Island's so called cottages and mansions preserved along the Cliff Walk, or read Charles Dickens to see the contrast between abused labor and conspicuous consumption by the families of the English and American oligarchs early in the Industrial Age. The wealth gap in American has widened as fast as new wealth has been produced since the industrial revolution began; in 2020 it is the widest in dollars and percentages as it has ever been in the history of America.

Modern philosophy is most often produced by oligarchs funding think tanks with tax exemptions producing teachable policies in the interest of corporations and dynastic families of wealth, seldom in the interest of the established justice or the common good.

Today America's key contentious economic issue is not the efficiency of capitalism to produce. That side of Smith's philosophical theory concerning free markets is proven. The battle involves three things. The first is defining the means and portion of increasing productivity to be distributed. Second, determining that portion of profits owed in taxes to government to ensure adequate and secure governance as well as the obvious need to end planned operating budget deficits that have led to a never-ending increase in national debt following each GOP reduction in the tax rates. Third and finally a rational return to a living wage to ensure a sustainable middle class in the United States. In doing so we must also ensure that risk taking has a sustainable return that is needed to continue to attract adequate capital investment without cycles of boom and bust.

What is desperately needed is a non-absolutist theory of sustainable distribution rather than absolute wealth accumulation rights for property owners without consideration of the nation's and its citizens' justly earned share of the value they add in the commercial process of a wished for rationally regulated market, in place of the golden idol of a free market that allows an ever expanding wealth gap.

My personal outrage is for those who support an ideology of freedom and property rights, yet cannot see or do not see opportunistic or coerced injustice as government allowed abuse. God created individuals, government created corporations. Today's GOP has allowed original intent to befuddle which is of God, and which is of the government of the few, having replaced Cesar.

Back in the eighteenth century, it is true that Adam Smith's insights did not fully anticipate how rapid growth of mechanization would affect capitalization. He did not foresee the ever greater demand for ever larger pools of money to capitalize the growth of industrialized capitalism. Starting mostly after Smith's time, improvements in productivity (meaning fewer man hours needed to grow or process a bushel of wheat, etc.), have often led to a reduction in employment in an industry (the usual product cited is horse buggy whips), or in a region (today coal mining in West Virginia). Today much of that disruption is due to the volatility of cheap labor exploitation by nations with governments dedicated to abuse of their own citizens or the high tech sector's computers, programmables, and/or robotic inventions, often sensor enhanced.

Unfortunately it also often means an increase in working class poverty even as profits grow. Today we are seeing another long round of reduced man hours to produce ever increasing outputs. Just in my lifetime, automation and digitization has reduced the number of telephone operators, meter readers, medical transcriptionists, longshoremen, each by more than a million wage earners. This is just citing four industries; dozens and dozens have been affected. A new technology on the horizon is driver-less vehicles. When it is perfected more than two million truck drivers will be unemployed. The need for more than philosophy, a need for mutually agreeable solutions is desperately needed. We may need to consider yet in the twenty-first century a guaranteed income based on taxes on automated industries for all Americans as a base income.

Only government intervention acts as a wealth distributor to ensure the nation is employed and/or funded in some way to maintain a civil society, especially if it is to be a society of free men. As an example, one of the responsibilities of the Federal Reserve beyond setting interest rates and managing inflation is to also maintain full employment, although presidents like to take credit for the economy and the GOP likes to define its corporate supporters as job creators, and they are. To a large extent it is government that plays the key role in the economy, and always when insuring a living wage for full time employed employees educated by tax payers. A living wage is not a right yet advocated by either party. This would solve the fight over access to healthcare and education and training equal to ability.

How can government justly act as a wealth distributor? One way is an employer mandate to pay a minimum wage to employees that keeps pace with inflation and the government's investment in educating them for the modern economy. If you think this is a bad thing, imagine what it would be like if you were trying to live on one forty hour week minimum wage job in the second decade of the twenty-first century without employment provided healthcare.

If employment levels are low and federalism to fund poor people in poor states is withheld, it is not laziness that causes hunger in children; it is the fact that minimum wage pays less than a minimum living wage. If millions of such jobs are needed in America, and that requires millions of employees earning less than a living wage, at what point do we stop the racial charade of laziness to explain away addressing the institutional reality of employment abuse being tolerated as a cause of childhood hunger, pain, and hopelessness?

Most people in that category qualify for federal assistance in housing, daycare, and food, so our tax dollars are providing these people money because their employers are not paying them a living wage.

A second way the government acts as a wealth distributor is by taxing profits, and using that money to support the people who can't get a living wage job. I am not making a moral argument here, or even a property versus individual rights argument; this is a rational argument for a rational and sustainable society.

Adam Smith and those who backed capitalism, starting with Hamilton at the birth of the United States, under-anticipated the opportunities and the risk of two kinds of capital that were barely mentioned before the nineteenth century; these are debt and equity. When they were finally leveraged, a man with a small nest egg and an idea could invest his funds. He could attract investors and/or lenders to his enterprise. This would eventually lead to industrial enterprises starting businesses instead of individuals, using the same small investment and large loans to bring ideas to market. They started selling stock in their enterprises, creating speculation. This was available to both fraudsters and legitimate promoters as we shall see.

Without regulation of investors or lenders, a major fly in the ointment became speculation on margin. This happens when one invests in stocks carried on company books as paid in capital, often overvalued by sellers and underfunded by buyers. If a stockholder's investment is actually largely debt, (in the case of a slowdown in growth) this triggers a margin loan call as a quick pay down is called for. Margin loans can cause distressed sales of stock, which cause the companies' book market value to shrink. The downsides of unregulated banking and stock markets bedeviled the United States for most of our first hundred and fifty years. When bank regulations were repealed by Movement Conservatives starting in the 1980s the practice returned, as well as the consequences of boom and bust which will be reviewed in Chapter 10.

The philosophers of the enlightenment had the stage set for the founding of our country as a going concern, based on the best thinking of the men of the Enlightenment and the compromises of our founders. Our history has constantly tested the compromise concept ever since, and as we all seem to agree, at this time we are again in gridlock early in the twenty-first century over the lack of ability or willingness to even consider compromise. Any politician in the modern GOP who considers compromise will be attacked in the next primary. They will face millions of dollars of outside money used against them in the next primary in their district, a recipe to ensure continuing gridlock.

Part II

U.S. History – Governance by Consent

Chapter 5 – U.S. Independence

This chapter includes a look back at the time after the English Civil War when Parliament was actually ruling England, during the time of the so called "deplorable acts of Parliament" that led to our revolt, defined as our intent in the Declaration of Independence. English troops were already in the field in Massachusetts. One by one the other colonies joined New England states in war under General George Washington from Virginia in combat against the Red Coats, often German mercenaries. Finally the French came to our aid after eight years and England sued for peace, which led to our founding as the United States of America.

Once the war was won, we suffered four years from 1783 to 1787 as states without a national federal government, without a constitution or any organized national government; adrift, no one was being paid, the war debt languished. The new states were doing business again; especially dangerous was the anger of the veterans who remained unpaid from the Revolutionary War; several uprisings worried George Washington, especially Shay's rebellion in Massachusetts.

Finally representatives of thirteen independent states met in 1787 to perfect deficiencies of what they called their Confederation without a defined and ratified authority to govern. It will take them until 1789 to agree on a constitution written and ratified, and the first government sworn in.

So far so good, but several states ratified the Constitution subject to a Bill of Rights enough to make the ratification official only if the demand was complied with, and there was still no authority to govern. Biblical Christians still believed in revelation that taught kings rule by God's will, but that authority has ended. Without a state church or a king, and a declaration that we will govern ourselves as freemen under the protection of the God of nature, we were committed to self rule.

There was no blue print for what comes next in the national government or the government back home in each state; most of the states had established a state government and a state constitution, while keeping a state religion.

In 1791 the Bill of Rights was ratified as part of a bargain in exchange for granting our elected representatives (all property owners) authority to govern "by the Consent of the Governed", the philological ideal proposed by John Locke; the property owners agreed to protect all citizens of the United States regardless of state of residency, from abuse by any state or state sanctioned entity.

In the same year the president and congress had accepted Hamilton's proposed economic system, capitalism based on the philological ideas of Adam Smith. Thank God for Washington, Madison, and Hamilton, even as regional party partisanship begins.

State churches were no longer legal; it would take a while to get all the new states up to speed with the new Constitution.

This chapter ties founding principles to much of our modern gridlock. Remember, this is a history to understand our gridlock as it has grown like an onion in layers, less than a traditional history of wars won and the resulting growth in our size. Our founding principles that are still at the base of how American governance is still organized owes thanks primarily to five men.

In order of importance I rank them as follows; first George Washington, tied for second are James Madison and Alexander Hamilton, third is John Marshall, and finally Thomas Jefferson. Starting with John Adams many played their key supporting role, but the five above played the key roles in founding the nature of the nation and its governing mechanisms we live in and with today.

Most key factors of government looked back to the Enlightenment or English Common Law; however, our new to be implemented economic system, capitalism, was no older than our revolt.

Opposition to factors of capitalism was the first issue of absolute gridlock in American history. The form of government and what a capitalist system portended in the minds of the southern founders was never addressed beyond their opposition to it as anti-republicanism was never fully addressed until the Civil War. The south did not want the national government to overpower the states and their distinct regional economy and culture.

Adam Smith was a contemporary of our founders. This is a good point for a look ahead at the three line introduction to his book *The Wealth of Nations* that was the foundation of capitalism, and two quotes from the book: one about distribution of wealth and prevention of oppression to those who add value by their labor, and the other about the rights of those who provide capital.

First the introduction.

"Of the causes of Improvements in the productive powers of Labor, and of the Order according to which its Produce is naturally distributed among the different Ranks of the People."

It will be another one hundred sixty-five years until FDR becomes the first president to pledge the United States government would address a fairer distribution of America's great ability to produce wealth; he called it his New Deal.

The second quote below from Adam Smith's book addresses what he called the system of natural liberty, which to him was a simple explanation of the magical outcome of free enterprise and free labor. He called it the invisible hand that unleashed the concept of private enterprise in the United State. His quote is as follows.

"Every man, as long as he does not violate the laws of justice, is left perfectly free to pursue his own interest his own way, and to bring both his industry and capital into competition with those of any other man, or order of men."

Of the founding concepts among our founders other than Alexander Hamilton, capitalism was the newest and least well known or understood of the enlightenment concepts they adopted.

Adam Smith also defined the role of government relating to wage earners better than any of the other key philosophers, as follows in his own words.

"According to the system of natural liberty, the sovereign has only three duties to attend to; ... first, the duty of protecting the society from violence and invasion of other independent societies; secondly, the duty of protecting as far as possible, every member of the society from the injustice or oppression of every other member of it, or the duty of establishing an exact administration of justice; and thirdly, the duty of erecting and maintaining certain public works and certain public institutions which it can never be for the interest of any individual, or small number of individuals..."

Conservatives only mention the second of these three, and ignore the first (justice and lack of oppression) which in this book I call the absence of abuse, and third, Adams defines what our founders called "the common good".

It seems obvious Smith did not see property owners as having the same absolute authority by divine right as God granted kings over property and his subjects, as he foresaw the future growing contribution to the growing demands of mechanized industry on labor and government.

Modern corporations only came into being after our Declaration of Independence that stated the intent of our revolutionary transition including a war in revolt, and ratification of the Constitution including the Bill of Rights which settled citizens' rights, and the federal government's authority to govern, with a remedy for abuse of citizens.

In 2020 corporations still claim employer rights over their employees, as the kings and their masters of old had over their serfs and peasants, with subsistence living replaced by lowest wages and minimum benefits and the level of safety the market will bear, solely at the owners' discretion.

The conservative ideology regarding these beliefs of old in the role of modern government, is that the federal government has no role to play. Conservatives claim employment law is reserved for the states constitutionally. Too often the U.S. Supreme Court rules as if the authority to govern bargain was never ratified.

Adam Smith's quote anticipated the reality that labors' knowledge, skill, and efforts add value to the property owner's investment. I read Smith to be stating it is therefore a natural right in justice that labor shares in the added income this knowledge, skill, and effort created.

The king only provided a subsistence level of living for his serfs and peasants; today corporations make a similar argument. They claim they only owe employees the lowest wage the market will bear. However, in reality the market is influenced by whatever level of investment the nation   spends to keep it sustainable, ensuring that the common good of sufficient infrastructure and an educated work force are fully funded to maintain the capitalist system. This must include a sustainable citizens' income, meaning sufficient tax income to close the loop and enough to support the national economy, especially as taxes on corporations and dynastic wealth are reduced.

I make the case in this book that failure to pay a just return on labors' value added, and tolerating unsafe and abusive working conditions for laborers is oppressive and therefore unjust; and it is the duty of the judiciary to ensure a remedy (if not by the legislature) by the court. Low wages jeopardize the tax receipts of the nation, and thereby the economy, and in the end "starving the beast" (Reagan quote in Chapter 10) destroys all.

I further argue that the many systems of labor American investors have invented and our courts have tolerated were oppressive and therefore too often violate the natural rights of those who labor for wages. The oppressive systems have included slavery, share cropping, prison labor renting, and the company store system. The continuing systems include casual labor for farm, construction, and domestic work, union show in schemes, and various non union industrial factory systems, any number of self employment schemes such as Amway, Uber, and Amazon's new delivery system known as the gig economy, as well as state sponsored right-to-work schemes. All but slavery were common after the Civil War until the New Deal, from about 1870 to 1935, many continue into the twentieth century.

Conservatives often equate Smith's use of the term "natural rights" as if he is talking about this as a factor as old as the Christian Bible and European feudalism, both introduced across Europe at the same time; he was not. Natural rights were only established as the intent of the God of creation during the enlightenment, after the reformation that ended absolute belief in Biblical revelation regarding the natural state of the universe. There were no natural rights of man in the concept revealed by the authors of the Roman's first Bible released as the Nicaea Bible. The only rights were the kings' and the churches' and they were absolute over all subjects "by divine right" and still the law of the state and the state church during Smith's lifetime in Scotland. Plato (as noted above) introduced the concept of natural rights the Enlightenment resurrected.

Capitalism was also the most contentious mechanism of governance between the northern and southern states. Smith and Hamilton both accepted that its produce is naturally distributed to the owner class once market wages are absorbed into the cost of goods sold without any consideration of sustainability.

A key future question for our modern gridlock will be, at what point do ancient natural distribution rights become unjust or oppressive for free men in a wage based economy of growing wealth production for citizens promised justice under the new authority to govern bargain made by our founders?

As the founders moved along down the path of sorting out how Washington's executive branch would operate day-to-day, Smith's theory of capitalism was adopted but his idea of natural distribution will be ignored for almost another hundred and fifty years. It will be the injustice due to the fact capitalism lacks a mechanism for natural distribution equal to the greater output of the invisible hand, that will dominate our last two chapters. The capitalists became rich beyond imagination, while wage earners remained in abject poverty.

There are those who see government only as a protector of property rights in defense of both contracts and the nation, and good order based on the moral teachings of Biblical Christianity as modified over the centuries by English kings until our founding. These few short paragraphs about Adam Smith's theory sums up why I see a need for a wider understanding of what America grew out of, going forward into the twenty-first century.

This is not a full history of our founding; it is the story of how common our gridlock is, and the fierceness of each inch of progress over the decades of America's history. The greater the wealth of the nation grew, the more fierce property owners became in demanding government allow nothing more than subsistence for the many who labor for wages, while protecting the wealth of the nation for the exclusive benefit of the few families of dynastic wealth and their managers, much like kings and their nobles under feudalism.

All they asked of us at Philadelphia was to compromise without resorting to gridlock, insolvency, or war. Every day of America's two hundred and thirty years of our consent as a people to be self governed, some half more or less of us have refused to fulfill this simple duty; it is as sacred as the oath our young citizens take when we send them into battle. No American can pretend to be a patriot, and remain intolerant of our fellow citizens or keep our government in gridlock. In my view these are the two most treasonous acts an American politician or jurist can engage in.

So let's review the outcomes of our first years as a nation in considering why I selected and ranked the five key leaders I mentioned above. I have read, researched, and studied the history of what each contributed, and how and why what they did together was sometimes compromised and became settled, and more often was not compromised and created gridlock or worse.

At our founding George Washington was not only their natural leader, he also was that most unnatural of men, a strong driven man who acted for the common good more than for his own enrichment or aggrandizement. Washington proved himself to be almost alone among the great men of history, a good judge of talent, strategy, and the interface of parts of a system equal to the task at hand. His final talents were patience and knowing when to get off the stage, trusting his creation was ready and needed to stand on its own.

Our Constitution, our economic system, our freedom of religion,

our fiscal system, our strong central well funded and armed national government, our divided government of laws not men, with checks and balances, our educated electorate, our bill of rights, and our authority to govern bargain "by consent of the governed" all owe their place in our success to George Washington; yet none of these but a well funded strong central government was his idea. Each was accepted unanimously in compromise when he personally supported each of these factors of American governance.

James Madison was the father of the United States Constitution and the Bill of Rights. Every factor of United States governance noted above except capitalism, and the means to Washington's requirement for a strong well funded central government we owe to Hamilton; a means of supporting our Constitution and settling what our laws mean we owe to Marshall, and our freedom of religion, our educated electorate, and consent bargain we owe to Jefferson.

Many men, John Adams, Benjamin Franklin, and others added gravitas, but the five mentioned above gave us the government; in the end two of them created the partisan gridlock we have endured since 1791, that continues over nearly the same issues the founders compromised for a minute to enact at the end of the eighteenth century.

If the first goal of our republic as Benjamin Franklin suggested is sustainability, such a nation must also sustain a large living wage middle class, a steady upwardly mobile dependent class, and an adequately funded class of folks too young, too afflicted, or too old to ensure survival at the poverty line for the economically noncompetitive. That can only be accomplished if we have a strong successful economic system adequate to the needs of a modern continental nation of plus three hundred million citizens. We all need to acknowledge the only such system known to man in history has been capitalism.

Those of us who support capitalism most must also acknowledge that while the incentive to invest for a return must be the first interest of those who represent corporate and dynastic wealth's interest, sustainability of our nation requires a mechanism of distribution of the fruits of the economic system adequate to the proportional needs of American families and government. Concerning those who cannot be self sufficient due to age, or who will not for whatever reason or will have difficulty because of their own shortcomings or some other factor of nature, or society norms, or even dumb luck, must be addressed within a share of distribution in the form of taxation that is built into the government's share of the distribution system. While there are good arguments against a planned economy, there are also good arguments against unregulated markets and unaddressed poverty also.

If you read the Preamble to the Constitution our founders wrote and the citizens ratified you can see that they stated these goals idealistically. Adams and Jefferson agreed a sustainable tension in balance between greed and virtue that adequately serves the common good and establishes justice was their goal in spite of their different view of the common man, the size of the government, or the nature of its economy. Nowhere will you find the founders intended to build a system based on every man for himself as a definition of liberty, freedom, or justice, or intended any class except slaves to be what we would term victims of abuse as a fact of existence. It is a knowable fact that there are millions of citizens born with limitations into abuse, unable to protect themselves or compete. They and their children live with hunger, fear, cold, without healthcare.

Governmental and societal tensions were discernible in the interplay primarily among Hamilton, Jefferson, Marshall and Madison, arguably the four most effective founders Washington depended on for establishing the government he turned over to us. I am referring to the actual government as it operates. They lived out their lives in the government they created in both tension and compromise. We still revere all five men in spite of each having no fewer human foibles than most folks, but in fact each possessed more reasoning power than most.

In 1791 James Madison, ignoring his own advice and Washington's wishes, established with Jefferson the first partisan political party in the south, which led to unending gridlock when both rejected Hamilton's national bank and economic goals, as well as Washington's goal of a strong central government. The south was less hostile to a state church than the north, Madison and Jefferson not so much.

Washington never joined a political party and advised he thought they were the bane of civil government. In reaction to the party of Madison and Jefferson, Adams and Hamilton formed a partisan political party in the north that accepted both Hamilton's and Washington's view of a central government and bank, and also accepted the Madisonian Constitution and Jeffersonian view regarding separation of church and state and the need for an informed educated electorate. Madison was satisfied with a limited electorate of men of property, Jefferson disagreed totally.

In the end for the most part each did compromise to ensure governing tension was kept out of gridlock at least during Washington's presidency, with a feeling that their base supporters would see the value therein. While the nation lived until the Civil War with declining willingness to compromise as the non slavery economy and number of states grew faster than slave states, we still do not seem to fully understand the folly of each renewed cycle of war, bust, or gridlock our founding gridlock has cost over the decades.

At the time of our founding, the United States of America became a nation with a lot (1,275 years) of baggage disguised as unanalyzed absolute beliefs, values, or norms as the majority belief system was or is called. We may not have discussed it at our founding, but in fact we inherited all of the political and economic ills of the Roman system legacies still intact, all the political and economic abuse of monarchy and state church autocracy, and all the ills of colonialism including slavery, mercantilism, and the class system of limited democracy. I will attempt to memorialize the effects of these legacies as our story progresses.

The key thing the new nation did have was a continuously growing arrival of striving individuals willing to start from scratch and earn their way out of landlessness, poverty, hunger, and fear, living on the slim diet of hope, belief, ambition, and the promise of a just system, and a willingness to live in freedom, work hard, and obey the law. The fact that happiness has become a reality for about half of all American families so far is why this nation is so great. I believe the reality of the half of families not there yet is the work left for the generations of the twenty-first century.

Our founders thought hard about what was wrong with other government systems. What they crafted assured reduction of, hopefully even elimination of abuse with better outcomes for all than the governance, economic, religious, or societal systems they had revolted against. That we are as far along as we are for so many is heartening; that we are in gridlock on how to address the other half is the hand on the brake in our quest to be seen as worthy of being called exceptional, let alone a fully just society of free men.

The most devastating outcome for those who are not accorded an equal or at least fair measure of justice is loss of hope. The cost of hopelessness is the worst policy outcome any nation can face short of losing a war to a nation led by a tyrant, or creating a tyrant of our own because he is good to our class of citizens – so far.

Our founders did not hate England, but like teenagers they demanded more independence at home, or as usually happens, they exerted their independence and vowed to do better than their parent in the life they would build. In time they also came to better understand their parents' limits, not as enemies but also not as models for knowing the ideal answers to the questions of life.

The founders created mechanisms for legislation as well as judicial change to address unknown future issues. They accepted the challenge to write and create an ongoing system of compromise for each new force at work against cohesion, while understanding that the full range of human emotions has always been an extra burden in finding the gumption to finish unsettled uphill battles calling for reason and measured progress against strong defense of established norms by the majority that injure the minority population in a state of intentional blindness or denial.

The founders made the best compromises to forge the best bargain they could. Happily they also knew the coming generations would grow in knowledge, understanding, and numbers, and would rethink the compromises and bargains of the eighteenth century. They even gave us tools to address change and inevitable vastness in creating in the first generation, and an independent three thousand mile wide continental nation with an amendable constitution.

They could not conceive of net neutrality, for example the cost of eye surgery for most folks who live into or beyond their seventies, or how best to fund it. They did give us an amendable system if we are wise enough to use it without always triggering a demand for regression back to the practice of explained away abuse of the many by the powerful and wealthy few, or still held in thrall to the proven errors of revelation.

Our revolution came about largely at the time and in the manner it did due to what became a debate over the logic of sovereignty. This was brought into focus by a series of acts of greed and shortsightedness the English Parliament imposed on the colonials, mostly in the 1760s. In the end the common name for these deeds became the "intolerable acts" as noted above. The worst in my opinion was called The Board of Customs Commissioners in 1767. This act of Parliament was approved by the king.

The Commissioners lived in the colonies and ruled over almost all aspects of government. What is intolerable will be rebelled against, and it was. I believe the founders revolted against their king when Parliament became arbitrary. Determined to effect change they had appealed to all four: the royal governor, the king, the Parliament, and directly to the English people, all to no avail.

Parliament assumed sovereignty in 1688 during the English Civil War (an interesting read in itself). They killed King Charles I, and created a prime minister, keeping the eventual new king as head of state only, still crowned by the state bishop (thus no new or changed authority to govern) while the Parliament became the head of government. This is still the English system of government today, also noted earlier.

In America we allowed a form of sovereignty to exist in each state as a republic. This became another of our forms of restraint on the idea of one autocratic man as ruler. The English system we revolted against has never been as complex or as gridlocked as we are, because there is both less freedom and less assurance of equality in the form of justice.

Our founders gave us a balance of both in tension and compromise.

Are we to squander both in gridlock? As I write England is going through the heartache of dealing with having joined a new system of sovereignty factors (the EU), and is now figuring out how to leave that trial arrangement without losing all of the trade advantages the arrangement created. We will see how the so called Brexit (British exit from the EU) works out.

We will not delve deeply into pre-revolutionary debates on sovereignty. For our purposes, authority to govern will remain our focus and the relationships among property owners, individuals as U.S. Citizens, taxes, and rights will form our background as to what was of concern and/or in dissent at the Constitutional Convention, that reignited once we were an organized government with authority to govern beginning in 1791.

One thought to remember: as each colony became a state its leaders realized it could not face the nations of the world alone. Yet they knew they also wanted a form of local sovereignty regarding local day-to-day life. Of the founders only Patrick Henry never accepted the idea that the United States could pass a law that Virginia disagreed with, and yet remain a law for Virginia citizens. Henry voted against the Constitution, and refused to serve in the new government. In the twenty-first century evangelicals have a similar problem to Henry's, this time regarding how the U.S. federal government can pass a law making an act they consider a sin to become a legal right for their neighbors, that they have to tolerate. That such acts take place in private are not mitigating to modern evangelicals.

Today's gridlock is as much or more about the constraints on local sovereignty regarding folks living in any given state as it is about gridlock over national sovereignty issues. Gun rights in NYC and in rural Montana are hardly the same, an example of where a national policy is difficult to administer in both a largely rural state and a large modern urban city, when the federal right belongs to every citizen of the United States no matter what state they live in. Note: Gun law is not the only urban versus rural governance dichotomy in the twenty-first century. The old 80-20 rule impacts every issue related to urban and rural realities.

Our founders wanted to move away from and beyond previous systems of abusive governance that were tolerated when the autocrats' authority was believed to be the will of God among the uneducated who were legally kept living in absolute fear of harm, hunger, death, and/or damnation.

We do not know to what extent the founders were aware of how entrenched the norms of the previous twelve hundred fifty years would remain in the minds of newly minted American citizens. No state church closed its doors on day one, and no woman had the vote on day one; it all has taken time and has been slow to be accepted as the new understanding of the bargains made became functional or not.

Would our founders be surprised that we have more hunger per thousand citizens in America today when food production is many times greater per person than it was in 1776? Are you? There was no welfare then, but there was a land grant system. Folks living on farms were otherwise poorer, but not hungrier.

To make an independent inquiry into the difference in longevity, height, and calories available between eighteenth century free men in colonial America who owned land, and feudal labor in England still living under what the Bible said was God's will, is interesting. What jumps out first is the difference in longevity. For instance, colonial subjects (before they became citizens) lived seventeen years longer in New England than feudal subjects in England in 1760 in a study I read; fifty-three years versus thirty-six years. Colonial America was a better life than for subjects still in England except the aristocracy, who still lived better than anyone else in any part of the Empire at that time.

The difference was land availability in the colonies that granted ownership of one's own productivity. In the twenty-first century we again see the effect of landlessness without a skill among the poor in modern America. The rights of land owners, and their government's willingness to set a low minimum wage, leaves full time working poor families hungry, while property owners are free to set a market price for food and rent. Hunger is a different issue today than in 1760 America, but not much better for the very poor than the 1870 company store system. They do toil less now, but have no greater dignity or quality of life in this much wealthier era.

The gridlock in the south was primarily opposition to Hamilton's solution for Washington's demand for an economic system sustainable against any future war with a European power. It remained for the balance of Jefferson's, Madison's, and Monroe's lives, in spite of Shay's rebellion for revolutionary war veterans' back pay, and the War of 1812, that reminded the founders of how easily rebellion at home or from across the sea could upset the balance they had created.

It was obvious that they understood greed, avarice, and opportunism along with tendencies toward self aggrandizement, aristocratic family dynastic tendencies, and national autocratic solutions to temporary frustration, so they did not expect a new Eden. They also understood well the idea of virtue, both of the moral variety such as they read in the Gospels of the four apostles, as well as the personal goodness observable among many of their fellow men as a non universal aspect of human nature.

Our founders instituted a government to accommodate what the men of the Enlightenment called Meliorism. This, in its simplest form, is a belief that the world can be made better by human effort. Meliorists (an almost extinct word) believed that people with individual rights will progress in understanding, thereby accepting changes made with an intent regarding outcomes that are in fact hoped to be victimless economic and political improvements; another example of what the founders referred to as the common good.

In other words, give people room and freedom to grow in wisdom and goodness and they will. They will also be able to discern between ideas that are in fact in their own interest, and those that are not. Sounds simple and reasonable; however in practice, in my view over eighty years of watching this in action, if anything this belief is a common failure making the uphill grade to be climbed ever steeper, especially for the least capable and/or competitive of at least half of us. Our chosen economic system which works to produce, flounders when it comes to outcomes for the majority of Americans as the speculative economic side is boom and bust while the distribution side is based on a marketing system defined as mutual opportunism. The system always errs on the side of guile, greed, and corruption. Folks with the most aptitude for each prey on those with the least. Only a government trusted to govern as a referee deserves the votes of the many. If that is not how the Supreme Court sees its mission, then you have a minority capture of the only hope the bottom half of wage earners have ever had.

Money spent on emotional speech in the interest of improved education, health, and living standards, if politically induced, will usually create more emotional heat than insight among those less endowed with an eye to sustainable goals for all of a nation's classes in a society with a dominant culture, even if not deliberate; when it is deliberate it is devastating for the poor.

The ideal of democracy supported the hope that people will vote for outcomes in their own best interest; the idealists did not always factor in the reality of emotions. It had long been the belief of economists that the wealthy, the wage earner, and the consumer will vote for outcomes in their own best interest; they did not always factor in greed. It was the intent of the law givers that legislators, judges, and rulers would always live by the rule of law; they did not always factor in self-dealing. It was the belief of theologians that bishops would always favor salvation for their flock over a seat at the table with the money changers and law makers; they did not factor in the seeming indifference bishops had for their own salvation. It was the teaching of President Reagan that bankers knew better than bureaucrats how to invest money; the folksy president did not factor in the risk inherent in speculation and opportunism among folks investing other people's money. In every case the people of limited resources were abused with the blessing of their own representatives and pastors, and left without a voice or a refund in the aftermath of the ever ensuing bust.

Among the Constitution, the Bill of Rights, and the Declaration of Independence, only the Declaration mentions God. The United Colonies declared independence to change our government and to live as free men as intended by the God of nature; they did not mention the God of any religion. The God of nature was defined during the Enlightenment as the creator of the universe; our laws reflect the nature of the universe, and man's place in it, as the intention of God. There is no factor of God's will having been revealed regarding human governance in American justice under the Bill of Rights.

Our Constitution was written to support the natural rights of man that the view noted above confers on each of us, in concert with our creation by God naturally in the course of time. Therefore we have a natural right to be free from abuse by any other power, as we go about our daily lives living in God's natural world subject only to our consent to be governed here on earth by the authority we grant to those we elect, in return for our assured mutual individual rights as citizens. As the outcomes of each era of American economic history plays out in our story, we will see the largest failure of any factor of American exceptionalism has been in our duty to those who labor for wages, and serve as enlisted combat soldiers.

The use of the term "under God" on our money, as our national motto, and in the Pledge of Allegiance were added in the mid 1950s. Our founders might have been appalled by the idea, not personally but as an act of government. If it was tested in court it would have to be as the founders so stated, and not as Biblical Christianity depicts, as the promoters seem to believe today and wish us to believe also. It does not matter as our nation was founded under the God of nature; the evangelical intent to introduce the Roman Biblical Christian theology "revealed" concepts into our schools and into the Constitutional rights judicial settlement process was and remains sacred and not secular. Jesus separated salvation from commerce, those who claim to love Jesus are determined to correct what they see as his error regarding commerce it is apparent.

We need a sustainable secular national government for as many reasons as we have citizens. Our Constitution was created to carefully keep what we consented to in equilibrium. This is a basic truth as well as a major insight that needs to be re-agreed to before we truly can get back to rational compromise let alone tolerance.

Most importantly we need some common understanding of the intent of the Constitution, rather than just finding ways to limit it. What do folks really mean when they say they want limited government?

Citizens already have judicial rights of dissent, some long forgotten but still viable. The key problem I see today is the court does not sort out legitimate conflicting citizens' legal rights, beyond accepting for adjudication a citizen's individual right. We will see as the battle over rights progresses in the last two chapters of this book, the court will make decisions regarding one citizen's rights conflicting with another, especially after 1964 when rights were extended to an ever wider subclass of citizens, such as blacks, women, gays, and religious objectors. All folks whose newly accepted rights were or are in conflict with societal norms, but are in fact secular protected rights equal to the most popular rights of the many, require tolerance if the concept of individual rights of free men is to remain as the founders intended in the Declaration of Independence and the Preamble to the Constitution.

Judicial activism is a fact of life today on both sides and has been at least since the Civil War era. Marshall's admonishment that a right deserves a remedy is no longer assured now that the Court (Hobby Lobby V Obamacare) will grant a right to a person (a concept introduced as mischief in the Fourteenth Amendment after the Civil War), and leave a citizen with an individual right without a remedy as a victim; it seems this should be judged a form of judicial error.

Historically, property rights in Roman and English law were developed as crown rights (the king's rights) not religious rights, but the king did have authority based on divine rights. In America's Constitution from 1791 there is no property right that is defined as superior to any individual American citizen's right regarding the consent bargain as part and parcel of the Bill of Rights. Jurists do not have authority to choose which citizen's right is most worthy; compromise must be forced by adjudication if it is to be assured in the settlement mechanism.

My daughter is an Evangelical Christian. She is concerned that her minister is going to end up in jail for refusing to marry a same sex couple. I explained that her minister is protected under the First Amendment. He is engaged in a legal church activity, and a civil activity. A minister has always and remains free to turn down a religious ceremony, such as marriage for the divorced in the Catholic Church. This has been happening for centuries and does so without incident. U.S. secular law does not allow court interference with religious ceremonies that do not harm any other citizen's rights.

In establishing the first American government, newly created citizens did not fear an amendment process to the Constitution or consider it a threat. They demanded it in the ratification conventions in the states as a protection from government abuse. Our Constitution was ratified on the belief that a way to govern had been created that was better than absolute monarchy. The ability to create amendments was acknowledgment of the possibility they had not gotten it all right the first time. The amendment process also acknowledged that changes in reality as well as insights might create a new or better understanding and outcome later in our history that was not available or understood at the time. That productivity would create unimaginable wealth was not known, that new forms of funding the massive at risk investments to develop a railroad, or to dam a large river, or to operate a large remote mine, also were not anticipated.

I hope this introduction to the government expectations we inherited from our founders is eye opening to those who may have found it difficult to get interested in civics in high school or were not exposed to the history of the thinking behind our founding in public school civics class, let alone schools operated by organized religions.

That a Catholic school kid like me had to search to understand American law, and how it differed from my family's church (canon) law, never surprised me. The faith-based are free to teach and believe American law is Biblical Christian faith-based, but like this quote sometimes attributed to Mark Twain, "It ain't what you don't know that gets you into trouble. It's what you know for sure that just ain't so". When they act on a belief that is not true, they threaten their freedom and mine, yours also.

In 1776 our founders stated it differently. They issued the Declaration of Independence which defined their right to institute not only a new government but also a new form of government. The thirteen united colonies, referring to themselves as the United States of America, declared themselves to be independent states.

Per the words of the Declaration, under the God of nature, referred to as the author of the universe by Jefferson in his writings, they also established a right of self-government. This government was subject to the will of the people (making the people the nominal sovereign), not by the will of God, but by the consent of the governed. This is the nation we all reside in, and pledge allegiance to its flag and Constitution, meaning the laws it represents. Even as we politically resist full implementation of democracy or justice for all, we recommit ourselves to our full founding intent when we recite the Pledge of Allegiance.

Thus ended the former colonial America's allegiance to the fourteen hundred year history of a European political and economic governance system based on a state and church form of government founded by the Roman Empire, and usurped by the English Parliament. This also ended the two hundred seventy-five year history of colonialism first founded by Spain, as adopted and applied to the American colonies by England. This was the beginning of our two hundred and thirty-five plus year old national government designed to be a self governed society of free men.

Our Revolutionary War is, for the purpose of this story, mostly unremarkable except for the outcome. The exception is noting that George Washington, commanding general of the victorious Continental army for eight years, became the first president of the United States. His chief aide, Alexander Hamilton, was the treasury secretary of the first U.S. government in 1789. They became the two most important drivers of our new government once James Madison had steered us through the Constitutional process.

The key lesson of the war for both Washington and Hamilton was the difficulty of fighting a war without a strong central government, and without the power to tax or conscript. There were many problems with infighting and refusal to adequately fund or man the war effort among the various confederated states.

This war experience was paramount in the thinking behind all of the decisions made in the first term of our government. It set the tone for all debates that have followed until current times regarding the role, intent, and relation of the federal government to the states. It also influenced the relationship of the people to their national government wherever they have resided in the nation. Remember, federal Constitutional law regarding individual citizen's rights apply regardless of your state of residence; no state law can legally abuse your assured Constitutional rights.

A new view arose two generations later with the settlement of the area west of the coastal mountains. To a large extent poor men were sent or chose to go west. Settled folks wanted a barrier between the civilized subjects of the coastal region and the tribes to the west. I'd define the key attitude of these so-called frontiersmen as a wish for freedom from government, the same government that granted them their land.

We will hear more about this viewpoint during the Jackson and Polk presidencies later in the next chapter. This will be relevant as we discuss the addition of Florida and the southwest to the United States that became the lower forty-eight states, along with the Louisiana purchase from Napoleon by President Jefferson.

Some colonies' boundaries extended to the mountains hundreds of miles inland, while the majority of subjects lived along the Atlantic coast, less than a hundred miles inland. Generally at that time migration moved inland along the rivers, as people were seeking arable land with natural means of transport back to the coast.

Cities were clustered at the mouths of rivers, especially if there was a protected harbor or bay. If the harbor could accommodate sailing ships, a major city often grew. In the interior, the best fertile farm lands with access to markets were along the shores of navigable rivers. Spring floods provided natural replenishment of nutrients to the naturally fertile soil.

In the mid 1770s, the total free population was not much more than two and a half million people. By 1775 hostilities had broken out in Boston. The colonies called a convention as a confederation. They voted to declare war by writing and signing the Declaration of Independence. They founded The United States of America in 1776, at least in name and intent.

An interesting reenactment of one of these early colonial debates is performed at St. John's church in Richmond Virginia every Presidents' Day weekend, which ends with Patrick Henry's declaration, "give me liberty or give me death". The whole debate takes half an hour, and is inspiring.

As we look back, I believe it is important to remember they did not declare war as thirteen independent or allied countries. However, in the same document they defined themselves as thirteen independent states. This is another precursor to regional disputes, and the vexing issue of dual sovereignty. It was not until well into the twentieth century that Great Britain settled their dual sovereignty issue with what became the Commonwealth system.

I keep a copy of the Declaration, the Bill of Rights, and the Constitution on my desk for reference. There are many good books on both views of the Constitution: the living Constitution and the original intent interpretation of the Constitution. Both views reflect the two major political parties' views. There is no one settled school of thought in America on how to interpret the Constitution; this is part of our gridlock. I have never read a good explanation of what the GOP which supports original intent thinks is the purpose of the amendment process.

The French-aided American victory was the last armed conflict between the new nation and the former mother country until twenty-five years later when we fought the final war with England beginning in 1812 and so named. This war taught the Virginia-born presidents the value of a central bank, but not the southern states, as we shall see forty-eight years later during the Civil War

There were three major contentions and one key concept during the Convention. There were also important contentions in the ratification process as each state voted to accept or reject the Constitution. Delegates from each state had difficulty resolving issues in the Convention. They had trouble with the same issues in ratification. The ratification required at least nine states voting, and a majority of five of those voting yes in order for America to become an independent nation based on the U.S. Constitution. Rhode Island and Georgia did not ratify until the nation was formed. The authority to govern was already predetermined as an intent in the Declaration of

Independence; "By the consent of the governed."

The first major contention was the need for a Bill of Rights. James Madison promised to make a Bill of Rights an early order of business in the first Congress. The original approval of the Constitution was ratified in many states subject to a request that a Bill of Rights be added; and so it was during the first presidential term and second term of Congress two years later in 1791.

The Constitution addressed property rights with implied protections in many articles but never as a directly stated right. English Common Law continued as state law in all of the new states; common law defined property law and replacement state laws continue to do so to this day. For example your house deed is registered in the county of the state you reside in, not in the housing department of the federal government as noted earlier.

I do not believe the men of property at the end of the eighteenth century ever wanted a central government with rights beyond those required to protect property and the borders of the states, and the nation. Congress added due process among other rights, and the amendment process, as well as the legislative powers; settlement by judicial review has also established additional rights and or remedies. A key insight in the remainder of this book will review conflicting rights in dissent where one right was allowed a remedy that left another abused right without a remedy. We will review two such cases involving corporation vs. women's rights. One will be the Lily Ledbetter right to equal pay vs. Goodrich Tire Company's right to privacy regarding wages. The other will be Hobby Lobby Craft Stores owner's religious right to not engage in the sin of participating as he believed birth control to be, versus female employee's rights; including tax free access to healthcare insurance only if employer funded (a Jim Crow legacy explained later), and her personal right as a citizen to reproductive family planning access to birth control medication.

Returning to the 1780s it was the farmers with small land holdings and the merchants who demanded and obtained individual citizen's rights, and we should all be forever grateful; such men were called the middling class at least in the north. This was the limited level of commerce Jefferson advocated as a preferred economic system for the United States, along with yeomen farmers, and export mercantile planters.

The second major contention was qualification to hold federal office. Most of the southern states, as well as the northern states except Rhode Island, wanted it limited to protestant Christians. This issue had the closest vote, but no state rejected the Constitution over this question, and it did not become a qualification for federal office.

This contention confirms the norm for the influence the state religions played in the cultural norms of our founding citizens. They wanted to form a government with separation of church and state, but wanted only protestant Christians to hold office. It seems a majority wanted a Christian moral code, but not "legislated morals". At least a majority then and now, separated civil criminality from sin as a state issue and police power.

All presidents to date have declared themselves Christians. The possible exceptions were Washington and Jefferson. They only declared themselves deists meaning believers in the concept of the God of nature cited in the Declaration of Independence. Like all other presidents, Jefferson never publicly wrote or spoke against Jesus; in his private writings he did question the divinity of Jesus, the virgin birth, the Trinity and the Resurrection. None of these questions ever became a factor regarding U.S. Law. There has never been a heresy law in the United States, which is a factor of a secular nation. In England with a heresy law there could only be one religion, the one chosen by the king. In America there are dozens of Christian and non-Christian religions and they are all legal.

The final major contention was the sovereignty question. The United States was defined as a sovereign nation. Each state also demanded retention of sovereignty within a federal system. This is the origin of the continuous arguing over states' rights versus federal rights. As Benjamin Franklin advised, "the founders gave us a republic, if we could keep it". The key issue not fully understood is where the state is sovereign and what the federal government is governing. The key contention is a lack of understanding that the state is sovereign over land, and the federal government is sovereign over citizens and interstate issues.

Having read the *Federalist Papers*, I do not know if the majority of founders, signers, and ratifiers anticipated the power of the terms "interstate commerce" or "necessary and proper" in the Constitution. Did they see the power those words would have in later years to authorize the scope of authority granted to the central government by the Supreme Court over the past two centuries?

This question was never settled in law in South America where they never became a republic with a large strong federal government. They have remained mostly poor in the global economy of the twenty-first century, in spite of vast resources, and a people who work hard when given the chance to immigrate.

As our nation grew, certainly each clause played a significant role in growth, power, and standardization, as well as the cost of federal governance. As an example we could have fifty different rail gauges, fifty discreet bank notes, fifty different sets of regulations for food and drug safety standards and customs departments regarding shipping and travel between states if absurdity had been carried to the nth degree. I for one appreciate how these two clauses have been adjudicated.

Areas of law left to the states to legislate are referred to as states' rights by those who want to define the scope of limits on federal rights. Their wish is to keep to the exact words in the Articles of the Constitution. The concept behind states' rights is known as nullification; any federal law any state did not like it could nullify. This has never been granted in the history of America.

The limited meanings of words from the British at that time are often seen as being in defense of states and property rights. It is possible leading men of property did not realize at the time how powerfully a majority of voters would feel about being protected from state government abuse by a majority of voters in the state where they live, who might not approve of their practicing a minority life style. Birth control is a good example and the least controversial and most common of these issues in the modern era.

States' rights supporters strongly declare their reverence for words' exact meaning at the time of our founding, as if there was ever a common understanding of any and all of the following discrete words: "freedom", "liberty", or "justice". The meanings of these three words have remained in debate from revolutionary times until the present. I see the words U.S. Constitution and patriotism as having a common meaning, yet do they in fact?

Liberty (named as a goal in the Preamble to the U.S. Constitution) is freedom from interference by an outside force in a nation's practice of its legal government. While freedom means a right to do as we each chose to pursue happiness as long as we break no law and do not infringe on any other citizen's rightful freedoms, freedom from abuse for individuals means freedom from abuse from our own national or state governments or entity they create. Corporations are state-created entities.

I argue that an abusive practice of a state created entity such as a corporation is in conflict with the Bill of Rights protection of individual citizens' right, and is now often overlooked in American court settlements. An example is abuse of a person's private enjoyment of an equal right to federal tax relief for the cost of healthcare. This factored in settling same sex marriage rights, but not in settling the Hobby Lobby case.

While freedom from abuse is justice in the U.S. Constitution living document sense of the word and in this book, liberty could be defined as freedom from third party abuse. This defines the intent of our rights under the Bill of Rights, but it is still in question in the twenty-first century as I believe the GOP ideology regarding judicial review rights to a remedy is concerned. Can a corporation continue to be free to abuse an employee's rights as a citizen without consequence in the twenty-first century? The Citizens United case settlement outcome seems so.

Freedom was an internal term, meaning protection for individual citizens to exercise their Constitutional rights, without abuse from any level of government. Too often folks who want to define freedom as freedom from government and/or taxation conflate patriotism and freedom as mutual statuses, opening debate and gridlock to a lot of misinformation about by whom, and how the U.S. Constitution can be interpreted. Piety is not a defining word for any U.S. Constitutional freedom or right.

The southern states, which were founded with different labor systems, religious loyalties and relationship to the crown have always resented this portion of our Constitutional rights and still do. Meaning that only the Supreme Court can define what the Constitution means regarding any right or law and how it is framed and used or enforced, hardly what a cock of the walk would-be strong governor such as Patrick Henry in Virginia would have approved. Funny, his own state constitution made him a weak governor at the hands of James Madison. John Adams, whom Henry and Madison both found problematic, gave his state governor the authority of a strong governor. I just find these outcome oddities interesting.

With the support of the modern Koch Network economics department at George Mason University, the modern GOP has defined freedom as "economic freedom". This "economic freedom" ideology adopted by the modern GOP does allow an individual who breaks through the economic barriers the right to accumulate great wealth, and thereby to rise in status, rights, and acceptance Many see that as freedom's Holy Grail. Another name for this ideology is Public Choice, the idea of private for-profit solutions rather than tax based public utility solutions for delivery of government services such as prisons, healthcare, schools, roads and bridges (tolls) and so on as common good outcomes.

Note regarding so-called educational tax exempt think tanks: Many wealthy individuals fund so called educational think tanks to study and provide input to legislators and administrative regulators. Such research is usually in support of an ideological political theory of the funding individuals, and it is safe to assume in support of an interest of the funding members of each institute.

The intent of such organizations include research, policy proposals, supporting documentation of the rationales, followed by funding to educate legislative folks, their staffs, the regulatory staff once a policy is enacted, and even judges once enacted and regulated policies are introduced if dissents arise. All of this is legal, tax exempt, and more successfully funded by the wealthy than by small donors.

The largest and most successful of these funding groups with the most institutes is known as the Koch Network, a conservative leaning group that is funded by a group of billionaire families, each in possession of dynastic wealth. For the most part the current members did not generate the original fortune, they inherited it. Among the many think tanks the Koch Network supports are a few large influential organizations such as the Enterprise Institute, The Cato Institute, the Manhattan Institute, and dozens of others that study issues.

At the state level they support an institute called ALEC that helps state legislators write legislation such as right-to-work bills, elect GOP members, and carry out gerrymandering once the GOP captures the levers of power in a state. They have switched over a thousand state house seats from the Democrats to the GOP since 2010. The Koch Network also funds political action organizations such as Americans for Prosperity that in effect function as lobbyists, and campaign influence to sell the think tanks' ideas in support of reduced regulations, reduced wage labor cost, and privatization of government services, among legislators and executive branch regulators and enforcers.

They also fund departments of economics, law, and others at George Mason University. We will mention other such organizations including George Soros' Open Borders Society supporting both conservative and liberal political agendas, but this is the key factor to understand how partisan ideology is developed, and the role it plays in whose priorities are heard loudest in Washington, on the internet and in political ads every two and four years.

Key issues we will discuss later in the book that originated with the Koch Network include tax cuts that pay for themselves, and for-profit healthcare, education, retirement, prisons, roads and bridges (tolls), and data based gerrymandering.

Often when we hear a politician discuss a policy, the data and the analysis will have been provided by an independent billionaire or group of billionaires, who also fund political campaigns. We will talk about others such as George Soros mentioned above, but all others pale in relation to the influence Charles Koch wields over the GOP in modern America.

To better know and understand how interconnected about fifteen or so of the richest families in America have become and how many aspects of every day life they have effected to the detriment of the founders' ideal they called established justice and the common good, read the book *Democracy in Chains* by Nancy MacLean. If you do not believe that the consequences of modern era GOP interpretations of freedom are dark, or that there are those who are working to return American governance back to the feudal mindset of the days of the divine right of kings, this book will be an eye opener.

The second of the three founding documents is the U.S. Constitution which established property rights as a state issue, but was mute on citizens' rights or religious rights. The Constitution was ratified in 1789 subject to Congress adding an amendment to be called The Bill of Rights, and it was ratified in 1791. As noted above the Constitution had established that all Americans were citizens of the United States; the Bill of Rights assured U.S. Citizens their rights would be protected by their government, as part of the authority to govern bargain. It also established our divided government. It did not define an economy or how each branch would carry out its mandate to uphold the Constitution.

Our third founding document was the Bill of Rights. Property owners remained free to own property used to create wealth, and pastors remained free to lead folks to salvation as each citizen chose or not, written as the establishment clause in the Bill of Rights, usually referred to as freedom of religion. Fortunately the Bill of Rights also established an amendment clause; it did not define the mechanism the Supreme Court would use to settle Constitutional dissent. The Supreme Court itself established a process they called judicial review that was intended to resolve a citizen's perceived injustice, or a conflict between the rights of various classes of citizens. America is often in gridlock over dissents having to do with old and new understandings of the governance of men as citizens or as employees, or borrowers. All citizens were established to be born with natural rights, a concept dating back to Plato, and no longer subject to revealed truths concerning subjugation by the state or the church.

In Chapter 10 we will review the outcomes of the Reagan era, the times at the end of the twentieth and beginning of the twenty-first centuries when the billionaires and pastors joined together to protect the old understanding against those who champion the rights of the citizens of the United States under our new constitutional order.

The GOP, the Koch family, and at least since the 1950s the many foundations that have evolved into what is now known as the Koch Network, have supported the most activist billionaire families who have created not only the governing ideology of the GOP over the past seventy years, but also the biggest think tanks, messaging systems, and campaign funding juggernaut ever in world political history.

In addition, this group of billionaires have helped fund the leading foundations that speak for the pastors, and has become a secret society that interfaces with national politicians in Washington DC known as The Family. The Family's full name is The Fellowship Foundation. The Fellowship Foundation was led by Doug Coe during his lifetime and he presided over the National Prayer Breakfast. Since 1953 every president from Eisenhower until the time covered by this book in the Trump presidency has attended the breakfast. The Fellowship Foundation, the organization behind The Family and The Prayer Breakfast has had the same goals as the Koch Network since the New Deal days of FDR. The also support an organization called the Federalist Society to groom young lawyers with their ideology for the federal bench, and have successfully packed the court into the mid twenty first century.

In Chapter 9 we will review how FDR for the first time in U.S. history addressed the meaning of federal rights for the many starving poor, mostly black, and abused working poor, mostly poorly or uneducated immigrants. Today the Koch's ideology and the theology of the Family overlap concerning market wages and charity as the only answer they accept for what they see as the natural expectation of poverty as a human norm.

Koch and Coe believe wages and charity are questions for

corporations and religion, as the province of the owners of wealth and salvation for believers. Neither see a role for the federal government to regulate or tax to fund wages or charity. To understand these alignments is to grasp the parameters of modern gridlock, and the dilemma of reaching compromise with absolutists, as ideologists and theologians so often are, especially when it comes to compromise.

The Bill of Rights does not grant nor deny the singular concept of freedom. It does confirm individual citizen's federal rights regardless of home state of residence. I think we are redundant when questioning if a law violates our liberty or our freedom. Liberty confers freedom. Large or small, government would just be political spin without Constitutional meaning. It is the absence of abuse that assures justice; reciprocally granting each other's rights and tolerance are the true meaning of equality.

However, absolute belief systems guarantee intolerance of those who are different, which they are free to be. This makes ideology and theology almost always non-compliant with the intent of the U.S. Constitution when viewed to include the Bill of Rights. Another Koch think tank we will discuss later actually focuses on the two years between the ratification of the Constitution and the Bill of Rights.

To me, an important change in the founding was the issue of duty. The Romans defined the duty of all subjects as accepting the rights of the masters, taught to be by the will of God. Their duty was to labor on the estate, and to defend the kingdom and the king when so ordered. The Constitution created a state with police powers (not absolute master's powers). Citizens had individual rights that the police could not do whatever they wished, because we were granted a new right defined as due process.

As to citizens' military duty, a militia was mentioned in the Second Amendment. However, many today see the Second Amendment less as a duty to serve the country in war, than as a right to personal protection. The nation has decided to leave our defenses to a professional army. A small but noisy group sees the Second Amendment as the right to keep arms to enable an overthrow of the government; if a mob decides, the majority is wrong. I address gun rights in the sixteen suggestions at the end of the book.

When I joined the U.S. Army in 1958, I accepted a duty to uphold the U.S. Constitution and I knew that when I swore an oath at induction. By the time I was separated from the military six years later with an honorable discharge, I further knew all of the following: I knew my oath included the intent of the founders in the Preamble, the Articles, the Amendments, and latent rights which could be recognized in the future. I understood that the Supreme Court has the power to define implied, i.e. latent rights, such as the Second Amendment's intent to allow private citizens to defend their property and person. I recognized the Constitution as an effort to settle law for governance of a society that one day would be millions of individuals across a continental nation of diverse free men, needing to fully respect each other's assured freedom from abuse, which defined my only duty towards all others, and theirs to me. I owe an American education and freedom of the press for my ability to learn all of this on my own merely by developing a non fiction reading habit.

As the first president Washington asked Alexander Hamilton from the north and Thomas Jefferson from the south to design a national government to be implemented into law for the nation under his leadership with the approval of the Congress. It would be another twenty years before the Supreme Court would approve all of Washington's decisions. It was from this smorgasbord of options that our initial introduction to the key founders was laid out early in this chapter.

The chief difference between the two proposals was first in the area of an economy. Hamilton proposed a mixed agricultural and manufacturing economy with a central bank and a national mint which he defined as Capitalism, and his critics defined as Debt Capitalism; once the nation became industrialized, I refer to it as Speculative Capitalism in this book. Jefferson wished to continue the economy of the south, as well as the export mercantilism that England had imposed on the south.

Washington selected Hamilton's vision of a strong central government in establishing how the executive branch would manage the United States government. He wanted adequate funding and manning in times of war. This power was and is subject only to the

Constitutional role of the legislature and the courts. There is no right of nullification to be granted any or all states, or their elected officials. This means that if the U.S. declares war, a state cannot opt out if it does not want to participate. This is a fact of our founding that was explored more fully by George Washington in his first inaugural address (worth a personal read).

Thomas Jefferson was not only the chief author of the Declaration of Independence, he was also the representative of the Confederation in France at the time the French came to the rescue of the colonies. He later became the first Secretary of State in Washington's cabinet. His Virginia vision of a limited power central government was rejected at the Constitution Convention, both by the ratifiers of the Constitution and by Washington as the first president.

The concept of limited government was adopted in the Constitution of the seceding Confederate states leading up to the Civil War. It led to their defeat in the Civil War when once again Jefferson Davis the president of the Confederacy was unable to require the governors of the southern states to fund or man the army adequately to meet the resources available to Lincoln in the north due to the founding policies of Hamilton and Washington.

In spite of the many defeats of small low tax government as the intent of the constitution, it persists as a belief system among a large minority of U.S. citizens mostly in red states over two hundred and thirty years later. Small government as a policy goal is as meaningless as "I want my country back" is as a political goal. Both are more an expression of emotion than rational governance. No major enemy of America in the modern era aspires to small, underfunded government, or to dissent from any of the various sub political regions in such a nation akin to our states.

During the years when Patrick Henry was the governor of Virginia he remained a singular advocate only for his region. This is different from his fellow Virginians Washington, Madison, Jefferson and Monroe, who played leading roles in the founding of the central government, helping create the strong national government that won WWII, ended the cold war, and still defends our nation to this day.

The sixth key player (but not to the same extent) was the first vice president and second president John Adams. Adams was a great, in fact the key contributor intellectually concerning Constitutional law and authority to govern, even as Madison is seen as the father of the Constitution. Adams, in helping define the state Constitutions, had gone a long way toward resolving sovereignty issues, but due to his thin skin and somewhat grumpy nature he was never tested as a legislator, and was less effective as an executive than his co-founders.

As a note on the reality of slavery at the time of our founding nothing ever impacted me more than reading a news report of a new ambassador from England witnessing a young black female slave being publicly whipped; the crowd cheered as he watched her agony and helplessness as her naked back began to look more and more like raw meat. The ambassador was particularly shocked that this abuse was administered not by an officer of the law, but by her owner's overseer, without appeal or limit. When it was over she and her wounds were left unattended.

I'm sure that if any southern leader at any level of government, or any pastor of a Christian sect at the time had raised a word of protest he would have been jeered and made an outcast. This dehumanization process remains a legacy in America over two hundred years later, passed down as a cultural norm among a self-described genteel God fearing Christian people.

Quotes in this book have quotation marks; this one about the whipped female slave does not, as I do not recall where I read this story, but I remember the shock I felt reading it. If this news story was true, it again proves how often folks are intentionally blind to the reality of what our norms inflict on our fellow humans. If not true it was totally believable based on what has passed as norms regarding open treatment of slaves during the history of slavery in America.

At that time Britain was a feudal nation at home, and a colonial nation around the world. The Brits committed this level of cruelty daily for centuries around the world and at home, while their ambassador seemed to be blind to where America learned this level of abuse of one people toward another.

Still, the first concept Patrick Henry stated he believed in and fought for was liberty, as stated in his famous quote "Give me liberty or give me death". Either men were at liberty to enjoy their homes, life, livelihoods, religion, opinions, family, and peace of mind as loyal subjects of a just government, or they were constrained to endure denial of these liberties by a police state, foreign or domestic, in subjugation. However, to my knowledge Henry never embraced the idea of being a citizen of the United States, nor ending slavery in Virginia.

Jefferson did define international independence in penning the Declaration; while lack of independence can also be a domestic issue, "either men are independent of unjust laws, suffering duress without redress, or they are dependent on arbitrary lawmaking which is a form of domestic tyranny, generally without a vote".

In America since day one as a country, all Americans, at least those who were white and propertied, have had the vote and redress in the courts, hardly factors of true or total dependence. Jefferson said it all first; independence as the founders announced it, in the new United States would ensure life, liberty, and the pursuit of happiness, an all encompassing concept much more important that it first sounds. Almost no society in history until Jefferson granted total freedom to marry whom one chooses, to pursue any field of work, live anywhere one choses; it was a level of personal freedom as a norm nowhere in the world at the time.

Patrick Henry understood the meaning of anarchy, which is the opposite of tyranny. Henry espoused anarchy in voting to revolt, yet his concern was more for the independence of his state than for his personal liberty or freedom, which his race, education, and wealth ensured if his state was sovereign.

The laws of Virginia did not give the governor a veto over legislation enacted by a majority in the legislature. States cannot vote to reject national laws, as we have seen recently in fighting over abortion as a privacy issue, and marriage equality (same sex marriage). Virginia's Governor Henry still felt dependent on the national government after independence from England; it was visceral and stinging for the rest of his life.

Henry thought a majority of state voters should be able to limit federal law in their state, in the best interest of the governed in their state (nullification). Henry was not concerned about rights for minorities. Rights for minorities were not a common concern anywhere in the world until a hundred years later, and were first enacted into law by a national government in Austria in the 1880s.

Until his final breath, Henry fought for strong states' rights. John C. Calhoun (staunch defender of slavery) and Jefferson Davis (president of the Southern Confederacy in the Civil War) also fought for the rights of states to keep slavery legal among other things. Most telling regarding the role slavery played in the founding of the Confederate States of America, Alexander H. Stephens, Vice President of the Confederacy delivered what is known as The Cornerstone Speech in 1861. In this speech he spelled out what he called the great truth that secession and war were based on. "Its foundations are laid, its cornerstone rests upon the great truth, that the negro is not equal to the white man; that slavery-subordination to the superior race is his natural and normal condition. This, our new government, is the first, in the history of the world, based upon this great physical, philosophical, and moral truth."

States' rights and nullification contentions were finally summed up by the new nation's vice president as they went to war. Nullification was the political posture of the former slave states, and the platform of the champions of the southern viewpoint. They were getting their people fired up over states' rights, while the real goal was to keep the slave system viable no matter how many other states outlawed it. They feared the free states would enact a federal law to deny slave states continued liberty to maintain their preferred labor system as the nation grew. Stephens finally told this fuller truth as the war began.

Modern political nullification advocates are not fighting abolitionists. To a large extent they are fighting individual citizens' federal rights they believe to be sins under Biblical Christian norms. In states that are majority Biblical Christian, they want to nullify the laws that grant an individual minority of even one person a right to sin, whatever the lack of secular police power interest in the so-called sin.

If this fight is successful, even once, all rights of minorities of any identifiable nature in America will be vulnerable to abuse by the police powers of the state. We object to the abuse of minorities overseas, such as Christians in Egypt, but some are fighting for the same abuse here (the ability to discriminate against, even punish minorities).

This is how all theocratic (government based on religion) and autocratic (power in the hands of one person, such as a dictator or an absolute monarch) nations have been in world history. We still see these today in theocratic Muslim nations such as Saudi Arabia and Iran, and autocratic nations such as Russia and China.

I do not know if the five GOP presidential candidates in 2016 who demanded an end to Supreme Court settlement based on judicial review knew they would were jeopardizing their own personal interpretation of the bible, which could lead to a return to heresy laws but they did express a demand for an end to judicial review which would overthrow U.S. prohibition of establishment of a defined single belief system among all the different Christian Church's.

However aware or not they are, the threat that would lead to adding religion as a department of government is the effect if they succeed in ending American secular law. They are well aware there is no national majority in support of this goal or they would make it a legislative and/or a platform goal. Neither they nor the GOP have gone that far yet; gerrymandering and spin are their preferred activism so far.

A political solution to increase the chances for single issue voters to be more effective will take compromise. It is almost impossible for Christians to agree to compromise on issues they believe are sins against the Biblical revealed teachings of the evangelical Christian God they worship. These doctrines are based on beliefs established by the Romans at Nicaea when they assembled the Bible and interpreted it based on Constantine's requirements for his Roman republic, empire, and kingdoms which were introduced in Chapter 1.

Constantine added holidays and rites including marriage, baptism, and a last rite before death as examples, to make acceptance of a universal religion more understandable and comforting for peoples across all of the kingdoms of the Roman Empire. He required new church holidays to reflect the norms of the pagan holidays of the subjugated mass of serfs and peasants, keeping them as cultural events in their lives and thereby more acceptable.

At the time of our revolution, the labor economy in each new state worked in a few different ways. Some men were employed by property owners as indentured servants, working for room and board only in exchange for future improved opportunity. Others were slaves working for base subsistence without appeal or relief for life. In the eighteenth century freedom was a labor term. Property owners, including those who owned single family farms were sometimes called yeomen, and were considered to be independent owners, not laborers. In opening the west from the early to mid 1800s, the term freedom was expanded. It came to be understood by those living on the frontier as freedom from government, and not just related to economics, at least until statehood was sought.

In this book I am talking about freedom as it relates to individual citizen rights including labor rights to hire representation, gun ownership rights, women's reproductive rights, and so on. I believe they are at least equal to property rights, requiring court ordered settlement to provide equitable justice in resolution. This is to insure individual citizen's rights, not to diminish legitimate property or religious rights.

At a minimum let's finally sort out abuse under a hierarchy of rights. Freedom from government always leads to rule by the strong man or the mob and ends in anarchy. This was not a concept Patrick Henry advocated nor Thomas Jefferson, nor even Andrew Jackson; not even Jefferson Davis advocated it. I am not sure President Trump has a definable set of norms beyond his own best interest which seems to embrace acceptance of rule by a strongman, at least as long as that strongman is himself.

It is difficult to know what is meant today by self-described patriots who demand economic freedom. It is too easy to see it as just a rejection of some individual right of another, or a level of taxes they object to, but as a baked in norm. I have a brother who goes ballistic if the question of Ruby Ridge comes up. The Ruby Ridge case from 1992 was a family revolting against government; it was mishandled on both sides and several people died, including a child. It is hard to get my brother to focus on the fact that the leader, Jeff Warren, was in contempt of court. The U.S. Marshals had a legal warrant, but they were afraid to serve it due to threats Warren had made. Warren, a survivalist living in remote Idaho who sold a couple of sawed off shotguns to FDI undercover agents at a Aryan Nation get together, was basically a white supremacist. He committed a crime then let it be known if the government agents came for him he would open fire on them.

I'm not taking sides in this case, nor excusing the death of Warren's wife and child. I'm just saying Warren played a key role in this legal dispute spiraling out of control. This was hardly a maverick government out of control, though folks like my brother easily spin it into a verbal assault on despotic government attacking American freedom. To be fair, Ruby Ridge was actually an assault on authorized government, just like the attack on the rioting prisoners at Attica State Prison under Governor Rockefeller; a longer standoff may have been prudent but in both cases it was hardly an unjust government out of control.

I'll take one more stab at political semantics. I see independence as meaning an independent nation. My take on liberty means citizens are free to pursue happiness within a regulated and understood legal system, with court protection of individual citizen rights. Freedom depends on and is subject to rational boundaries such as warrants and trial by jury, a means of redress such as judicial review, all under a concept of due process. This is not freedom from government, but freedom from abuse by an unjust or arbitrary government.

The most complete theory I know of regarding Constitutional government in existence in 1786 was a work by a thirty-eight year old French writer of the Enlightenment, Baron de Montesquieu. It is titled (in its English translation) *The Spirit of Laws*. Montesquieu defined three forms of political systems. The first was republican, which included those which broadly extended citizens' rights. He called them democratic republics. The other two political systems in his definitions were monarchical and despotic meaning no restraint

119

whatsoever on the ruler except possibly the military, but no Constitutional rule of law, and no religious law restraints.

Montesquieu did not address economic governance other than guilds. There was no inkling of private enterprise or private markets for another hundred years after his death. He may have liked the concept of guilds, as they were secret societies sworn to acceptance of God and king, and Montesquieu remained loyal to his king and his religion; he made the case he did anyway, the same conflict as my dad.

Many of the founders I mentioned never believed the stone masons played a meaningful role in our U.S. founding. However, others believed differently. The skill of the masons gave them special standing with the kings and bishops, who relied on them to build their castles and cathedrals. A mason could discuss a risky political idea with more expectation of safety, since they were hard to replace. This helps explain why many early thinkers joined with the masons, and over time turned it into a society of leaders in debate, not just stone workers. It hid their conversations from being seen as seditious.

Back to Montesquieu. He recommended an untried system of government he defined as a constitutional government within a democratic republic, which is what we became.

Imagine creating a new government based on a philosopher's idea. Many people must have wondered how we could have order, safety, and security without a king? How could it not lead to anarchy?

I have not read to what extent James Madison was a student of Montesquieu, but he was a Princeton graduate. He was the lead advocate for a constitutional system at what became the Constitutional Convention in Philadelphia, and it is obvious that he advocated for and adopted much of the Montesquieu model. Having trained at Princeton instead of the Church of England's University of William and Mary, Madison would have been exposed to the published works of the Enlightenment thinkers, even a Catholic thinker like Montesquieu. Montesquieu was also a favorite of Franklin, and Franklin in many ways was the elder sage at Philadelphia.

Almost all states empowered with absolute authority by a bishop and/or a general (religious or secular) will become despotic in the end. I believe this is the threat that would evolve in the United States if unconstrained religion or a president for life was ever allowed to dominate our government. America would most likely become nationalistic and/or theocratic.

Why would a just God create a universe finally populated by man if His only intent was to reward those He selected to own property, if that was how He intended it to work, deciding who was to be rich and have dominion over the other men He created, only to labor on the property of a few greedy tyrants, neither Godly nor just? Only an unjust God I'd say which I find unbelievable.

Our founders supported property rights meaning the freedom to own property and use it. Cash wages had never been a huge factor in the colonies, so setting the pay of laborers was not a priority. Our founders based citizens' rights on a belief in the rights that the creator of the universe endowed to all men. Jefferson said all men are born equal; they all knew that did not mean equal talent or opportunity, but an equal right to opportunity and justice, regardless of rank in society.

If you were smart or talented enough to acquire property, you were entitled to that protected privilege as a natural gift from the God of nature. To me this is not a belief from the Enlightenment, but a carryover from the English Common Law system; they had always accepted their own right to own and use property. It may explain why men of both greed and virtue as they saw themselves did not divine a need to address distribution equal to the added value of labor as a factor of justice to be assured as a duty of governance.

Justice as a factor of distribution based on property and labor was a kernel of an idea in the mind of Adam Smith. I've never read about any other man of the enlightenment nor any of the founders except Hamilton and then only as a student of Adam Smith, who had the same idea; they focused on the ownership of the output side of property, not so much what was due to labor even though labor supplied all of the manual toil and skill in the production of wealth.

This would be perverse in the extreme with the vision of hindsight, but that is what the founders seem to have believed. The corporate world and the families of accumulated dynastic wealth spend billions of dollars a year to defend this as a God given right in the twenty-first century. As donors they find plenty of willing politicians and judges to affirm that is what God and the founders intended. None of those who espouse absolute property rights ever mention the difference between Nicene rights for the few and the God of nature creations for the many.

That millions of evangelicals in effect accept that God's and the founders' only intent for them was salvation later if they stick to submission even unto abuse as a duty, is astounding. This is no different from the spin Constantine put on religion many centuries ago, admittedly in a time of widespread ignorance. It is time to stop the madness, as an old ad campaign used to sell goods.

Unlike the above, Montesquieu and Locke believed secular law should ensure civil liberties. Political institutions should reflect the society and geography of the community to be governed (remember how different the north and south were at our founding). Washington opted for a new national norm, which was only possible if states were not permitted to nullify national federal law. Even today the European Union struggles with balancing the whole versus the parts.

A majority of citizens at the time of our founding truly wanted independence. Almost none of them knew of or demanded the many concepts of freedom and liberty offered to voters today. Try stopping people in the street today; how many could explain these concepts? Only a secular education on the meaning of and concepts behind secular government that would be a requirement for graduation in American high schools might help educate the American electorate of what their rights mean one to another.

Montesquieu wrote that civil and criminal laws must ensure personal security of body, life, and property. He also said that constitutional laws must ensure personal rights. His highest praise was for a democratic republic, meaning beyond the Greek concept of democracy, with a willingness of the citizens to put community interest above personal interest.

Unfortunately, we Americans, in all our greatness, have not demonstrated that this final concept has taken root. President John F. Kennedy's famous quote "Ask not what your country can do for you, ask what you can do for your country" comes to mind.

One last insight of Montesquieu I find worth mentioning is his thinking on "political liberty"; the term is his. He defined it as personal citizen's rights like our Bill of Rights, which are a set of laws protecting defined rights of each individual. Our founders did not include political liberty in the Constitution at Philadelphia as noted earlier. It was fear of defeat at the Virginia Ratification Convention that led to the Bill of Rights, causing Madison to relent, as enough warmed to ratification of the new Constitution. It still gave political authority to property owners (originally, only white male land owners could vote, which was still a big improvement over nobody being able to vote) but in the end it was meant to assure citizens justice even as it was ignored, just as kings ignored the Magna Carta for hundred of years.

The Bill of Rights goes beyond democracy. Democracy only gives a say in selecting leaders, and replaces the old concept of masters by God's will. The Bill of Rights defines a limit on the restraints government can place on an individual within the law, even if the majority of elected leaders approve it. It is the difference between illegal and unconstitutional. Illegal only defines contrary to legislated law; a new legislature can change the law and thereby change what is legal if the president agrees, or they can even override the presidential veto if enough legislators vote yes. Constitutional means it is part of the by consent of the people bargain; the meaning of the Constitution can only be settled by the Supreme Court, or an amendment to the Constitution which must be approved (ratified in the states).

The breaking point for America was taxes without representation; why was such an abuse legal in England? Our founders revolted not only against the tax, but also the system that sanctioned it. The founders did not overreact and outlaw religion or Christianity due to the king's and his bishops' long and excessive greed, or only revolt against taxes. If they had they would not have created a new government with the ability to self govern including adequate taxation within a system that also promised individual justice to all citizens.

At the U.S. Constitutional Convention and in the ratification process, two approaches to sovereignty were proposed. One was by James Madison, who proposed sovereignty only for the central government; Madison was the only one I'm aware of who also concerned himself with the tension between private rights established justice and the common good. The other approach to sovereignty was by Patrick Henry in the ratification process for Virginia, who proposed it only for states, demanding states rights including nullification of federal law in dissent. Madison won and Henry lost the Constitutional ratification debate in his own state.

The negotiated compromise was the concept of enumerated powers and a republican form of government. Two hundred and thirty-five years after the forming of our first government this "solution" has continued to divide our regional visions of governance. Many of the contentions still deliberated by SCOTUS (Supreme Court of the United States) remain rooted in regional and/or state divides as old as the life of our nation.

In revolt against Parliament's right to extract taxes without representation, did our founders have to reject the executives' divine rights, the state church coronation, and King James Bible as a state document? No, but they had become a new nation and they decided to attempt to establish a new and in their eyes a more just form of governance for what is now our nation. This nation began on day one with many sets of norms among the variously founded colonies, as well as the various state constitutions of the new states.

How were slaves to be represented without being defined in law as citizens? The Bible and colonial law allowed them to be defined as property. English law in the colonies had also allowed slaves to be defined as property, an economic asset that could be pledged as collateral against a loan and sold individually outside their family group.

Politics and negotiated compromise explains the convoluted

reasoning behind the two thirds decision to include slaves in the count establishing the number of House of Representatives seats for each state. It was also agreed that each state, regardless of size, population, or wealth, would have two votes in the Senate.

The key issue regarding slavery at the founding was economic and political, not racial; there was no one north or south who acknowledged slaves as equal human individuals or human persons; they were property.

The south raised labor intensive crops that needed massive amounts of cheap labor; the north did not. The slave issue ensured there would be two Americas from the founding; ensured or not, disparate cultural norms eventually ensured contention, conflict, gridlock, and finally war.

How could such complex issues be compromised at the founding, and almost no issues get settled in the twenty-first century? The founders too feared loss of cultural norms. They did not know for sure a Bill of Rights would be added to allay concerns about lack of due process let alone assured individual rights before ratification.

This caused folks to be less sure of outcomes than those we struggle with today. One issue they could not have known is that property right norms would put labor rights in contention with the still argued belief that property rights were and are absolute. Another is that a religious ban on a human practice seen as sin could become a legal right and therefore legalized as a cultural norm. We spelled this out earlier; however, the conflict was skillfully neglected from 1791 until the 1930s. Again we see the effect of regression among folks whose political mantra is "I want my country back".

I can image they thought at the time that states' rights and the primacy of property rights over labor rights would always remain the understanding. This was the norm for most at the Constitutional Convention, before ratification and the enactment of the Bill of Rights. The amendment clause was based on ideas not yet imagined in 1791; only in making the Constitution amendable were they planning for future unknowns.

No one knew then about corporations, or what secular (civil) law would actually mean. No one knew that healthcare or mechanization would each make defense spending devour more than ten percent of the total production of the nation. Who knew that the average voter would expect to live in a heated home, with clean running water, and sewers, eating two thousand calories a day, and that each child would be educated until the age of about eighteen, just as a norm of citizenship? No one. Who does not expect these norms today as a civil norm for their own family? Of course we all do. One huge hurdle is that we should expect national affordable healthcare for all as a family norm. Not all citizens agree.

At the time of our founding, the planters compromised for political balance between regional issues. The merchant class was happy to settle for peace and moving on as a nation. Those without property had little say for most of American history. The new nation ended the king's absolute control (ownership) of property. Property law became based on Locke's views of labor, property, and nature, which said that ownership of unused land could be earned by investing one's labor in the land to make it productive. In America, homesteading was based on this theory's view of men, land, and nature per the author of the universe's (God's) natural rights of man.

In the end, with no religious test for office holders, a compromised definition of the status of slaves, and only a promised Bill of Rights, the Constitution was ratified in 1789. The Bill of Rights followed two years later. It was initiated in the House of Representatives and ratified by the thirteen states, already each a state of the Union in 1791. This Bill of Rights included the establishment (freedom of religion) clause.

Madison made one more attempt at the nullification of law under the Constitution. He wanted to give the federal government power to veto state laws. What we wound up with is settlement of such conflict in the Supreme Court if the law leads to dissent. Madison's stronger federal right or veto was rejected.

The new Constitution was in place and any state's right to nullify federal law remains unconstitutional. The concept that states could nullify federal laws died in fact, but has remained somewhere between a belief, a wish, and a demand. This sovereignty debate, states versus federal government, is totally resolved yet the decision remains alive in dissent, and in gridlock as GOP jurists treat corporate rights absolutely superior to citizen's rights

For a good read about living late in the age of feudalism, read a history of the life and times of Catherine the Great of Russia. This is a great story of the leaders of all three state powers, church, state, and military, and the propertied class called nobles in the times of a labor force of serfs or peasants. Catherine believed her subjects lived with abuse and wanted to end their misery, but she could not find a rational political or economic means to win support from nobles, the church, or her military leaders.

Reading about Catherine is insightful in trying to understand the economics of the labor system that abused peasants and serfs, and how hard it was for the few men of property to conceive of another economic model that could possibly work. No one could until the early Industrial Age created the phenomenon of productivity, as has been mentioned before. It was Adam Smith who finally conceived of capitalism, which conceived of labor as a factor of value in improving the outcomes of production for all, the state, church, nobles, military, and labor as "wage earning consumers".

Within less than a hundred years capitalism did produce vast wealth. It did not (at least without government stepping in) improve the life of laborers. It actually mostly created new forms of misery for laborers, even though they were no longer slaves or serfs; they were free men and wage earners but without defined labor rights. Hunger remained a motivator.

My father learned this as a child laborer in the work camp of the Anaconda Copper Company in Butte Montana. Being raised in misery without labor rights, he became a life long grateful member of a labor union as an adult, even as he saw the police power of the state shoot to kill in protecting the rights of the property owners at the Detroit auto plants in the 1920s and 30s where he migrated to escape the mines.

Like most U.S. corporations before the New Deal and the Wagner Act in 1935, the Anaconda Copper Company had made Butte Montana a nightmare for teenage boys. Boys like my dad, as young as thirteen, went down a deep mine shaft every morning for a twelve hour shift that provided none of today's norms for a typical miner. His meager earnings did almost nothing for the family, beyond feeding them and providing a bunk without running water or heat in the sub zero winters. Miners' boarding houses had a wood stove on the first floor; a hole in the second floor brought the only warm air upstairs from below.

The norms of my father's life in the 1900s and 1920s in a mining family in Montana were atrocious. This changed soon after when Franklin D. Roosevelt (at the urging of Frances Perkins his Labor Secretary) ended child labor and twelve hours shifts, and allowed representation funded by union dues to negotiate with the mine owners, and a newly legal right to withhold their labor (without pay) if negotiations stalled. This was their first and only power. It lasted only seven years as an absolute legal right.

Francis Perkins was FDR's only Labor Secretary and we will meet her in Chapter 9. In my mind she was the most influential woman in American history. Both labor hours and child labor were addressed earlier in the twentieth century, but it was only in the 1930s that FDR got them approved by both Congress and the Supreme Court.

Before, during and after the 1930s, miners were not supported by either their pastors or congressmen in their fight to raise wage labor above poverty level servitude for life, without rights, job security, or safe work sites.

To better understand the political and economic contentions of the colonial period, read histories of the sugar or cotton industries in North America or the Caribbean, or the poppy and opium trade in India and China. Nowhere was, nor is, the concept of rights for those who labor or their families, a consideration by the leadership of the church, state, business, or the wealthy.

In 1789 George Washington appointed his first cabinet with only five departments to administer in the Executive Branch. Today President Trump in 2019 oversees the administration of sixteen Executive

Departments. Hamilton and Jefferson the only founders in the first cabinet both agreed the functional government was to comply with the Constitution. However, the Constitution contained few defined mechanisms of operation for the executive on day one, let alone the legislature or judiciary.

The Constitution covered legal limits subject to interpretation, mandated duties of a general nature, assigned a few rights, and basic goals such as a more perfect union, to establish justice, and to provide for the common welfare (the common good). The Preamble as a goal was never defined or reviewed as a serious concern until the 1930s. Keep in mind they couldn't look at other countries and see how this was being done elsewhere. This new government was a blank slate with new limits seldom if ever before established in restraint of the authority and rights of the head of state. No head of state in history ever had sub sovereigns with rights outside the authority of the supreme sovereign, meaning the thirteen state governors and legislators.

We don't really know a lot about the founders' discussions at the Constitutional Convention. Talking about intent is difficult beyond the Federalist Papers. Madison's notes are the only record of the Convention and he edited them for years thereafter, therefore no true contemporary record remains that was voted to be approved as a record.

Washington's first task was to define a plan for the operation of the U.S. central government. He was well aware of the differences in approach to land, labor, economics, capital, industry, taxation and reliance on sacred text in the two predominant regions (slave south, and wage north) regarding economic norms. There were also religious differences between the south and the north. The elders in the north and a king's bishop in the south were the heads of the state churches.

Only the primacy of property and limiting voter eligibility to white male property owners were in sync between the two regions, as well as those who made up the first Executive Branch and the first Legislative Branch. Washington appointed the first Supreme Court, and it was not "his" Supreme Court. Once the Bill of Rights was enacted in 1791 the first government was a work in progress. I mention "his" Supreme Court because of President Trump in the twenty-first century seems to have difficulty understanding who the Attorney General represents and by extension wants a Supreme Court that is protective of the president, as opposed to what Madison created and Washington understood had been ratified as the law.

During Washington's two terms as president there was no discussion or dissent regarding what was or was not constitutional about his chosen process. No one at the time referred Washington's proposal to the Supreme Court to challenge the structure of the central government and that structure still survives, with a four hundred percent increase in the departments in the Executive Branch. About twenty years later the Supreme Court did adjudicate and settle Washington's founding decisions with a unanimous vote beyond the economy we discussed earlier.

The government did have the authority, and as it turned out the fiscal means due to Hamilton's system, Washington's endorsement, and Madison leading the Congress to unanimously approve Washington's chosen system. We also must include Chief Justice John Marshall in this process when he led the Supreme Court to unanimously approve all of Washington's proposals as enacted. In 2020 Washington's shaping of the national government endures.

It may be funny when TV comedy shows interview Main Street or college campus folks and show how few can name our three branches of government, or name the vice president or Speaker of the House. It is less funny when ill-informed folks vote and we live with the fruits of emotion and misinformation because we did not elect legislators, we elected partisan absolutists who claim their gerrymandered election constitutes a mandate.

That we as a nation spend over seventy five thousand dollars educating each of these know-nothings is a recipe for disaster. I grew up in Michigan and I have lived in California, Louisiana, Connecticut, Mississippi, Texas, North Carolina, and now Virginia. Kindergarten through twelfth grade educations cost from barely sixty thousand dollars per student in Mississippi to as much as one hundred twenty thousand dollars in California. The earning power of California graduates versus Mississippi reflects the return on this investment. Income per capita in California is sixty-four thousand dollars and only forty thousand five hundred ninety three dollars in Mississippi (2015 data). An extra twenty-four thousand dollars a year for forty years is five hundred thousand dollars per citizen. Which came first, low investment in education or low earning power of the future voters?

A couple of personal notes here. Transfers were a part of corporate life in the 1960s-70s, so I moved quite a bit. My children attended public schools in Michigan, Connecticut, Louisiana, Texas, and Massachusetts. They saw the difference. I have lived the longest in Massachusetts and have seen the difference in education in so-called red states and in so-called blue states. Based on my personal experience, in the red states the schools strive to instill regional norms. In the blue states they strive to instill critical thinking. It is not surprising the blue group spends almost twice as much on education and pays twice as much on average in wages (if benefits are included this gap would be even wider). The blue states have both the highest income and the lowest poverty rates among the states.

The blue states remit as much as more than twice what the federal government spends back into their states out of the federal treasury. Delaware for example, pays almost two dollars in federal taxes for every dollar in federal benefits they get in return. So the remaining dollar goes to funding the military and federal government in general including block grant federalism, a form of welfare to the mostly red states whose economy does not generate enough money to fully fund their own state budgets.

On the other end of the scale is South Carolina. For every dollar they pay in federal taxes, they receive two dollars and eighty-seven cents in federal benefits. States such as South Carolina, Mississippi, Louisiana, and Alabama are therefore paying absolutely nothing to fund our national defense.

What is so great economically about living in a red state? I don't know, but they do in fact want the blue states to change their economies to lower the cost of the federal government. It seems mindless beyond reason to weaken our national military and to end funding the poor in the poor states, but that is the politics in red state America in 2020. Federalism was expanded beginning with President Reagan and will be discussed in Chapter 10.

Michigan is an example of a state that does well overall, but suffers in certain areas. It was and remains segregated in its urban former industrial cities. The Michigan cities of Flint and Detroit are examples of pockets of folks who are unready to govern or earn a living wage on average. Much of it comes back to generations of less money spent on education and white flight out of these cities including white led industrial corporations ending living wage job opportunities.

Intentionally under-educating a large minority of the population so they graduate unready for either the needs of a complex economy or government remains costly and unacceptable. This was part of the "separate but equal" education debacle in the south, and is still a major problem. It has been arguably the most costly "savings" in the history of America, intentionally educating minorities to be less ready for a meaningful place in a complex economy and government, as Strom Thurmond and Billy Graham defined the black population in America since 1948 (reviewed in Chapter 9).

Lower taxes do not guarantee better economic outcomes for a state, nor higher incomes for the average family. Nothing in life provides more freedom for adults and opportunity for children than a family finally earning a living wage with healthcare.

We will see that it was a long time before any change of status for minorities was addressed by federal legislators or U.S. Courts. Labor rights, voting rights, equal pay and family planning for women, among other abuses are all still works in progress in twenty-first century America, only addressed in America between 1935 and 1980, and still awaiting reversal of the current reactive trend.

None of the improved opportunities for blacks or women came about as a direct and early result of freedom or justice values espoused in the American Constitution or Bill of Rights. They all were due primarily to early mid twentieth century New Deal legislation, regulation, and adjudication, and all were opposed by a majority of the majority population in a large minority of individual states, and among regional majorities of Biblical Christian faith based voters.

These improvements in the rights of citizens were more the result of the policies, primarily of three presidents, Franklin D. Roosevelt, Harry S. Truman, and Lyndon B. Johnson, than their party. We will also see the reversal of this, although parties do tend to ride the coattails of popular presidents, successful or not.

By 1789 a Constitution was in place, based on Madison's Virginia Plan modified by the New Jersey Plan. The small states insisted on establishing the United States as a hybrid, both federal and national government, that gave them equal representation in the Senate (the branch that represented states) meaning as a compromise states could not nullify federal laws, and the national government could not veto state laws. If a state law violated the Constitution, then only a national veto could result from a successful appeal to the Supreme Court. The small state compromise saved the Constitution. Benjamin Franklin, not a noted Christian at the moment of peril called for a prayer and an adjournment. The next day after a night of reflection the delegates compromised and the Constitution was enacted and sent to the states for ratification.

With a government in place, we will next take a look at the first seventy-five years of America as an independent nation of declared self-governed men living in a secular nation.

Chapter 6

Bill of Rights

1791-1865   America's first 75 years: Washington, Adams, Jefferson, Hamilton, Madison, Marshall, and Jackson; Davis; the Civil War initiated by the southern states; ends with the end of slavery and the assassination of President Lincoln.

In Chapter 5 Washington began the first seventy-five years of the United States of America as an organized government, with ever growing regional tensions as a legacy from events covered in the first five chapters. Those civil and church legacies formed the minds of our founders and citizens alike as retained societal norms, while life finally began for Americans as citizens of the nation, and state leaders too often continued as leaders of their state and region in contention with the new national government. Federalism versus nationalism continues in gridlock to this day.

As for the post Civil War effort, the economics of the colonies were as difficult in victory as was the plight of Washington at his home; both worried his mind the eight years of war, his short retirement, and his eight years as president.

The revolutionary army had been plagued by short enlistments, a shortage of weapons and ammunition, poor roads, a blockade against shipping, as well as overall reduced imports, no banks or credit, no authority to tax, inadequate manufacturing capacity, and thirteen colonies reluctant and or unable to fund the effort. In the end the Revolutionary War was fought with borrowed funds.

Washington never joined a party; his views were more as a realist than any personal or regional ideology, religious theory, attachment to an economic system, or knowledge of a structured authority for governing. He knew the financial burdens on the southern states under the English imposed mercantile system where England set prices and exchange rates on imports into and exports out of the southern states. He knew the hopelessness of the Confederation as a governance system with no central government authority and its field commander with no access or right to demand resources of any of the thirteen colonies that were now declared states engaged in war as a nation under new untried state Constitutions, some with strong governors and others including his Virginia without.

Those who may believe that the day-to-day duties of the president, the size of the federal government, or the day-to-day work of the president's cabinet flowed from the Articles in the Constitution, are under informed as to what was defined as Washington's rights, limits and duties for the executive operations of the president or his office. The Constitution gave each branch authority to define their own operational mechanisms, only the sphere of authority of each was spelled out. Over two hundred thirty years later in 2020, our president and our house of representatives are in conflict over rights and duties.

Laws and budgets had to be passed to define expectations, limit costs, and set goals subject to Congressional oversight. Dispute resolution among the parties from the people to the states, to the legislature and the executive, would all need a means for court ordering such disputes. As an appellate court the Supreme Court chose judicial review as their mechanism to issue majority reports, as each issue over the centuries have been adjudicated in review, argued in private, and voted in settlement.

Washington's first administration included John Adams as the first vice president with a very limited defined role in the newly established United States of America government. Washington was the unanimous choice for president. I believe all or nearly all had a favorite son for vice president, as Adams, a graduate of Harvard University, was of the north. He was the best or nearly the best known northern founder as he had helped every colony with its state constitution, and he easily won the vice presidency. To my knowledge Washington was not close to his vice president in any meaningful way. The first federal government was set up with a cabinet of secretaries, and they included as key secretaries the following with a short introduction.

During the war effort Adams had spent time in France and in

Holland as an ambassador and was sent to borrow money. Adams replaced Benjamin Franklin as our second ambassador to France. Thomas Jefferson was the third and final. Adams acted as the ambassador to England. Funds and men, ships and arms were all supplied by the king of France during Jefferson's years in Paris; France made the difference in ending the war in favor of the colonies.

Thomas Jefferson, our first secretary of state, was a graduate of William and Mary College which was affiliated with the then state Church of England. William and Mary trained both clergy for the pulpit and attorneys for the law. Jefferson was an attorney by education; he had served in the Virginia colonial government in several capacities, and was as mentioned the author of the Declaration of Independence.

Jefferson was also a Virginia planter and slave owner who favored strong states rights, with limited rights for the central government. Jefferson not only spent the Revolutionary War period in France negotiating the loans and military assistance that finally enabled Washington to defeat the king and his army, he served in France again during the French Revolution, so he played no role in the Constitutional Convention. He developed an affection for the French, and for the rest of his life was the most interested of all the founders in the common man. The American revolution was for the most part a revolution initiated by property owners; in France the revolution was for the most part initiated by the common people against the elite property owners and the king. Surprisingly, given the level of wealth held by the church and the level of support for the king extended by bishops, the French people did not overthrow the bishops. France remained a Roman Catholic nation, and remains so to this day.

Until Jefferson became the third president he viewed Virginia and by extension the southern states in the new government primarily as an agricultural based, rural, slave labor, warm weather export crops based economy, among a like region of several states in the new nation, totally distinct from the reality of norms in the northern states.

There were other non planters such as Franklin of Philadelphia, but he no longer played a active founding role once the Constitution was approved.

As noted Alexander Hamilton became the first secretary of the treasury. He had excelled as a man of commerce before entering what is now Columbia University of New York and that experience mattered in setting right the new nation's funding. It was Hamilton who as the first secretary of the treasury introduced the economic system we still enjoy in the U.S. to this day, capitalism, with a national bank; also, an ability to tax created an ability to create debt. It replaced the English mercantile system in the north at our founding and in the south after the Civil War. He also paid off the states' Revolutionary War debt based on having established tariffs. Capitalism flourished in the north as manufacturing grew for the home market.

A key element to note here is how the differences between the northern and southern states that became the United States were settled, as exemplified by the first two cabinet secretaries Washington chose.

The states in the north were mostly settled by folks looking for freedom from the state church, or because of a lack of advancement opportunity in their mother country. They had arrived from England indentured to mercantile enterprises chartered by the Crown. As these men earned their freedom and became middling prosperous by English standards with a bit of land, they continued to hold to protestant sects other than the state Church of England.

Their church supported colleges reflected dissenting theological views which made the enlightenment concept of separation of church and state compatible with their disenchantment with the mother county. This was memorialized in the first amendment to the Constitution as the Establishment Clause in the Bill of Rights. Madison from Virginia was a graduate of a northern protestant university, Princeton in New Jersey. His boyhood tutor was a Princeton man and his father accepted his recommendation; it was Madison who wrote the establishment clause.

The southern land holders were mostly descended from families indebted to the king for land grants and as such were formerly loyal subjects of the king. They also attended or supported the state church headed by their benefactor. Southern men became wary of monarchy and the church that supported it, in the control of what they saw as the greedy men of property who led Parliament by the time of the revolution.

William and Mary College in Virginia trained men from the south who were less in league with the northern view of the establishment clause in the Bill of Rights. Southern graduates had to compromise their belief system to institute what they saw as a more rational relationship to government in service to its citizens, than a church in service to monarchy. Jefferson was an exception, being more of a deist than a practicing Christian. Many Scotsmen had migrated to the south for opportunity but not in leadership roles, and the Presbyterian Church also became well settled in the south, followed in numbers next by Baptists, both after the evangelicals. George Wythe taught law at the College of William and Mary, and his views informed Jefferson, Marshall, and Monroe.

Owning "servants and/or slaves" was also more natural to the sons of noblemen in the south than to the lower classes of settlers in the north. There were in fact slaves in the north in the early years, and yeomen did from time to time employ farm laborers as bondsmen or even own a slave or two.

A quick note here about slaves. They were often the most valuable property owned by southern planters. In 1807, Jefferson as the third president ended the importation of slaves from Africa. Hardly a move against slavery, as the Virginia planters' slaves now became the breeding stock for the future supply, increasing each slave's value. I have read that one of the few work breaks any slaves ever were given was for pregnant women after 1808, to ensure as many live births as possible for commercial reasons when they were intentionally kept pregnant as a cash crop.

Note: when Madison our fourth president died his wife Dolly moved back to the Capital, and over time allowed her son from a first marriage to sell off Madison's slaves to support her final fourteen years of life as a well loved social hostess, and her only son to live out his life as an alcoholic gambler. None of Madison's slaves were ever set free as had been his wish.

As more land was cleared of native people or timber or swamps, slaves became a growing cash crop for sale into the newly opening border lands expropriated from and then cleansed of the indigenous population, as they spoke of the process at the time. This reached a peak after the founding generation had past. The peak land cleansing efforts as we shall see later in this chapter occurred in the 1830s and the 1840s in the lands from Florida to Texas to California across the American south and southwest into the Union.

As settlers from both the north and south moved west, new states were created. To maintain control or regional parity in Congress it became important for a balance to be maintained regarding representation in Congress between slave and free economic labor system states. A powerful central government was a growing threat to the southern way of life and the economic system it rested upon, especially as anti-slave sentiment grew in the north. This threat grew as regionalism destroyed what little sense of nationalism remained in place from our founding.

Washington and Jefferson both wrote about slavery and recognized its limited ability to produce meaningful cash profits (mercantilism was basically a barter and credit system). They also occasionally noted a vague recognition of what the almighty might actually think of the institution. Studying their commentary caused me to question the southerner's true devotion to their unique way of life, yet seventy years later they went to war to maintain it. As in most human endeavors, established norms are seldom rejected outright. This truth is one of the fascinating realities about how completely our founders changed economic governance norms at our founding, from mercantilism to capitalism, even if slow to become the going concern it became in time, contrary to the southern states' long traditions.

In the year 1800 America moved beyond our founding years, even though the next three presidents would all be founders from Virginia who each served two four year terms. Presidents Thomas Jefferson, James Madison, and James Monroe served eight years each, and all were lawyers, owners of slave worked plantations, students of the classics, and lived their lives in debt under the mercantile system. All three thought they believed in limited government yet they grew our nation into a three thousand mile wide continental nation. In this book as we attempt to understand how and why we live in gridlock in spite of great might and wealth, we will limit our review to the major happenings of their times. We will compare them to the failures of the other great revolutions of the early nineteenth century, and see how the second half of this first seventy-five year era of the American experiment in self government progressed spectacularly in wealth creation, territorial growth, political gridlock, and creation of an ever growing human tragedy treated more with intentional blindness than anything our laws and religious traditions taught regarding common decency, let alone the ideal of justice.

John Adams served only one term; his greatest contribution to the nation was the appointment of John Marshall as Chief Justice of the Supreme Court, another founding father and along with Jefferson, and Monroe, a William and Mary law graduate in Williamsburg, Virginia under the tutelage of George Wythe, America's first law professor, and in my mind one of the greatest and least known of our founders.

In 1803 John Marshall wrote the first opinion that became the foundation of how laws are declared settled by the Supreme Court in the United States under a process called judicial review. The case is known as Marbury v. Madison. Once again I'll not walk us through the details; what was at stake was settled law.

Adams had appointed Marbury to a minor office; the warrant was signed but not delivered. Newly inaugurated President Jefferson began his presidency attempting to cancel and overturn this signed legal appointment that was left undelivered on President Adams' desk in the White House. Jefferson wanted the appointment to go to a member of his political party and not Adams' party. Jefferson asked his attorney general to cancel the appointment; Marbury sued the attorney general. Marshall established that even the president is subject to the law, and created the process to resolve such conflicts in final settlement.

This process has only been defied once in U.S. history by a sitting president, Andrew Jackson in the 1830s, which we'll discuss later in this chapter. However, as an example of how legacies are a factor in

U.S. law, just such a situation shaped up in 2019 regarding President Trump's emergency order to move Congressional appropriated military funding to fund the building of a wall on our southern borders, funding the president had requested and the Congress rejected. The Supreme Court's five GOP members gave the President partial relief, based on a Congressional approved right to declare an emergency and move funding. Marbury so far is still the law and the U.S. House of Congress remains the only approved political entity of the American Government able to approve spending. The legislature needs to reconsider what constitutes an emergency under this legislation.

During the same era in our early years as a nation the French revolution was to a large extent led by the starving masses. The famous line of Queen Marie Antoinette who was soon beheaded, "let them eat cake" when there was no bread to feed the masses, comes to mind.

Over the next few years without the leadership of a George Washington or James Madison there was chaos in France. What came to be known as the "terrors" caused the French Revolution to spiral out of control. As always happens in times of chaos a strong man arose, Napoleon, who over the same period of time our nation was settling into steady growth under a set of agreed laws, Napoleon was engaged in a plan to "make France great again", to coin a phase. Another great read regarding the folly of chaos and would be greatness under a strong man is the life of Napoleon.

All would-be great autocrats' efforts always lead to debt and the wasting of the youth of their nation in war. Napoleon had a few victories and then led his troops to Egypt where his men died of thirst, and to Russia where men died of exposure, and finally attempting to quell a slave rebellion in Haiti where his men died of dysentery.

Before the French people finally put an end to this reign of self glory, Napoleon needed money for his wars, and out of the blue offered to President Jefferson France's rights to what was called the Louisiana Purchase. In brief Jefferson sent ambassadors to make a deal for New Orleans, to enable navigation of the Mississippi. Napoleon offered the whole territory all the way to the Rockies and all of the unexplored plains states. Jefferson's ambassador accepted the deal subject to approval.

Jefferson, the champion of small local government, fearful of over reaching presidents, advised only by his friend Attorney General Madison and his Treasury Secretary Gallatin, closed the deal. He did so without a vote in Congress. Thanks to Hamilton's banking and tax systems this purchase was funded without any referral to Congress even for an appropriation.

This single decision ensured the end of slavery and the long run up to the Civil War, and in the end new layers of gridlock and the creation of new bastardization of the founding promise of the governance bargain, and new means of subjugating black citizens; the war over slavery took another fifty-six years to come to a head.

We will see in a later chapter, one hundred seventy-five years later that General and later President Dwight Eisenhower during his presidency after WWII saw the need to build a national military highway system; it became the U.S. interstate highway system that American commerce and tourism depend on today. Hamilton planted the seeds that made Eisenhower's vision possible to sell as an idea, and to fund it as a defense budget item. A president with vision can do big things and change the nation, but such change agents must have a great idea and the people behind him. In the twentieth century we will meet four such presidents (FDR, HST, LBJ, and Ronald Reagan); all but one of them did more good than harm as we shall review in Chapters 9 and 10. Some would include Teddy Roosevelt and Woodrow Wilson; I agree they began what was called the Progressive Era. However, as initiators they did not live to reach the level of impact of the four later transition presidents.

A few years later during the presidency of James Madison the question of what a state (in this case Maryland) could or could not do if a majority of its voters' representatives disagreed with a federal law Congress had approved, came to a head in my favorite Chief Justice's court, John Marshall. As noted above Marshall was appointed from Virginia by President John Adams of Massachusetts, the first vice president and second president.

The case involved Maryland trying to nullify the federal law that allowed a national bank office in Baltimore. There was no national bank at the time as Madison had allowed Hamilton's First National Bank to expire. Congress had voted to put an office of the Second National Bank in Baltimore that Madison requested after he had struggled to defeat England in the war of 1812 without a national bank. Maryland claimed an abuse of federal power as they believed this national bank branch created unfair competition for their state banks.

Maryland appealed to the Supreme Court based on two arguments; first the Constitution does not mention a national bank, second they claimed the national bank was not necessary. The Marshall court settled the law, first agreeing the Constitution did not directly authorize a national bank. Second the Court ruled the Constitution did allow the Congress to manage the money of the United States, and allowed that Congress has a right to do what Congress considered necessary, not what the state considered not absolutely necessary. The Court went further and stated that the state of Maryland could not refuse, tax, or oversee any federal bank that opened an office in Maryland.

The Marshall court found that Congress was free to do what it deemed "proper and necessary" to carry out the business of the federal government under the "Proper and Necessary" clause in the Constitution. The Court at that point confirmed that the national government's rights were superior to the rights of a state, if the federal government found its action to be necessary. That ruling still stands and still chafes in some regions of the nation, even though it has worked to the advantage of most states and the nation, under the concept of federalism.

Federalism is a term we will explore in more detail as it becomes the most costly domestic non military federal spending program in the American budget early in the twenty-first century, as we look ahead to how a founding legacy can create unexpected issues of gridlock as our history moves along, and a president reinterprets a federal program. This becomes one of my sixteen suggested changes for the twenty-first century.

Madison became the fourth U.S. president. He agreed with Jefferson; neither were fans of a national bank. However, Jefferson in the Barbary Coast wars and Madison in the War of 1812 came to see the value of a national bank during times of war, for the same reasons Hamilton proposed it and Washington approved it to counteract the unwillingness of each and all of the states to fund the national military even in time of war.

Again in the twenty-first century the GOP has refused to tax to fund the three terrorism wars we have engaged in since 2001 and that continue into 2020; all are funded by debt, only possible because of the Hamilton system, and the Marshall settlement of the differences between Hamilton's view of governance and the southerners' view of government and taxes, without concern for the sustainability of the nation, from the revolutionary war and continuing.

The charter for the First National Bank, as Hamilton had proposed and Washington approved and the Congress enacted, was based on a charter Washington approved with a sunset clause that allowed the bank's charter to expire in 1811, and Madison allowed it to expire one year before going to war again. The lessons of the war of 1812 led to the Second National Bank being approved in 1816 which lasted through the balance of time of the Virginia presidents for another eight years, as well as that of John Adams' son, John Quincy Adams.

Neither Jefferson nor Madison was a veteran of the War for Independence. Then as now presidents who have served in war seem more sensitive to the cost of war in both treasure and blood, and the needs of both generals and men in the field, than those who have not, in the view of most historians.

There was no new debt; however, each state owed debt from the time of the revolution. Hamilton recognized the value of credit and insisted on paying off the debt from the revolution, which he did over the objections of most of the states. He invented federal bonds, using his tariffs to fund the interest.

As the Virginia founders began their twenty-four years of governance, states were still deeply in debt and without a path to solvency accepted by Jefferson, Madison, or Monroe. Only because of

Hamilton's tax and bond system based on the nation's ability to tax, were the three presidents able to approve post roads to be built, the mail to be delivered, and ambassadors dispatched and funded, while political parties continued to debate the system that was working, a true sign of a divided nation then and now.

Many of today's debates continue to reflect the same issues of these early national contentions regarding rights and regulation of labor, banks, property rights versus individual citizens, sovereign states versus the central government, as well as funding with debt, spending Congress has already approved, in spite of a nation wealthy enough to self fund if the political will can be found to tax.

There has never been a balanced budget amendment to the U.S. Constitution. The Constitution allows the Congress to use debt as well as taxes, tariffs and fees to fund the government.

Since our founding days it has been an issue to get enough taxes approved to enable appropriated bills to be paid with taxes, as opposed to debt. Then as now the cash poor southern states voted no on taxes, but voted yes on appropriations. Even when Hamilton used federal money to pay off Revolutionary War debt of the individual states, the southern states objected; look it up, this is true.

In addition to asking Congress to pass and fund needed programs as he saw it, Washington as were all presidents was also the head of the executive branch of government (in effect the manager of the day-to-day government). Presidents since Washington have always administered their executive duties under the oversight of cabinet secretaries to regulate the carrying out of laws affecting each secretary's area of responsibility and appropriated budgets, with expertise. These departments operate under legislation, funding, and oversight of the House side of the Congress. The modern GOP's evangelical faction objects to oversight, another source of never ending gridlock outcomes.

In feudal state church England in 1776 when the Declaration of Independence was written, England's governing class was primarily continued generation to generation under inheritance laws, known as primogeniture i.e. the oldest son or male relative inherited one hundred percent of the main estate. Today the families of dynastic wealth primarily accumulated by successful families in control of corporate holdings fund think tanks as educational entities to spread the output of the think tanks ideologies to ensure continuation of the national wealth gap, in their favor.

Another use of what is now referred to as dark money is lobbying to ensure that accommodating federal legislation especially concerning labor law (right-to-work), inheritance law (estate planning), tax law especially of non earned income (interest and capital gains) is treated with more favorable rates than ordinary income such as wages, commissions, and professional fees. Legacy beliefs remain even as realities change.

Another decision made in 1810 during the presidency of Madison was that all of Washington's founding decisions regarding the executive branch were declared Constitutional by John Marshall's Supreme Court. America has operated under a federal system with a strong central government from its beginning, and that tradition has been upheld as the legal government of the United States ever since.

Before we move on to the presidency of Andrew Jackson, and the opening of states west of the eastern mountains, let's consider what is to come as Jefferson returned to his home in Charlottesville Virginia and considered what the Louisiana Territory purchase portended. Jefferson had established and sent an exploration of his purchase called the Corps of Discovery, also known as the Lewis and Clark Expedition.

Jefferson knew that much of the new territories would become states with a different crop base that did not require slaves. He also knew a national repeal of slavery might be just, but he did not want to see it because of what he saw as his and his region's best economic interest at the time.

Jefferson had no means of estimating how many states would be carved out of his purchase, or what labor system they would adopt at the time he signed the deal, or if in time they would vote with the north or south. His private thoughts were usually more expansive than his public comments; he made a smart decision in capturing the

Louisiana Purchase for the United States, but he did not crow about it at the time. If you visit Jefferson's home in Virginia today you will see the skins and native American artifacts and western maps displayed that were the legacy of the Lewis and Clark expedition.

Yet with this deal Jefferson's purchase sealed the fate of the slave based economic system in America. He knew it might not happen in his lifetime, but he knew what was coming. There would be future fights over the increasing number of free states in the new territories that could lead to war, and finally an end to slavery in America.

We will not review in detail the nineteenth century presidency of James K. Polk. However, like Jefferson he was a southern slave holder who in only one term added about as much land mass to the United States as Jefferson. Between a showdown with Britain over the Oregon Territory, annexation of Texas, and the California Territory of Mexico that was ceded under settlement of the Mexican War, Polk expanded the United States to much of the full territory of today's lower forty-eight states; this did not effect the fate of slavery to the degree Jefferson's acquisition did.

In the end, adding all this territory was not the fairest thing for Mexico, nor the smartest thing for the cause of the slave states; it was one of the great factors in what some call America's Manifest Destiny. Many consider Polk the greatest one term president in history, and usually one of the ten best ever; however, he may have eradicated more Native Americans than any other president, even if the general consensus is that Jackson was the worst friend Native Americans ever had, usually based on his "trail of tears" removal of the Cherokees from Georgia to present day Oklahoma.

By comparison to any other executive decision impacting the nation, this decision by the states' rights champion Jefferson sealed the southern states' fate. Jefferson in fact grew the size of the United States, institutionalized the executive prerogatives of a determined president, and marginalized the southern governing norms as new states were carved out of the new territory. Each state that was added became a labor system showdown regarding Congressional representation.

We will not go into the weeds on this, but read a history of the Missouri Compromise or Dred Scott to better understand how we unraveled the first time as a functional government. If it ever happens again, as many or more folks could die if mishandled. It will be driven by ideology and absolutism I fear, not by fighting for a better outcome regarding the common good, or to establish justice.

The only executive order that has had anywhere near as significant an economic impact on America was Ronald Reagan's executive order decision to allow unfettered free trade from Asia including China in 1985, to be discussed in Chapter 10. This was arguably the most expensive mistake in American history, for the most families and towns and the economic health of the nation. To listen to GOP spin in the twenty-first century it would be easy to believe President Reagan was the best friend working families ever had.

A compromise that accepts Washington's decisions in favor of a system for operating the federal government as well as an end to a governance role for religion has to be understood or America's Constitutional system is doomed. We need to reconcile, not reject, the reality. I'm not sure where this comment best fits in this narrative, but I want to add it before we leave the founders' era behind.

In the first seventy-five years of American history most citizens of New York, Virginia, or South Carolina felt more pride in and would have defined themselves sooner as a citizen of their state, than define themselves as an American citizen.

Anyone who feels more pride as a Texan or as a southerner than as a citizen of the United States is a factor in what I see as an attack on our founding documents, and what they represent. This is true for many in the south, less so for folks in the north, east, mid America, or the west. It is hard to know what patriotism actually means in any region where this is still true.

By Washington and Congress having accepted Hamilton's proposal for a strong central government with a capitalist economic system along with eventual settlement of these decisions as law by the Supreme Court, America became the most wealthy and powerful nation in the world. Washington, the sometimes stoic general, proved to be a man of vision beyond the norms of his class, region, or life experience.

By way of comparison, South America's first president, Simon Bolivar, presided over what remained a cluster of small fiefdoms; his creation of greater Columbia never gelled into a wealthy or powerful continental nation. It failed as the United States most likely would have if Washington had accepted Jefferson's proposal of a small weak central government with thirteen strong state governments, once nullification had created thirteen different systems of governance across America.

In my opinion Bolivar failed due to a couple of realities. First, the Spanish colonial system never bought into the enlightenment or developed a strong parliament with some local administration allowed the colonists. Second, South America remained by choice an export crop or extract industry mercantile economy in service only to the property class in the colonies and at home. Spain never developed a strong group of chartered colonies that were self governed for a long period of early history. South America never had a Plymouth Colony, or such a local compact among the colonists, even granting a limited form of religion, as Spain also was never affected much by the reformation of Christianity as was England. In the end the governors of the separate states in South America remained sovereign. In the end Bolivar was believed to have been poisoned for demanding to be president for life. In America Washington retired to his home after two terms.

Madison did not think in terms of political parties, or his and Congress' preferences in Washington's first term; he saw his duty was to lead Congress in enactment of Washington's proposals, a tradition that endured until 1993 for most Speakers of the House. Tip O'Neill was the last Speaker who saw that his relationship to an opposite party president was meant to be collaborative, which to O'Neill meant giving the winning president a chance to try the ideas he won on.

Newt Gingrich was the first to introduce absolutism as a tactic in the Speaker's role; however, he allowed John Kasich and Phil Gramm to do business in compromise with Bill Clinton, as we will review in Chapter 10.

There was dissent of course. The founders had created a co-equal legislature and there was still concern over the problems they had suffered at the hands of a sovereign absolute king, but it was not shared by Madison who prevailed for his president and nation in that first term.

Patrick Henry turned down Washington's offer to be Secretary of State in his second term, in protest against Washington's strong central government decisions. Henry feared Hamilton's federalist government would be a problem for states' rights leaning governance in his beloved Virginia. Seventy-one years later Virginia voted to secede from the Union in agreement with, and over the loss of the nullification battle Calhoun waged for South Carolina at the beginning of the 1860s.

Henry died in the same year as Washington, only one year after Adams was elected. However, as the terrors of the French Revolution unfolded in France in Adam's first year in office, Henry supported Adams, a federalist and a northerner, as the second president of the United States. His support for Adams helped ensure the Supreme Court settled Washington's design of the Executive Branch, as Adam's appointed John Marshall to be the deciding Chief Justice of the Supreme Court, the court that judicially reviewed Washington and the founders' decisions in applying the Constitution to governing and approved all of the founders' decisions as settled law. Most of it still intact.

Henry's refusal to serve Washington made no sense to me. I just assume it was a protest statement against his fellow Virginians for not rejecting Hamilton's influence, but I concede it could have been love of being governor, or a grudge over having lost the nullification argument. Henry did not serve in the revolution and routinely voted against adequate funding of the revolutionary army. I see Henry as penny wise and pound foolish in terms of the cost of freedom; he has not been the last in our history. I guess I really do believe he loved being Governor of Virginia more than any satisfaction any national office could have given him.

Today, Henry is as close as the Tea Party comes to having a patron saint. Patrick Henry's family homestead is in the district where a Tea Party candidate in 2014 toppled the majority leader in the House of Representatives, a fellow Republican but not absolutist enough, having failed to refuse to fund the United States debt as a form of protest. Henry's home, tavern, and law office across the street from the Hanover Court House and jail in Virginia where he practiced law still stand, and can be visited; it's worth a visit.

By the 1830s Hamilton's tariffs which Jefferson supported were a burden for the south. By 1850 the imbalance of free labor states to slave states became an overwhelming fear in the south. We will see this contention come to a head in 1860. The Republican Party (GOP) was formed by abolitionists in 1854 to intentionally address slavery in newly formed states, beginning with the Kansas-Nebraska contentions, and to support abolishing slavery in general. 1860 was an election year; the last compromise president Buchanan was a lame duck. President-elect Lincoln had said a house divided against itself cannot stand; the meaning of Lincoln's commitment will be fully explained by the end of this chapter

Andrew Jackson had allowed the Second National Bank to end. During the Civil War Lincoln set up a third national bank again with a sunset clause. Recessions followed the end of each national bank. There was no other national bank until enactment of the Federal Reserve under Woodrow Wilson in 1913 which survives to this day. Each of these first three central banks was allowed to lapse. We will see that the true role for a national bank only fully emerged due to the need to capitalize industry and to recapitalize banks after periods of war or economic collapse.

The third value of a national central bank relates to the money supply, interest rate setting, and inflation rate rationalization. Each time the central bank was allowed to expire it triggered a twenty year boom and bust economic cycle as an outcome. Each time repeal was based on ideology, not economic reality, just as the latest two boom bust banking failures were at the end of the 1980s (Savings & Loans) and the 2000s (Wall Street and Freddie and Fannie). In some ways any central control or oversight was a concern of each state, but was central to the whole idea of independence in the south, and freedom to many individual southerners still today.

If you think you support original intent as to how the Constitution should be interpreted, consider that our so called small government founding guru Jefferson argued a central bank was unconstitutional. However, no state bank could ever be large or strong enough to recapitalize a state's economy after a national collapse due to speculative capitalism or a world war, or even a huge natural disaster.

Based on experience, we would need a Constitutional amendment if the legislature had not instituted a national bank. No nation could exist in the modern global economy without such a function. On the flip side of the coin, Jefferson was the key defender of a wall between church and state if a society of free men was to function. In 2017 the last attorney general from a southern state defined this separation as unconstitutional. Settlement of these basic questions are paramount if we are going to function as a national government equal to the task of a modern world power as an economy as well as an alliance partner with credibility.

Today the Libertarian wing of the modern GOP still seeks a Jefferson model of governance; if they ever succeed they will destroy functional funding of the capitalist system they like to believe they champion. We will see additional examples of the mischief original intent (also known as strict constructionist or original meaning) can lead to in Chapter 10.

Washington approved a central bank because there was very little money or credit available to fund his army, especially from the all but cashless, credit dependent, slave labor, debt barter system England used (inflicted on) to manage tobacco and cotton growers in the colonial agriculture mercantile economy of the south at the time.

Hamilton wanted a central bank because he saw the need for stable money and credit in the coming capitalist economic system in the north and the needs of the even larger nation and economy that he believed would evolve under capitalism. He wanted to be rid of the royal governor, the king's troops and Parliament's taxes; he also wanted to function as a fully funded and independent nation.

We will see in 1907 a time of boom and bust without a central bank that J.P. Morgan bailed out Wall Street and New York City himself with President Teddy Roosevelt's concurrence, once the nation was a large industrial nation, and the industrialists pursued speculation in an unregulated market to the point of collapse.

I often jump ahead this way tying founding era issues that recur, until a sustainable solution is enacted legislatively, or settled by the court at some point in our economic governance history. I hope it is more helpful than distracting. I really see this whole seventeen hundred years as one evolving story of ever recurring issues that were routinely ignored whenever possible.

I am personally more interested in workable policy outcomes that do more good than harm and I am in ideology, another reason for writing a book that is looking for compromise to replace gridlock, as well as improved understanding of how the American economic governance system really came about, how it works and why, with a few examples of failure based on ideology. Improvements in our system always have been based on lessons learned over time, seldom if ever on an absolutist belief system turning out to have all the solutions for all classes in society.

In effect the same drives that produce wealth when left unregulated historically have repeatedly collapsed based on speculative greed, first booming fueled by debt, followed by a devastating bust. This is what Allen Greenspan, Reagan's Chairman of the Federal Reserve, called irrational exuberance in the boom George W. Bush triggered in 2004 that foundered in 2007. My antidote is a theory called rational boundaries, which can be found in a book titled *Mechanisms of Governance* by Oliver E. Williamson.

FDR is the only president in our history who instituted adequate regulation and social insurance to make banking safe in America, designed to have rational boundaries as a factor of policy making. If the earnings are more modest, the absence of crashes make it a bargain for all who bank across all banking relationships, as net debtors, savers, or investors, on either side of the ledger.

Jefferson, Jackson, and Lincoln in the nineteenth century, and Reagan in the twentieth, and again George W Bush in the twenty-first, each ended or deregulated a key form of central banking leading to an overwhelming speculative bust, with inadequate ability for states and state banks to recapitalize themselves. The recurring outcome has been years of abusive misery for the innocent citizens affected.

These main contentions dividing Hamilton's vision for the national government from Jefferson's remained over their lifetimes and continue to this day. The ideas Hamilton suggested, still in place as our central government system, include a central bank as a sustainable means of wealth creation to fund appropriations without external debt, capitalism as the system that produces the adequate wealth and federal infrastructures that meet the needs of interstate trade and to fund military needs including a standing national military. Quite a legacy for Hamilton and Washington if you judge them on outcome!

The main method of resistance to the Hamilton system that has replaced the states' rights and nullification arguments in our current economic governance era is intentional debt budgeting used as a "starve the beast" level of taxation, even in a plus twenty trillion dollar economy. Deregulation and deconstruction of the administrative state are based on ideological arguments to intentionally undermine government and judicial review, to nullify individual citizen rights in favor of opportunism for the wealthy, in fact if not in law. The wealth gap is intentionally being allowed to widen, as property rights now seen as corporate rights dominate fading acceptance of individual citizen rights.

No policy ever seems to be politically settled based on policy outcomes; ideology is still the political norm in governance when all three branches in the political process are controlled by a single party.

We will see when we cover the Civil War at the end of this chapter that Jefferson Davis did fight a war with all of the limits from which Washington protected the federal government's future presidents, and never acknowledged the lesson.

The Confederate States of America (CSA) allowed states' rights to dominate the CSA Constitution which was adopted almost word for word otherwise. Davis was smart enough to comprehend how lack of funds and supplies, even authority over the state militias, led to loss of the war to the better funded and better supplied north; yet even this loss did not change his ideology. Davis died proud of his Southern Honor Code beyond all else, even in ideological defeat and poverty, as the face of an unsustainable system of independent governors.

Nullification was disallowed by the Supreme Court under John Marshall as noted. The last champion of nullification before the modern Tea Party wing of the GOP was John Calhoun in the run up to the Civil War; it is still a dream in the U.S. south to this day, especially to the evangelical wing of the modern GOP.

The concept of judicial review was not a Constitutional question; Hamilton and Jefferson both agreed with the concept of a judicial branch with the task of upholding the Constitution and the authority to adjudicate disputes, what Marshall called a remedy.

Hamilton backed the concept to ensure settled law in the United States. I have never found a written opinion of how Jefferson thought Constitutional debates were to be settled by the Court. Jefferson, who backed nullification, did not want state legislated law subject to federal judicial review anymore than Marshall wanted nullification.

The term judicial review did not make it into the Constitution; however the role assigned to the third branch of government was defined "to uphold the Constitution". Marshall defined that to mean judicial review disputes between parties with rights under Constitutional law in the United States were to have final settlement. That is still the settled law as to how the Constitution is to be upheld by the Court over two hundred years later. The dispute is, should the settlements be based on the reality of life in 1791, or the modern era's expanded knowledge and understanding of what is today's reality for most individual citizens.

Tension between states' rights advocates, and the Constitutional enumerated powers of the federal government are still argued in each session of the Supreme Court of the United States including the current term in 2020 convened at the new budget year for the government, October first 2019, as the start of the 2020 court's operational year ending June thirtieth 2020.

The party of Jefferson ruled for the next twenty-four years, through his two terms as well as Madison's, and then Monroe's ending in 1825 with the election of John Adams' son, John Quincy Adams, whose single term ended the federalist party at the presidential level. John Quincy Adam's one term was no more remarkable than his father's. John Quincy Adams returned to the U.S. House of Representatives after the White House.

In practice none of the Virginia presidents rolled back or replaced Hamilton's economic governance design of how the Executive Branch would conduct the nation's business. The next time the north won the presidency, the standard bearer of a northern party was Abraham Lincoln as a (newly formed political party) Republican in 1860. Andrew Jackson followed John Quincy Adams as a Democrat Republican, the party of every president thereafter until Lincoln.

Andrew Jackson is still well regarded by many in spite of his near tyrannical approach to the presidency. Jackson may have had the most domineering will of any U.S. president in history. As a man of the frontier he was personally rugged. If you visit his home in Tennessee it is a mansion for the time and place. Jackson as a general in the militia in the War of 1812 distinguished himself for life as a hero. As a president he was like Reagan in the twentieth century, a reaction to the headlong changes of his era.

Jackson played a holding place between the founding and the Civil War. In the south he began the wholesale clearing of southern land of native Americans. When the Supreme Court overruled him he still sent the army south, and told the Court to enforce their order if they could, the only time in U.S. history a president has ignored an order of the Supreme Court. Jackson allowed the charter of the Second National Bank to lapse, and twenty years of recession set in.

In the end Hamilton agreed to move the national capital from New York to a southern location as part of Madison getting the south to support Washington's choice of the Hamilton system in the first Congress. Washington DC was the compromise. Both Hamilton's system and Madison's capital survive.

Before, during, and after the Civil War until the 1930s when FDR regulated and insured federally chartered banks, state banks continued to flounder from time to time and to fail, triggering bank runs; they also provided less credit than the rapidly expanding industrial economy required.

Tennessee's Andrew Jackson was the first western president, meaning west of the Allegheny and Appalachian mountains. Jackson was a teenager during the Revolutionary War, but did participate as a messenger as I remember reading in his biography. He went on to be a city founder (Nashville), a plantation owner, an Indian fighter, a militiaman, an officer, then general in the War of 1812.

He also served in Congress before being elected president. Famous as a ferocious fighter, he defeated the British in the last battle of the War of 1812. Less known among his exploits were his efforts quelling the Indians in Florida, and then just ignoring orders and driving the Spanish out of Florida, taking it for the United States. America did eventually make a payment to Spain of five million dollars to settle the Florida dispute.

Elected twice as president, Jackson was none the less a divisive figure during his tenure; he was famous for the "trail of tears", a series of forced eastern Indian tribes' relocation, opening their lands for settlement of a new slave state producing cotton for the British. The Cherokees were marched over a thousand miles to the Oklahoma Territory. There were Cherokees in what today are western North Carolina, southeastern Tennessee, and northern Georgia. Over sixteen thousand Cherokees were uprooted; about a third of those forced to migrate perished that first year.

Jackson was the first president of the newly formed Democratic Party. This party was made up of former members of Jefferson's Democrat Republican Party, along with former Federalists who were sympathetic to the southern cause.

There was a short lived Whig party in the north for former Federalists, mostly individuals less sympathetic to the southern states. Within twenty years the Whigs were replaced by the Republican Party; their first president was Abraham Lincoln. Today's GOP now supported by the southern states is the modern version of the party of Lincoln.

Jackson is a true transition figure in the United States' first seventy-five years. Elected just past the halfway mark in 1829, he served until 1838. Jackson was the first true National Party candidate. He was the first Democrat; as such he needed votes from both southern and northern factions of the party. Thus began thirty years of compromise presidents, none of whom distinguished themselves as they tried to contain the growing demand in the south for a way to keep the balance between slave and free labor states, or to leave the Union. The possible exception is President Polk, who is worth a read of his own.

A process was set in motion in 1820 by the Missouri Compromise, which admitted Missouri as a slave state and set a northern limit for new slave states as they were carved out of Jefferson's old Louisiana Purchase just north of the thirtieth parallel.

In the 1830s Jackson held the Union together, but the die was cast for eventual secession across the southern states. By the 1830s abolitionists were gaining a louder voice in the north. The Missouri Compromise was becoming strained, and it was finally undone by the Kansas Nebraska act of 1854 which allowed residents of Kansas to decide for themselves if they wanted to be a free or slave state. Kansas became a battleground state with local uprisings as a result.

South Carolina was the chief agitating state reacting to the abolitionists with nullification votes and threats of secession. The south had not monitored what British policy would be if the south seceded, or went to war with the national government, in preparation for any interruption of supply. This was an oversight with consequences when South Carolina fired the first shots, and to the surprise of many in the south, Lincoln ordered the north to fire back. It was a great surprise and calamity for the south as the civil war it initiated would prove to be in the end.

Unbeknownst to the southern planters the British were already hedging their bets on how long they could depend on the slave based price of cotton they enjoyed; they encouraged cotton crops in Egypt and India, and other colonies where they maintained a relationship.

Between Jackson's and Buchanan's presidencies which ended with Lincoln's inauguration, senators became regional leaders and pushed regional agendas. During this period presidents often tried to be conciliators, and seemed weak when compared to the strong willed senators who made a name for themselves during the run up to the war, such as Henry Clay of Kentucky, Steven Douglas of Illinois, Daniel Webster (born in New Hampshire, but famous as a Senator from Massachusetts, a three time Whig candidate for president, and the most out-spoken of them all), and John C. Calhoun of South Carolina, known as the Great Nullifier.

The final year before the war, the last of the compromise presidents, James Buchanan of Pennsylvania, sat all but idly by as the first seven states voted to secede from the Union. Buchanan fancied himself a strict constructionist regarding the Constitution. He had made his fame in his home state as an effective attorney, and was even offered a seat on the U.S. Supreme Court which he declined.

The last fateful event that triggered the election of Lincoln, who was more of an absolutist about the Union than an abolitionist regarding slavery, was triggered by the Dred Scott decision, which was unpopular in the north. It is an interesting read on its own, but the crux of the matter was Dred Scott was a slave who lived many years with his owner, a military man in northern states. He sued for his right to be free based on his years in the north. The issue was the south's demand for enforcement of the Fugitive Slave Act.

The Chief Justice was Roger Taney of Maryland who wrote the majority opinion that Dred was still a slave, and went on to explain once a slave always a slave. He added injury to insult explaining in detail how low an opinion he had of the black race, adding in conclusion that black folks were not worthy of any rights. Not only were the abolitionists in the north livid, what would be called moderates today were also truly offended.

It was rumored that President Buchanan had let Taney know that a strong ruling might be helpful in keeping the south in the Union. It all backfired, and it riled the north, leading to the election of Abraham

Lincoln. Calhoun went home to push his secession agenda. The Civil War filled the final four years of the first seventy-five years of the American experiment in Federal Republican Democracy.

The Confederate States of America (CSA) was established in 1861. A Convention was held in Birmingham Alabama; a new government was made up of the eleven states that had voted to secede from the United States of America. They adopted a Constitution, and declared a state of war existing between the CSA states and the United States of America. Birmingham became the first capital of the CSA. The new Confederate States Constitution ensured states' rights senior to central government rights, with a slave based labor export crop agrarian mercantile economy much as Jefferson had advocated in Washington's first term for the nation.

They elected a U.S. Senator from Mississippi as the first and only president of the CSA, Jefferson Davis. Davis was a planter, a graduate of the United States Military Academy at West Point, a former general in the U.S. army, and a hero of the Mexican War, and a U.S senator from Mississippi. Jefferson Davis was not in attendance but anticipated he would be called to service. He sent a telegram to the convention saying "Judge what Mississippi requires of me, and place me accordingly".

It took weeks before he was notified of his election, and due to the state of the road system at that time in the CSA, it took him another seven weeks to arrive in Birmingham.

Davis was a true man of the Old South. He believed in states rights, believed "it was God's will that white men had a right to own members of the Negro race", a belief held until the end of his life, many years after the Civil War defeat. He had moved beyond worrying about a balance of representation in the national government that formed the arguments between the end of Jackson's presidency and the inauguration of Lincoln, and agreed with his friend Calhoun that secession was the only recourse left to the southern states.

He was outraged that the honor of the South had been insulted by the abolitionists as their numbers and influence grew in the north. The abolitionists' attacks were felt across the south, instilling Jefferson Davis's sense of duty; he was prout to accept the presidency of the Confederate States of America.

That sense of outrage and duty was common across the South. That his trip to Birmingham took seven weeks due to the inadequacy of roads and an inadequate rail system in the south was not a key concern for him; it seems shortsighted for a professional military man.

Like much of the south, Davis believed that Lincoln would not want or would be unable to field troops for a long war. Davis believed that Britain, the major customer of the south's cotton plantations, would recognize the new government within weeks. Davis also believed he would appoint a Secretary of War and that he would select the generals for the CSA's Army himself. He trusted southern men would fight and acquit themselves well. He was correct on only this last point - the rebels fought like hell.

Davis was able to move the national capital of the CSA from Birmingham to Richmond, Virginia. That would be about the only thing that worked out as his vision took shape that first year of his presidency.

He was correct about the willingness of southern young fellows to fight for their homeland. Southern Honor not only accrued to the slave owning planters in the old south, but it accrued also to the poorest of white men and women as well, the same sense of honor I suggested above that still prevails in much of the old confederate states.

Most folks have read or absorbed a sense if not biographical knowledge of President Abraham Lincoln. Not so much of Jeff Davis. If you read a good biography of Davis you will be amazed at the grind his presidency became, without any change in his views about Lincoln's willingness to quit, or his belief that England would enter the war on the side of the Confederacy. Davis never grasped nor acknowledged the problems of managing a war under the handicap of the CSA states' rights dominant ability to ignore the wishes of the president of a weak central government system for which the south has always expressed an ideological belief.

A small central government with a limited mandate is as a matter of course weak, and an inadequate government in time of war, just as Washington had explained his experience fighting for the confederated colonies which ruled with limited authority. Southern politicians are still intentionally blind to the downside of weak, now referred to as small, government, in spite of nuclear arms availability around the globe.

The governors had done little enough to prepare eleven strong states' governments as they headed into war without a strong central government, or a defined system of coordination between the individual states and the new nation. Their near sole focus had been on limited federal power, and the CSA became a failed experiment of what should have been recognized as an unworkable wish. The idea remains an idealized wish, sustained as I suggest only by intentional blindness. If not, why is misinformation and political spin its proponent's chief forms of advocacy?

If Lincoln had allowed dissolution of the Union before the war, I believe there would be less animosity today between the regions than the resentment that grew out of the reconstruction period (in our next chapter), but Lincoln, a lawyer, read the text of his oath to uphold the constitutional pledge to mean preserve the Union.

Reconstruction was a twelve year period after the war while the Union troops occupied the south, before white citizens totally recaptured the governments and economy of the south. A compromise settlement of the 1876 presidential race gave Rutherford B. Hayes the presidency in return for his removing the troops and allowing white leaders to fully implement Jim Crow across the south, ending any consideration of implementing the intent of Lincoln's three amendments regarding rights for black citizens of the United States.

South Carolina demanded the surrender of Fort Sumter; Lincoln rejected this demand, and the governor of South Carolina ordered the Charleston battery to open fire on the Fort. Lincoln declared it an act of war, and the American Civil War commenced.

Davis too slowly learned the meaning of limits on a small central government, including insufficient authority to tax or draft troops, appoint generals, borrow money, set up a bank and a mint to create money acceptable to creditors, contract legal debt with a means to ensure payment, or conduct foreign affairs, beyond the concessions he could coax out of the eleven independent governors. Unlike Washington, Davis had no commercial lawyer like New York's Hamilton, or international trader like Philadelphia's Morris to help fund the war such as Washington enjoyed in the Revolutionary War.

Davis had no means to compel any cooperation or support beyond personal skills; information traveled slowly, and face to face meetings were rare. The fact that the CSA carried on for four years is a testament of Jefferson's resolve, the CSA military men, southern pride, and the fact that Lincoln was a military novice. It took time for him to learn to judge military leaders for himself. Nothing surprised Davis more than the resolve of the American president. Abe Lincoln defended the unity of the nation he swore an oath to preserve all the way to victory.

Beyond reading a good biography of Jeff Davis, his White House is now a museum and is open to the public in Richmond, Virginia. It is a very worthwhile place to visit, with a book shop as a resource. I bought seven or eight books there and have returned to them often over the years, including while writing this book, not so much for ideas, but to ensure I had the sense of what he felt. You will have to search for the hopelessness I find in the nullification argument and in Jefferson's presidency; it has very little spelled out as such in the biographical material I have read.

In the CSA every governor was also a commander in chief, so to speak, as the head of a sovereign state government's militia. Having eleven separate governors' view points frustrated issues of funding, manning, and supplying the CSA, and created mindless issues regarding the appointment of generals to lead state militias and deciding where and when they would fight. Each governor retained the right to appoint his preferred general to lead his state's militias, as the CSA was not allowed a national standing funded and manned army. Virginia's Army of the Potomac under General Robert E. Lee late in the war was as close as Davis came to full authority as a

Commander in Chief; too little, too late.

The generals he did appoint were old cronies from West Point and the Mexican War, and they turned out to be more interested in saving their armies early in the war than going to war as fighting generals. When actual battles did ensue, the men of the south distinguished themselves with uncommon valor, and were usually victorious in the early years based on pure grit.

In this area Lincoln also had his own early problems with generals who were more politician than warrior, at least until he found General U.S. Grant. The south did have one real fighting, General Stonewall Jackson, no kin to the former president. Sadly for Davis, Jackson was killed before the war ended.

Over the next four years, Lincoln never backed down from insisting the CSA states had no constitutional right to secede. Lincoln simply explained his policy by saying I took an oath to preserve the Union, and I will. And he did, at a cost in loss of life of half a million men on each side of the divide in this early American test of endurance that was meant to settle the economic and governance divide between the two regions, including the contentious one of labor systems and the societal norms afforded free men in the north versus slaves in the south.

Britain had foreseen the possibility of an interruption in their supply of the south's cotton to feed their valuable cloth making industry, anticipating an abolitionist war, or a slave insurrection. The south's cotton was of excellent quantity, quality, (soil, rain, climate and seed type were all excellent in the U.S. south), along with the low cost of slave labor by the 1840s. But as noted before, unknown to Jefferson, England had enhanced the cotton growing capacity in their colonial lands in India and Egypt to develop an alternative source.

Neither Britain nor any other European country ever recognized the CSA as a sovereign nation. Jefferson never ceased assuring his Confederate citizens that Britain would soon recognize the CSA, and aid in the defeat of the north. Those supplies the CSA did obtain from Britain were from commercial sources.

England did not recognize the CSA; they also did not officially block military imports mostly to Wilmington, a port on the Cape Fear River in southern North Carolina. The entrance to the Cape Fear River was protected by Fort Fisher that overlooked the mouth of the river as it narrows with gun placements on both sides. Fort Fisher remained very effective until late in the last year of the war, keeping the Wilmington docks on the Cape Fear River open thirty miles upriver. The remnants of the fort are well preserved and a very interesting memorial to southern resolve and ability to stop hostile military travel up the river.

Too late in the war Robert E. Lee became in effect commander of the CSA Army, but by then the south was overwhelmed by the Union's many advantages. Lee however, was seen by most as the best general on either side during the entire four years. In the end he lost to Grant, but no one including Grant, who was more than anything a tough and competent warrior general, ever had a bad word to say about Lee. There are those who will argue that General Sherman was the best general in the Civil War, but for our story regarding Lee, I agree with the majority opinion. Like all of us he had his flaws; among them was how he treated his own slaves.

I will not go into the 2017-18 issue of the legacy of CSA monuments across cities and battlefields of the south, except to say that the partisan divide we are reviewing throughout this book disallows either side to be anything but an absolutist in gridlock on resolving how to honor the value of millions of American ancestors' valor, without enraging millions of our historically abused ancestors' families today.

In the end the south conceded as Grant's forces overran Richmond. Lincoln had already emancipated the slaves, and offered the men of the south a right to regain U.S. citizenship with a right to reclaim their homes and lands and the right to vote, if they would sign a pledge to accept and swear loyalty to the U.S. Constitution which included the newly minted Twelfth, Thirteenth and Fourteenth Amendments that dealt with the status of the freed slaves as citizens of our nation, founded as a self governed society of free men.

If you tour the homes now open as museums on the Charleston South

Carolina waterfront, one of the mansions has both an original copy of the owner's reinstatement of citizenship and another of his property, both signed by Andrew Johnson the new president, Lincoln's vice president at the end of the war. It gave me goose bumps when I read them.

President Lincoln was assassinated at the end of the Civil War, and Vice President Andrew Johnson became president. Johnson had been a compromise selection to run with Abraham Lincoln; he was a segregationist, and sympathetic to the south. He initiated policies in blow back to Lincoln's Civil War Constitutional amendments, and was impeached by the Republican Party, but not convicted.

Lincoln was a great transitional president who did not live to implement his policies; we will review similar blow back again against another transitional president FDR, who led America to military victory in WWII a hundred and eighty years after the Civil War. The Civil War amendments were greeted immediately by blow back in favor of the south and against ex-slaves. FDR's new deal transitions were in favor of working men and small town banks and families. It was not until thirty-five years later when the blow back against the new deal was birthed with the election of Ronald Reagan in 1980 and racism would again be a key factor of resentment that led to the blow back.

Most southerners did sign the pledge in the end. However, Davis himself never renounced the CSA nor accepted repatriation as a U.S. citizen, not even to escape jail time when he finally was captured a few years after the war.

I'm going to jump ahead three years here, to Reconstruction for a short insert.

At the end of the Civil War the south effectively remained occupied. For any state to rejoin the Union, or for any individual to be granted a return of his real estate and become an American citizen again and regain the right to vote, that citizen had to pledge an oath to the Constitution as noted above. Three amendments to the Constitution addressed freedom for the slaves who immediately became citizens, and in plain English defined the limits on any state that denied due process, or that denied equal protection of the law, and remedied any state's abuse of any Bill of Rights freedom enjoyed by all other U.S. citizens. Seems pretty clear, so how have these three protections for former slaves been used in practice over the past one hundred and fifty years?

Since the end of the Civil War these three amendments have been used to enforce the rights of corporations about four hundred times more often than blacks in the judicial branch of our federal government. Corporate rights are not mentioned in the Bill of Rights, nor in the Fourteenth Amendment.

Even in the north it took another fifty-five years for white women to gain the right to vote. It was exactly one hundred years before any blacks had the unfettered right to vote in the United States. Today states that lean toward states' rights still look to disenfranchise the black vote in their states; even in the north some states have joined in passing voter ID laws and gerrymandering congressional districts. The GOP has become much more skilled at these tactics but the Democratic Party has joined in the practice when they hold the state house, after every ten year census, when redistricting takes place.

The modern GOP majority Supreme Court ruled on the question of the constitutionality of this new means of controlling elections in their 2017-2018 terms as it affects the concept of one man, one vote, in our democracy. The 2018 decision was not definitive, and the issue was returned to the states with advice to do a better job. The GOP with a five to four majority seems to see gerrymandering as a states' rights issue; the Democrats see this as a national issue for U.S. House of Representative districts, accepting that representation in the Senate is a federalism compromise and therefore a states' right issue, as I understand the law. The U.S. House does not represent the states or the federal government; it represents the citizens. If you did not know this, it is not surprising; too many Congress persons seem not to realize it either. The Supreme Court outcomes in the twenty-first century usually have been pro states rights in support of corporations as Fourteenth Amendment persons, versus citizens' rights.

Note: I'm inserting a twenty-first century issue here to make the point that rights often conflict in our complex economy between citizens' rights and what were called property rights at the founding, a time before corporations and wage labor issues often affecting thousands or millions of employees in labor rights disputes ever reached the modern Supreme Court. The Lily Ledbetter case is one of two recent labor disputes based on U.S. Constitutional dissents, caused by conflicts in laws or regulations that pit an employer's rights as a person against an employee's rights as a citizen. The other is the Hobby Lobby case already mentioned.

The dissenters in these two cases each sued for justice: the employee who saw her equal pay labor rights abused, and the employer who saw his religious right to not support birth control he believed was a sin abused.

The Supreme Court saw two civil or regulatory law inspired Constitutional Bill of Rights dissents. Lily's corporate employer saw its privacy rights challenged as well as its statute of limitations on being sued abused. The second corporate employer was in fact abused; however, so were his employees who lost their tax exemption and group price of their birth control, which is another abuse going back to 1951 and the Jim Crow solution to Congress's racial rejection to universal healthcare. All of these abuses caused by conflicting rights that were ignored by the legislative and/or the executive branch were referred to the Supreme Court for settlement. The court that intended to be nonpartisan and independent has become partisan and thereby less than judicious. The justices have allowed themselves to become the evaluators of primacy between competing rights that should be addressed by the legislative branch in the first place when enacting a new law, or in the process of regulating how the law is to be implemented and/or funded.

If this is not trouble enough for the justices to cope with, we have another situation that is hard to fathom, known as the Chevron Deference Principle relating to administrative law cases that reach the Court. Not being a lawyer here's what I understand. Congress still creates federal law; however, those laws once enacted are managed by Executive Branch agencies, which in effect write the rules of the road for compliance and enforcement. The Court must rule on what is or is not unambiguous, or ambiguous about such writing when a dissent is heard by the court. I kid you not.

The Court is thereby losing its non political status, and its relevance which can only lead to greater gridlock. Either the legal profession must resolve this or the judiciary branch of government, or the Congress. If not, all such conflicts must be referred back to the legislature, or the executive if the cause of the dissent is a presidential order. In both cases noted here, the women were ruled against, and the majority vote was a partisan 5-4 decision. All four parties had Constitutional rights; corporate and religious rights were upheld, while the women who labored for wages were abused in fact and in law, in both cases without recourse.

I'm arguing the court is now politicized to the point of settling conflicted executive branch regulations, and cultural questions in the workplace that conflict with employees' healthcare, labor, and family planning rights by allowing a cultural and/or religious belief to deny women's constitutional and/or legislated rights; this seems to call for referral back to the legislature to fix. Surely the Supreme Court should not be defining corporations' and religious folks' right to deny women employees equal due process under the law. This issue is included in the sixteen suggestions I make at the end of the book.

Back to the 1860s. Almost immediately the south began to test due process and equal rights for newly freed citizens, eventually establishing segregated schools under a concept of "separate but equal", the Jim Crow laws that limited almost all social and civil activities of black citizens across the former slave states from the mid 1870s until 1964-65.

Within about ten years after a time referred to as reconstruction, the southern representatives in Congress (now all members of the Democratic political party, the opposite of Abraham Lincoln's) made their segregated and separate but equal forms of individual rights owed to black citizens felt in almost every department of the federal government, as well as their home states.

Most of these new issues understood to be racial were not addressed as issues needing reform for another eighty years. Harry Truman desegregated the U.S. military only in 1948 (WWII was fought including black troops, but they were not in the same outfits). From about 1880 after the Civil War until the end of WWII southern Boll Weevil Democrats maintained their states as bastions of segregation, within the Democratic Party by quiet agreement, based on a view in the Biblical Christian south that the black man was of an inferior race.

I worked in the south from mid 1966 until 1978, except for one year 1969 in Connecticut, a total of eleven years in Mississippi, Missouri, Louisiana and Texas. I worked in manufacturing, and as American manufacturing moved south, I was sent south to transplant factories in right-to-work states before manufacturing moved on to China and Mexico in the 1980s, by which time I was self employed in a job shop, now called supply chain manufacturing.

I worked in the metal working industry for thirty-eight years. There was little difference in the job north or south. There were meaningful societal differences between the two regions, very few of which I saw as superior for wage labor working families in the south.

Our next chapter will look at the second of three seventy-five year eras of American history following the end of the U.S. Civil War. The north and south differed in their understanding of the changes that ensued in American politics, economy, and government, as industrialization changed the understanding and expectations regarding wealth, property, and labor in a time of abundance. All norms were mired in pre-industrial productivity reality norms, and pre-revolutionary property right norms as well as the role of church and sin and individual citizen rights and cultural norms. All were impacted by displacement and opportunity as well as opportunism.

During reconstruction, then industrialization, productivity-based growth in income, wealth, government, wages, taxes, and its effect on the relationship of the citizen to his (and at a point in time her) government and employer, changed faster than cultural norms.

In the United States' second seventy-five years, the challenges of wealth growth, speculation, market crashes, regulations, and distribution of wealth to property owners beyond profits, all came to a head in 1933. It will be our third seventy-five years, affecting race, gender, sexual preference, medical, and marital norms that arose as political issues. It will not be until the third seventy-five years as

America changes many times faster than norms adjust, that culture becomes as disruptive as nullification was in the first seventy-five years or the economic disruptions we are about to review in the second seventy-five years, and becomes the focus of political disruption. It was not until after WWII that a new political and economic model emerged in the south. Rationales changed more than viewpoints or cultural beliefs.

As we move past the Civil War era, the concept of Honor in the South grew faster perhaps than an understanding of the evolving role of government. This will be the noted reality of the second seventy-five years of American history. It will be seen there was little reassessment of long held beliefs; instead, reconstruction in the first ten to twelve years after the war was a period of mixed resentment and opportunism for most folks on all sides of the questions at that time.

Perhaps if Lincoln had lived he might have brought some civility and gravitas to the process, but he was gone, and chaos ensued. Emotions will remain the driving force in the politics of the common citizen regardless of how much progress is made in education, productivity, science and wealth creation, even as New Deal and WWII spending in the south improved life for an ever larger percentage of society.

Let's move on as the war is over, and see how we governed ourselves through the recovery period after the war.

Chapter 7

End of Slavery, Jim Crow, Industrial Wealth, Subsistence Wages

The Civil War was over. In the south reconstruction, Jim Crow, and eventually the Supreme Court Plessy Decision (separate but equal) legalized segregation as the law of the land; a favor to the political will of the southern states.

In the north industrialization. Wall Street introduces an early form of holding company called trusts, and speculative capitalization based on debt which fuels so called "booms", and unheard of wealth accumulation.

In 1887 the Interstate Commerce Act consolidates, moves anti-trust activities from the individual states to the federal government. In 1890 the Sherman Act gives the executive branch the tools to deal with the worst outcomes of the Trusts, in 1914 the Federal Trade Commission gives rounds out the early efforts of the government to regulate commerce in the U.S.. Regulation of industry will be a key goal of FDR's reform efforts, stymied by the Supreme Court. Anti-trust is another area of abuse worthy of separate study.

The trust ideology of un-regulated consolidation of industry to insure monopoly pricing and profits leads to many boom and bust incidents with the first nationwide economic "bust" of the twentieth century in 1907. This speculation driven boom became nationwide devastation, and since has been know as boom and bust cycles in U.S. history, never driven by policies based on outcomes. Always based on a GOP ideology called speculative capitalism, which rejects any regulation of corporations, banks, the stock market, or credit, always in the name of so called free markets.

This chapter covers only the first forty-five years 1865-1910 of our second seventy-five years of the American Governing Bargain; the outcome of speculative wealth creation is covered in a short Chapter 8.

In this brief forty-five years the reality of life will change more than in the 1585 years from the founding of organized governance and religion by the Romans until the ending of the U.S. Civil War. From candles to electricity, from swords and arrows to machine guns, from wooden sailing ships to steel battleships, from hoes and scythes to tractors and reapers and so on.

This will be the beginning of modern politics between the two partisan political parties. The final thirty years of this second era after our founding will be covered in the next chapter; we will review the onset of the struggle between maintaining the old economic limits on labor cost without slavery, the introduction of segregated education, while religious values based on Nicene Christianity avoid coming to grips with new understandings about latent individual rights, and racial control norms in the culture of the south replace public whipping with fear of lynching in secret.

Meanwhile in the north, we will see the onset of industrialization, opportunism and productivity, increasing the need for both unskilled labor recruited from domestic farms, and via a new class of immigration the poor and uneducated from southern and eastern Europe, as well as development of skilled and college educated technical and scientific employees to design products, make tools and molds, man the machines, and handle the distribution jobs on the shop floor, on the docks, and at the wheel of trucks across the country.

So far our story of the United States has been a story of North and South, and the push from the Atlantic Coast to the Mississippi River. The West from the Mississippi River to the Pacific Ocean had been acquired; the Civil War years were also the years the North began building the Transcontinental Railroads. Beginning in 1862 the Union enacted three laws to accommodate the questions of right of ways, and funding to build the first of what became three Pacific Coast Railways, first the Central, then the Northern, and finally the Southern, all connecting with existing railroad lines from the east coast to the Missouri River, and later further south to the Mississippi.

Nothing demonstrates the difference in mindset concerning big government versus small government, than the reality of what the strong federal government accomplished building these railroads while defeating a collection of weak state governments in the south.

The south has not yet reconciled what the Union government accomplished with their defeat. The winning mindset, meaning continuing to open the west and developing industrial might to defeat the south, building a continental railroad by making and laying the track to open the west, while preserving the union, and enabling the nation's future destiny. This reality is huge. The Union made these investments not to enrich their region, but on behalf of the nation's future.

It's 1865 and the Civil War has ended. In the south anger, confusion, fear, and poverty for the former Confederate States of America (CSA) among white nationalists becomes the reality.

The feeling of resentment and loss remains, especially concerning the changed status of newly freed slaves. The changed status of the former slaves hardened the opinion that the black man was in fact inferior to the white man. This inferiority bias as a taught fact in the American south officially only began to end in 1948 as we will review in Chapter 9.

We will not review here in any depth the early years of the short lived period of blacks holding office. If Lincoln had lived and carried out his design for the returning states, the long nightmare of re-subjugating the free black man may have been different. As it was, within ten years a combination of practices emerged, de jure, meaning practices that are legally recognized (black codes) and de factor, meaning societal norms understood by all but not addressed in law.

Eventually these state codes, laws and norms became known as Jim Crow Laws, affecting every aspect of both black and white life in the southern states. They were as major as segregated schools, and as minor but demeaning as separate drinking fountains, or as riding only in the rear of city buses in southern cities. Jim Crow laws not only had major impacts on daily life in society, but personal living standards as well, such as city water and sewage, employment opportunity, housing, and medical treatment. In spite of the new Constitutional Amendments (Twelfth, Thirteenth and Fourteenth) defining the new citizens' new legal status, their rights in the states where they lived negated any new national rights they were entitled to until 1964. The southern states had never accepted the Bill of Rights for their white citizens let alone black less than citizens as they saw it before and after the war.

In fact the south was dirt poor for white folks as well as black. There was no "State Bank" money, and little in the way of U.S. currency or coinage. Most farm equipment was unusable; there were few farm animals, meaning every aspect of day-to-day life was a constant struggle, and opportunistic Yankees were arriving in droves. Some came as troops to keep order, some as "carpetbagger" opportunists who too often saw the need for "managing" reconstruction (dollars) as their meal ticket; some came as sharks looking to buy assets for pennies on the dollar. Almost none were welcome, or helpful.

Radicals and moderates in both political parties were involved in the many dissensions, which led first to an attempted presidential impeachment, then to the failure, by most measures of reconstruction itself. Within ten years dissent and loss of coherence led to a full economic depression affecting both the north and the south.

Lincoln's national bank had been allowed to lapse, with a return to unregulated boom and bust speculative economies rising and falling through the remainder of the first one hundred and forty-five years of American economic history into the early 1930s.

By the mid 1870s southern white politicians were back in control of the southern state houses, their senators and representatives were back in the U.S. Congress, and the southern state legislatures were passing the restrictive laws called "the black codes" noted above. The codes were enacted to again control and marginalize black labor, now legally wage based and free, but in fact still coerced and most often working under a debt based, prison or barter employment scheme.

The percentage of black folks working for cash wages grew slowly in the post war economy of the southern states. In 2018 a Starbucks manger created a stir when he called the police on two black men who were waiting there for a third friend to join them. The two black men were "loitering"; that was a black code violation in the 1870s in

U.S. southern states, punishable by a sentence of hard labor which was sold to local farms and plantations. It is a legacy that still continues to be over-policed.

Slowly black labor became a system of casual labor (day-to-day with no security which continues into the twenty-first century, often debt based in a mostly cashless economy). No one was expecting to re-institute slavery, but low cost labor was still the norm as a mindset across the southern economy and remains so. The overriding goal was to re-institute a place in the economy for freed blacks as low cost labor while maintaining segregation of the races.

The south tolerated civil neglect regarding employers who coerced their laborers; no longer could the young black girl be whipped in public. However, lynchings at night became a new terror for black men. A sense of fear among the black population was actually tolerated by the police as a helpful norm. This fear-based management system infected city government and county sheriff departments, as well as both commercial business owners and citizens' oversight groups that emerged as re-enforcing tiers of control.

Large farms and the county courthouses blended into another black male labor coercion system. Segregated black churches were encouraged; white church pastors and bishops re-enforced the total belief blacks were Biblically inferior to whites in God's eyes, and were created to be the servants of their betters.

The most pressing issue was to restart economic activity, but southern white folks had no money, and no means to re-capitalize state banks. There was no money for wages, and there were few who wanted to pay wages even if they had money. Blacks were now free but most could not afford to own land, equipment or farm animals, and subsistence was the extent of what was ever acknowledged as due black labor, however skilled or arduous the labor.

As noted the first employment schemes in the new south were based on debt; the most popular scheme in the agricultural south was called share cropping. It lasted for about ninety years with poor whites also becoming share croppers. Land, twenty to forty acres with a shack was rented for a share of the crop, and a shared rented mule helped till the soil; seed was advanced on credit and the barest subsistence diet and basest work clothes were also advanced.

At harvest time, first the debt was repaid and then the owner's share of the crop was collected. Finally, if there was any cash left over it was taken as a credit on next year's rents. Often there was still a debt at the end of the year, or at the end of the tenants life, insuring even hungry families were not free to exit the bargain. Thus a life based on working off a never–ending debt ensued for millions, much as the surfs in feudal Europe had lived, hungry, cold, and in the dark, in ignorance and fear, inter-generationally. Hope did not die among southern blacks, it never existed.

The south combined coercion, fear and debt to ensure continued control of subsistence labor costs as well as all other black activities. Shacks sprouted up in clusters, often in low areas subject to flooding where no one else wanted to live. Christianity was encouraged in the black churches, and began its long slow activity of providing what little hope folks could find in not in the U.S. south; at least it would be found in the next life, the same as the king's subjects. Many coalesced into communities on the edges of towns, with the women working as domestics, men as day laborers or any farm or town work that was available, usually the hardest, hottest, and dirtiest, and most dangerous.

In the north the idea of debt labor was also being adopted under a system of subsistence wage control referred to as "The Company Store". It worked much like colonial era mercantilism. The company (mining, factories and mills, and large scale farming) all followed a similar structure; it provided a small house, a "tab" or credit, or if wages were paid it was in "script" printed by the employer that could only be spent in the company town or at a company store. The employer not only set wages, but also rents and prices at the store to ensure the family remained in debt for generations, much the same as the share cropper system. This system was my family's first taste of American "freedom" away from the era of famine under the English colonial system at the time in Ireland.

The company, just as England did in colonial pre-revolutionary times, set the hours, work conditions, and pay. If done properly the free wage labor work force was now in debt to the company; folks could not quit until their debt was worked off. In the twenty-first century President Reagan reintroduced the anti consumer ideology of unfettered usury in the form of pay day lenders to again trap wage earners in perpetual debt schemes.

Millions of folks including my grandparents' families left rural poor and hungry landlessness in Europe for a ticket to America, and a work promise that became never-ending toil, exposure to hazardous conditions, living weary in worry and in debt, but for the most part no longer hungry.

In both cases the employee "borrowed" rent and food (seed also if a share cropper) in subsistence from the employer, and then worked off his debt, usually for life This was the level of greed that was a norm for much of late nineteenth and early twentieth century America. Political, religious, and employment leaders, not even jurists saw anything abusive about these debt schemes, and still do not.

The Constitutional promise to protect citizens from abuse applied only to government abuse, but practices that abused labor were never adjudicated as abusive no matter how abusive the practice, and failed to recognize that the entity abusing U.S. Citizens was sanctioned by a state.

This mindset still is reinforced to this day, memorialized in the ideology of politicians who advocate anti-labor and poverty legislation, and pastors who advocate pro-family anti-sin legislation but support anti-family living wage and healthcare legislation, in continuation of support of the Nicene Christian belief, which supported coercion of subsistence labor as granted to those entrusted with property rights as God's will. Reciting the Nicene Creed or continuing to support a Christian religion that supports it is what our founders' Declaration revolted against, not just taxation without representation.

Overcoming these mindsets was the task that faced folks born at the end of the era we are reading about here when these coercive practices were being established and enforced, even as wealth was finally being produced in millions and then billions, and today trillions of dollars for the property class.

Most major southern protestant religious denominations accepted the concept of Biblical sanction for the limited role allotted black citizens. Southern church leaders continued teaching that God's word, as handed down in the King James I Bible version of Nicene Christianity, held that one of Noah's sons named Ham was outcast to Africa. Thus the status of the black man as inferior in God's eyes remained a norm in the south until 1948, to be explained in Chapter 9.

Vigilantism posing as fraternal groups also emerged; the most famous of these was the Ku Klux Klan (KKK) which introduced unique forms of fear, the most effective being lynching, which continued for almost one hundred years. A warning sign was a burning cross in a black man's yard. Such fear based societal control patterns were tolerated by local mayors and police departments, as well as local voters, newspaper editors, and pastors across the south well into the late mid twentieth century, mostly without condemnation or interference.

Southern honor as a sustaining source of pride remained intact throughout reconstruction along with a return to local white rule after the Civil War and continued into the eras of the KKK, Jim Crow Laws, Separate but Equal, and White Citizens Councils, always with an intent to keep the races segregated as the key tenet of the whole post Civil War social, economic, religious, and political belief system. Segregation was in place de facto in the northern states as well, but not as open, therefore less well observed. The level of indifference to abuse of black citizens in the north did not really became knowable until the post Civil Rights era after the 1960s, and was laid bare for all to see in the 1970 with the school busing decision.

Mistrust of the north and the federal government was handed down father to son in the post Civil War southern states. This is a historical review, not an attack on southern folks. However, I want to recognize our history as well as the wonder of the system of government we established, and how that system allowed, for the first time in history, a nation to address long periods of injustice, if only in incremental steps.

Every system of government has been guilty of similar injustices throughout history, as those capable of acquiring and managing property became the idealized upper class and most worthy citizens in control of almost every society on earth. The United States to its credit was the first and perhaps still the only nation to agree to officially end its unjust former governing norms and laws, if not fully rectifying the impact on those abused, among a majority population who find it easier to excuse themselves as not being alive in those days, than to fully end the dysfunction that is still a curse on as much or more than half our black citizens. It is also a huge negative cost to maintain the economic and personal scourge of welfare for poor individuals, federalism for poor states, and the cost of policing and imprisoning our most dysfunctional young males.

I understand some military and some religious leaders have gained control of nations from time to time, and too often gain civil calm at the cost of loss of personal freedom for those they govern. In the end, it is always those who control the source of wealth and/or the wealth of a nation who control the government directly or control the political leadership, usually both.

A third non-cash economic employment issue was the traditional jobs that slaves had performed other than tending cotton and other warm weather crops; it dealt with former tradesmen on the plantations. A black carpenter or mason and so on, not only worked on his master's plantation, but was hired out for wages paid to the owner. These skills were needed for rebuilding; there was no cash available to pay wages to a laborer, but there were less meaningful or obvious ways to use debt for control of these useful discrete skills. Some skilled craftsmen were caught up in the prison work schemes, many others became the first blacks to combine bartered labor for land and eventually became wage earning freemen of property.

A number of other coercive non-slavery schemes were put in place in the south, much like the company store system in the north, only segregated and poorer. They included black apprentice programs. Men moved to a place of business, and then spent years as free labor, in debt to a company store and/or rental in company provided housing (shacks). Brick production, road building, mining, cabinet making, and forge shops are all examples.

Another labor coercing system was arrest and conviction for minor infractions under arbitrary civil laws; the sentence would be a long period of forced prison labor, hired out by the court to help support the legal jurisdiction, usually a town or county, as well as to rebuild the town, and/or to recapitalize a white owned enterprise. The prisoners were hired out for a low dollar payment that kept men working on a chain gang and/or overseen by a man on horseback with a shot gun and dogs. There were twelve hour work days in a form of enslavement by scheme rather than a free status, a scheme that might have allowed wages if there was cash available in the system. Stump removal, turpentine production, swamp drainage, and timber harvesting were all examples of this work.

Over many years of a combination of inducements based on fear, lynching, cross burning, whipping, and other humiliations, along with entrapment forms of labor contracting, a normalcy to southern workday life returned to pre Civil War norms.

Black women regained their positions as domestics in southern homes. Because black women were not as feared as black men, there was less severe management of black women's labor; coercion of black women was most often sexual instead of the whip or the rope, but whipping black women was not unknown even after the war.

Southern white folks hated the new Republican Party of Lincoln that included the abolitionists, and joined the Democrat party. As the parties grew over the rest of the century southern democrats had little in common with Democrats in the north especially after the Plessy separate but equal segregation decision thirty years after the Civil War. From Woodrow Wilson forward Democrats in the north were progressives; the south has never been progressive, but they were not going to vote for the party of Lincoln.

The south voted for the Democratic Party, and their electoral college votes ensured the north control of the presidency after the great depression and in Congress By shrewd use of the seniority system, the south increased their power as the selection of Committee Chairmanships gave them control of distribution of federal funds, and the money flowed like rivers, south.

Untold millions of dollars were redistributed to the southern states in return for votes. The south liked some of the issues in question, but would also agree to support policies that were not seen as harmful to the southern way of life. This ended in the 1970s as we will review in Chapter 9; it only took about ten years to replace the seniority system and the end of earmarks also known as pork barrel redistribution of federal tax receipts from large high wage northern states (now called blue states) to poorer states, now replaced with less obvious new block grant federalism which now transfers much more money than earmarks ever dreamed of transferring, a gift from Ronald Reagan for joining the GOP.

The south was not then, and is not now, particularly introspective regarding outcomes from policies in which they have invested honor and values as they spin it. From time to time you will hear me refer to this lack of introspection as "intentional blindness". We all do it to some extent, but in politics it can become an art form, and lead to self inflicted wounds, or as now in the early twenty-first century, to national gridlock.

The statement above is not history such as is relayed in a book about a Civil War battle; this is opinion but it is observable to the casual eye as well as students of sociology. Belief systems regarding governance, regional honor, and the wrath of God on our nation beyond individual salvation, remains more important than individual freedoms or economic policy outcomes to millions of voters in modern America in red states.

Jefferson had always believed in the common sense of hard working voters. Adams always believed emotions overcame common sense and led to rashness. As presidents they both governed based on their own reasoning and never trusted the fury of the mob, let alone incited it, as we are now seeing happen nightly on cable news in the twenty-first century.

I've read that at the end of the Civil War there were about four million "Negroes" as they were defined in the old south. As the country recovered from the post war depression and moved into the growing industrialization of the 1880s, the need for ever more black agricultural workers reversed and dropped quickly. Hunger was a common fact of life for millions of former black slaves, just as the folks put off the farms in England experienced as portrayed by Charles Dickens in his books about this transitional period across all the western nations after the 1860s.

As the north industrialized in this first wave of mechanization, industrial growth and new wealth creation, blacks began moving north for work, and west for freedom. It was not until after the great depression that black migration north became a serious resettlement of blacks from the third or fourth generation born in freedom and poverty in the south.

When one of my grandchildren once asked why so many blacks moved north from the south, I told her tractors and other mechanized farm equipment; men without work always migrate if they can. My Irish grandparents migrated in the nineteenth century. Hispanics have migrated from the still dirt poor regions of Mexico and Central America since before WWII, encouraged by the needs of American industry both agricultural, construction, and manufacturing.

That such migration creates cultural conflicts is also a common norm. Reacting to such issues emotionally is just as common. Personally I think a guest worker program for some job descriptions such as agricultural labor and seasonal resort work makes sense as a rational compromise, i.e., an annual guest worker program for seasonal work, and a lifetime guest worker program for DACA unregistered young taxpayers in any job they can qualify for. We taxpayers have paid to educate them, while their parents provided cheap labor for U.S. employers.

The phenomenon of productivity is a simple concept; fewer folks needed on the farm, whites in the north, and blacks in the south. American labor changed from the nineteenth to the twentieth centuries from almost ninety percent farm labor, to over ninety percent non-farm labor, while food production increased by several hundred percent as did the growth in production of goods first, and eventually services as well; the tractor I mentioned above is a simple example.

This happened once folks were earning money working long hours and needing services performed for them, all in less than one hundred years. The pace of productivity and therefore output and wealth have only increased since, almost exclusively for the owner class, at a far greater share than for labor or government.

Factories sprang up to produce each new mechanical aid that provided more wealth, absorbing millions of immigrants as well as poor white men from the border states, and northern states' farmers into the factories and mills, while black men from the deep south mostly found day labor jobs, often called casual labor without assured work. White men generally held wage jobs referred to as permanent employment, earning a low daily wage in the growing and prospering north.

Casual laborers then and now usually suffer from irregular hours, sporadic work, no benefits, and no ability to develop credit, preventing any thought of home ownership let alone private transportation, assured retirement, or access to healthcare beyond what eventually became the free care pool, requiring hospitals to stabilize sick and injured poor folks before release.

As an example of productivity's impact on southern farms, if one man with only a hoe can farm a few acres, and one man with a mule and a steel plow can farm forty acres, one man with a John Deere Tractor and a gang of steel plows can farm hundreds of acres. Each incremental improvement is increased productivity. The operative belief in the Libertarian wing of the modern GOP in Congress and in the federal courts is the value of the increased output belongs only to the owner. No longer was there a need for large families of slaves; with just a handful of part-time (planting and harvesting seasons) field hands, using mechanized equipment the job was done. The belief in the south was they will stay if they are hungry and only basic subsistence nutrition is provided. It took little or no education for this level of lifetime employment expectation.

Those who remained in the south were for the most part the most skilled and ambitious, living most often as working poor folks but assured of food for work as needed employment. Less skilled and/or least ambitious folks remained casually employed, living in hunger year around. Later they often accepted free one way bus tickets with a sandwich and twenty dollars and a bus ticket to a northern city.

Two excellent books regarding this hunger level of family poverty in the south are Pat Conroy's first novel about teaching in a poor rural black school, and Lyndon Johnson's authorized biography, each telling of a first teaching job, Conroy teaching kids in South Carolina on a so called Gullah people's island, and the future president in Texas teaching Hispanic kids in a rural farm district in the hill country where he grew up. In both southern states the kids came to school hungry each morning. It made a lifelong impression on both men; their stories made an impression on me.

For President Johnson forty years later it led to his War on Poverty, out of which grew the modern food stamp program that LBJ introduced in 1964. It provides nearly fifteen percent of all Americans on average about four dollars a day per household member. This program has been an economic aid to farmers and the grocery industry in America, as well as a sad testimony to the wages allowed to be paid to poor folks in America, below the poverty line in millions of jobs in low wage industries.

The question for LBJ when he announced his Great Society legislation that was intended to end hunger for these poor mostly rural or inner city kids in America, was how to overcome Americans' aversion to social solutions to human dilemmas. Those who opposed welfare then and now espoused market solutions, meaning jobs for the so-called lazy.

The south never had a natural economic advantage in natural resources, so its economic advantage became cheap labor, an abundance of arable warm weather crop land once cleared of forest and the native population, and an accommodating if opportunistic customer. Even that market was reduced after the Civil War, at least until New England built dams and mill buildings and America began its own cotton cloth production.

The south remained an economic backwater from about 1865 until after WWII and really into the 1960s. Electrification, modern highways, and adequate school funding to prepare and train young adults for factory and military labor needs, all required funding from the federal government from the 1930s on. Finally, once there was electrification and the beginning of a true wage economy, air conditioning made southern factories, warehouses, and offices comfortable work sites. Interstate highways made them accessible.

By comparison after the Civil War the north had a national bank, had enacted an adequate war tax system, was in a good transportation situation with adequate ports, canals, railways and roads. They had created standing navy and marine corps, and had established manufacturing including arms and munitions at the outbreak of the Revolutionary War that were mostly still in place. No Civil War battles interrupted farming north of Pennsylvania. War profits had even left many northern areas prosperous.

The north had avoided foreign entanglements other than mutually agreed commerce, while maintaining diplomatic relations with most of the European courts, including the south's old customer England.

In the north an ever expanding need for mines, factories, and mills required millions of workers. As we have noted American farms became mechanized allowing young men to leave the farms migrating into the cities seeking factory work. Across Europe the strongest of the landless poor immigrated, leaving home to settle in American cities, producing cloth in Boston, steel in Pittsburgh, soon autos in Detroit, manning slaughter houses in Chicago and so on, while others mined coal in the eastern mountains, and copper and iron ore in the upper mid-west and western mountain regions.

The last key factor of subjugation of freed slaves to a regimen of separation from participation in the social, economic, and governance of freedoms and justice of American life after the end of the Civil War, took place in the Supreme Court in 1896. This was the separate but equal Plessy decision noted in our introduction to this chapter.

In 1896 the U.S. Supreme Court stepped into the middle of the subjugation of former slaves, agreeing to hear a dissent to a transportation law in the south. A gentleman named Plessy believed he was denied his equal individual rights regarding separation of seats on interstate railroads based on separate cars for white and black passengers in Louisiana.

Many readers will remember Rosa Parks nearly sixty years later refusing to give up her seat in the front portion of a bus in Selma Alabama as an early act that led to the U.S. Legislature finally ending legal segregation in America.

Few Americans have ever read about the first state legislature that faced the question of a railroad selling separate tickets to ride on its trains in cars that were designated either white or colored. You might be surprised to learn it was in 1838, in Salem Massachusetts. That case went to the state legislature, where Charles Adams, the son of John Quincy Adams, and grandson of John Adams the second and sixth presidents of the United States, was a leading voice in the assembly. Adams was more concerned about two other issues than the fact of separation of the races or the rights of colored folks.

Adams was reluctant to interfere with the property rights of the investors in the railroad; he was concerned about a backlash among white male voters who were against politicians who put the rights of black citizens ahead of the preferences of white folks who preferred separate cars. In time the practice was ended by the railway itself in Salem and eventually across the northern states.

However, segregation was a cultural mandate affecting blacks in the south. In Louisiana on an interstate train a light skinned black man bought a ticket for a whites only car, took his seat, and refused to leave.

In 1896 this case was heard by the U.S. Supreme Court in a famous foundation case known as Plessy v. Ferguson, introduced above. The question was, were state segregation laws constitutional. The Supreme Court at the time was made up of mostly judges from the north. The decision was eight to one against Plessy; the rationale was, it was legal as long as the service provided was separate but equal.

This decision was one of the most anti-individual rights decisions in American history. It was not overturned until 1954 by the Supreme Court in the Brown v. Board of Education decision that ended legal segregation of schools in America. No decision in American history has had more political, legal, and illegal blow back, or for a longer period in history than the ending of separate but equal. Plessy was a nineteenth century segregationist solution to force a separation policy on the nation that some folks would now see as abuse in the twenty-first century. Now that gay marriage is legal, the old southern idea of separate but equal is once again the fallback. Southern pastors have been selling to politicians and parents support for the sacred rights of marriage, but are promoting a separate (and again not equal) solution they call Civil Unions. Gays and honest judges are having none of it, but the evangelical minority are once again demanding they are entitled to make the majority accommodate their brand of abuse. When it is mixed with religious intolerance it seems a sacred duty to the absolutists among us.

After twenty years the courts stepped in again as the pace of compliance was less than snail paced. The new court order became the school busing issue of late twentieth century turmoil in America that came to a head in the 1970s, and again put on display the level of racial resentment in the north as well as the south.

As the twentieth century began, in many ways Teddy Roosevelt was an odd reformer. Perhaps the most imperialist president in American history, Roosevelt did in fact break up the trusts. In the process he created what became Wall Street and the Stock Market as the first, then later regulated markets in America, with government oversight added by FDR in the 1930s in reaction to speculation that had never been brought under control in America until then, and then only for fifty years of safe mortgage banking.

Roosevelt also engineered the severing of Panama from Colombia, and the building of the Panama Canal. Before becoming president, Roosevelt led the fight in Congress to go to war with Spain. In the process he became famous fighting in Cuba, and backed the United States' acquisition of Puerto Rico and the Philippines, which the U.S. then subdued.

Cuba first became a U.S. protectorate and then independent in 1902, with U.S. rights to intervene if the U.S. Congress opposed Cuban governance. The U.S. supported Boston's United Fruit Company's takeover of the sugar industry in Cuba which they ran as a fiefdom for over thirty years.

The U.S. Marines invaded Cuba to protect the assets of United Fruit Company which owned the Cuban sugar industry until 1934, when the Cuban military revolted and reclaimed Cuba. This was during the depression when America was in the middle of prohibition. The U.S. Mafia (with a blind eye from Congress) corrupted the Cuban Army and its leaders, and built hotels and casinos on the beaches. During the time alcohol was not legal in the U.S., the mafia also smuggled millions of dollars worth of alcohol into Miami. In 1959 a communist supported dictator overthrew the Cuban Army and the rest is history.

While Teddy Roosevelt oversaw the sending of a great fleet of America's great coal burning battleships around the world as a show of force, the world was leading up to WWI; the American Congress remained politically isolationist in outlook and would continue until well into WWII.

Europe had continued to fight internal wars particularly between Germany and France over steel and coal regions they both bordered, as well as over colonial dominance, into the twentieth century. The Ottomans still controlled the Middle East and its Suez Canal, as well as the world's largest emerging oil field(s) in the Middle East. The Hapsburgs still controlled much of Eastern Europe, especially the Roman Catholic areas from their strongholds in Austria and Hungary.

The czar still controlled Russia, and lusted for a warm water port on the Mediterranean Sea as well as domination of Poland as the Romanov's tried to hang on to autocracy (nobles ruling by God's will; this was true of Orthodox Catholic governments in the east including Russia, as in the Roman Catholic west including our mother nation England) in an emerging world of industrialization, and representative government.

Serfdom had only just come to an end creating surplus farm labor as even Russia industrialized and in the late nineteenth century, serfs who were no longer needed on the farms headed to the cities, much as in Europe and America.

The German states were being formed into a nation, with tension between protestants and Catholics. Just when things were going well for Teddy Roosevelt, America suffered the third largest crash of the twentieth century in 1907, just another twenty year speculative boom and bust cycle without a national bank it seemed at first. This bust was so severe it became the trigger for America to develop a twentieth century central bank, soon followed by a tax system equal to the cost of mechanized war, which had already been introduced across Europe due to industrialization creating mechanized war (tanks, ships, machine guns, and so on, all more costly than the already expensive infantrymen and cavalry brigades).

When President Lincoln's wartime National Bank was allowed to end, America did not re-regulate banking over the following forty-two years, nor the stock market, nor create a national central provider of liquidity. From the end of the Civil War until the 1907 crash America had suffered through at least four major national boom and bust periods of debt speculation and overreach without meaningful reform.

Concerning the crash mentioned above, the billionaire (in today's dollars) Augustus Heinze who controlled some Butte Montana copper mines as well as the Knickerbocker Bank in NYC, tried to corner the market for the stock in his Anaconda mining company. As so often repeated in the history of unfettered (meaning unregulated) capitalism, Heinze and friends were not satisfied with just great wealth, so along with their New York banks they created a copper bubble using debt to drive up the value of his holdings, which then burst, tossing America in 1907 into the worst depression so far in U.S. history. This is the same Anaconda company I noted earlier, in Montana where my father was born, and where all of the profits eventually ended up going to a one hundred year old single daughter, while Montana and its miners remained poor.

History repeatedly teaches that unregulated greed drives gorging to the detriment not only of an industry and its stockholders, but also crushes their customers and their employees, which leads to ordinary people and their local banks becoming insolvent or busted from a deposit withdrawal run on the bank until cash liquidity runs out and the banks close. Without banking the local businesses also close and small town America, where as much as half of all American jobs are located, dries up as these small businesses close their doors.

Acknowledged by many as a great man of finance and a key , thought to be the richest man in America, J.P. Morgan personally re-liquefied the New York banks and ended the panic at great profit to himself, and great cost to the nation and its people. This led Congress, under the leadership of Senator Nelson Aldrich, to form a congressional commission that led to the creation of the Federal Reserve System in 1913, signed into law by Democrat President Woodrow Wilson. It worked well enough in spite of Congress not adopting a form of depositor insurance until after the still unregulated stock market again crashed in 1929.

Back to the onset of the twentieth century. There remained a never-ending ideology that title to land confers all of the profits made on that land ever after to the title holder as long as it is owned, with no consideration however great the profits, or the increased cost to labor or government to secure those profits. The Bible supported this belief as revealed by what the king and his bishop believed was inerrant knowledge in our mother country before and after the English civil war; remember the parable of the just vineyard owner, all labor decisions accrued to the property owner. Even the title of this parable displays the bias of church support of property rights. All of Europe sold a subjugating labor system from the pulpit based on a so called "just" owner, as if that was a norm.

This became a carryover from English common law into U.S. state courts, as the founders of our national government separated the absolutist systems of kings yet retained much of English common law as the basis for law in our new states, including registration of deeds and incorporation of commercial organizations, called corporations.

Moving on in our timeline we will next review the epic changes of economic and governance norms in the time between the two Roosevelts, which could also be titled the time between the first two great speculative debt fueled financial collapses of the three twentieth century collapses. The first occurred from 1907-14, the second from 1929-40. America ended speculative debt capitalism in 1933 under President FDR. The third collapse occurred fifty years later from 1987-1993 when President Reagan deregulated President FDR's banking and capital systems after the great depression, each to be discussed in the appropriate timeline ahead.

So let's take a look at this major change in America as President Teddy Roosevelt and Woodrow Wilson, the early progressives looked for solutions to the issues behind the colossal 1907 collapse that ruined almost every family, town, and bank in the nation. In modern twenty-first century, America Progressive is a derogatory name the GOP calls Democrats who advocate a government role in regulating the economy for the common good or to establish justice. In the early years of the twentieth century it was first a Republican and then a Democrat who were each looking for a solution to the devastation of boom and bust capitalism that in spite of producing great wealth, was not only not sharing the fruit of the good times with employees or the nation, they were actually causing the collapse of the nation and its working families every twenty years or so.

Chapter 8

Theodore Roosevelt to FDR

The Federal Government adds an income tax to supercharge and stabilize America's economic outcomes for all Americans.

Income taxes, the Federal Reserve, WWI, an end of three massive empires, the czars in Russia, the Ottomans in the Middle East, and the Hapsburgs in Eastern Europe, followed by reparations imposed on Germany, partition of the Middle East, and a postwar boom that led to a postwar crash and the Great Depression, all between 1913 and 1929.

Chapter 8 will be the chapter covering the fewest years of American history, yet one of the most momentous sixteen years in world history.

A last hurrah for imperial empires and gold as the settlement exchange of world trade, clashes among the reordered empires, and early growing pains in the democracies, the rise of corporate empires clashing with the growing demands of organized labor to be recognized.

In America progressive political policies lead to reactive GOP resurrection of speculative banking, and capitalism, and a return to boom and bust outcomes, this time the largest in history. The collapse of the nation's economy in the Great Depression will lead to the New Deal, followed by the rise of Hitler and WWII, then in the return of the victorious veterans the rise of the first living wage middle class in world history.

As usual the GOP will plan its return to limited government, speculative banking, crushing labor gains, and this time adding a war on the income tax system as a war on "big government".

The transition from the nineteenth century to the twentieth century really marked the beginning of America as a global power and a maturing nation at home. Teddy Roosevelt was born just prior to the

Civil War into an old wealthy New York family and died just after the end of WWI. The Civil War was fought on foot and horseback, and even with the millions of men who served in the trenches, WWI was fought with tanks, battleships, and airplanes, and most devastating of all for the foot soldiers, machine guns and mustard gas.

No man could have been a more appropriate leader for the era than Teddy. He was America's first progressive, he was a reformer, and the first to introduce regulation of commerce, railroads, and food inspections. Teddy was also the first to address the concerns of average American born eligible voters who by the time Teddy became president, in most parts of the country, had at least an eighth grade education. Teddy offered American voters a square deal, meaning a guarantee of fairness, not well defined but he was the first to even consider the concept.

Really he was the first president to even give lip service to the stated intent of our founding documents including the common good, and to establish justice, equality of opportunity as the meaning of assured federal civil justice, and the need for reliable fiscal and monetary policies for a stable economy. He was also the first president to seriously value America's public land as a national trust for the good of the nation and its people, beyond exploiting America's natural assets for profit alone, accruing only to the investors in the exploitation scheme.

Many of Teddy's policies were popular, including ending the trust arrangement of interlaced stock manipulation that created huge monopolies in oil, coal, steel, railroads and other industries including copper, that in the unregulated era in the early decades of the new century were open to unregulated speculative capitalism.

The authorization for the executive branch of government to regulate industry and markets was the Hepburn Act of 1906. Teddy had asked for regulation of railroad rates, and the Congress complied with this new bipartisan Act. This Act gave authority to the ICC (Interstate Commerce Commission) to regulate railroads and other factors of transportation such as bridges. Remember during the Civil War the federal government funded three railroads across the west to the Pacific.

Forty years later, folks were moving west and building towns, the railroads had a monopoly on transportation and true to form, the investors who captured the new railroads gouged every user as if they had owned the land, and funded the whole enterprise from the beginning, ignoring the treasure and blood shed of the generations of Americans who had made it possible, while considering any taxation to be confiscation.

Under FDR executive departments became regulators, and each agency added thousands of regulators, becoming the mechanism of governance to regulate commerce across all commercial and industrial activities. To a large extent this is what the modern GOP rails against in the twenty-first century, calling regulators the "deep state".

In Chapter 9 a little over fifty years later we will read of Barry Goldwater as a member of the John Birch Society making the same argument over again against government regulation, defending his Arizona where he and his wife inherited almost three hundred million copper mine dollars. He railed against confiscatory taxes, demanding we all see how their grandparents had done it all themselves. Forgetting the war with Mexico, the railroads, highways, and Hoover Dam that actually made it all possible using east coast states taxes at the time.

The crash of 1907 that set so much of the progressive ideas of the early twentieth century in motion was caused by the bust when the boom of speculation based on debt crashed. What was so bad or unique about the crash of 1907 is that it wasn't just another cyclical boom and bust. Over the hyper growth at the end of the nineteenth century and into the onset of the twentieth century, with the lack of stock market and banking regulation, without a central banking system, only the industrialists themselves controlled all the wealth of the nation, the states, and the national government. The mass of the people limped along on subsistence in good times, and in hunger and debt in the aftermath of each bust.

In Europe the central bankers who controlled each nation's gold supply controlled the economies. In America our currency was based on gold, but only our treasury played a role in managing our gold; the treasury played no role in providing liquidity to our capital markets. Among our industrialists, some like Ford, Rockefeller, Edison, Carnegie, and Vanderbilt were concerned with building huge profitable monopolies designed to control markets, industries, and generate profits. Others such as J.P. Morgan were bankers dedicated to profiting off of the sale of stocks, bonds, and manipulating mergers and acquisitions, much as Wall Street does today. However, unlike today there were few rules or regulations and no or little oversight or enforcement of the few rules of the time.

In 1907 the trusts were besieged for cash as an attempt to corner the copper industry in America was crashing as noted above. Industry had grown so fast new capital was a constant need. Without regulation, stocks (purchased equity capital as opposed to loaned debt capital) were being sold with only ten percent down on margin, a form of debt sale.

Any bad news about a stock drove down confidence and therefore the price, and the margin (portion of a stock) purchase bought on credit came due; a fire sale in a downturn became a disaster.

New York banks loaned funds to smaller city banks across the nation and acted as a depository at harvest time, a function now performed by the Federal Reserve. There was no Federal Reserve in 1907. In fact the crash of 1907 caused Teddy Roosevelt to have Congress establish a special committee to study how to end this threat to the American economy. When a failing stock market would cause Wall Street to make cash calls on margin buyers, the demand for cash would escalate quickly, causing the NY banks to make calls on their deposit loans to smaller banks, and the cycle would escalate into a nationwide bank run. Savers withdrew funds from their banks, which meant small banks withdrew their funds from the bigger banks that funded Wall Street to return savings to towns folks, and the whole house of cards came tumbling down with no way to refresh the banks until confidence was regained, which could and did take years.

Teddy Roosevelt was hunting in Africa when the first of the Trust Banks failed; confidence dropped and the money market center of New York became insolvent within days. There was no central bank;

industry had grown larger than the amount of gold in the world could fund based on agreed valuations. Much of this new wealth was held not in gold, but in debt based speculative bond investments.

As the richest and most trusted man in America, J. P. Morgan saved the Trust Banks, bailed out the Wall Street banks and then the city of New York, but the stock market was set to collapse when Tennessee Coal, a key stock at the time, started to fail.

J.P. Morgan saved that stock in a deal he set up with U.S. Steel, but he needed Teddy Roosevelt's assurance that there would be no anti-trust complications, and he got it, to Teddy's credit. There was one more GOP president after Teddy, President Howard Taft, who later repealed Teddy's approval, but by then the stock market was saved and the economy had rebounded.

There were no consumer banks, few personal loans, or mortgages for homes or farms in 1907. They were all unregulated and had to be held by the local bank with very large equity invested up front, making home ownership very difficult for working families, almost impossible.

From 1907 to 1912 Congress studied the dilemma in both the House and the Senate Banking Committees, and drafted bills to create a new Central Bank, making money more elastic, which means liquid; velocity of money means the number of times a dollar turns per year in a given economy. These are factors of transactions requiring money in the economy, as opposed to wealth held in non-liquid assets such as land.

At the end of Teddy Roosevelt's two terms the GOP was still popular; the two term limit was not yet in place that followed the four elections of FDR. William Howard Taft was a jurist on the Federal Appeals Court; Teddy had appointed Taft to his cabinet, and successfully supported Taft to run in 1908. President Taft was more an administrator than leader. In 1912 Roosevelt ran against Taft as a Progressive in what was called the Bull Moose Party. With the GOP vote split, the Democratic Party candidate Woodrow Wilson won.

Woodrow Wilson was president of Princeton University before he became the second Progressive president, this time as a Democrat. Wilson would finish the job Teddy had started to remake the fiscal and monetary needs of the U.S. economy adequate to our new industrial might. As we shall see, the needs of wage earners, small towns, and home town banks adequate to the needs of farmers and home owners were not addressed by either. That didn't happen until the 1930s with the election of FDR.

In 1913 the income tax was established and the size and interest of government expanded as fast as industrial wealth was created. The lowest tax rate was one percent on incomes over four thousand dollars which left almost all hourly wages earners off the tax roles.

This change was signed into law by the second Progressive Reform president, Woodrow Wilson, just as the Federal Reserve was in the same year. Of as much importance to the industrialists as the government, and today for all of us, the Teddy Roosevelt study regarding the effects and reforms needed from the 1907 crash led to the founding of the Federal Reserve, and modern levels of liquidity in America separate from the value of, or the size of, the national stockpile of gold.

Until the twentieth century no nation taxed incomes, as there was so little in the way of cash income. Tariffs, duties, and taxes on crops were the primary income of most governments. It was the mechanization of war starting in 1914 early in the twentieth century that caused the cost of national defense to escalate as fast as the wealth being produced by the same new realities.

Tanks cost more than horses, and machine guns cost more than rifles. Steel ships cost more than wood ships. The need for increased government income was acutely felt in America in waging WWI across Europe. Fuel costs became a factor of magnitude as naval power expanded beyond the limits of sailing ships, while the cost of naval armament and electrification also exploded.

From our founding the federal government was funded via tariffs, taxes on imports that were often set high to protect native industry. This assured even larger profits for the industrialists and the bankers who funded them, who also came to own the ensuing interest as additional accumulated profits (a process known as compounding), allowing vast dynastic family asset based fortunes to accrue.

Tariffs created higher prices for consumers, while those who set wages could continue to keep wages low. No wonder early progressives who first raised the living wage issue as a labor right were resisted by business folks in the north, and by growers in the southern and plains states.

The internal combustion engine, the steel industry, oil industry, auto industry, electrical energy industries, ocean going steam ships, aerospace industries, and machine-produced cloth all became major wealth producing industries while wages and government taxes barely advanced.

Taft, as the last of the GOP presidents before the first Progressive Democrats, did not take an active role in getting a central bank crafted for the new economy. Teddy turned out to be the only Progressive Republican president in U.S. history. Some give Nixon credit for some progressive measures in the early 1970s but he was basically a conservative Main Street Republican by nature.

Arguably the two smartest men to hold the American presidency were Virginians: Thomas Jefferson the third president early in the nineteenth century and Woodrow Wilson early in the twentieth century, who more than most American presidents straddled the nation's two cultural norms, the growth tendencies if not the politics of the north, while being men of the south. Jefferson founded a great university, the University of Virginia, and Wilson was president of the elite Princeton University in New Jersey.

Wilson became president in 1913 and asked his Treasury Secretary and the chairman of the Banking Committee in the Senate, a fellow named Owens, and in the House a fellow named Glass, to work out what became the Federal Reserve as his first act of government. He called Congress back into session and kept them there until December when he got the bill he wanted, all but pulling teeth to keep them at their task. The Federal Reserve was established.

About the only thing the Democrats wanted that they did not get was deposit insurance. The second Progressive Democrat FDR signed that into law in 1935 after folks saw another run on the banks following the crash of 1929, more than twenty years after Wilson signed the Federal Reserve Bill into law.

The combination of bank risk regulation, the ability to create liquidity, set interest rates as a mechanism to control inflation, and ensure full employment, all these tasks set for the Federal Reserve were met, and served the nation well without a bust until the 1980s GOP relapse.

I will not go into it in this book, but for over a hundred years there has been a constant right wing conspiracy theory in America that European Jews own or control the Federal Reserve. This is not a key factor in U.S. gridlock, but it certainly contributes to modern right wing Nationalism, to be more fully discussed in Chapter 10.

The detail of the 1907 banking crash and the creation of the Federal Reserve is worthy of a more in-depth study, and well worth finding a good history book that explains the tale of how J.P. Morgan cleaned up a speculative mess that led to a loss of depositor confidence, before we had a central bank in modern industrial America. For every historical factor I introduce, I recommend a deeper look; if you are interested there are several excellent books on each subject available from the regulators to the bankers, and how the system works. There have always been conspiracy theories concerning the Federal Reserve's founding; a good read should clear up those wild conspiracy theories as well.

A few years later after WWI and the crash of 1929, the Feds' role was expanded, which enabled it to support FDR's reopening the banks in 1933. This is a historical event we will review in more detail in Chapter 9.

As noted earlier, the old subsistence labor systems produced so little wealth that no concept of sharing wealth or distributing a portion of it to laborers had ever been envisioned, not in the Bible, not in English Common Law, not in the U.S. Constitution. We are summarizing a constant theme, but it becomes so much more meaningful in the last two chapters, as a factor of family income, gridlock, and voters hearing spin and too often not knowing who to blame for the mess or the gridlock. Koch educated modern GOP jurists have made so called dark money from mostly the rich as a means of spreading distorted interpretations of both policies and outcomes, and the gridlock noose around the neck of American self government democracy has tightened with each election cycle.

Distribution of new wealth as a factor of justice was practically a non issue politically before the 1929 crash. FDR and New Deal Democrats made it a political factor after the end of WWII. However, distribution beyond subsistence is still in dispute today in the twenty-first century with the top one percent of families owning over ninety percent of all wealth in America. Property owners, the GOP and for the most part Christian pastors still support the concept that nothing is owed to labor beyond the lowest wage the market will allow, nor to the federal government in taxes beyond defense and orderly policing domestically including settlement of contracts, set at hardly more than subsistence for both even as productivity, profits, wealth, and inflation ensued.

By the beginning of WWI in 1914, oil was the most expensive new cost of war. Iran, Iraq, Saudi Arabia, and the smaller Arab states have played a growing role in the supply and cost of oil. All have been in turmoil for over a hundred years and counting, and the availability and cost per barrel of oil have affected all modern costs. The relations and tensions set up with the settlement of WWI and the tribal and religious Muslim sects have all remained in play, all with partisan interference from Europe before WWII, then including the U.S., Russia, and China since the end of the cold war.

The cost in human terms as well as wealth remains a challenge that still reverberates daily, both economically based on who controls the oil, and politically based on the leadership put in place including military. This role has escalated since the Middle East created OPEC in the 1920s and again when America invaded Iraq twenty years ago. The opposing factions contained in the WWI borders set by Britain and France with Wilson's concurrence are still in place and in contention; this reality will dominate much of the rest of this book.

In 1914, the second year of Wilson's presidency, the income tax and the Federal Reserve were established, and WWI broke out in Eastern

Europe. Then as now nations had alliances. Over the next year all of Europe and the Ottoman Empire (that defeated the Roman's Eastern Empire nine hundred years before and controlled the Middle East since) were at war. America joined the fray in 1917, a year before the war ended. It was America's first military foray on the east side of the Atlantic Ocean since Jefferson.

At the turn of the twentieth century in the eastern half or more of Europe, the ruling powers included the following: the newly formed German Empire, the long reigning Hapsburg's Austrian-Hungarian Empire, the new nation Italy (the home of the old Holy Roman Empire and the Papal States), the Russian Empire of the czars, and the Ottoman Empire which ruled parts of the countries east of the Adriatic Sea including modern Turkey.

Within the first twenty years of the new (twentieth) century, three major eastern empires would cease to exist: czarist Russia, the Turkish Ottomans, and the Austrian Hungarian (Hapsburgs). The United States would be drawn into redrawing ancient borders, as well as keeping the peace among vastly different cultures including civic, moral, and economic.

President Wilson did not lead isolationist America into WWI until 1917, only a year before it ended. It took another half a dozen years later before all of the treaties and settlements were worked out. Wilson went to the peace conference in Paris with a fourteen point plan. The peace, if you could call it that, was engineered by Britain and France, and signed off by Wilson who was less than insightful in spite of his first rate mind. The inequities in the settlement led to the German lead up to WWII some dozen years later, and left the U.S. with many of the issues still bedeviling the Middle East today.

Among Wilson's fourteen points, one of the few ideas proposed that France and Britain entertained, was a League of Nations to be a source of diplomatic solutions for the nations of the world, as regional differences grew into threats of future wars. A conference was held in San Francisco and the League of Nations was formed. The U.S. Congress at the time was controlled by the GOP which was still led by isolationists. American membership in the League was rejected, and the idea failed. We will see a similar organization come out of the settlement of WWII (the United Nations) operating with mixed reviews to date.

Among the outcomes of the WWI treaties, France took control of Syria, and Britain took control of Egypt and the Suez Canal as a short cut to India, and established a mandate to settle European Jews in Arab Palestine. Britain also took over northern greater Syria and formed two new nations, Iraq and Jordan, taking control of what became the Iraq oilfields . Britain also retained control of Iran's oil, and what became Saudi Arabia's oil. Jordan and Iraq were newly decreed nations with an Arabic king in each, ruling a diverse people in Iraq, and ninety-five percent Palestinians in Jordan.

While the Jordan population was and is a Palestinian majority, the Jordan king is actually a Hashemite from the Arabian Peninsula, and he is now an ally of Israel in their standoff with the Palestinian peoples, based on Israel coming to the aid of the Jordan king when Jordan's native population revolted and staged a coup led by Yasser Arafat and his Palestinian Liberation Organization.

In America, the Palestinians' revolt to recapture their homeland was and continues to be defined as a terrorist organization coup of a legitimate government, and not a civil war of liberation. This view is based on Palestine's refusal to agree to Israel's right to exist. What are all wars if not an attempt to legitimatize the new government by one group of people, who go to war against another government that claims the right to govern the people of such nation?

Every one of these decisions created political, military, economic, and humanitarian nightmares that continue to this day, and America has wound up playing a key role in all of it, as we'll follow in both Chapters 9 and 10, primarily because the world became dependent on oil for energy, and it was discovered that the largest deposits of oil in the world were and are in the Middle East. I remember an old joke told as if George W. Bush said it; "I don't understand why God put our oil under their sand"; this is satire, but it captures the feelings about the need for oil in the western democracies.

World history and America's evolving role in it slowly pushed a growing list of unresolved foreign issues down the road for decades.

It is little wonder we are embroiled in so many Middle East dilemmas today. America did not become an internationalist country until WWII, and now America is in the late stages of a nationalist regression, led by a large minority political cultural movement on the right.

In the U.S., farm labor from family farms in the north and from plantations as well as share cropper farms in the south, continued to migrate to cities in the industrial north seeking jobs. This led to urbanization, a key issue for the twentieth century that was never seriously addressed, as suburban open spaces allowed what became known as white flight to let the reality of black hopelessness simmer on a back burner. Aggressive policing, massive prison construction, and aggressive discriminatory sentencing were part of the stall. Without job access so-called do-gooders even managed to enact feeding schemes, subject to back lash against those seen as lazy.

Acknowledging the despoiling of our land, rivers, and the environment have been concepts treated with the same skillful neglect as the sharing of wealth from productivity improvements with labor, or acceptance of paying meaningful levels of income taxes on accumulating dynastic fortunes even in time of war among the wealthiest few thousand dynastic families of billionaires in America. These are some of the gridlock issues I refer to as outcomes.

One by one each of these areas of national life needed improvement, and it fell to the federal government to play a key role, first as the change agent and then as the regulator, and finally as the enforcer. Each time an issue intruded on the safety and security of the life of the nation, as an economic, cultural, regional, religious, or governance norm, most if not all American citizens were riled on one side or another. More mutual denigration ensued than progress until the introduction of the New Deal in the midst of the complete collapse of the national economy after 1929.

President Teddy Roosevelt was the first president to introduce concepts of ecology and environmentalism. He also saw the need for an honest valuation of stocks for investors, the need for disclosures to benefit consumers, and a growing concern for the well being of those who labor for hourly wages. All of this led to the need for the government to play a role in regulating stock trading, as well as safety issues for employees and consumers, and the setting aside of national heritage lands for preservation as parks, forests, and wildlife reservations, the establishment of labor rights, and adequate taxation to fund not only growth in wealth, but also the growth of a consumer economy fueled middle class and infrastructure.

This would have to wait for Teddy's cousin Franklin to become president almost thirty years later, to find a constitutional right for the federal government to assume a meaningful role in improving outcomes of these issues based on insightful policies. As can be expected, fifty years later even the more good than harm outcomes of the New Deal were followed by blow back sold as the government being the problem, not the ills of society they acted to alleviate if not solve.

Constantine so well established the king's absolute right to all of the property in every kingdom, and Englishmen so ingrained the concept in the common law after the English civil war, that future property owners and future forms of property all insisted that only they had an absolute right to all of the income produced as a function of property of any description including but not limited to land, machines, tools, patents and knowledge. This carried over into our founding, allowing states to keep absolute property rights in spite of the new Bill of Rights assuring citizens' property rights free of abuse as the nation grew.

Everything pre-mechanized man had known about wealth, power, politics, labor, government, religion and rights of all the various classes of interest required a new understanding and re-thinking of the impact on citizens and governments, as the needs of corporations and men of wealth demanded greater efforts from employees, and greater services of government, all the while demanding the right to not share any of the newfound wealth with those who provided the added value produced by labor, or the support services provided by government.

Additionally, a new class of merchant bankers arose whose rights were based on the realities of property norms that had almost exclusively meant private real estate property in England and her colonies for centuries, as corporate industrial wealth surpassed the value of all the productive land in each nation, as well as the gold supply at agreed values.

Teddy Roosevelt became the last GOP president with a primary interest in how to address these realities, from ecology, to labor, women, public education, and minorities, on the farm and in the inner cities, but Teddy lacked theories, mechanisms, and policies, as well as support for the intent of his new ideas.

In Europe there was no concept of citizens' rights based from their civil war that granted equality. However little it had been asserted, America had been founded with all citizens entitled to governance in compliance with rights based on assured justice, while the southern states equally demanded the Bill of Rights did not apply to them. The Civil War settled this, yet the south has since ignored labor rights in every way possible.

It seemed that growth in productivity which created a means of producing wealth beyond menial output would be a natural boon to all, but when has change that effects settled norms ever been automatic? The greed of man, the nature of governments to protect property rights over individual citizens' rights, and the relationship between kings and bishops originally, and now pastor organizations and corporate leadership, all have shown constant support for the owner class.

This is a primer on American historical gridlock and not a history of Europe. Yet we cannot know how America became who we are and how and why the world became as it is, with the problems we are now reviewing from a hundred years ago, without an understanding of the changes impacting the world.

Great wealth ignited new tensions between and among the factors of economic interests: those who sorted out sourcing, extraction or growth, and capitalization, and those who provided the knowledge, skill, and toil needed to produce and deliver energy, food, labor, and even men and supplies in peace time and for wars as international ease of transporting large crowds and freight. This impacted all of the settled norms of cost around the nation's issues noted above.

Government, banks and markets, invention, manufacturing, construction, cost, prices, and distribution of infrastructure, populated living centers, and funds were all as if in a boiling cauldron.

Additionally America had a more complex problem than anywhere else based on our unique Bill of Rights, which had been treated as hardly more than an afterthought until the twentieth century. The oligarchs will have their comeuppance, as will those who prosper based on control of cultural norms. They will not take intrusion on their turf without blow back.

In my family we often talk about old problems of beliefs regarding religion, tribe, and/or governance rearing its head again when a person whose opinion is absolute, in spite of not knowing the history of what happened, or how some dilemma developed, or how it was treated in the past, is confronted by the demands of a minority group that gains its voice and finally demands to live without a form of abuse as a norm.

Most of what ensues is what I call skillful neglect, intentional blindness, opportunism, and/or spin in a world of change. In the work environment, sometimes out of mismanagement or greed, most often the outcome is a byproduct. It can be what union folks or Catholics, or the Irish, or welders, or what all of us have in common.

I hope to present the final eighty-seven years from 1933 to the present day of our history, occurring during most of my life and more than half of all the pages in this seventeen hundred and five year narrative work in a way for us to compare how we see them, hopefully as they are, and not as they are spun by one side or the other. Spin is too much a part of modern political life in America. I believe it does much harm and little good. Social media has immensely enhanced the ability of spin to do harm and distort what is knowable daily and accumulative, especially since the reduction of print oversight in the digital age with the loss of an editing factor.

At this point in our history, we are in the second term of Woodrow Wilson in the early 1920s. Over the last ten years in our time line exuberance has overtaken that portion of the economy driven by opportunism. Wilson suffered a stroke, but citizens were not told.

Over the next ten years the Republicans retook the White House led by one term President Calvin Coolidge, known as silent Cal, whose ideology could be summed up as the less government the better. I'm not sure who interpreted our founders' embrace of limited government, checks and balances, as meaning small government, but Coolidge got that message. I will make the argument in Chapters 9 and 10 that none of our founders wanted a small or weak federal government in the dangerous world they understood, even if they feared its eventual impact on their region's labor, religious, economic or cultural norms.

The south never really recovered from the Civil War over fifty years past now in our story, but it had settled into a slow paced normalcy of small town life and values, based on agriculture, faith, family, segregation, schooling that reinforced traditional values and eschewed science, and of course resentment of loss of the war to the Yankee north, and respect for the men who had fought for the south in the war.

After one term each, Presidents Coolidge's and Harding's impact on the outcomes of the twentieth century is not worth mentioning. Then came GOP President Herbert Hoover, a brilliant mining engineer with a basic trust in modern industry and finance, and a basic GOP belief that the president actually was granted little authority under the Constitution to interfere in the economy or the life of the citizens of the United States, as practiced in each of the several states.

For the first seven years of the post war GOP economy, the paper wealth of the industrialists and speculators soared. These times were referred to as the roaring twenties. Then the inflated balloon burst, as if a mighty dam broke and a river of destruction carried away everything and everyone in its path. America entered the Great Depression in October of 1929 in the first year of Hoover's term. He hardly caused the depression, but based on GOP ideology he sat like a deer in the headlights watching without acting. This experience shaped the fears of my generation's (the first to come of age after WWII) parents and grandparents for life.

Among the worst five presidents in history based on ideology alone,

President Hoover insisted he had no authority granted by the founders to do anything, and so let misery, hunger, and hopelessness ensue for most of the next three years with little improvement.

Our current domestic political gridlock developed from this point forward. First we will review the actions taken by the most successful modern democratic president in history, Franklin Delano Roosevelt, known to history as FDR, to address relief, then recovery, then reform (FDR's famous first term three Rs) followed by WWII, and then the FDR era of four Democrat and three Republican presidents who for the most part kept world peace, and the new consumer driven American middle class economy, as he and his heirs envisioned and enabled.

America really did have a small government relative to the problems, as wealth, industry, immigration, births, the economy and cities had all been encouraged to grow many times faster than the government, and it all crashed at the same time, again based solely on a GOP flawed ideology of speculative lending, while another disallowed flawed ideology prevented any relief or recovery. We will discuss the GOP gridlock in opposition to FDR's plan to reform the American system of a total wealth gap between rich and poor with very little in the way of a middle class.

FDR's New Deal was the number one cause of change in economic outcomes in American history for the most people ever, introducing a safer and fairer economy. The GOP true to ideological form opposed every single improvement in the life, wealth, liberty, and every citizen's improved opportunity to pursue their idea of happiness.

And so the American story of our economic governance history over the eras we've covered has brought us to the great depression and the election in 1932 of Franklin Delano Roosevelt, the thirty-second president of the United States (1933-1945). He was the only president who was elected four times. He died only a few months into his fourth term and was succeeded by his Vice President Harry S. Truman.

FDR's New Deal era addressed banking, labor, retirement, and areas of federalism such as road and dam building reforms in the 1930s, as well as pre-war efforts leading up to WWII which finally pulled the U.S. fully out of the Great Depression.

So let's move on to the FDR New Deal era, personally my favorite era since the founding of our always great nation.

Part III

Latest 75 Years, FDR New Deal V. GOP Blow Back

Chapter 9 - The FDR Era

The New Deal - FDR's forty-seven year Economic Governance Era of Relief, Recovery, and Reform. The only era in U.S. history of sustained middle class growth; the first time wage labor shared in America's ever growing national prosperity.

Stabilization of the banking system including social insurance protection for safe banking including depositors, legalization of labor unions, temporary jobs to relieve families, crop support for farmers, the largest public works construction in history, and early aid to Britain as WWII was coming to a head. The GOP fought FDR on every issue.

This era saw the winning of WWII, the end of world colonialism by European nations, the rebuilding of the U.S. as twelve million troops came home to a GI Bill that educated and provided a living wage to include affordable ownership of a family home based on low down payment government guaranteed mortgages, most implemented based on FDR programs by President Harry Truman following WWII and the rebuilding of Europe. Then perhaps most disturbing to the south and white male hourly wage earners, during the presidency of LBJ (Lyndon Baines Johnson) the FDR Democrats legislated equal individual rights for women and blacks, and finally full voting rights for blacks.

The building of the American middle class took off. As fast as the middle class grew with new rights for labor, women, and blacks, so did a new anti New Deal GOP coalition including segregationist evangelical leaders in the south based on a new definition of white supremacy, funded by leaders of dynastic wealth families from across the nation in support of renewed property rights demands, calling for immediate cuts in taxes . This movement (The John Birch Society, an organization founded by many of the fathers of today's

Koch Network) will finally lead the GOP to elect a champion of their conservative ideology to repeal all the economic gains of American working families the New Deal had enabled.

The blow back against about a hundred million working poor and desegregated blacks still living in poverty, will be nearly as harsh as the blow back against former slaves after the civil war, and still in full battle mode we will see as our tale ends in 2020.

Much of the support for the idea to defeat these newly recognized legislated as well as Supreme Court recognized working and middle class rights came from the voting decisions of a large majority of the beneficiaries of these New Deal changes, often over their political and union leaders' recommendations, i.e., white union men who became known as Reagan Democrats.

This portion of our narrative will be a cautionary tale of ordinary folks voting against their own best economic interests based on cultural norm reactive emotions beginning in 1968 as we shall see in the Democratic primary campaign that year to replace LBJ.

Between Truman and LBJ a successful general Dwight David (Ike) Eisenhower was elected GOP president in the middle of the era; he appointed the two Dulles brothers, Allen to head the CIA and John Foster as Secretary of State, both were strongly anti communist, committed Christians, and the most imperialistic GOP leaders since Teddy Roosevelt. President Eisenhower also built the Interstate Highway System, appointed a moderate GOP led Supreme Court that ended separate but equal segregation in the United States; Ike's chief justice added a right to privacy for women making their own reproductive decisions, which includes a controversial right to first trimester abortion.

In the 1970s this era will introduce the age of OPEC oil independence in the Middle East, causing rampant inflation in the US, and Cold War containment of Russian after WWII by Harry Truman.

In March of 1933 Franklin Delano Roosevelt (FDR) was inaugurated as the thirty-second president of the United States, deep into the worst nationwide economic depression in American history, for the second time in the twentieth century. Both were caused by unregulated speculative banking and margin debt funding in the stock market of less than fully regulation of Wall Street, using debt capitalization on margin (a form of borrowing to purchase stocks, looked at as equity ownership, but at high risk in a downturn) to invest in an unregulated stock market.

This was the second major boom and bust (speculative investing) in America in twenty-two years, the traditional outcome of the pursuit of growth beyond the natural increase in consumer demand which was at the time primarily driven by consumer spending which depended on rising incomes.

FDR's first initiatives dealt with the shuttered banks and the broken cash economy of out of work wage earners, which came to include almost all of the banks and over half of all hourly wage earners across the nation.

FDR had accepted the nomination of his party by discussing the "Forgotten Man". He compared the depression facing the nation to what was called for in a nation facing a war. He pledged to rebuild the country from the ground up by putting the infantry (meaning the wage earners at the bottom of the earning pyramid) back to work under a number of not yet named programs. He reminded America that farms were being foreclosed due to farm prices being lower than the cost to grow. FDR promised a farm price support program and delivered.

He promised to be a good neighbor internationally, but the GOP's Smoot-Hawley Tariffs were so high that other nations had stopped buying farm products from the U.S. FDR stated that only reciprocal relationships produced healthy non-destructive economies in balance, and called for repeal of the tariffs. It might have been a good idea if President Trump had read a bit about FDR policy ideas.

As noted earlier in our narrative, business leaders supported by bankers, most GOP political leaders, and evangelical and Roman Catholic pastors, claimed one hundred percent of any share of the nation's wealth belonged to property owners who were often stock holders, claiming men who labored had no right to secure income or job security. FDR promised a New Deal, and he stated his intentions as a pledge.

FDR's pledge promised a more equitable opportunity to share in the distribution of national wealth. I'm writing this book in the twenty-first century and the daily discussions on partisan cable TV debate shows are asking Democrats if they believe in "capitalism"; the answer should be yes. It provides all of the wealth and that is its job. At the state level the owner is entitled to one hundred percent of the profit over the lowest market cost the owner can enforce; this goes back to the Biblical Christian idea of feudalism which ended at our founding, and English Common Law which is based on the King James Bible's views regarding kings, their nobles, and the peasants indentured for life on the kings' lands managed by his nobles, all reveled to be God's will since the Council of Nicaea.

The talking heads also ask twenty-first century Democrats what their views are on "social" solutions to economic dilemmas, is it not plain old socialism? The answer is hell no. FDR gave the answer that supported both capitalism's role and equitable social justice as a political philosophy.

That is the answer Democrats must learn again. This is not a trick question and the New Deal made it work for all of Americans for forty-eight years, better than anything in history, except perhaps for the families of dynastic wealth accumulation, who now have turned the tables by capturing the ideology of the modern GOP.

Here is FDR's New Deal pledge that created the American living wage middle class:

"Throughout the nation men and women forgotten in the political philosophy of the government, look to us here for guidance and for more equitable opportunity to share in the distribution of national wealth; I pledge myself to a New Deal for the American people."

FDR did not say "redistribute"; he intended just distribution insuring sustainable profits for property owners, wages for labor, and taxes for the nation, all built into equitable pricing in the U.S. market.

FDR did not want to undermine capitalism, he wanted the American economic system to be dynamic, sustainable and just to all who made it possible. Democrats should resurrect this as their enduring legacy, ensuring only an earned equitable share. If the middle class man our wars and man our factories, mines, and farms, they should by right and equity share in the rewards in line with the value they add in peacetime. That was a universal norm as an American value after WWII after 1945 except for returning black veterans in the U.S. South.

FDR stated that "The only thing we have to fear is fear itself". FDR knew the two most important factors to relieve day-to-day fear was a living wage family income, and safe functioning banks. FDR established the basics of relief for lost employment which was a common cycle during post civil war years of recurring boom and bust speculative banking.

From the time of his election FDR's cabinet members were designing the early actions the administration would take in the first one hundred days followed by three major efforts they would initiate, each as early as possible in his first four year term. FDR called these initiatives his three R's program, **Relief, Recovery, and Reform.**

Most of the relief programs were planned, funded, and implemented in the first one hundred days; however, recovery of the national banking system was their most immediate task. Ordinary borrowers had withdrawn their savings from home town banks, and put their money under their mattress as the saying went. That was if the small town banks were still open and solvent. Thousands had closed, and savers had lost their life's savings.

At the time no American president had ever asked the Federal Reserve to re-capitalize American banks. Most Republicans doubted it was constitutional, and the Supreme Court, dominated by Republican appointees, had never considered the question.

Conservatives have always accepted the outcomes of boom and bust as normal business cycles, and have resisted all attempts at regulation in the stated interest of growth as the greatest good. However, more often than not, the success of these policies on the upside have accrued to the knowledgeable wealthy. The misery of failure has impacted uninformed investors, commercial bank depositors, net borrowers, and families who depend on steady wages for day-to-day living expenses.

Each new bust was larger and more devastating, but no one ever really made the injustice of the system to ordinary citizens a major political or Supreme Court issue before FDR. How could policies that led to recurring abuse of millions of innocent working folks not be an absence of justice?

To reopen the banks required re-capitalization, which is a role of a central bank; however, consumer banking was as unregulated at the time as commercial banking. FDR regulated both forms of banking as well as mortgage banking, ending boom and bust cycles followed by runs on the banks and collapse of the national economy. He used a concept his team called social insurance to insure bank deposits. Hamilton had proved the huge credit worthiness of a large nation that can tax, and the usefulness of credit to a large nation in times of distress, not just the stress of war, but also the stress of economic collapse.

Even before taking office, Roosevelt asked Hoover's top finance men to send a bill to Congress called The Emergency Banking Act, which Congress passed the same day. This Act opened most of the Federal Reserve Bank's systems within a few days. FDR set up oversight on insurance operations within the government that guaranteed funds deposited in federal insured banks who agreed to defined banking standards (regulation), and FDIC insurance and safe banking were born. Today eighty-seven years later the FDIC successfully insures and regulates consumer banks which continue as the safest banking system in the history of the world, without a major failure. This is an outcome of a policy, and an example of how I will compare FDR's outcomes to Ronald Reagan's.

Federal insured banks have never gone broke, or collapsed, or caused a national depression. A small insurance fee is charged and deposits are guaranteed up to a limit of two hundred and fifty thousand dollars per depositor. I do not know of a single American in either party who opposes this system.

This type of national benefit to citizens funded by the by citizens who earn the benefit and not from income taxes is known as social insurance, such as Social Security. It is the only form of socialism that the Democrats have ever implemented. I wish Democrats would teach its newly elected members this history lesson; if not the party, who will?

The only times in history the U.S. Government has borrowed to fund a social insurance program are the two times the GOP deregulated the risk side and both crashed the national economy. Reagan had lowered lending standards for savings and loan banks, while leaving government insurance in place at safe banking rates, and George W. Bush did the same thing with Freddie and Fannie.

In both cases a special entity was set up including the Federal Reserve as the lender of last resort. In both cases Hamilton's central bank idea and America's authority and credit provided a means to bail out the guilty (of malfeasance) GOP. In both cases the entity (The Resolution Trust in the 1990s) bailed out Reagan's crash from the 1980s when he injected speculation into his drive for economic growth, and then used money loaned to the entity to fund the gap between salable assets and bank losses. In the case of Freddie and Fannie, a government re-lending bank was re-established with Federal Reserve loaned money to take over deflated assets just as Wall Street sharks do, and saved the economy, the jobs, and made money selling off the assets when they reinflated.

The GOP is so dedicated to speculative growth with outcomes on the upside for speculative billionaires and so opposed to safe banking and safe mortgages for wage earning families, that they voted against the bailout when Obama a Democrat was president. The GOP did vote for the bailout when George H. W. Bush was president, but did not re-elect him, because he also raised taxes to help fund the recovery.

FDR set up a number of systems for federal insured type banks. A few that FDR set up that remained solid until deregulated by Ronald Reagan and later George W Bush, were allowed to use speculative risk while keeping FDR's federal insurance in place, and these went boom and bust. All of these banks were mortgage banks of one type or another.

Bank failures dropped from over two hundred thousand during Hubert Hoover's final GOP term before FDR, to a few hundred during the entire forty-eight year FDR era. For the rest of this book I'll be demonstrating FDR policy outcome improvements such as these on which my appreciation of presidents and party policies are based, or demonstrating GOP policies in a similar manner that did not work, for purposes of comparing outcomes.

I'll specifically point out examples of GOP ideological policy outcomes that fail, such as bank failures leading to economic crashes, and tax cuts that led to national debt increases, along with free trade induced unemployment increases, while the wealth gap widened between rich and poor in America, an arguable example of unjust abuse of the governance system itself.

The key insights over the seventeen hundred years of this book, and especially important in the current era, from the crash of 1929 to the recovery from the 2007 crash, are the failure cycles under each GOP president, and recovery cycles under Democrat presidents. Partisan yes, factual also yes.

We will compare the reaction to these outcomes. Simply stated we will see irrefutably that Democratic policies have done more good, and GOP policies have done more harm to more citizens when reviewed without spin, and compared based on the most good for the most citizens for the longest time. This is what the founders idealized as the common good intent in the Preamble to the U.S. Constitution.

Gridlock to a large extent remains rigid in modern America as the reality of the above bank outcomes in the past few decades has been allowed to be ignored as policy outcome failures based on GOP spin. We will not move away from these ideology based policies until the outcomes are acknowledged and subjected to objective variance reporting, between stated intent such as "growth". If in fact a tax cut along with deregulation of banking creates hyper growth, and then leads to over supply and collapse, we cannot just brag about the growth and spin the collapse as a partisan exercise. Sustainability must become an established justice and common good goal if we are going to end grid lock and constant rancor.

Before asking the Federal Reserve to recapitalize the community banks, the farm banks, and the savings banks, Roosevelt by presidential order ended exporting gold outside the United States without permission of the U.S. Treasury, and established a fixed price for gold at thirty-five dollars an ounce, about fifty percent higher than the then market exchange rate for U.S. dollars.

This provided the Federal Reserve with the needed liquidity without inflation that recapitalization required. Additionally, bank recapitalization was assisted by how well the public responded; hundreds of millions of stashed savings came out from under the mattresses and back into the banks during the first few weeks.

The modern GOP opposes these successful programs that citizens love based solely on ideology. Their chief means of fighting these "common good" programs is to spin the programs as either socialism, or the cause of America's twenty-first century huge twenty-two trillion dollars and growing national debt. This is actually the result of another ideology distortion concerning GOP tax cut policy, under a theory they originally called supply side economics, and they still call "starve the beast" debt as Reagan nicknamed it before they began to insist they opposed it, and blamed it on "entitlements".

FDR did not use the term but he addressed the effects of supply side economics on farm incomes without regulation as huge changes in the economy that occur from time to time in every nation's history. The farmers had huge supplies, but there was no demand at the price needed to break even, let alone make a profit. This is the ever thus down side of supply side economics.

As soon as FDR took office in 1933, his Economy Act fiscal reform was passed into law to effect much needed fiscal recovery and to fund relief. It began with a fifteen percent reduction in the pay of federal employees who had not lost their jobs during the depression, as well as veterans' pensions.

This freed up immediate cash (five hundred million dollars) to fund temporary make work programs that would put men back to work.

These funds were funneled through the political system allowing local governors and mayors to not only entice voters, but also making them popular even for mayors who did not like FDR; even the mayors FDR did not agree with were seen to have the most local knowledge of where the failures of banks and businesses had put the most men out of work. I say men as at the time most men worked and women were homemakers. This also reassured some in both parties in Congress that FDR was not just planning a huge socialist spending spree with borrowed or printed money. I'll state here early in the FDR era he did not try to fix the economy and racial injustice at the same time; racial inequality was not addressed by the Democratic Party until 1948 under Harry Truman.

FDR's request for fiscal policy to stabilize commercial bank confidence was as noted above the creation of social insurance depositor insurance, administered by the Federal Deposit Insurance Corporation (FDIC). This system also set interest rates, and usury limits at eighteen percent.

The most popular of FDR's social insurance programs, the Social Security System, today is in surplus by some 2.7 trillion dollars, and some plus sixty million retired Americans depend primarily on their monthly earned Social Security benefit to stay out of poverty. This surplus is now loaned to the U.S. treasury to help fund the debt created by GOP tax cuts in times when spending appropriations are higher than enacted tax rates produce.

Another FDR bank innovation to promote trade and create income and jobs from exports was the establishment of the Import/Export Bank, which provides funds to support corporate exports when local lending in the buyers' country is not available. This program started in 1934 and has created trillions of dollars of exports, produced millions of jobs, and has turned over to the U.S. Treasury billions of dollars of profit. Not a single net income tax dollar has ever been used to fund Social Security, FDIC or the Import/Export Bank. In effect social insurance allows American citizens access to the leverage effect of the economy that their income taxes and wage income spending have built in our consumer economy.

The modern GOP likes to conflate FDR's social insurance programs which are self funded and thereby earned by citizen beneficiaries, such as the FDIC and safety net welfare programs, as socialism and welfare for citizens who cannot or do not successfully participate in the private economy, in a deliberate effort it seems to blur the line between earned benefits and true need based welfare.

Earned benefits are never welfare or socialism, as the FDIC proves. It was established as a separate entity that charge a fraction of a percentage point fee on each deposit to protect depositors' funds with government guaranteed insurance. These insurance premiums fund the cost and the government, and since the Baltimore bank decision Supreme Court has had authority to not only tax and assess tariffs, but to also assess fees. The first deposit limit per depositor insured was twenty-five thousand dollars; today the program is still in place and the limit on each account is two hundred fifty thousand dollars. The program regulates bank reserve funds, underwriting standards, and mandates an agreement to abide by all the regulations of both the FDIC and the Federal Reserve, including supervision and takeover for liquidation if mismanaged. This social insurance system, as well as mortgage insurance based affordable home ownership are sometimes referred to as the utility value of the nations funding power and authority; these programs are treated in the marketplace much the same as a U.S. Government Bond.

All Americans can deposit their money in non FDIC savings accounts called money market funds that pay slightly higher interest; they are not insured by the federal government. However, when George W Bush crashed the economy in 2007 by deregulating Freddie and Fannie, money market depositors were so frightened that he adopted FDR's safe banking idea and guaranteed money market funds for a few years.

The stage was set for what became a sustainable set of regulations to correct the ills of speculative debt greed, and risk driven unregulated Wall Street stock sales on margin, meaning part of the purchase price was borrowed from the investment bank authorized to sell corporate stocks and bonds; both sides of the concept were unregulated and without oversight. Capital was being bought with debt, a sure recipe for boom and bust throughout America's banking history until FDR, then again after Reagan repealed FDR's security regulations, but not his insurance regulations, which turned Reagan's deregulation of the Savings and Loan Banks into a disaster for the economy and the tax payers also as we will review in Chapter 10.

FDR's banking success provided the opportunity to introduce his other new concepts, referred to as progressive policies, regarding regulated American capitalism, meaning regulated sustainability to end boom and bust. FDR knew that the wealthy invested money beyond what they needed to live in comfort, often taking risks with their money that they could afford, frequently making huge returns, sometimes going broke. The working class seldom had any surplus funds beyond savings for a rainy day. Working folks could now deposit money to keep it safe until it was needed. Individual banks could go broke, but the depositors' funds would not be lost, and the towns and businesses where they lived and worked would still have safe banks that would replace the failed bank.

FDR recognized that unregulated capitalism produces ever growing wealth on the upside, but is subject to cyclical periods of boom and bust with a downside; about once every twenty years was the norm. FDR also recognized in his time there was no theory or mechanism conceived or seriously advocated during our past one hundred and forty-four year history that provided an avenue for a portion of this ever increasing new wealth to be shared beyond the owner (property rights) class with labor, or to meet the growing demands on the federal government to support the public cost of growth as noted repeatedly throughout any meaningful review of America's fiscal and monetary history, including this one.

This was especially true in the newly emerging age of much more expensive mechanized war. We have mentioned this since the fourth century when the Romans wanted to cut the cost of legionaries. Finally in the 1930s FDR pledged to address these recurring and destructive norms, while his opposing politicians in the GOP have always equated taxes with loss of freedom; today it is a GOP ideology supported by the Freedom Caucus in the U.S. House of Representatives called Economic Freedom, also to be reviewed in Chapter 10.

Among the new concepts of regulated factors of the American

economy in FDR's first two years, some like FDIC were established as permanent reform programs. FDR also set up temporary agencies to provide relief for men out of work, among them the Public Works Administration (PWA) that created work for over three million men, working on over thirty-five thousand programs. Some built public facilities such as roads, airports, dams, as well as post offices, courthouses, and so on.

Most areas in the U.S. south in the 1930s remained rural without paved roads or electrification. Another program was the Rural Electrification Program, and the Tennessee Valley Authority that built dams using turbines to generate electricity as well as a distribution system. These efforts not only electrified the south, they also provided very low cost electricity in the still cash poor southern states. The Farmers Relief Act was another relief program for rural areas. A more long term program for farmers was called the Agriculture Adjustment Act (AAA).

We mentioned that the GOP ideology regarding growth in the economy does not look to the demand side driven by wage growth that is spent to enhance middle class life in America, called the consumer economy. Demand side economics was favored by FDR and the Democrats, especially at the time FDR's Labor Secretary Frances Perkins was crafting many of these programs for FDR. The GOP favors tax incentives to drive production called supply side economics. It creates speculation growth until surplus inventory begins a slow down that turns into a crash, and then a longer term collapse, thus the term "boom and bust" as we've noted several times now into the fourth century of American history, from the eighteenth to the twenty-first centuries.

Mechanization of farming naturally increased productivity on American farms in the first third of the twentieth century. By the time of the election of FDR, over production was a factor of supply side phenomena. The new mechanized productivity increase produced so much food (eventually a great source of international trade income) that prices dropped to the point that the cost of production and transportation was greater than the market price without sufficient demand.

The AAA program paid farmers to keep land out of production to lower it enough to drive the price back up and end the foreclosure of the thousands of farms being taken over by the banks every week across America.

This program was instituted in 1933; three years later the GOP controlled Supreme Court found this program unconstitutional. FDR changed the concept and paid farmers to plant soil enriching crops and then plow them under, enriching the soil, a concept the Court approved. Farm relief was to be a temporary program under the New Deal and it worked. It worked so well that it continues to this day of corporate farming, and is still maintained due to support of farm state congressional representation as a corporate welfare program into the twenty-first century. This actually is a form of socialism, but the party of the farmers, the modern GOP, treats this form of welfare with intentional blindness.

In fact, in the *Wealth of Nations*, Adam Smith conceived his system (capitalism) based on his insight that labor would replace property as the greater value factor in wealth creation, a concept we today call value added. He also predicted the success of capitalism would create a growing demand for the central government to play an assuring role in the needs of capitalism to function; by assured he meant an ensured or safe system of debt, credit, settlements, courts, defense of sea lanes, and monetary unit such as a sound dollar, and so on, requiring access to an adequate or sustainable portion of the new wealth to fund this new and growing capitalism that only a large government could manage in a large continental economy.

Since our founding, today's GOP and the southern states regardless of party affiliation have advocated a small and limited role for the federal government that continues today in both Houses of Congress. Limited government is a mantra of the modern GOP. FDR proved only a large funded government can keep a large nation both wealthy and secure, regarding both defense and income levels among the classes of citizens equal to a minimum living wage.

FDR set out to establish a balance to the upside of unfettered capitalism's unique ability to produce unbounded productivity and wealth in the American economy as well as boom and bust disruptions; along with the unsustainable inequities regarding labor's and government's right to an agreed share of the new and increasing wealth, both Hamilton and Smith did express the insight that new definitions of distribution rights would become a growing need.

It never happened until FDR, and it created immediate blow back from those who absolutely represent property owners, who of course have an acknowledged first and largest share of the interest pie. However, these absolutists deny the earned rights of labor or government an equitable and sustainable share of the pie, also absolutely. They reject FDR's concept of balance; this is a minority position but with gerrymandering and other schemes we will see they control governing early in the twenty-first century.

So far we have reviewed FDR's first one hundred days stabilization of banking and security sales in 1933. The fiscal reforms bought credibility for FDR as a practical man, as his relief efforts put men to work, found the money to fund them, and provided relief to rural areas in the south as well as farm areas across the nation. Some of these programs were intended to be temporary (relief) and most ended in 1937 at the end of FDR's first term; others were intended to become permanent and they have.

We now move on to the second two years of FDR's first term and on into his second term. We will look at longer range recovery, labor rights reform, and retirement poverty reform for the elderly. Many programs were rejected by the GOP appointed judges on the Supreme Court, sometimes referred to as the First New Deal, followed by a Second New Deal based on changes in the court and the Administration's reconsideration of how they presented solutions, much as noted above in the changes resolving the aide to farmers.

An interesting side factor in the politics of the FDR era versus the Ronald Reagan era is the issue of the Press in modern times. The Press, now the Media, is used by both of our two main political parties to introduce "spin" both positive and negative, one era to the next supported by the ever growing use of money as speech, now settled by the GOP majority Supreme Court in favor of the rights of corporations as Fourteenth Amendment persons.

Money is now legal as speech but only for corporations and as a practical matter the wealthy, who also fund evangelicals and gun owners as long as they vote to support the corporate agenda that is supported by the GOP. As I write, corporations and the wealthy are free to use money as speech as a new judicial norm, most often in support of property rights that are at war with individual citizen rights. Labor unions specifically cannot use members' dues money as speech, while corporations can use share holders profits as speech. Hard to find either an original intent, or equal justice for labor and employers in this GOP adjudicated settlement.

This was the issue addressed by Hamilton's quote on the first page of this book, among the quotes of our founders defining my understanding of their intent. Hamilton reminded us that the few will attempt to control the many if they ever gain control.

FDR was wheelchair bound; he was elected president four times, yet most Americans did not know the president used a wheelchair as the result of adult onset polio. FDR, Ike, and John F. Kennedy among other FDR era presidents had extra marital affairs, and again the voters were never told. This was only some eighty years ago, but quaint by twenty-first century media realities.

For better or worse the 1930 Press reported sanitized news with less opinion or spin. Both opinion and spin are key factors in reporting today's presidential news. Part of that is the style of the times, and part is the growth of media and the types of media available today; all successful politicians must master or be consumed by these processes. All voters must learn to discern or be lost to a meaningful role regarding the key need of a sustainable democracy, an informed electorate that votes.

FDR was the first president to use the media for nationwide broadcasting as it became viable in the electronic age that evolved early in the twentieth century. The first national electronic medium was radio. FDR fully embraced presidential addresses he called fireside chats, which he used to explain and teach the public what his proposed changes were intended to accomplish, and to report on his progress, and to counter his adversaries.

One more aspect of life in the 1930s was the worldwide struggle among communism in Russia, fascism in Europe, colonialism around the non-white world, and America's democratic isolationism. There was a standoff between corporate conservatism and socialism and even some communism among the uneducated working poor in the United States, overtones of which reverberate into the twenty-first century.

The range of conservatism in America was defined by isolationist, low tax favoring, anti union labor, and anti-regulation corporate as well as main street GOP legislators in the north, and evangelical theology and segregationist ideologies, mostly among the southern wing of the then Democratic Party.

The range of liberalism in America was defined by pro-labor, anti-racist, pro-women rights, anti-capitalist, in favor of an end to prohibition, pro-secular tolerance in public education, a growing support for FDR's policies, and sympathy for the intent of Marxist reform struggling in Europe to deal with the recent end to serfdom in Russia.

The Democrats were more concerned with policy outcomes than with locking in a manifesto which the segregationists published signed by political leaders across the south, or the manifesto of corporate owners, *Conscience of a Conservative,* published with Barry Goldwater given credit as the author. We will review these position documents as the New Deal blow back continues to the end of this book.

In 1935 FDR turned from relief efforts to address long term labor reform by establishing robust labor rights for the first time in American history. These rights were requested of FDR by his labor Secretary Frances Perkins, and passed on by FDR to Congress. This effort was the most meaningful for his promise of a New Deal regarding a fair portion in the distribution of the fruits of production of wealth in America for those whose labor and the men who produced the ever growing output due to productivity, as added value to the fruits of capital investment.

FDR asked Congress for a bill to allow American labor to associate democratically, and to collect dues to fund legal representation in negotiating with property owners as employers do regarding wages and working conditions in the work place, across companies and plants, and across any industry nationally, by trade, as well as general labor unions, as a latent constitutional right.

Latent rights are a term for ideas that form a right not spelled out originally, but left for the amendment process. Rights can be legislated and then settled by the Supreme Court. In 2008 a latent right for private gun ownership for personal protection of home and person was challenged and settled. This aspect of gun ownership under the Second Amendment was not spelled out in 1791. The 2008 U.S. Supreme Court found it was not the founders' intent that private citizens on the frontier had to depend on a militia when there was none available for hundreds of miles, and that in fact it was intended even if unsaid that citizens could own and bear their own guns for personal protection.

This was the same as the latent idea regarding a woman's right to family planning regarding reproduction; women were naturally found to have a latent private right to make these decisions themselves in private, alone or with their doctor. Also regarding labor, if stockholders could pool funds, elect representation, and hire professional representation for negotiations, so should groups of hourly value added providing employees.

Congress passed what came to be known as the Wagner Act with all of the above provisions in 1935. Two years later the Supreme Court upheld the Wagner Act.

Most of these FDR ideas were formulated by Labor Secretary Frances Perkins. Perkins was at the forefront of every area of FDR's and the Democratic Party's social insurance and worker rights political, legislative, court battles, and success stories during the only forty-seven years of American history when wage earners lives improved year after year as a percent of the national income.

Perkins began her career as a chemistry teacher, and later became interested in factory safety after witnessing the infamous Triangle Shirt Factory fire in NYC in 1911. Over one hundred women sweatshop workers (as they were called) died of smoke, flames, or from jumping from upper floors; there were few safety rules in 1911. The doors were locked to keep the women in the building on their full twelve hour shifts. Hence there was no escape from the smoke and flames other than jumping.

Perkins took what today would be her master's degree at Wharton in economics and sociology. Her first labor related job was with the state of New York dealing with factory safety. In 1929 Governor FDR who had followed Perkins's career in NY State government appointed her as the Commissioner of his newly initiated New York State Department of Labor. When FDR became president four years later, he invited her to become his Secretary of Labor. As such she was the first female Cabinet Secretary in American history. When FDR invited Perkins to interview for the job, she arrived with ten demands. They were as follows:

One: Unemployment insurance.

Two: A Public Works Program such as WPA as an immediate relief program.

Three: Outlawing child labor.

Four: A standard eight hour work day.

Five: A minimum wage.

Six: Workers' Compensation Insurance.

Seven: Allow the federal labor secretary to work with state departments of labor.

Eight: A right for laborers to associate as unions to organize pool money, and hire representation to bargain for wages and working conditions.

Nine: Old age pensions which became Social Security.

Ten: Universal health insurance (never enacted as yet in 2020).

Frances Perkins proposed and drafted legislation and regulations, and saw them through Congress; nine of the ten labor programs she proposed became law, only number ten failed. FDR never allowed her to propose it because of southern opposition to healthcare for black citizens residing in their states.

After FDR's death Perkins stayed on for a while in Truman's cabinet, but she was pushed out by the southern wing of the Democratic Party with the support of the AFL and CIO Unions. Truman liked her and her ideas but he was a politician and was trying to rebuild Europe and contain Russia; he needed all the Congressional help he could get.

Later Perkins was appointed to the Civil Service Board by Truman. She ended her working years as a professor at Cornell University. Today the Labor Department building in Washington D.C. is named for Frances Perkins, one of the few remembrances of a true hero of labor in American history. For all her contribution to the working men and women of America and their families she is intentionally persona non grata with the American labor movement. I can only guess this relates to the fact that she was a women, and in the 1930s women were not welcome in union halls.

An irony of her tenure is the shortsightedness of the American labor movement. The AFL (American Federation of Labor) and the CIO (Congress of Industrial Organizations), the two largest industrial unions in America opposed her appointment and sought to have her replaced throughout her plus ten years of service, even though she achieved the most legislative wins for the labor movement and the working man in the history of the Department of Labor.

Labor leaders demanded that Truman replace Perkins with an experienced "labor leader", which he finally did. The "labor leader" he appointed who was recommended by the AFL and CIO soon failed; during his short tenure he did not get a single labor bill enacted. I will not even add his name here as he is not worthy of any recognition. He was never criticized by labor for his lack of performance; Perkins was never lauded for her contributions. It is a defect of the movement that they never seemed to understand their own best interest.

Even though Frances Perkins's name is on the Department of Labor Building in DC, almost no one knows who she is. There are good biographies available, but especially for professional women hers is one of the most inspiring in American history. To me she is the most interesting woman and the single most effective and meaningful woman in American history from a governmental policy point of view, especially for hourly wage dependent families at the peak of their share in America's capitalist system of wealth creation.

In the 2016 GOP debate on CNN the last question of the night was, who would each candidate like to see on the new ten dollar bill? This question was relevant because putting a woman on the bill is in discussion currently at the U.S. Mint. No one mentioned Frances Perkins, the woman who almost single handedly expanded the U.S. middle class to include hourly wage earners (the working poor). I know of no more important woman in American governmental history than Frances Perkins. No GOP candidate in 2016 seemed to know of her, and why would they? Few women of her own Democratic Party know of her achievements. My Democratic Party again fails to enlighten its members in Congress, even with the newly elected one hundred plus women in the 2018 Congress.

To this day unions seldom mention or acknowledge Perkins' accomplishments in any way. Wage based union labor in America left the Democratic Party during Lyndon Johnson's presidency in 1968. In my home town of Detroit in the presidential primary the UAW voted seventy-three percent for George Wallace, a southern white supremacist and right-to-work governor from Alabama. The UAW members voted against a pro-union, pro-living wage, pro- healthcare lifetime New Deal candidate Hubert Humphrey. Twelve years later these union Democrats would become known as Reagan Democrats.

On that day in 1968 thirty-six percent of American private sector wage laborers earned a living wage with fully funded family healthcare. Today four percent of private sector jobs are union, and almost no unskilled hourly wage laborer in American earns a living wage, or is provided fully funded healthcare for his or her family. There is no group of white voters in America less well informed than white union men, although many other groups are just as ill informed, especially those who are retired on pensions no longer offered to wage laborers, who owe their Social Security and pensions and their Medicare to Frances Perkins and FDR's invention, Social Insurance.

When FDR signed the Wagner Act into law it led to the establishment of labor unions with authority to vote, associate democratically, elect officers, collect dues from all who voted yes or no as long as a majority voted yes, and to use the dues to hire legal advice and representation in negotiations with corporations that were required by law to bargain in good faith. All of these "democratic" processes were enabled under Clause 7 of the Act. As a result, after WWII America became the first nation in the history of the world to create a majority middle class earning what became know as a living wage, with healthcare benefits for most, and retirement funded benefits for most.

At its peak about thirty-five years later over a third of all wage earners in America were employed by private employers, belonged to unions and enjoyed the above noted standard of living. This system grew until 1985.

The first blow back by the GOP to cripple wage growth keeping pace with the effects of productivity, inflation, and profits after WWII occurred in 1947. It was called the Taft-Hartley Act, which ended union members' rights to democratic participation or association across state lines as national unions, or across industries or employers beyond a local plant in any state. This law enabled the creation of right-to-work legislation at the state level. It ended the legal basis of Clause 7. Nothing would improve the wealth gap more than repeal of Taft-Hartley and reinstituting Clause 7 rights for hourly wage earners. Taft-Hartley enabled state chartered corporations total authority over wages in any state that so chose. The Supreme Court has abandoned any role in providing a remedy to any citizen abused in a labor dispute in such states. Why should this be allowed to stand?

The most popular FDR program (noted above as part of our living wage discussion) introduced by Frances Perkins also in 1935 was the Social Security program . It was and is a self funded earned inter-generational social insurance program that ended old age poverty in America. It is the most voter supported and beloved social insurance program in the history of any social insurance program in the U.S.. It is safe to say it is also the best supported political decision in American history.

These elderly retirement and healthcare social insurance programs are still debt free, fully funded for at least the next fifteen years, and still fully supported by the Democratic Party and a majority of Americans. By law they can never borrow money. This does not stop the GOP from blaming their tax cut debt on these debt free programs.

My generation grew up hearing praises in most of our families as they retold stories of their coming of age and seeing their parents' progress from hunger and fear to a paycheck and hope, especially during FDR's early make work era of relief in his first term in the mid 1930s, the early years of my parents' marriage, followed by the years of union growth, and for their retired grandparents living on Social Security, at least for white citizens born between 1920 and 1960.

One last area of reform we will introduce before we end review of FDR's first term and the end of relief and how it was spun by the GOP, is the social insurance support of low down payment mortgage insurance for home ownership. This became the means of home ownership for hundreds of millions of Americans, and also thanks to inflation became the largest source of wealth accumulation for middle class American citizens and families in history. One day the 401K tax free savings industry may supplant home ownership in wealth creation but not until wages are high enough to allow participation by the lowest forty percent of wage earners.

The president created two types of social insurance programs for home ownership, one pure government and the other a hybrid private bank for recapitalizing small town mortgage banks; all of them remained functional and popular for the rest of the FDR era. We will see in Chapter 10 the GOP deregulated three of them, and all three failed within three years of deregulation, another less better outcome of the little known Reagan era legacies.

FDR's second term began in 1937 when England already knew war was imminent. The last program of the Three Rs portion of FDR's New Deal impacted farmers, food processors, food retailers, and the poor; it was the food stamp program. Because it helped so many people and directly affected citizens in every Congressional district, it was very popular in spite of being a form of socialism and welfare, as spun by most GOP and segregationist true believers.

The first food stamp program was enacted in May of 1939 and lasted into the second year of WWII. It was proposed by future vice president Henry Wallace, Secretary of Agriculture at that time.

We noted above the farmers could not sell their crops at a price equal to even the cost to produce, so FDR was paying the farmers not to grow and sell a crop, just to enrich their soil until better times, a form of sustainability rational boundary thinking seeks. FDR and the New Deal created the FSP (the Food Stamp Program). It helped farms, unemployed hungry families, and the food industry at a level that included the corner store in every small town in America, what the founders had meant by the common good.

Today with America a million times wealthier, the GOP ideology sees the unemployed, the children of low wage Mexicans the food industry entices to illegally immigrate, and the seventeen million children of low wage poor families that go to bed hungry and disparaged as lazy, and the billionaires demanding tax cuts for themselves, as well as food stamp funding cuts for the lazy, and demanding a freeze in the minimum wage for over twenty years. This is the difference in outcomes from the policies of the onset of the New Deal, and the end stage of the GOP blow back, for the victims without hope in 2020.

Like the Labor Department building in DC named for Frances Perkins, the Agriculture Department building in DC is named for a key former player in the history of the department, Jamie Whitten of Mississippi, the second longest serving member of the U.S. House in history. For most of those years until he retired in 1991 Jamie was the chair of the Appropriations Committee and chair of the Appropriations Subcommittee on Agriculture, a low level committee assignment.

But he had an impact on the hungry black children in the American south in the second half of the twentieth century. For twenty-five years Jamie denied any food stamp payments to any black U.S. citizen who lived in Mississippi. No one filed a dissent on behalf of these abused citizens; the Supreme Court offered no remedy to these children for their unequal treatment by their own representative to the federal government.

Jamie's district in Mississippi was more than fifty percent black. When the Supreme Court overturned as legal, rights called "separate but equal", the southern politicians including Whitten signed what became known as the Southern Manifesto. It promised to fight integration forever and warned that integration would lead to the ruin of the nation.

In 2020 his home state Mississippi has the highest percent of state residents who qualify for assistance based on poverty participation rate in the modern EBT (for profit manager of the current funding system), twenty-one percent. The program was expanded throughout the New Deal era; cut backs only began in the 1980s when Ronald Reagan poisoned the national approval for this program referring to "welfare queens in their pink Cadillacs".

In 2020 the number one reason for voting the GOP I hear from white folks in my generation who live on Social Security and Medicare, funded partially today by poor folks who do work and pay FICA taxes, is they resent the lazy people who collect food stamps. Of course there is no such thing as food stamps and has not been for many years, it is now SNAP (Supplemental Nutrition Assistance Program). In the 2021 budget that starts October first, five weeks before the next election, the GOP is proposing to cut about eight hundred thousand recipients from the SNAP program. I believe this is the most disgraceful of all GOP blow back success stories of any FDR relief, recovery, or reform program of all the good the Democrats did in the FDR era.

The second great challenge for FDR beyond the depression was to support England as Germany began to round up Jews and threatened war with Poland in 1938. To understand what FDR and the nations of Europe faced from the two fascist nations, Germany and Italy, I'll insert a short overview of the rise of Adolf Hitler and his Nazi Party from the 1930s.

Let's start with the issue of Germany's authority to govern, a dilemma that interrupted the FDR era beginning in the first year of FDR's second term, to demonstrate how seductively grievances can be harnessed to create a political majority driven by emotion.

Adolph Hitler came to power with a nationalist message that he would repudiate the unjust (from the viewpoint of most Germans) WWI reparation debt as demanded and enforced by England and France with the approval of the United States in settlement of Germany's defeat.

Hitler consolidated his authority as a dictator by calling for an election to vote on two issues. First, did the German people agree that the reparation debt should be repudiated as he and his party proposed in their campaign; on this issue he received a plurality of about ninety-six percent. Second, should Hitler be granted whatever power he found necessary to succeed in his repeal of the reparation effort; this second question passed with more than a three quarters majority approval.

Hitler now held absolute authority over the German state, the government, the nation, its military, its policies, and the lives of all individuals. Hitler assumed authority as an empowered autocratic, as or more powerful as any European king or emperor in history. Hitler almost immediately put into motion several parts of a form of nationalism that allowed him to create fever pitch enthusiasm for the internal policing he established.

As for external grievances he led a demand that all abutting nations restore to his national government every factor of German life in their lands that had ever been a part of German history. One way or another Hitler sought revenge hundreds of miles in every direction beyond what had finally become Germany late in the nineteenth century.

No enemy of Germany and the Aryan majority population was more despised, more scapegoated or destroyed with greater vengeance than the Jews. Ethnic cleansing was pursued day and night for six years, killing more than a million Jews a year, several thousand every day for almost two thousand days. Never doubt or underestimate man's tolerance for hate fueled, emotion driven depravity.

Externally Hitler blamed the Jews and their banks for Germany's distress, as well as France and Great Britain and their policies. He also resented lands east, south, and west of then German borders with Germanic populations that were not part of Germany. He announced his intention to repatriate them into a new greater Germany, called the Third Reich.

Hitler's initial internal programs included containment of the Jews, and the development of two paramilitary groups in the country, the Storm Troopers and the Gestapo, in addition to the German national military. One group was to whip up fever pitch resentment, hatred, and fear of Jews; the second group was to create an internal spy ring to garner distrust and finger pointing, adding new levels of fear across the country and the region.

Hitler launched a campaign of manufactured paranoia based on conspiracies that built mind-whipping levels of nationalistic patriotism. The intent was to right every conceivable wrong; he focused national hate as his first step toward what he referred to as "the ultimate solution". Hitler held himself out to be the only one who could bring the real German people the revenge and restitution they deserved. It became apparent that Germans "wanted their country back".

The traditional army that was loyal to the German president was tasked with recruiting and rebuilding its armaments, which had been curtailed by WWI settlement terms limiting the proud German army to only one hundred thousand personnel. This placated the army led by an ambitious general who sought Hitler's favor more than he supported Hitler's ambitions. The General was Ernest Rohm; he was soon assassinated along with an acknowledged seventy-seven others, with perhaps as many as several hundreds more, for power grabbing attempts in what was known as the night of the long knives. Hitler at this point held absolute military as well as civil power over the German nation. Germany was no longer a nation of law; it was simply tyranny, setting in motion what would become WWII, leading a devoted cult dedicated to extracting revenge as well as inflicting subjugation.

The so called long knives preemptive purge muted any pockets of opposition that might have still existed going forward. Hitler's support from his elite police and intelligence departments finally gave him absolute dictatorship without any mechanism for review, oversight, or constraint; his authority to govern was by consent of those who approved total annihilation of all who opposed his dictates. Throughout human history this level of autocratic authority has always come to power only with destructive intent.

This raising of the blood ire of the German people was engineered by Hitler's two chosen spy masters who became famous during the run up to the second world war and going forward in conquest, only ending due to total and crushing defeat. These masterminds were Generals Himmler and Goring, Hitler's closest generals in conducting both WWII and his ultimate purging of Jews and other so called undesirables in the systematic roundup, transporting, and annihilation in death camps. This was Hitler's program on behalf of German nationalists' blood purification program, the Holocaust. Hitler sought a pure Aryan race of Germans ruling all of the Europe continent at a minimum. The German people declared war not only on Jews, but also on white Christians who were not Germans.

It is a cautionary tale to me that absolute forms of nationalism still burn in the hearts of millions in many countries around the world in the twenty-first century. Some want a dominant tribe, or political party, some a race, or level of property ownership. Allied by tribal, true religion belief, language, race, or economic status, my dad's norms noted on the back of the book reflected the nationalist emotional components of a majority of folks in the world without much deeper thought. This is just pride, even perhaps useful pride, as long as it does not spin out of control. It is always driven out of control by a demagogue inciting emotional resentment. Hitler is the ultimate example in world history.

World War II began in 1939 with all departments of the German State loyal first to Hitler, and then to the Fatherland. Germany was and is a Christian nation almost equally divided between Catholics and Lutherans; both sides remained loyal to Hitler and his vision for Germany throughout the war, along with the support of their pastors.

There has never been a nation in history that denied its nationalist dictator his war, once they are convinced he is fighting it for them, and share his vision of what he will deliver for them, which is to validate their culture as righteous.

Napoleon was given three chances to destroy his nation before defeat of his errant vision was finally accepted by the people. Just like the Germans about one hundred twenty-five years later, the French allowed their savior Napoleon to destroy their nation's youth and wealth for a full generation, and all this just a few years after rising up and destroying the aristocracy with its absolute power to abuse.

Ignorance and emotion seems to favor revenge more than quality of life. The longing for warrior leaders has been mesmerizing in almost all nations across the world since history has been recorded, and it is arguable that it lives on into the twenty-first century.

Like WWI, WWII can also be a lifetime study. Reading a good history of each is good preparation for understanding much of the conflict in the world following each war that still affects the never-ending speed bumps among nations and regions across the world to this day. Did control of the Suez Canal or invention of the machine gun create a solution to problems for European nations, or did they create new and more dangerous problems for the peoples of world? Did either create more reasons for leaders across the world to adopt reliance on reason over emotion that is the hallmark of our founders' wisdom? I believe we ignore their belief in tolerance and compromise as the price of freedom for each of us to pursue personal happiness at our peril.

In 1939 as WWII began with the German invasion of Poland, America was still an isolationist nation politically and militarily, as was reflected in both major political parties but more so in the GOP. This is typical of conservative governments the world over; they controlled the U.S. Congress during much of this era in, actually in league with the southern wing of the Democratic Party even as Democrat party presidents led the nation.

From 1939 through 1940 FDR was increasingly involved in attempting to assist the soon to be English wartime prime minister Winston

Churchill in arming for the war that soon included the German bombing of London, while the Congress remained committed to keeping America out of a European war. 1941 was the turning point of FDR's Administration.

January 1941 saw the New Deal phase end as FDR's key focus became wider with his four freedoms introduced in his State of the Union speech; they were Freedom from Fear, Freedom of Worship, Freedom from Want, and Freedom of Speech, which have been honored by his party as a focus ever since. Germany was threatening the freedom of all democratic nations and FDR needed to expand the world view of his fellow lawmakers if America was going to help ensure defeat of Hitler's intent.

March 1941 saw enactment of a Bill to Promote the Defense of the United States known as Lend Lease, designed to lend money and lease equipment to the nations who became our allies, mainly England and Russia. Over the next five years America funded the war effort against first the Germans and their ally Italy, and then Japan.

August 1941 saw the signing of the Atlantic Charter, a joint statement by FDR and Prime Minister Churchill on behalf of Great Britain and the United States. It laid out eight principles the two nations pledged as goals for the nations of the world; these were what their objectives would be in settlement after their enemies (the Axis), were defeated by America and its allies.

The pledge of the charter included the following:

1. No territorial gains.

2. Any territorial adjustments would be made with consent of the citizens considered.

3. Self determination is a right of all people.

4. A concerted effort would be made to lower trade barriers.

5. Advancement of social welfare and economic cooperation would be

recognized.

6. Work to establish freedom from fear and want.

7. Freedom of the seas was acknowledged as a goal.

8. They agreed to work to disarm aggressive nations.

In December 1941 Japan attacked the United States at Pearl Harbor on the Island of Oahu, Hawaii. Germany had already attacked Russia, and soon declared war on the United States. America was at war into the middle of 1945 in Europe and Asia and on all the seas of the world.

In 1945 by the end of the war America had provided over eight billion dollars to the war effort, primarily to England. In the end the equipment was left, and the debt was settled as a one billion dollar term loan. The war finally ended the depression as the war effort put not only men back to work, but as the men went to war, for the first time millions of women went to work for wages and continued in peace time. By the end of the war FDR had been dead for less than a year, and Churchill was defeated for reelection soon after the war.

FDR always believed in a balanced budget; he fought WWII and taxed to keep debt in check. Eventually the top income tax rate in America during the war was ninety percent on all income over four hundred thousand dollars per year. Truman and Eisenhower (Democrat and Republican presidents) would continue high taxes into the rebuilding of the U.S., Europe, and Japan after WWII, creating additional political blow back on top of the continued rejection of the New Deal among business conservative Republicans, and segregationist Democrats in the south.

FDR was not only willing to try new ideas, he was willing to take a second look at new ideas the court rejected, as well as re-thinking old ideas that were not working. When his first attempt at reform was rejected by ideology based bias, even in the face of starvation due to failure of the ideologist policies that led to the Depression, he did not give up, he persevered. He reworked the legislation until the court allowed him to put men back to work, banks back to lending, factories back to producing, and families back to believing in their and the nation's future. In the end he put the democracies back to defending themselves, and gave folks hope at home and across Europe that they could persevere to a more rational relationship between rich and poor at home, and between nations world wide.

The Conservatives did not like a single fiscal (government finance) or monetary (Federal Reserve) idea that FDR bought into, especially temporary deficit spending now known more or less as Keynesian pump priming. The employer of last resort is an example; government borrows on the short term to refinance the economy, and then taxes during the recovery to pay down the debt.

It is frustratingly interesting that the GOP has adopted an ideology that taxes so low it's intent is to create deficit spending on purpose to destroy the American government's ability to fund the common good or uphold established justice, which by definition almost always lessens the ability of the nation to ensure justice.

FDR created two budgets, one balanced to cover traditional government programs, the second funded with debt to be repaid when the economy recovered. He created a temporary Keynesian budget to help fund an alphabet list of temporary make-work programs intended to have sunset end dates in his first term, and then to win WWII in his second term. FDR then increased taxes sufficient to cover nearly all Congressional appropriations going forward after 1940. It was another twenty years later in President Kennedy's first term before taxes seriously began to be returned back to prewar levels.

Sustainable taxes driven by war profits finally funded the FDR recovery from the great depression, then funded WWII, and finally the rebuilding of America and Europe after the war. A high level of military spending continued for another thirty-six years to fund Cold War containment of Russia.

One last comment about the story of how FDR accomplished his latent rights goals in his second attempt at the New Deal, with the turning of one southern judge's vote who accepted FDR's preamble understanding of upholding established justice and the common good as an intent argument, and a compromise with southern congressional chairmen. An example of FDR's latent rights argument was labor rights, mentioned early. At our founding not enough wealth was produced using just human labor to worry about a share for labor beyond subsistence, and this had been true since the founding of feudalism. Men at the time worked long and hard just to feed themselves and provide shelter. However, once mechanization led to industrialization and one man could produce many times more value added wealth per day, the laborer had a latent right (unrecognized until the reality changed) to a portion of the new wealth. No one in the leadership class, owners, managers, legislators, pastors, or bankers agreed. They all saw that one hundred percent of the new wealth still belonged only to the few among this property owner supporting class of national leaders. I see this as ignoring the preamble intent to establish justice.

This is still pretty much the ideology of the GOP, its supporters, and those they influence. There is little support for the expanded mission the government must uphold to make an economy and to provide the services needed to keep the wheels turning across all the settlements. Only government can enforce these settled issues of rights across the contributions of our society of free men, making millions of exchanges every day, including assured mail deliveries, a strong dollar, enforceable contracts, stable interest rates, and stable exchange rates, that ensure a stable global economy. Only government can and does provide that degree of discipline, fairness, assurance, and the cost is a bargain compared to the chaos when government is not up to the task.

No emperor, philosopher, king, pope, or constitution of any country in the history of the world, and no other U.S. president in all of my reading has ever promised a share of national wealth as a goal for the wage laboring peoples of his country, let alone delivered, until FDR. His was the most transitional idea any president had introduced since Washington endorsed Madison's form of government and Hamilton's form of economy as our national government in 1791, and then gave the example of retiring back to life as a citizen.

In terms of U.S. governance, FDR's opponents managed to find loopholes to end labor rights without attacking the intent. Meaning no one says we want to destroy families' living wages, but they are comfortable to say democracy is not a proper labor union vehicle for enforcing membership dues for anyone who votes against paying dues, and some always do. However, no one ever refuses to accept the higher wages or better working conditions.

As mentioned, FDR did not live to see the end of WWII. In photos of FDR at Yalta, the last meeting of FDR, Churchill, and Stalin, he looked like a living ghost. Harry S. Truman was sworn in and oversaw the last five months of the war. He was a rational man and defined both the new consumer order in the United States to the benefit of the twelve million victorious young military men and women who returned, and the rebuilding of Europe in defiance of the old men of Europe who wished to return to the good old days of class privilege and colonialism, not to mention wars as common among themselves as boom and bust speculation among American billionaires since the golden age of the late 1800s.

Harry Truman had only been to lunch with FDR a few times and had not been briefed on the key strategies that led to the end of the war in Europe under General Dwight Eisenhower (who would replace Truman as president almost eight years later). Neither had he been briefed on the war in Japan led by General Douglas MacArthur (who Truman will fire over leadership of the Korean War six years later) nor the secret atomic bomb project called the Manhattan Project that would end the war once Truman made the final decision regarding the use of a nuclear bomb on two urban civilian populations in Japan.

The final three plus years of FDR's fourth term in 1946, 1947, and 1948 led by Harry Truman, was the beginning of the re-creation of Europe, Asia, and the United States, individually and interdependently. Order out of chaos, the world was divided half and half between free and captive by ideology, religion, culture, economics including wealth, education, and more than anything the leadership of rational men in the American government who were determined to create a new reality for the peoples of the world, and the relationships among nations.

In late 1945 America was led by one of the least well known or respected national leaders in the world, Harry S. Truman, a captain in WWI France, a failed haberdasher without a college degree, a ward politician from Kansas City, Missouri, selected by a ward boss in 1933 to become a nondescript senator, who only five months before had become a little known vice president of the United States.

On day one Truman had leading his cabinet the best known, respected, and capable United States general since George Washington, George Marshall. On day one no president could have had more respect for his Secretary of State. By the time President Truman and General Marshall retired from government no general ever had more respect for a president than did George Marshall for President Truman.

It may be hard to believe based on the paragraphs above but if there ever was a better Secretary of State in American history than Marshall it was in my opinion Dean Acheson, who was Truman's Secretary of State from 1949 until they both left office in 1954. If anyone ever had more respect for Harry Truman as a man and president than George Marshall, it was Dean Acheson. The achievements of these three men, Truman, Marshall, and Acheson, and their beneficial effect on the world created the high level of respect I have for this trio.

In 1970 Dean Acheson wrote his biography of their lives together, called *Present at the Creation*. If you only read one more book in your life, make it this one for sheer awe at just how great America has been at its best.

The book opens with this quote by Alfonso X of Spain who died in 1284: "Had I been present at the creation I would have given some useful hints for the better ordering of the universe".

As Harry Truman recreated the world after WWII for the better of us all, no one gave more or better suggestions to Harry than his friend Dean. Harry had also inherited FDR's so called brain trust including Henry Morgenthau and Harold Ickes, men who had already played key roles in creating the New Deal, and saving the American economy after the Great Depression.

I'm going to include the 1944 Bretton Woods Conference at this point as it was at the transition point between the two presidents led more by the team FDR had assembled in his cabinet including Acheson, that Harry Truman inherited in 1945. It introduced the first of the international agreements the western allies entered into for the governance of the relations among the allies for life after WWII.

FDR had stopped the movement of gold out of the U.S. as noted previously. In 1944 the Allies met in Bretton Woods, New Hampshire, at the Mount Washington Inn to work out an agreement for reestablishing trading, lending, and settling of international payments between each nation's monetary unit, the dollar, the pound, and so on pegged to an agreed price of gold (thirty-five dollars an ounce), with all agreeing not to devalue their currency against the set value they agreed to.

A lending entity was established called the International Monetary Fund (IMF), that was funded with agreed upon apportioned shares by the signing nations with leadership rotating among them. An international settlement bank was also established. This system worked for over sixty years, parts still do; the rise of worldwide trade and daily settlement by wire finally led to a new program for the twenty-first century.

From 1945 forward we will be on track to understanding how President Truman remade the world based on FDR's objectives of what I call rational boundaries and what Harry Truman called his Fair Deal domestically, his Marshall Plan and other such recovery programs among our allies and former enemies, and finally his containment policy regarding Russia and the spread of communism.

The outcomes of these three sets of objectives became the most successful eight years in history, affecting for the better the lives of billions of world citizens, and all with relatively little debt in the end.

At the time FDR died in February of 1945 and Truman became President, Germany was on the ropes but the war was not yet won; it would only be a matter of weeks in Europe until May 8th for the total surrender of Nazi Germany. The final peace conference of the war was held at Potsdam, Germany, where Truman attended his only meeting ever with Stalin. FDR had thought Stalin would be reasonable after the war, but Churchill knew better; Harry agreed with Churchill, after they met.

Stalin was already setting up satellite governments in the Eastern

European Capitals of the nations that abutted Russia. The United States was mopping up the Pacific Island portion of the war with Japan. Truman would authorize dropping the atomic bomb on Japan in August, and WWII was over. Stalin insisted on dividing Germany and Austria into four zones of control. President Truman spent the rest of his nearly two terms in office rebuilding Europe, America, and Japan, containing Russia, and sorting out the decolonization of the Continents.

To start our discussion of President Truman's post war contributions to America's future, as well as Europe's, I'll first list his major timeline decisions by title and year. We will then discuss these changes as they effected the various balls Harry and his team were juggling. Finally we will discuss the outcomes as well as the growing blow back by those who feared the loss of their cheap labor, oil, and low taxes, and those who resented the loss of their segregated privileges reestablished after the end of the slavery era in the American south.

I do my best to make my insights clear and understandable; some will agree, some will see bias, or retreat into intentional blindness. But this is the tug of war we have lived through during my eighty year lifetime in America, and it is ready to explode if the pressures continue to grow, as the most arbitrary third of Americans demand obedience to a shiny object they have elected president, who faced both impeachment and reelection in 2020. They demand first to destroy (deconstruct) what they now hate, even before they have a new improved plan. How they will remake the Constitution is no more thoughtful than their healthcare plan to replace Obama care was in 2017.

Here are the timelines of Harry Truman's plus seven year key actions and decisions by year with a brief comment. I have subscribed to the Miller Center of the University of Virginia's Study of the American Presidency Project for many years, and this list is their list, composed after Truman's decision to drop the atomic bombs and end WWII, and close enough to what my own list would be for the purpose of this book.

September 1945: a twenty-one point plan was formulated for re-conversion of the economy to peace time. A lesson in human nature and greed, all war contracts were canceled, war production ended, forty-five million men's and women's jobs were thereby also terminated, and twelve million military men were coming home with low job prospects.

Corporations wanted to end price controls and cut taxes. Truman held fast to both to allow time for the transition. Unions wanted an end to wage controls and a wage increase, and again Truman held fast for the same reason. Folks were angry, and unions went on strike, including major ones affecting every coal and railroad company. Truman announced he would take over the railroads and put the returning troops to work running them. The following year in frustration the nation elected GOP majorities in both houses of Congress.

September 1946: In his State of the Union Address, Truman called for a five point economic bill of rights for citizens regarding universal access to healthcare. The second major event of 1946 was Churchill's Iron Curtain Speech, defining Stalin and Russia as an isolated menace and calling for a plan (to address the threat).

March 1947: Truman (HST) announced his Truman Doctrine. This will become our national policy leading first to arms for Greece and Turkey as Stalin attempted to add these two countries to his invasion and capture of Eastern Europe after WWII, and later the Berlin Airlift in defense of a divided city, and still later the defense of the two Asian nations partitioned after WWII, Korea and Vietnam when the communist north invaded the democratic southern half.

June 1947: Two major actions; first the Marshall Plan is announced to rebuild Europe, second Truman vetoes the Taft-Hartley Bill; Congress overrode the veto, which ended union members democratic rights in Clause 7 of the Wagner Act that made unions legal (this will be a major if little remembered beginning of the end of labor unions' living wage gains in America).

July 1947: Truman created the Department of Defense, the National Security Council, and the CIA. These three agencies fought and won what became known as the cold war over the next forty-six years until nearly the end of the twentieth century, and have fought the twenty-first century war on terror at the onset of the century. The Democrats' policies funded the cold war era with taxes even when we had GOP presidents, and the GOP policies have funded the war on terror with debt even when we have had a Democratic president.

April 1948: Truman asked Congress for the first Civil Rights Bill in reaction to how returning black veterans were again being subjected to intimidation, coercion, and physical abuse. In July Truman desegregated the U.S. Military.

May 1948: Truman recognized Israel as a nation and the Palestinians' right to a nation, approving a UN resolution.

June 1948: On the 24th the Soviet Union blockaded West Berlin, a divided city in the divided country of defeated Germany after WWII, leading Stalin to reopen the city.

Note: 1948 was a re-election year, and against all odds based on the midterm outcome two years before when all the frustration of re-conversion had put Congress in the hands of the GOP, Truman was re-elected and the Democrats even regained Congress.

At the 1948 Democratic Convention in reaction to Truman's civil rights actions, Strom Thurmond the segregationist governor of South Carolina, walked out of the Convention, and ran against Truman as a "Dixiecrat", winning four southern states. Strom will play a key role in creating the new GOP anti New Deal southern strategy conservative GOP that finally elected Ronald Reagan who pledged to repeal the New Deal in 1980.

It was only in the 1980 presidential election the Democrats will learn how little hourly wage union folks understood or cared about the concepts behind labor rights and law that FDR and Frances Perkins had worked so hard to implement. The emotions and cultural bias of folks who lived lives of physical labor overcame any supposed best interest beliefs of economists with PhDs about citizens in voting booths.

HST began his first elected term as president with a State of the Union speech on January 5, 1949, asking Congress to send him a new set of bills to sign to implement a program he called his Fair Deal Act.

1949: NATO was formed. Of all of Truman's team ideas after WWII, this is one of the most successful of his many enduring and civilizing ideas during his post WWII leadership years. The key concept was Article 5, an attack on any member is an attack on all members. Europe went from almost never having a period of more than twenty years between wars for around a thousand years, to no war in Europe between NATO countries for the past seventy plus years.

August 1949: HST issued his white paper on China that established America's China policy for the next twenty-five years until Richard Nixon and Henry Kissinger opened China again to international diplomacy.

October 1949: Peoples Republic of China was established.

October 1950: McCarthyism and red scare of the GOP, and the American Medical Association (AMA) began and has continued to control healthcare policy in America, with cash to legislators, and spending on negative ads against any control of healthcare cost.

October 1950: The Federal Minimum Wage Program began.

October 1950: North Korea invaded South Korea. HST ordered the U.S. Army to Korea to stop the invasion.

April 1951: HST fires General MacArthur for insubordination regarding MacArthur's plan to invade China; Truman fought in WWI, ordered the dropping of the Atomic Bomb to end WWII, and believed in containment to end the cold war with communism without starting WWIII. By then both the U.S. and Russia had the atomic bomb, and China had a million citizens to man a military effort, and Russia and China controlled nearly half of the land area in the world, making such a war potentially a total human disaster.

1951: Greed continued, Truman nationalized the steel mills over strikes during wartime.

1952: The Supreme Court ruled nationalizing the steel mills was unconstitutional.

1953: Truman worked out a backroom deal with southern segregationists who defeated universal healthcare during Jim Crow, to provide family healthcare for white men who won WWII. The scheme was to make healthcare funding employment based. The U.S. Government would help fund it with a tax deduction only for the corporation or referral union (unions who collect the pay of their members from the employer and pay wages and benefits after dues deductions). A secondary reason Truman was so determined to establish universal healthcare was the terrible health of American men drafted into the military to man WWII. Men were drafted between eighteen and forty-nine years old. Of those eighteen to thirty-four years old about thirty-five percent were unfit to serve due to poor health, and of those between thirty-five and forty-nine about half were unfit. Most of the issues were preventable if rural America had had access to healthcare.

In the time of Jim Crow, unions and corporations practiced de facto segregation (not by law, but by agreed practice) meaning they did not hire black citizens as employees. In 1964 healthcare became more widely available to blacks and women once the Civil Rights Bill was signed by President Lyndon B. Johnson (LBJ), ending under law all segregation policies in America. Black citizens who had access to employer tax exempt healthcare funding after 1964 saw their access diminish after Reagan's Free Trade decision in 1985 decimated union jobs in manufacturing once they had to compete with wages from China.

It is ironic that in 2019 the GOP defended this racially biased solution to government help funding health insurance only for white employees. Nearly seventy years before the GOP had called Harry Truman's healthcare concern for the American people as socialist at best and communist at worst. At the time Harry let the IRS quietly allow this partial solution for white people only; it was never voted on by Congress or signed by a president as an administrative decision. It is still discriminatory against all non union and corporate employees, as they are still the only folks entitled to this national tax break to access healthcare.

In 1952 before he left office Truman addressed the AMA, the John Birch Society, and the GOP's use of the term "socialism", as a pejorative with this quote:

"Socialism is a scare word they have hurled at every advance the people have made in the last twenty years. Socialism is what they called Public Power (electric power dams). Socialism is what they called Social Security. Socialism is what they called farm price supports. Socialism is what they called Bank Deposit Insurance. Socialism is what they called the growth of free and independent labor organizations. Socialism is what they call almost anything that helps all the people."

We mentioned North Korea, North Vietnam, and the People's Republic of China, as containment conflict points during the Truman years. In all three countries Stalin played a role in supporting a nationalist to lead a communist takeover after WWII in these former colonial countries.

We have already noted that in the Middle East and India England wished to continue their empires after the war France did also in Vietnam as well as in the Middle East and countries in North Africa. Four presidents played increasing roles in decolonization between the end of WWI, until Dwight Eisenhower made his decision to support France, and sent military advisers into Vietnam forty-one years later.

America became a free nation by revolting against colonialism, and ever since has created business interests around the world, and in the process has had some serious influence and interest in colonial or former colonial nations being pursued by Russian influence among nationalist leaders. Over the rest of this book we will review the conflict for America as native peoples revolt against the leadership that controlled commercially valuable crops, mines, and so on. Too often America will see native folks revolt as terrorists. At times we will defend our own corporations as the newly free natives wish to nationalize their warm weather crop land and extraction industry raw materials.

While there was little knowledge in such countries of the concepts of democracy or capitalism, or communism for that matter, there was resentment of colonial masters, and of the local families who had gained control of local wealth with the support of the colonial nations, usually England, France, the Netherlands, Belgium, and Portugal. In most of these occupied colonial countries the leaders became businessmen, Christians, wealthy, spoke English, and gained control of the nation's military such as it was.

Their armies were hounded by nationalists branded as terrorists and supported by Stalin. America was committed to independence as well as support of trade partners, and was partial to Christianity over godless communism. There were no good choices. Whatever Roosevelt thought he had gained by inserting some anti-colonial issues into his Atlantic Charter, England had no commitment to this provision. Truman supported independence for India, and he had influence as he was helping England recover after having helped them defeat fascism.

We will see these issues come to a head in the Eisenhower Administration, largely in a less than admirable manner under the Dulles brothers, Allen as head of the CIA, and John Foster as Secretary of State; America will deal with the fallout for the rest of this book. These types of issues are factors of today's gridlock in 2020.

Democracy is an American ideal, but never advanced to the extent that capitalism and Christianity have been exported as civilizing concepts by American or European interests, just as the wealthy in America have not fully supported full democracy or individual citizen rights much beyond due process in the courts here at home in the domestic politics of the United States, and then only for white citizens. Such is the nature of best interest politics among leadership that truly understand and can afford to fight for their best interests. Examples include America backed leaders Syngman Rhee, a Methodist business man in Korea, and Ngo Dinh Diem a Catholic business man in Vietnam. America went to war in both countries in the 1950s, and lost over fifty thousand American soldiers in each war, without changing the nationalists supported by Russia during the cold war. The war weariness in twenty-first century America is largely a legacy of these years of containment. The alternative would have been WWIII.

In Korea the people of the south became successful after the war was won. In Vietnam the people north and south supported the northern leader who chose communism, and disrespected the southern leader who lost in spite of our support. In both cases our men died to ensure that Russia and the world knew America was dedicated to keeping communism contained, and nuclear war at bay

Democracy in poor countries with majority illiterate populations is problematic as Thomas Jefferson knew at our founding, especially if first time local voters favored nationalists whose stated primary concern was land repatriation over outside economic development. All of these WWI and WWII leftover issues continue to be troublesome to America in the twenty-first century, especially in the Middle East, and Central America.

While we are still in the second term of HST let me add a note about Harry and the union men he helped who did little to provide oversight of their new organizations. Too many unions were taken over by thugs, while too few developed into professional organizations that did a good job of representing their members. I believe there is a role for the union movement in America's future for want of a better solution. It will take as much regulation of labor leaders as is required for bank leaders and for the same reasons. I mentioned referral unions in connection with payroll tax breaks for healthcare. A key factor of referral unions became pension funding. These funds were administered by the unions, the largest being the Teamsters. Just ahead we will review the role corruption played once union leaders had access to billions of dollars. The greed came easily, the outcome contributed to the loss of support. Any resurrection will require solving the working man's problems with greed among the folks who become their fiduciaries. They have been let down by Wall Street, unions, corporations, and U.S. politicians.

FDR's philosophy of "social insurance" was later endorsed by President Truman who introduced it in Europe as we Americans funded rebuilding Europe, established NATO, and introduced new constitutions that embedded sustainable distribution of wealth sharing as a national goal in most European nations; what we define as Social Insurance, they define as Social Democracy.

Here at home at best modern GOP Movement Conservatism is an ideal of individualism. At worst it defines the New Deal as anti-Christian and anti-capitalism, seeing too many of its supporters too comfortable with socialism and/or communism as a future economic philosophy for the nation.

If the right ever acknowledged they understood the difference between state ownership of asset socialism, or state central planning control of all aspects of the economy (which defines communism), and FDR's New Deal Social Insurance, they never admitted it; in fact they freely equated them as three peas in one philosophical pod, the ultimate spin in American political best interest history.

To recognize what Teddy Roosevelt, Woodrow Wilson, Franklin Roosevelt, Harry Truman, Lyndon Johnson, and Jimmy Carter understood, and the GOP treats with skillful neglect, is to understand what a modern nation must know about wealth and economic security before it can establish rational boundaries instead of mutual opportunism as the economic rationale for the nation.

Wealth building requires a system of courts and regulations to ensure orderly business transactions, not to mention the cost of defense of our freedom from outside domination. There is also the cost of investing in an educated workforce, and the value of access to America's three hundred million plus consumers. America has maintained the world's safest monetary system since its inception as reviewed in Chapter 8, and it has proven so even in times of world wars and major economic crashes. It is the safest economic system in the history of the world to this day in spite of twenty-two trillion dollars of debt.

I started and ran a successful business for almost thirty years. I acknowledge I could not have been successful without all of the government supported factors that I made use of daily, from educated employees to roads, cheap secure mail service, and safe affordable banking, with courts to protect my assets and contracts, even safe water and sewer systems, and a stable currency, all these factors among other daily services I was hardly aware of day to day.

I always felt safe to quote a fixed price for a product I would not deliver for months, even though I had to purchase the materials within days, and fund my labor costs for weeks, and then wait additional weeks for major corporations to fund my invoices. A central bank was established in 1913 that routinely met a daily goal of a stable money supply including predictable interest rates in normal times. Anyone who threatens to not pay our debt is a fool, and they are common in our current Congress.

Back to our time line. What was Strom Thurmond up to back home in the south after running against Harry Truman in 1948? Strom redefined the rationale for subjugation of the black man based on the teachings of the Rev. Billy Graham. Billy preached the black man was not inferior to the white man, he was in fact a child of God just like men of all races. However, Billy believed that because America had a very complex economy and form of government, segregation was still acceptable due to the fact the black man was not yet ready to play an integrated role.

How did this new understanding fit the post war anti New Deal Movement Conservative ideology? Leading off the eastern wing of the GOP led by William F. Buckley, aligned with Movement Conservatives led by Bob Taft in the mid-west and the Libertarian John Birch Society's first generation corporate wealth accumulators in the west, now superseded by their sons and daughters as the Koch Network, all bought into and accepted Billy Graham's and Strom Thurmond's justification for what they were satisfied was a more humane justification for segregation.

Strom's use of this new insight for testing GOP leadership to see if the party would welcome conservative voters if they enforced a form of segregation that did not deny the black man's place in God's creation, just the level of participation he was ready to assume, led to the south becoming known in the GOP not as the segregationist wing of the GOP but as the Evangelical wing of the GOP, as the GOP welcomed the religious south anti secular, Biblical disdain for the bill of rights, in concert with the GOP corporate wings Biblical disdain for labor rights, preferring a return to the just vineyard owners' authority to set wages.

Two Senators, one a member of the John Birch Society as a member of a dynastic wealth family, Barry Goldwater, and the other Strom

Thurmond of the old segregated south, became friends and co-founders of the marriage of old family money, and old reliable conservative evangelical voters. In the GOP the Birchers became the Koch Network, and in the South the evangelical pastors joined together in an alliance to return the United States to how the world would be if the ratification of the U.S. Constitution in 1789 had been unconditional. They have never set a goal of overthrowing the U.S. Constitution, they just want to nullify the Bill of Rights. That battle, already won once in the Civil War, is the battle we will review again over the balance of this book.

Note: The Koch Network and George Soros will each play an important external role in the ideology of the two parties, Charles Koch in the GOP and George Soros less so, but a similar role from the 1960s on.

I'll comment here as Koch's input will be a factor over the remainder of the book. I do not agree with the ideology of either Koch or Soros, however I say this early as each party uses the other as a scapegoat. Charles Koch's father was a genius chemist and made a fortune inventing jet fuel, among other things, and Charles and his brother have increased the family fortune since the father died, and I say good for them. However, I do not understand their all but absolute rejection of the idea that families of dynastic wealth owe a duty to pay a fair share of the taxes to support the nation that has enabled their success, or a living wage to employees in the nation who do all of the hourly wage value added work required to support our plus twenty trillion dollar economy.

George Soros made his own fortune by escaping from Hungary where he was born during the occupation by the Nazis, to London where he lived into his teen years under the communist domination of his country after WWII ended Nazi occupation. Based on his early life I do understand the Soros Open Border initiative. Koch seems without empathy for the working poor and wedded to greed, while Soros seems to be a rich victim who can afford to demand what no or few nations will ever agree to, and that is open borders; it would be a form of national madness, but he longed for them all his early life.

Once again back to our time line. Not in order of sequence or consequence but as a free flow recollection of how this all evolved, let me add the following. Truman approved the formation of Israel and its inclusion in the United Nations, and successfully steered this through Congress. At the same time Truman also approved Jordan with a ninety-five percent Palestinian population as a homeland for the Palestinians, a fact no longer acknowledged by anyone other than the Palestinians and the UN.

Israel's neighboring nations had resisted the settlement of Israel since the end of WWI. Russia which was now an oil exporter saw an opportunity for a role in the Middle East, especially in oil rich Iran, and they wanted a warm water port in Syria. As an ally they successfully established a foothold in each. Today the United States is involved in a most complex stalemate with Russia over the Middle East, even more complex than our long effort to see the re-establishment of the eastern portion of the Hapsburg Empire that collapsed along with the Ottomans as independent nations at the end of the First World War.

The Iran oil issue between Britain and Russia became worse in the Eisenhower presidency, more so than in Truman's. Arab Muslims engaged in terrorism, oil disruption and anti-Israel feelings as a mix of unresolved grievances, continuing still as I write.

The Middle East is dominated by a singularly narrow church state approach to authority to govern and absolute loyalty to a religious law doctrine that creates acrimonious relationships with most of the non-Muslim border and trading nations they come in contact with.

This has the West in a desperate standoff with non-state terrorism, supported religiously by the religious side of Islamic Law, and supported financially by the state side of Islamic law. As we reviewed early in this story, only in Islamic states are church and state joined in law based on the nation's and the religion's singular founding document, the Qur'an, a fact that is impossible to reconcile as a legacy of colonialism for many young Muslims who are living in modern democracies in the west.

My father puzzled to understand his loyalty to America and his Catholic Church. Similarly, Muslims who served Britain in the colonial past were given passports to protect them from retaliation once the British left India and the Middle East, and today their grandchildren are British, but do not fit in the national culture; they feel alienated. They are too often open to ideas of revenge for the frustration they feel.

Truman was aware of the need for trade and rebuilding not only the infrastructure of European countries, but also their economies, treasuries, military, and world vision. After the war he replaced FDR's Secretary of the Treasury Henry Morgenthau with Fred Vinson who saw the implementation of the Bretton Woods economic, trade, settlement and exchange systems into the rebuilding of Europe, along with NATO, mentioned above.

In Europe Truman did some of his finest work. Truman forced Britain and France to forego the reparations they once again wished to impose on Germany. He invited all three major European nations to accept a stable arrangement that eventually became the European Union. As we noted previously, FDR's Secretary of State whom Truman loved, General Marshall, was finally replaced by Dean Acheson, who may have been the most successful Secretary of State in history. Acheson oversaw Truman's successful rebuilding of Europe's governments, infrastructure and institutions.

Although the Germans were not permitted to have a standing army they were the key manufacturing support country in Europe, and were an important aspect of making NATO successful in containing Russia during the cold war, as opposed to continuing to fight France and Britain every twenty years. The NATO-ensured peace is still working, but President Trump casually discussed ending our role in the NATO alliance as it has existed for seventy years. Trump called for a review and/or an update of the role NATO should play in the twenty-first century, using a funding showdown as a negotiating tool. Let's hope NATO endures as long as Russia operates as a political, economic and military threat to the West, while armed with more nuclear devices than the U.S.

Most of Germany's factories had been appropriated and moved to Russia as part of the western allies' settlement with Russia in Eastern Europe. Russia had played the largest role in defeating Hitler. Stalin, the Russian dictator, attempted to assert his authority over Eastern Europe by ordering a blockade of all Berlin, which had been divided into eastern and western controlled sections within East Germany at war's end.

Truman had General Marshall oversee air shipments of supplies to the besieged Berliners which became known as the Berlin Airlift. It successfully ended the blockade and froze in place a "cold war" between free western nations and a ring of satellite subordinate buffer states under Russian control known as the Union of Soviet Socialist Republics, better know as the USSR.

These buffer states lived in isolation from the rest of Europe for the next forty years in what became defined as the Cold War, meaning no open warfare, and no normal relations including trade, travel, or even communications on the peaceful side of international relations, and no diplomatic, military, or alliances on the diplomatic side of international state norms.

Truman forced France and Germany to accept sharing the coal and iron fields that bordered both countries and had been fought over for hundreds of years. This helped confine Soviet (Russian) influence to the eastern half of Europe only. The dividing line between the Soviet-dominated communist countries and the independent countries, the so-called Iron Curtain, came to symbolize the lack of communication between the two regions. This Iron Curtain held for almost fifty years after WWII until the fall of Soviet communism in 1991.

In spite of Truman's many accomplishments he faced fierce opposition as he ran for the Democratic nomination for president in his own right in 1948. In his own party Henry Wallace the former vice president and socialist threw his hat in the ring. At the Convention Truman accepted civil rights into the party platform for the first time in either party, as a nod to northern governors and mayors coming to grips with growing black populations migrating from the rural south.

It was federal tax money from wealthier northern states that was used to fund southern hospitals, schools, and other community funding for police, fire, and public buildings such as country court houses and jails, and city halls, and other public use equipment and buildings. The goal was to always take the money, while denying federal government oversight of any subsidy money the Congress authorized. This was the federalism money the south craved while hating the oversight that came with it.

Subsidy money in poor states is a strong desire; abiding the source of the funding and U.S. Congressional oversight of how it is spent is another matter. Each new lowering of the wall between church and state in secular law America is a cautionary tale, as "pork" not only went to state houses and town halls, but also to religious schools after 1954.

If evangelicals are successful in maintaining access to federal taxpayer money while denying oversight to the representatives of the taxpayers from the twenty wealthy blue states, and if we allow block grant federalism as well as tax money to continue to be used to support tax exempt Christian academies, then every non-evangelical taxpayer from a blue state will be subject to abuse under the Constitution, as state welfare money allows segregationists to continue to deny jobs and food stamps for black citizens while using federalism interstate welfare to educate segregated white children.

1948 was a landmark year in U.S. political history that reverberates to this day. Senator Robert Taft of Ohio's wing of the Republican Party saw the New Deal administration of FDR, and what followed in Truman's administration as filled with communists and their policies, or as socialists at best if not communists in fact. The reason for Senators Taft's suspicions was the legacy of flirting with communist theories of social justice by early union labor leaders in America in the face of what amounted to domestic imperialism by industrialists.

Taft as the GOP leader of the Senate was as opposed to labor rights in 1948, as he had been in favor of isolationist policies before the war, and against pump priming during the depression. Remember, Taft was the leader in getting the anti-union Taft-Hartley Bill enacted in 1947, which enabled right-to-work laws in the southern states.

Another factor was Taft's tolerance for demagogues if it aided his political advantage. The Taft wing of the GOP long held a belief that

Roosevelt, as a sick man at Yalta, gave away too much to Stalin. This split came to a head when a junior Wisconsin Senator was allowed to engage in false accusations in a process that came to be called McCarthyism, taken from the last name of their demagogic committee chair of the Senate Committee on Un-American Activities. Taft announced his decision to seek the Republican nomination for president in 1948, along with New York's Governor Dewey.

The Main Street Republicans were less arch conservative than the Dixiecrat Democrats in the south who were also strongly white nationalist, or the anti-communist Taft Wing of the Republican Party in the Midwest and northeast, where a new conservative ideology was forming.

This was a cross between what became known as Neocon military hawks (another hybrid mix of policies that favored the military) who were absolute supporters of property rights over individual rights, and supported a corporate advocacy form of conservative orthodoxy led by the media mogul William F. Buckley, and the members of the John Birch Society among others including the father of today's Koch Network leaders, and Strom Thurmond of South as the leader of evangelical Christian segregationists in the states of the old south.

The Neocon faction as well as an emerging Libertarian wing of the GOP were dedicated to preservation of the rights of corporate families' dynastic accumulated wealth as a political power base. Both would be led by sons whose fathers operated as publishers of supportive political magazines, Bill Crystal and Steve Forbes among others. At the time and into the 1970s there was also a strong Neocon faction in the Democratic Party led by Senator Scoop Jackson of Washington state, and Sam Nunn of Georgia.

After the 1952 presidential election a war hero, General Dwight Eisenhower, ran as a pragmatist Republican. Tensions grew between Main Street Republicans like Dewey (who the GOP ran for president in 1948 defeating Robert Taft, the founder along with Thurmond and Buckley) and a group of western state conservatives who were primarily Libertarians of what was known as the Movement Conservative in the 1948 GOP primary campaign.

The last and most influential funding wing of this new movement ran their first presidential candidate in 1964, Barry Goldwater. More about Goldwater (an anti communist, anti union member of the John Birch Society) in the 1964 time frame of this book. These pro-business, pro-military, anti-union wings would form the reactionary core of America's next economic era. They aligned with Strom Thurmond's evangelical, segregationist, right-to-work wing in the Reagan Era (as I've called it for the purpose of defining key eras of economic governance in American history).

There was one key exception to isolationism and the focus of a communist scare by the Taft Wing of the GOP in Congress after WWII. This exception was the support Truman and his key team, General George Marshall as Secretary of Defense and Dean Acheson as Secretary of State, received from the GOP Chairman of the Foreign Relations Committee Arthur Vandenberg, a Senator from Michigan.

For the most part Vandenberg is forgotten today, but he was essential in the containment of the U.S.SR, and the establishment of NATO and the United Nations. These became possible only with Vandenberg's support of Truman's foreign policies, and would have been all but impossible to implement without Vandenberg's support and leadership in Congress as a GOP Chairman, with the GOP the majority in the Senate. This is the kind of bipartisanship every nation needs more of regarding big decisions at times of transition that has become impossible in the twenty-first century as absolutism has become the governing norm.

Stalin was trying to push Greece and Turkey into the Soviet sphere of influence at the end of WWII, and Vandenberg supported Truman's decision to draw the line with the Soviet Union over both countries. Vandenberg, Truman and Truman's team kept western Europe free from Communism and prevented a possible WWIII. Shortly after Churchill's concept of the Iron Curtain and Truman's concept of Containment fell into place as another piece of the puzzle of post WWII, America came together. We see most issues were not settled by just one factor of national and international life. The same issues arose over many different settlements, and often the same players were involved. This is how it evolved between 1945 and 1965 as the Democrats put post war American in place, and the GOP reacted time and time again just as angry about the rebuilding of the nation as they had been about rescuing the economy and the families destroyed by GOP speculative banking and capitalism using regulations.

A few thoughts about the relationships among Russia, the Orthodox branch of Christianity, Eastern Europe, and the Ottomans. We usually think of the Ottomans as Muslims with dominion over the Arabs. In the West we do not think much about their role in the Orthodox areas of Eastern Europe. As for Russia we do not give much thought to their impact on western governance until 1945 and the end of WWII. We have seen already that the Ottoman and Hapsburg Empires struggled to govern Eastern Europe, yet neither was an Orthodox Empire.

The Turkish people, who became first the Roman Empire in the East and today the nation of Turkey, were and are considered among the best warriors in the world, and the most effective armies over the centuries. Today they are part of NATO, uneasy in the alliance. They were and are Muslim with a secular government. There have only been a few, Iraq was another until 1979.

The orthodox Christian countries were all small and/or had weak governments, again a cautionary tale as are some countries in South America for those who advocate small or weak central government. They had been dominated for seven hundred years until Peter the Great of Russia defeated the strongest western Europe protestant warrior king, surprisingly Charles XII of Sweden in 1709.

Two years later Peter was nearly defeated by the Ottomans when he as leader of the orthodox countries and fought and nearly lost a war with the Ottomans, who ruled over several orthodox countries under Muslim rule at the beginning of the eighteenth century. The Russian czars ruling by divine orthodox rights were finally overthrown by communist revolutionaries in 1918.

Russia was ruled as a form of nationalism defined by a political party, more than a philosophy of communism, as a dictatorship which ruled by domination, eventually leading to militaristic control of all abutting nations in a socialist union that functioned like a colonial empire. Empires are always seen in this book as domination, which is an imposed authority to govern and never includes equality or freedom for the citizens of colonized nations. It is a system of coerced labor, and loss of national treasure under direct or purchased police or military control.

The authority to rule was based on party control of the military. This central form of governance lasted from 1918 until 1991, collapsing due to failure to create enough wealth and having never accepted capitalism, the only economic system anywhere that can produce enough wealth for all to be happy depending on limits on distribution. However, capitalist countries seldom have happy citizens, as money legal or not politically limits just distribution of the great wealth.

Back to President Truman's post WWII rebuilding of Europe and containment of Russian aggression in Eastern Europe and Southeast Asia, as well as a form of domination of former Ottoman countries on the Black Sea and south of the Russian border in the Muslim countries west of Turkey and the Black Sea. This is an area still in contention under current Russian president Putin who continues the Russian empire instincts of controlling all Russian border states. However, in the twenty-first century he seems to be striving to create a similar system of nationalism among eastern oligarchs in league with national religious leaders, much as the GOP under Trump as a unitary president and McConnell and the Koch Federalist court is doing in the U.S. Israel, as small as it is, seems to be in cahoots with this scheme.

Truman himself was proud to give his friend Arthur Vandenberg the credit he deserved. Today, Vandenberg's contributions would not be possible since President Reagan introduced absolutism as a governing tactic, imposing domination in place of our Constitutional system of divided government. In 2020 Donald Trump is in battle with the to determine if America will continue as a democracy or become a white apartheid government.

The Reagan brand of absolutism has not been used to govern or to advance the American economy or security, but rather it has been used as a tool to build a loyal reactionary base for the GOP. Today's Freedom Caucus and the gerrymandering that supports it would not be possible without absolutism, and as we will learn, a disastrous loosening of the committee system in Congress in the 1970s. The source concept behind Reagan style absolutism germinated in an American corporation where Ronald Reagan worked in the 1950s before his rise to fame in GOP politics in the 1960s.

During the Truman post war era, Chinese communist/ nationalist Mao Zedong, supported by Russia, ousted the Christian pro-business leader of China, General Chiang Kai-Shek. Chiang was the chairman of the nationalist government of China at the end of WWII. His political party, the Nationalist Party, was formed after the revolution that overthrew the Chinese emperor in 1912. The reason I mentioned the fact that Chiang Kai-Shek in China and Diem in Vietnam and Rhee in Korea had business and Christian credentials is because of how the Asian branch of the State Department developed during the first half of the twentieth century.

America did business in Asia, and where ever American businesses were established, American missionaries followed. Many of the sons of missionaries went to Princeton's School of Diplomacy and into the State Department after WWII. American diplomats backed Chiang Kai-Shek in China's civil war, while in the north Russia backed northern leaders in nations that shared a border with Russia. The third key civil war country besides China and Vietnam was Korea. Again American diplomats backed Christian business man Sygman Rhee in Korea's capital city Seoul. None of these American backed leaders had the support of the Korean, Vietnamese or Chinese people, almost all peasants.

The small still divided country of Korea played and still plays a large role in the standoff between the United States and China. Korea was ruled by Japan from 1910 until the end of WWII when it was divided into two states, communist North Korea and democratic South Korea. Both countries were supported by their sponsor during the Cold War, and are now allied with their former sponsors as independent nations.

The Russians and the Chinese supported the communist leader of North Korea. The U.S. supported South Korea's leader Sygman Rhee. In the middle of Truman's second term in 1950, North Korea invaded South Korea beginning what is known as the Korean War which Truman referred to as a Police Action.

Truman sent General MacArthur, who had fought and defeated Japan in WWII, back into battle and the U.S. drove the Korean communists all the way back to the Chinese border.

MacArthur wanted to end communism in China, but Truman refused as he only wanted to contain communism, not start a nuclear WWIII. In the end MacArthur engaged the press and Congress behind Truman's back, and Truman fired him. The Korean War slogged on until a truce was called along the thirty-seventh parallel in 1953, over a year into President Eisenhower's first term. That war is still in a status of truce, with troops along both borders.

Truman's doctrine of containment of communism was supported long past his presidency, through the end of the Korean War, the Vietnam War, during the presidencies of Eisenhower, Kennedy, Johnson, Nixon, Ford, and Carter. Reagan continued this policy on steroids, just as a new communist leader was recognizing the failing state of the domestic Russian economy, Mikhail Gorbachev.

Today as an oil and gas exporter with a former KBG (secret police) president, the communist party and the Russian military are back to interfering with any country that abuts the Russian border. Since 1998 Russia under Putin has continued to bluster on the world stage, remains distrustful of NATO's concern with Russian objectives in Eastern Europe, and remains a nuclear threat to be engaged with caution. President Donald Trump has a confusing relationship with President Putin. So far he has been less than forthcoming about his long association with sales of condominiums in the U.S. that are bought with laundered money through offshore banks into NYC lawyers offices associated with the Jewish wing of the so called Russian Mafia. That relationship has been reported for about twenty years. Dozens of hotels and thousands of condos have been sold in this manner by Donald Trump's business over the past twenty-five years per the book *House of Putin, House of Trump,* and the New York Times. In the 1990s Putin took control of Russian mineral and oil assets, and became an oligarch and a dominate leader of Russia.

In America in the 1990s Donald Trump, heir of apartment wealth in NYC, took control of gambling in New Jersey and became a desperate debtor in possession of distressed real estate. A private mutually beneficial relationship that formed in the dark in the 1990s came to light as Donald Trump became president of the United States and Vladimir Putin served as president of Russia at the end of the second decade of the twenty-first century. If this was all an aboveboard relationship or was nefarious is a key issue as America's two dominate political parties ramp up the 2020 presidential campaign.

In the Middle East, Nixon, Ford, Carter, and Reagan all dealt with containment of communism, lasting until the fall of communism in Russia in 1991. It was renewed in the twenty-first century in a less virulent manner, due to the European purchase of Russian gas and oil. However, as Russia has been involved in Muslim country issues for three hundred years including warm water ports and abutting nation concerns, America's Middle East dilemmas make them Russia's dilemmas also.

Truman rebuilt Europe without putting the European countries in debt, which allowed them to fund universal health care and free college tuition, among other social programs that are not enjoyed as yet in America. In my view our healthcare system is our financial Achilles' heel, being funded primarily as a payroll cost in what is now a global economy.

The non-corporate employed more or less half of American hourly wage families who almost universally have inadequately funded healthcare access, without any government tax consideration. This is because all corporate employed citizens enjoy a government tax exemption that non-corporate employed Americans are denied. This abuse was instituted as a racial legacy that denied equality, a legacy of misuse of the Fourteenth Amendment that established blacks freed from slavery as citizens, but still denied participation in the economy and government of the nation. All of which will be fully explained in Chapter 10 as GOP jurists vetted first by the Koch supported Federalist Society become a majority on the Supreme Court.

Today America lives with gridlock regarding poverty without access to healthcare as a right, and a legacy of racial reality remaining stalled in transition. This makes the complex stepping stones that inform this legacy, many of them set in cement and in the dark, difficult to spell out in simple terms. As Trump said, "who knew healthcare would be so hard".

In my summary I'll advance a two part solution for a fully funded universal healthcare system that does not involve payrolls in the global economy, or income taxes in a time of anti income tax sentiment. I do support a public option as a stepping stone if America is going to keep healthcare a federal issue. I believe it is time to consider making it a state issue; this would almost for sure make abortion, one of the most gridlocked policy fight in the nation, a state issue also.

Truman is not particularly well remembered for his civil rights accomplishments but he did desegregate the U.S. Army in 1948, and accepted a civil rights mention in the 1948 Democratic Party campaign platform as a nod to big city Democrat mayors, who by then had sizable black populations in their cities migrating in from the newly mechanized agricultural south. Jobs in the northern cities were mostly working for corporations directly or assigned by a trade union. Under Jim Crow laws in the south and by tradition in the north, neither corporations nor unions hired black folks.

As early as 1948 three years after the end of WWII the south was mechanizing, and the available jobs for agricultural workers were falling fast. The surplus workers were being shipped north, usually with a bus ticket, a bag of sandwiches, and twenty dollars. This was the precursor to today's inner city dilemma.

Three years later in 1951, with the concurrence of industry, labor, and all factions of his party, President Truman quietly instructed the IRS to issue a new benefit for white employees across America but the word white was never mentioned. In the days of Jim Crow blacks were barred from employment by corporations and unions, so in fact the new benefit only applied to white citizens.

This so called employer provided health insurance tax break is still in place, and remains the most expensive and the most discriminatory tax exemption of any tax break ever granted. Truman's Treasury Department's IRS tax collection division in 1951 granted this tax deduction for the employer and employee if the employer chose to offer paid healthcare as a benefit. The cost was tax deductible for the employer, and the prepaid insurance was a tax free benefit for the employee.

In the run up to the 2020 presidential elections some Democrats are supporting an ill defined policy they are calling Medicare for all. This is a disservice to what Medicare is and is not, and what universal healthcare or a single payer system provides including cost savings. All Republicans who have spoken out, and even some Democrats are noting that more than sixty percent of Americans have employer funded (fully or partially) healthcare and do not want to lose it; politicians who think this is true do not want to lose the support of these voters. No one is saying if Medicare would still be prohibited from negotiating drug prices with drug companies who are allowed unlimited spending on political speech that is used to fund scare ads to protect their greed, even as citizens die for lack of access to high cost drugs as inexpensive to make as insulin.

This benefit continued as a basically fully funded system from enactment in 1951, and only came to include newly employed black folks after President Johnson passed the Civil Rights act in 1964. Tax exempt employer based healthcare funding is still a factor in the healthcare of over half of all American families, but usually no longer fully funded, meaning there are now deductibles and co-pays in the global competition of the twenty-first century.

Once American employers and employees lost fair trade tariff protections to the open borders of modern free trade, another Reagan policy implemented without Congressional hearings or a vote, manufacturing employment was decimated. American wages and benefits could not compete with Chinese wages. This fact will be mentioned time and again in relation to the various aspects of life that are affected, as policy around the various issues are discussed.

Note: In his first term President Trump tried to put the tariff genie back in the bottle, and he promised American manufacturing jobs would return and that it would be an easy win. Trump put tariffs back in place in 2019, and China retaliated against American farm products, causing farm bankruptcies. Trump doubled down, and China has deflated its currency. Trump rode Obama policies that produced seven years of slow but steady growth for another two years. Trump's policies caused the first stall in confidence in nine years, and the market displayed the first signs of recession since the collapse of mortgage banking and wall street beginning in 2007. Trump's deficit spending tax cut was intended to stall this trend and it did, into the 2020 election year.

Let's move on to the election of General Dwight Eisenhower in 1952 as President of the United States, the first Republican president elected since 1928.

Eisenhower had been the commander of the Allies' D Day invasion in Europe and was an American war hero. His actual Five Star Command was the European Theater of Operations or ETO. Ike is famous for having introduced and pushed through Congress a national military highway system that became America's Interstate Highway System; this was Ike's signature domestic accomplishment.

However, not all went well over the next eight years. Ike had seen that operation and maintenance of modern weaponry had become very technical. He also had seen how unprepared American high school graduates were for the tasks required in a modern mechanized, electrified, even aerospace military. Every aspect of modern warfare required understanding hundreds of new technologies from high compression engines, diesels, and many new uses of electrical assistance, and all of it required maintenance. To address this need for a better educated military, Ike established a new federal department in the executive branch, the Department of Education.

Regarding the reality of outcomes of local schools, Ike, like Truman on healthcare in rural areas, became aware that young men educated in rural schools dedicated to education that focused on local cultural values first, and math and science second (if at all), were not prepared for our modern military. The new Education Department began a program to fund technical subjects in public schools, primarily math and science as well as mechanical aptitude dependent shop skills.

It was and remains agreed that American education is best run by local officials; I personally question if this is in the best interest of the nation or the students. At first national money was a Godsend in rural poor counties. However, most rural poor counties in America were also strong links in the so-called Bible Belt. Salvation was as strong as patriotism, and for sure stronger than patriotism to the federal government in rural America in the mid twentieth century. The curriculum reflected the values of VFW members, pastors and congregations of the local Bible based churches, and the town fathers who almost to a man also made up the White Citizens Councils, all equally in lockstep without conflict on the principle of segregation of the races as a core principle.

It seems Ike almost unknowingly opened a can of worms. Standard practice was to teach local values and beliefs as fact in local schools, which in rural America was not always in sync with emerging scientific realities. Much of the money coming into the federal government was provided by modern large industrial states that had a broader base of norms and values than did small rural agricultural towns across the south and Midwest. Industry in the north had become mechanized along with the military; tradesmen who had mechanical skills and apprentice training knowledge were commonplace.

At about the same time Ike established his new Department of Education, he appointed a GOP Governor from California as Chief Justice of the Supreme Court, Earl Warren, who held office during a period of major changes in U.S. Constitutional law, including race relations and legislative apportionment.

Reaction to the Warren Court as it is usually referred to is still a key contention in current U.S. Politics. Many latent citizens' rights found in the Amendments to the Constitution remain well supported by the majority of U.S. voters, but are hated by a large minority of Americans with nationalist leanings based on backlash to cultural norm changes.

This skewed our understanding of reality regarding the history of democracy and our Constitution including the Bill of Rights. The absolute beliefs of political and religious leaders have created a mistrust of secular national government which mans and funds keeping America free in a dangerous world. This leads to millions of folks voting against their own best economic interest to protect the idea that the purpose of religion is more than personal salvation; it must ensure government is compatible with salvation and sin is a rationale for defining crime in America.

Remember, in reviewing Barry Goldwater's book *The Conscience of a Conservative*, we read his adage that America must return to the old "revealed" truths, i.e., the revealed truth that was the authority of the Romans to govern by God's will since the founding of Nicene Biblical Christianity which was the absolute authority of the king our founders had revolted against over one hundred and fifty years before. Simply put, from Nicene to English Common Law, the purpose of government had not been the common good of citizens or to establish justice, it was and is the protection of property rights and guiding subjects to accept a subsistence existence in return for salvation.

There are at least three examples of conflicts federal money created in small town America. First, it was a problem for school administrators. Second, there were conflicts for affected pastors if what was taught all week at school was in conflict with what was taught in church on Sunday. Third, there were conflicts for public school teachers who for the most part agreed with local norms, less so the teachers who taught biology, geography, and civics.

Within twenty years all of these oversight conflicts would be understood and hardened. At the outset the money was welcome and the oversight was ignored. Eventually the oversight was resented and resisted, and another layer of gridlock set in. In 2020 the GOP is resisting oversight by the House of Representatives as defined in the Constitution, in open revolt by the GOP president and supported by GOP Senators. At this time they offer no restraint on absolute authority.

The Southern Democratic senators had become chairmen of key congressional committees and brought home the bacon, including the building of military facilities in the south. As long as these key senators remained committee chairs they could tamp down any interference from the federal government. Beginning in the 1950s this factor of southern political life would end within twenty years; the tensions grew as Ike's new Supreme Court became more liberal, while the Democrats had a last eight years of New Deal activism beyond the Eisenhower years, under LBJ after John F. Kennedy was assassinated.

Ike was out of step, or maybe it was the other way around; perhaps the south was out of step with Ike's experience in the field in WWII, just as Washington had been out of step with the beliefs of the planters living in an all but non-cash mercantile system in the south during his eight years in the field in the Revolutionary War. Both led as experienced heroes with hard won knowledge based on that experience.

Neither was a maintainer of the societal norms that were in place afterward that reflected their community norms. They did not have much say about wages, benefits, or curricula at schools for teachers, nor regarding economic decisions about commerce or clinical decisions in hospitals for nurses. They both reacted strongly and positively regarding what the nation needed going forward that was lacking in the war just won the hard way.

By mid century teachers in public schools and nurses in non-government hospitals increasingly felt unfairly paid, and overly limited regarding best practice in their own field of expertise. Unionization of nurses grew as this movement grew, especially among those employed in for-profit hospitals as that phenomenon grew after the introduction of HMOs in the 1970s, and later as President Reagan introduced the GOP ideology of for-profit fulfillment of common good public services they call Public Choice, by favoring for-profit healthcare. Public Choice (for-profit) solutions to government services never considers the Preamble intent to establish justice.

Teachers are usually employed by a local school board. Local school boards are funded based on local property taxes. School boards in most states became subsidized with state funds, especially if the state set up a lottery for this purpose. From the 1950s on the federal government also subsidized education. These professional women sought union representation as had many of their blue collar husbands. Too often male dominated school boards carried the prevailing belief, and did not see women as heads of households, perhaps impacting not seeing teachers as decision makers in their own workplaces.

Nurse and teacher pay, benefits, and classroom and hospital work rules all reflected this view, which led to a common practice of promoting males to school principals and hospital administrators, even though males were a small percentage of professionals in these two fields.

Voters also reflected this view when asked to support a local tax increase. In the fifties and sixties after WWII male blue collar unions, first skilled then unskilled factory workers, out-earned these primarily female professions by an ever widening gap.

As much as the new federal money was welcomed, southern states did not want northerners telling them how to treat black employees. They preferred a low wage economy, and backed an anti-union program they called right-to-work.

In the second year of Ike's presidency, the Supreme Court integrated schools with the Brown v. School Board decision. This decision was resented in the north and the south. To Ike's credit and in spite of never having really discussed his thoughts on segregation or integration, Ike decided to uphold the court. He took the first major step in what would become once again a total upheaval in the norms of the nation as compared to the regional norms of the country, particularly the racial norms of the southern states, when he sent troops to Little Rock Arkansas to enforce integration.

When I lived and worked in southern factories in the 1960s and 70s, support of public education was strong. The southern states at that time supported separation of church and state to keep taxpayer money from going to private Catholic schools.

Now, to fight desegregation and/or to ensure freedom from mandated curricula that is resented such as sex education or the theory of evolution, privatization of K-12 schooling is desired using public tax money with a hope to nullify oversight. Such changing "values" are hardly more than situational opportunism; to call them principles is an insult to intellectual values.

Resistance to these so far unconstitutional demands has been spun to be, and sometimes actually believed to be an attack on Christians, while most non-evangelicals see it as an attack on the U.S. Constitution, without a working understanding of the intent of the Constitution or how the body of judicial review settlement informs today's politics, or settled constitutional rights.

This has been mostly a fight at the legislative and judicial review level of the federal government. The war on the Bill of Rights at the presidential level has been related more to executive power, in such areas as the media and in the Justice Department's special prosecutor investigations of four of the past nine sitting presidents, primarily for misrepresentation, secret activities, or obstruction of Congress.

As soon as busing was introduced into the desegregation equation, Christian academies became a serious factor in the towns where I lived and raised my children in the south. A demand grew for vouchers based on tax receipts that would allow parents to make public money available for voucher funded private schools. It has been my anecdotal observation that much of the drive to redefine the legal status of separation of church and state stems from these voucher issues. I'm sure if this effort is successful without destroying our current system of governance, prayer in public schools and teaching the infallibility of Bible based revelations as fact will follow.

As a Roman Catholic attending Catholic school in the 1950s I was taught the Pope was infallible when speaking on faith and morals. Not taught was the fact the Pope had been upheld by European kings as being infallible regarding all knowledge as revealed by God. As we reviewed earlier in the Age of Discovery the church faced a dilemma upholding this teaching when geocentrism was proven false. It took about three hundred and fifty years for the Pope to change the meaning of infallibility, adding the words "on matters of faith and morals", ending the Pope's claim of infallibility concerning all knowledge, which at the time included what passed for scientific facts.

Evangelicals have now applied a similar principle of belief, not to any church leader or prophet(s) but to the Bible, itself a creation of men purporting to have infallible revealed knowledge, as opposed to scientific provable knowledge, thus the acceptance of belief as a base factor for being considered an evangelical Christian.

I have no need to argue against Christian beliefs, as I believe constitutionally and personally in each citizen's right to pursue salvation so long as it does no harm to other fellow human beings' rights. They see an intended war on Christianity. What I see is an intent to declare war on all other Americans' Constitutional secular rights and activities they see as a sin against God. In fact it is a war on a secular Constitution including the Bill of Rights, and thereby the U.S. national government. To end secular law is to end the United States government. Their simple plea is we have to throw it all out and start over; this would be domestic treason, except for their right to free speech, actually a right to be protected.

I see the difficulty for evangelicals to be tolerant citizens accepting non-evangelical citizens' rights if America is to remain a republic. They seem to believe Jesus ordered every evangelical Christian to spread the words they believe to be absolute truth to all people in all nations including their own. As a result Biblical truth that conflicts with anyone else's Constitutional rights cannot be tolerated. Only evangelical leadership can solve this dilemma, and the dynastic billionaires have made it in the pastors' economic interest to refuse tolerance as a norm.

The GOP seems to have accepted these gridlock inducing norms as positive vote seeking factors, ignoring the abuse caused to fellow citizens, or the war on the Constitution evangelicals are engaged in, meaning the war on the Bill of Rights. The southern states had this fight over slavery and lost. They had it again over segregation and lost Now it is over secular rights and the wealth gap. They must lose again or the nation is unsustainable.

When an evangelical claims America is at war with Christianity, no one seems to ask who is the protagonist in this war? It is the evangelicals rejecting the rights of others. Gridlock cannot end without a truce, as long as tolerance remains an impossible goal.

It was my impression living in the south that segregationists found it less difficult to defend Christianity than segregation and changed the parameters of the fight, but not the goal of the fight, meaning to continue the norms of the southern culture. No way to prove this, but it is the only rational reason I can find for the change of position on separation of church and state. In the 1960s it was gospel in the south in their stand against Catholic Schools, and later their reversal in support of evangelical school academies being allowed to use public funds for private schools. In any case I think we've covered why I think Ike's establishment of the Department of Education created a larger dilemma than he ever knew.

Ike took up Truman's goal of ending colonialism after WWII, and forced Britain to relinquish its control of the Suez Canal. This had been a lifeline for Britain to India and other colonial holdings, and for France to Vietnam and their other colonial holdings as well. Barry Goldwater was personally not invested in these two policies, public money for Christian Schools and Truman's and Ike's concerns to end colonialism. However, he was just as effective as Strom Thurmond in fighting for the new limited goals of the GOP, once he became a U.S. Senator in the 1950s.

Goldwater's family was a wealthy Arizona department store owning clan. He married the heir to the Phelps Dodge Arizona Copper mining fortune. He only became a politician in the early 1950s, and in 1956 he won the Arizona U.S. Senate seat as a well known newcomer to national politics, as Ike carried the state in his popular reelection bid.

Barry asked to be on the Commerce Committee and the Defense Committee as a merchant and a fighter pilot in the Arizona National Guard. Instead he was assigned to the Labor Committee, in the middle of one of one of the worst labor disputes in America history, a UAW strike at the Kohler Company in Cheboygan Wisconsin led by Walter Reuther, an icon of the union movement and one of the more respected and most honest of America's union leaders.

In Arizona as a merchant and son-in-law of the copper kings, Barry had come to resent if not hate the whole union movement. As a conservative military guy he believed unions were socialist at best and communist at worst. We won't go deep into the weeds here, but corrupt unions were being investigated in the 1950s by Bobby Kennedy, a lawyer working for the Labor Committee. As noted above, unions had overplayed their hand after WWII with thousands of wildcat strikes demanding raises, matching the greed of the industrialists demanding price increases before the nation was back on its feet, after making vast fortunes in war profits.

On television Bobby Kennedy was grilling the man believed to be the most corrupt and mafia infiltrated union boss, Jimmy Hoffa of the Teamsters Union, and America was glued to the TV. Then the Kohler strike became a long battle with hired thugs on both sides, in spite of a great family business on one side and one of the best unions on the other. The UAW and Walter Reuther were under attack. Barry Goldwater for whatever reason asked Bobby Kennedy to get Walter Reuther on the hot seat. It took a while but he did. They never destroyed Reuther, but they did manage to seriously muddy support for the union movement across the nation.

Strom Thurmond was a foe of unions and a Movement Conservative leader for the New GOP along with Barry Goldwater. Both believed in right-to-work as a state policy and allowed it to become one of the bedrock ideologies of the new GOP Southern Strategy. New Deal backlash was growing in the dark. It would be only ten years later in 1968 that the UAW voted against the Democratic Party and all that Walter Reuther had accomplished for his membership and their families. The UAW rank and file voted for the right-to-work segregationist George Wallace in defiance of the recommendation of Walter Reuther, their own union leadership who had helped FDR get the help he needed from back home in Congressional districts that the union had delivered.

The UAW's rank and file embrace of segregation was the tripping point that led to the destruction of the American middle class. They proved they loved labor union rights less than they hated welfare for blacks.

This was the most costly mistake any group of men ever made in American history, comparable to the Confederate States' decision to secede which destroyed the southern economy for five generations and has kept it comparably economically poor ever since.

The three key issues Taft-Hartley ended were the keystones to

279

insuring hourly wage earners could sell their wages in the market for the value they contribute as opposed to the least that the market allows. The first was Clause 7, democracy, which we have discussed; the second was the end of check-off and the closed shop. The closed shop meant if the union got fifty-one percent of the vote, all employees had to be members of the union, and check-off meant dues were a payroll deduction delivered to the union. The third was the right to strike. These were the three factors of the New Deal Wagner Act that had empowered unions

Taft-Hartley ended sustainable living wage incomes, making the nation unsustainable for over half the nation's families earning less than a living wage including funded access to healthcare, a failed standard of living in the largest and wealthiest nation on earth. It is unbelievable to me that as Americans we did this to ourselves.

I managed factory employees under such agreements at Dresser Industries and dealt with hourly folks who wanted their plant to succeed; they were smart and knew their jobs depended as much on the success of the plant as did the profits of the stockholders.

I managed these folks and sat across from them in union negotiations. The only differences in how I managed a union shop as the son of a union leader as opposed to most corporate managers I met were twofold: first, I approached them as a member of the Dresser team, never as us and them; second, I openly discussed the fact that the only concern on both sides from eight to five in the plant was mutually beneficial income. I stressed the more profit we generated, the more money I could be successful in getting management to agree to include in the package I helped negotiate between their representatives and my management. I found this to be more effective than only driving ever increasing production goals. To be successful I had to remain credible; this could not be just a game. The most destructive words I ever heard in a company boardroom were, "Okay, this is what we are going to tell them".

In business I always told my sales staff "never say dumb things to smart people", and that is what so much of what I heard from management that was ideologically anti-union as opposed to being pro the best deal we could make for every aspect of the business.

It was management at war, instead of best practice planning how to manage labor's resentment on the shop floor and in the office among the hourly union office staff. Industrial relations were taught in American universities to be adversarial instead of best practice for the needs of each side. I cared about work rules, the employees cared about income and fair treatment; we could negotiate this-for-that trade offs that allowed us to better utilize our staff including cross training, and elimination of jurisdictional fights on the shop floor after the contract was settled. Human nature creates gridlock just as much on shop floors as it does in mega churches, and political parties, and large unions.

As a committeeman for Local 13 in Detroit's Printing Pressmen's Union, my dad was on the bargaining committee during several negotiations of new contracts. At age sixteen or seventeen I asked him why he always talked at home about the handful of pressmen who were alcoholic deadbeats whose jobs he preserved; asking him did that not destroy his own legitimacy. He told me that issue had been raised several times by the chief negotiator for the joint newspaper owners' negotiating team. He said he always replied, "I know the names of those you would request we allow to be removed; you also know the names of your foremen who are both alcoholics and abusive. You act first and I will agree to join you in resolving the problem of alcohol addiction in your press rooms, if we can agree to find a way to provide a fund for long time employees of the union and the News Company".

It never happened; in every company where I managed hourly employees I was always told our first duty as factory managers was to uphold the first line supervisors, meaning the foremen. My solution was to find a place for long time employees in both management and labor who were no longer productive for whatever reason, move them into a non-disruptive position, red line (freeze) their pay for the rest of their time to retirement, and end their ability to disrupt. I understood I still had to meet my approved budget, and found labor peace and low employee turnover to be more manageable than disruptive and difficult ever escalating shop floor resentments caused by troubling employees on both sides.

We lived to the contract and disciplined both foremen and rank and file employees who strayed; shop floor peace is possible, but not if either side starts with an adversarial attitude on day one. I've visited more than a hundred factories, with and without a union, and I can sense the tension or lack there of within a few minutes. Political gridlock and union contract gridlock are, from a human nature point of view, second cousins.

What I knew about unions I learned from my union activist dad. He always told his team two things: never strike for money, only for principles, and in money negotiations it is as important for the union's future as it is the company's that the employer remains competitive and profitable. In union contract negotiations, the first item on the table is seldom money, although both sides will have defined money goals at a point in time, more often late than early. Both sides also need to keep in mind the cost of living and the cost of doing business. Negotiating teams are usually made up of representative(s) of one or more local team managers the corporate staff see as knowledgeable of local issues, and one or more staff labor lawyers who are knowledgeable of corporate employee relations policies. It's important to remember that in this type of negotiating there are four parties: corporate management, local management, the union, and the local employees, unless it is a national contract, in which I was never involved.

In the 1970s I was on the corporate contract negotiating team representing the local factory, along with a corporate labor lawyer representing corporate management during an initial union negotiation at a Dresser Industries factory in Alexandria Louisiana where we manufactured industrial valves. The corporate management negotiating team withheld the employees' negotiating teams' check-off and closed shop demands which the union wanted, until our team had secured the manning and work rule demands that management wanted, to ensure we could maintain improved work force output after settlement, based on agreed expectations.

As difficult as it may be to believe this produced a more productive and satisfied work force, and an improved bottom line for the company. I always argued for a smarter relationship with the hourly wage employees, and for avoiding the adversarial relationship I saw too often over my years in management. Just as I look at political policies I looked at outcomes and not ideology on the shop floor.

These two, check-off and closed shop, were not unfair burdens; they were mutual motivational tools to arrive at compromise. The union representatives kept their own cookie jar of trade offs to sell what turned out to be the last best deal they could get. Then they had to satisfy their membership, just as we had to satisfy the needs of the corporation to remain competitive in the marketplace for customers, as well as Wall Street for stockholder satisfaction without falling into the gridlock. Absolutism works for stockholders perhaps, but it never works to the benefit of all factors of settlement of mutually beneficial agreements, which I call rational boundary outcomes.

One last thought on corporate-union or management-labor negotiations. They are much like our national governance. Both types of negotiations have a choice between compromise and gridlock. I saw this in my many years doing business with GE, both seeing and reading about how GE chose absolutism just as the GOP has politically. As noted elsewhere in this book the GE labor negotiations policy was to make one offer with limited money up front, take it or leave it; if not acceptable the plant would be closed.

On the short term it made GE the most profitable corporation in the world; in the long run it left the corporation a shell of its former self, and today its stock is worth less than ten cents on the dollar from its high flying days as it was destroying itself from within. To my mind Reaganomics and GOP absolutism on taxes, trade, and regulation of speculative banking and capitalism have set in motion the same fate for America as befell GE. This will be discussed in more detail in Ronald Reagan's introduction to the GE system in Chapter 10.

Back to union and management contract settlements. In this union members mimicked corporate stockholders who grant their board members the ability to do likewise for the benefit of the majority of stockholders, whatever the political beliefs of some stockholders, or however they prefer the corporations profits are spent. The Wagner Act Section 7 did not address child labor, hours of work in a day or week, or pay for overtime; FDR's labor Secretary Frances Perkins had resolved all such issues already and they had been legislated and adjudicated. Section 7 only addressed the right to organize, collect dues, and use them for the benefit of all members. It would seem under the concepts of democratic action and First Amendment rights the majority of the members were within their rights to carry out the majority members' negotiating goals as a give, in a give and take process.

Wagner (the Democratic Senator who sponsored the New Deal workers' rights act in Congress) used the concept of "democracy" to justify mandate; if fifty-one percent of workers voted for a union, all had to join. Granted that democracy is a mechanism of governing, but boards of all sorts of organizations grant fifty-one percent of votes to apply to one hundred percent of members and/or beneficiaries.

Section 7 provided employees with "the right to self-organization, to form, join or assist labor organizations, to bargain collectively through representatives of their own choosing, and to engage in other concerted activities for the purposes of collective bargaining or other mutual aid or protection…" 29 Y, S. C. – 157 (as noted on the American Bar web site). This was the clause the GOP sought to destroy, and did, starting with Bob Taft in 1947, and the last nail was driven in the coffin by Ronald Reagan in his absolutist ending of the PATCO (federal air traffic controllers) walkout, which we will review in chapter 10, our next and final chapter.

As I write, my home state of Michigan, once the most unionized state and Walter Reuther's home base as head of the General Motors branch of the UAW, has legally outlawed closed shop and check-off as negotiable rights seen as benefiting the union, as if that is different than helping the members. Michigan has now joined the ranks of right-to-work states.

Taft-Hartley ended democratic type voting rights for labor unions. A lawyer cleverly named the concept for one of the pro-Bob Taft wings of the GOP as "right-to-work", and it is still the anti-union monster idea that the GOP was looking for.

Both right-to-work and free trade are GOP ideological and campaign policies in support of all corporate income beyond market. If this was not true, the GOP would allow Medicare to negotiate drug prices.

Property owners have never recognized that any employee has any say or right to negotiate, or to withhold work to resolve labor versus management disputes. The hourly laborer in America has no means of dissent left to appeal the abuse of corporate rights to set wages at what ever the lowest the market will allow; this is the definition of abuse. However in the twenty-first century we still have Supreme Court justices who do not fully uphold the Bill of Rights as Constitutional.

In fact the U.S. economy is mutually dependent on all three. It is dependent on the contributions of taxpayer funded infrastructure and court ordering in support of a robust commercial and consumer economy, the ideas and investments of owners and operators of legal businesses seeking profit, and wage earners seeking a living wage income. These three are the factors that provide the three legs of a strong consumer based economy.

The Democrat party sees this as a common good and a factor of establishing justice. The GOP sees this as denial of economic freedom, without defining a constitutional authority. It is supported only as an ideological best interest of the members of the GOP, without concern for the majority or the nation.

I will add here that the GOP ideology of right-to-work is no less harmful than the equally abusive policy of free trade in a world of disparities of rights, laws, labor systems and economies. U.S. labor needs to have a protective barrier for the cost of its level of rights and laws, or a right to use reciprocity, meaning no nation can sell more dollars of its exports into America than it purchases for import into its economy from America. Either one allows a balance of trade payments equilibrium, and a cost of living sufficient for sustainability.

Few people talk about the two concepts that were key to union busting (right-to-work and free trade), but Strom Thurmond led the anti-union idea of "no northern union leader coming down to Dixie and telling us how to pay our blacks" that helped take the south into the GOP once these two ideologies were enacted.

The political and practical demise of the union movement began the day LBJ signed the Civil Rights Act into law in 1964. I bet my dad that his union would vote for a right-to-work president within twenty years; it took only four years to vote for a right to work segregationist (Wallace) for president, and sixteen years for my dad's union brothers to become Reagan Democrats.

One more comment here on the 1964 Civil Rights Bill that LBJ persuaded Congress to pass. Since that day the GOP has courted the south's vote by supporting racial politics. The GOP is adamant they are not racists, and I don't accuse them of that. I just relate that racism has been the outcome and they are not sorry it is so. The south talks in terms of freedom in addressing the ideology behind their having created a belief among the base that prompts them to only state "I want my country back". It is a form of freedom that has poverty as an outcome for the majority, hardly what an informed voter would chose, so it is in fact deceptive, always the intent of spin, and always starts with "here's our talking points", the equivalent of management stating "here's what we are going to tell them", the GE system Reagan adopted for the GOP (to be expanded in Chapter 10).

The 1964 Civil Rights Bill had seven goals; number seven was equal employment opportunity. Three southern states, Mississippi, Louisiana, and Alabama funded a joint action committee against goal number seven; it was called the "Coordination Committee for Fundamental Freedom". They also included goal two, equal access to public accommodation. I do not address that issue in this book, but it was all part of the battle for continued segregation. Senators actually complained about being phoned by Christian clergy from the south advising them that they and their flocks were opposed to the Civil Rights Bill.

I left Dresser Industries to own a private business, the kind that creates the jobs the GOP likes to remind folks about. I never had a union in my tool and die shop, but we had a written set of norms for the plant manager and the employee representative committee of three key folks elected by the three major groups: skilled workers, laborers, and administration. Every factory has meetings in the restroom, if not openly structured. Only a few disputes a year were brought to my office. I had a theory: it is just as hard to find a good boss, as it is to find a good employee. Being one helps keeping the other. Not everyone liked me, but few employees resigned, and none brought an organizing signature card into the factory that I ever heard of.

I knew growing up in pro-union Michigan that it was just as segregated as Thurmond knew his home state of South Carolina was. By the time busing was creating turmoil in Boston Massachusetts I was living and running a business in a Boston suburb. I was no more surprised by riots in South Boston than I was by desegregation riots in Alabama. It is a legacy of our legal history in the south, and our cultural history in the north. It will take a long time to work through these issues, at least for the rest of the twenty-first century. We need to do it with as little human and financial cost as possible, and with as much compromise in incremental fashion as possible.

In the meantime in Congress in the 1950s, attacks alleging unproven communist membership were being made against individual Americans by the conservative Taft wing of the GOP. Before he was disgraced, Wisconsin Senator Joseph McCarthy was allowed to use his Senate committee assignment to wreak havoc on thousands of American lives. McCarthyism was coined as a term to describe these accusatory attacks on individual American citizens, although no evidence was ever produced. McCarthy even accused former WWII General and then President Dwight Eisenhower of communist affiliations, as usual without proof and just as usual without a reprimand from the GOP leaders in the Senate at the time.

In the same anti-communist era of overwrought fear mongering, and seeing a communist plot behind any social concern for the plight of wage laborers and/or blacks, Dwight Eisenhower chose odd leadership for the CIA, the organization responsible for international intelligence gathering that President Truman had created, as well as to head the U.S. State Department.

President Eisenhower selected two brothers, both corporate international lawyers, from the largest and most successful international corporate law firm in the nation, Sullivan and Cromwell, referred to earlier.

He chose Allen Dulles, a former OSS spy as his CIA Director, and his brother John Foster Dulles as his Secretary of State. At the time John was serving as an appointed senator from New York State, having been appointed by former governor of New York and losing GOP presidential candidate in the 1948 presidential race against Harry Truman, John Dewey. Like former Democrat President Woodrow Wilson, the two brothers were raised in a missionary family. Their father was a Presbyterian minister, and they were dedicated to the conversion of the Asian people to both Christianity and Capitalism. They believed the business of America was to make the world safe for free trade, with open access to all markets of the world to American corporations. They both saw communism as a double threat, first to the idea of Christianity, and secondly to capitalism in general and American free enterprise in particular.

The Dulles brothers were both partners in a law firm that had represented international divisions of American companies overseas, as well as in Washington, long before lobbying became an industry. Their best known client was a Boston corporation that imported bananas and sugar, the United Fruit Company; they even served on the UFC board.

United Fruit Company controlled many third world former colonial nations that grew crops not viable in the U.S., or not at third world prices. Other corporations including extraction industries like oil, or mining such as uranium, were all of interest to both the U.S. and Russia during the cold war, and had been of lifelong interest to the Dulles Brothers' law firm's clients.

The issue for the national leaders of such nations came down to two concerns. These nations had become colonies because they held commercial interest for their former European colonial masters. In almost every one of these countries those who cooperated with the colonial master were hated by the nationals, citizens who were not involved in colonial schemes at best, or were abused in colonial schemes as business as usual.

There was almost always a natural leader on both sides of the equation. Those who worked with a colonizer nation became rich, and those who worked with the United States, who just controlled the economy and thereby the country without the full trappings of colonialism, who also became rich.

The U.S. was not a colonizer nation in the sense that we did not occupy these countries, but we did contract with owners and leaders who controlled the local economy, government, and military. The key local leaders became businessmen, nominally ran a limited form of democracy, and became nominally at least, Christians. This was a key concern of the American government after WWII as almost all U.S. diplomats in those days had been selected based on a willingness to also be proactive in allowing Christian missionaries safe rights to convert the natives of these nations, in non-Christian countries, especially in Asia.

Usually the original European colonizer nation had already introduced Christianity into these nations. In Central and South America, from Eisenhower forward the GOP played a key role in keeping fruit and sugar prices low and communism out, eventually arming the ruling families, and introducing mercenaries into the equation to insure low wages and docile workers. Russia was only too eager to arm the rebels; corruption, chaos, and abuse of the native population have continued in Central America, impacting our Mexican border ever since.

Newly independent nations were allowed to hold elections. For the most part if Americans dominated the export economy of a country, the cooperative leadership controlled the elections. Most nationalist leaders who won elections were enticed by Russia to consider communism in return for economic and military support. Many leaders stated they wanted neutrality.

Egypt claimed they wanted neutrality, but neither Russia nor the U.S. allowed it. I assume it was the same in Russia, but in America Secretary John Foster Dulles did not trust or believe such leaders. When the wrong side won, America developed a new term of State; it was called regime change.

Just as many of the problems around the world are a legacy of the end of the colonial wars, many of the issues America has dealt with around the world since the end of WWII go back to the clandestine deeds of the Dulles brothers, all done with the concurrence of their sponsor, President Eisenhower, who in all other ways seems to have been a successful middle of the road Republican president. Eisenhower was never embarrassed by the actions of the Dulles brothers. They supplied him with what is known in statecraft as plausible deniability.

I do not take sides here as to the rightness of this process in assuring the containment and eventual collapse of communism. The cold war was still war. However, the legacy this strategy left in Central America, the Middle East, southeast Asia, and Africa is severe.

In the far east, China was a special issue in total severance from America for thirty years. China finally adopted a form of capitalism, and today China has favored nation status yet remains communist in its form of government. The next several paragraphs are some of the least known and problematic legacy issues America deals with to this day in our international and border issues.

Regime change was an American policy, and as practiced by the Dulles brothers it included elimination with prejudice (assassination). The Dulles brothers shared deep respect for American trade, especially as practiced by the exotic fruit and extraction industries in third world emerging, and often former colonial countries even as the GOP party remained isolationist. John Foster Dulles made sure that bananas, oil, and ore mining investments made in former colonial countries were of national interest to the U.S. government.

John and his brother Allen made sure that post colonial governments were led by Christian businessmen, as opposed to nationalists seeking neutrality internationally, which usually included land redistribution to native populations locally. John forced emerging governments to choose between the two; he did not allow neutrality at all. It was assumed any neutrality would lead to communist affiliation, if not already in place.

The first incident of the Dulles brothers' intervention in a former colonial country to prevent nationalists from nationalizing foreign investments once an election was won by a nationalist, was in Iran. This took place in Ike's first year as president (1953). John Foster Dulles saw the world as divided between the good of Christianity and capitalism and the evils of Islam and/or communism.

John had even supported Hitler as preferable to Stalin into the early 1940s as Stalin became a U.S. Ally during WWII. Iran had oil, and a king (Shah) who was cozy with Germany. But Germany was at war with Russia, and Russia had a border with Iran, five hundred percent more troops and equipment, and was allied in 1941 with Britain against Germany. Russia and Britain invaded Iran and together deposed the Shah, installed his son who was more pliable, and divided Iran, Russia in the north along with a couple of groups associated with Iran, the Armenians and the Kurds. Stalin, Churchill, and FDR had met in the capital of Iran, Tehran, and Stalin and Churchill had both agreed to exit Iran six months after the war; Churchill did, Stalin did not.

After the war Truman and Churchill forced Russia out. It did not take long for Russian to return. The Mullahs forced the Shah out, and the military forced a "democratic vote". The new Prime Minister of Iran was former general Mosaddeq. He wanted to nationalize Iran's oil wells.

This is a lot of detail for a small part of our story, but it set the stage for the GOP in the Middle East from Eisenhower to become a daily concern of President Reagan, over both of his two terms, and for the two Bush presidents, and had a profound effect on the concept of regime change in the mind of George W. Bush's vice president, Dick Cheney.

The Dulles brothers helped Britain assassinate Mosaddeq, the elected head of Iran's government when he announced plans to nationalize Iran's oil fields, and they installed the Shah as our friend who would leave British oil concessions in place. Iran has been a burden to every U.S. president since, it is fair to say, most devastatingly to President Jimmy Carter as he granted the Shah, who was suffering from cancer at the time, asylum in the U.S. as a former ally,.

Dulles was the only post WWII Secretary of State who did not want to just contain communism, he wanted to defeat it as Godless and Socialist; this was closer to Goldwater's view than Ike's. A popular comment regarding this view when Goldwater ran for president was he viewed the world through rose colored bomb sights. Dulles treated newly elected nationalists of smaller countries who were caught in the middle during the Cold War as either with us or not. Remember containment was based on Harry Truman's doctrine to prevent WWIII in the nuclear age; Ike allowed the Dulles brothers to act as more than just assuring containment.

The Dulles equation left nationalists with only one choice, to allow American and allied nations' key families to continue to own the land and commercial rights in these newly freed countries, protecting what he saw as "American wealth producing assets". If they refused they were seen as collectivists who were sympathetic to communism; if need be such leaders were to be overthrown, or if necessary, assassinated.

The Dulles brothers obtained Ike's permission to use assassination as America's covert method for regime change. Ike did not want WWIII, yet concurred. Eventually they carried out or participated in eleven overthrows or assassination attempts, starting in Guatemala where the elected President Arbenz nationalized one hundred percent of the land owned by only fourteen families who plundered the labor of the peasants, and ending with the Democratic Republic of Congo's president named Lumumba over Uranium, with a twelfth planned in Cuba to assassinate Castro, as Ike's second term ended.

Truman had called for an end to colonialism, but did not fix the property rights issues regarding nationalism versus the assets of colonial nations' corporate investors in these nations, as part of his resurrection of the European states, while supporting colonial nations' rights to become free nations.

This dilemma played out in former colonial countries in Asia, South America, Africa, and the Middle East from Eisenhower's presidency through George W. Bush, while a commitment to containment of nuclear Russia was maintained. President Obama spent his entire two terms in a similar pickle in the Middle East, as Russia reasserted herself in the ongoing Middle East quagmire.

Let's look at the second incident, in Guatemala, as the only other example we will review in some depth. It will demonstrate the Dulles brothers' interference in other countries' politics. The United Fruit

Company was a key Dulles client at their old law firm of Sullivan and Cromwell; the firm represented United Fruit for most of the first half of the twentieth century.

Guatemala was a very poor country, and most of the arable land (over eighty percent) was owned or leased by the American firm United Fruit from one of only fourteen Creole (of full Spanish origin) families, whose property rights went back to Spanish colonial rule. In 1954 Guatemala elected a nationalist president named Arbenz.

Arbenz had run for office as a reformer against the ills of colonialism. He billed himself as a nationalist, and neutrality between capitalism and communism, or in other words America and Russia. Arbenz was overthrown by the CIA under the direction of Allen Dulles, to protect the interests of an American corporation over the rights of a newly democratic nation in our hemisphere where the Monroe Doctrine was still in place. America was and is officially the protector of all nations in our hemisphere from outside interference.

In America in 1950, all nationalist leaders who wished to be neutral in the Cold War between the U.S. and Russia were treated as communists. Dulles disputed neutralism in every possible way. Under 1950s U.S. policy for all intent and purpose, only leaders of emerging nations who were Christian and capitalist in belief and actions were accepted as being non-communists. Remember the leaders America supported in South Korea, South Vietnam, and Taiwan (Nationalist China).

John Foster Dulles claimed to hate colonialism but did not see that American corporate imperialism amounted to the same thing in the eyes of the nationalists and the landless in South America and Southeast Asia. When asked how he knew that nationalizing land reform in Guatemala was communist inspired, Dulles said he could not prove it, but it was the natural tie-in.

Dulles made self-interest of other countries' leaders a litmus test of suitability for office with himself as judge, jury, and executioner, all with Eisenhower's benign neglect at worst, and deniable plausibility at best. To put their citizens' economic interests ahead of America's corporate interests became a death sentence in most of these former colonial nations in the 1950s. This was the prelude to the Contra (Nicaraguan counter-revolutionaries) thirty years later.

Back to our tale of the United Fruit Company, a tale of how American interests were being focused at the time after WWII isolationism had died in the GOP. While Arbenz was still in office there was a discussion of what should the company reparations be for their investment there for the value of the company's lands in Guatemala if they were to be nationalized. Meaning how much were they worth if the ownership of the land was transferred to the Guatemalans. In plain English, how much compensation would the United Fruit Company receive from the Arbenz government?

The first parcel was valued by the company at about 1.8 million dollars for tax purposes. The Company's friends in the pre-independence government had agreed to allow the company to set its own valuation. The company set its own depreciated value as the tax value, as opposed to the market value of the annual crop, assuring the corporation would have to pay very little in taxes to the nation or the people of Guatemala, an example of plunder long after the Roman legionaries.

The Company set the buyout price at the market value for nationalization, or ten times more than what they paid taxes on, or eighteen million dollars, and demanded the Government pay up; both sides still wanted to sell Guatemalan bananas in the U.S. market.

Dulles protested that the "market value" was many millions of dollars greater than the "tax value", and demanded that tax value be the starting point for reparations. The U.S. Secretary of State, not United Fruit's corporate lawyers, negotiated the settlement of this commercial venture.

In 2020 UFC rights are owned by Chiquita brand. Guatemala still produces bananas, sugar, and coffee, but does not grow any crops to feed its citizens Over half of all citizens live in poverty. President Trump in 2020 is building a wall to keep Guatemalans out. Those who show up at the border asking for asylum have their children separated from them and held in for-profit prisons.

Eventually John Foster Dulles asked Ike for permission to overthrow or remove Arbenz, the first democratically elected leader of Guatemala. Ike approved, subject to plausible deniability which protected Ike from knowledge or blame, according to the history I've read on American intervention in South America.

How the facts of the Dulles regime change overthrows and assassinations came to light will be addressed shortly. I give credit to Ike for keeping communism out of South America, but as the Dulles brothers used their capitalism in the process is part of the legacy of resentment and a feeling that America owes these countries for all they have suffered, that we still deal with today. Today's refugees from the failed State of Guatemala that President Trump is dealing with go back to this and the Contra era of dysfunction in the Americas. We will review in Chapter 10.

These secrets (American government sanctioned killings) got out; pilots and paramilitary folks were captured and so on. Newsmen do not give up, people eventually write memoirs. Over the next seven years, the Dulles brothers attempted or in fact murdered six more nationalist leaders: Ho Chi Minh in Vietnam, Sukarno in Indonesia, Nasser in Egypt, Lumumba in the Congo (they succeeded in getting Lumumba killed), and Castro in Cuba; the attempts on those they did not manage to kill left America with a black eye among the citizens of these nations.

The Bay of Pigs invasion of Cuba was planned under Allen Dulles in the last year of Ike's term, and approved by the next president John F. Kennedy who then fired Allen Dulles when the attempt failed. John Foster Dulles himself died in the last year of Ike's second term, so Castro was their last assassination attempt, which also failed as did the four mentioned above.

Many Americans believe we were once respected around the world but are no longer. We went from an isolationist nation to a reluctant warring country to a war weary country in fifty years, as America increasingly invested in projecting military might, beginning under Teddy Roosevelt at the start of the twentieth century. Presidents may have been too driven to be overly militant to avoid being seen as weak on communism in the past, or on terrorism now.

Korea was our first war "fought only to contain communism without triggering a nuclear WWIII". Korea ended in a truce after three years with a democratic South Korea and a communist North Korea remaining. The truce is still in place, and may only be settled in a renewed effort; no one will be surprised if Korea remains a problem well into the future.

Twenty years after Korea we muddled nineteen years from 1954 to 1973, attempting to contain communism in North Viet Nam, which ended in first our exit after more than fifty thousand deaths, and finally the communist government adopting capitalism while keeping a communist form of governance.

Meanwhile the cold war continued to increasingly become the focus of our military spending and diplomatic rhetoric. The truth in Viet Nam would have been to state we are not going to start WWIII or withdraw, so we will bomb the North without limits, which President Eisenhower started, President Johnson escalated, and President Nixon continued. It allowed North Vietnam to sustain the resistance beyond the American public's willingness to fund a costly stalemate with blood and dollars. This changed America's tolerance for boots on the ground containment and the draft.

When did wage labor families finally begin to join the middle class? Slowly after WWII, and then WOW! Between Truman's GI Bill with its GI loans and FHA, housing developments popped up in most states around almost all cities. The soldiers came home, got married, went to school on the GI Bill, and made baby boom families. They wanted homes, cars, appliances, and within a few years TVs; the consumer economy was born. These were mostly Truman policies but giving Ike credit, he continued them including the taxes needed to fund them.

Greed does not just drive plunder, it also drives cost avoidance. The major presidential candidate of the cold war era backed by the new Movement Conservatives was Barry Goldwater who ran against LBJ in 1964. Then success in 1980 when Ronald Reagan won. Reagan and Goldwater shared the same low wages, low top tax rate side of greed as basic bias. I'm talking about the cost of government to address the problems of the previous GOP era dealing with the 1929 depression, followed by non partisan WWII, and the aftermath of not only rebuilding devastated Europe, but the reintroduction into the U.S. economy of the returning troops.

Truman the Democrat from 1945 to 1954, and Ike the Republican from 1953 to 1961, both believed the returning troops had earned living wage jobs, healthcare, affordable housing, and education, all of which would also make the United States more equitable and wealthier over all, and thereby stronger. Ike was the last GOP president who thought in terms of what was good for the troops was good for America.

The Movement Conservatives including Robert Taft's anti-communist crusade in the Senate, Barry Goldwater and his John Birch Society, William Buckley and his conservative college crusade, and of course the segregationist politicians and the new evangelical preachers in the south all joined forces with a basic message that low taxes, small government, Christian values, and unfettered speculative capitalism were the original intent of the founders and the revealed truth we inherited from posterity that America should hearken back to, forgetting this was what we revolted against.

In the end the GOP theorized FDR had created security for all financial classes in America only to make them dependent on the Democrats, as if it was a false bargain costing them their freedom to escape poverty and insecurity, for a living wage, secure employment, and access to safe banking, and retirement.

This deviant theory would reoccur in explaining LBJ's safety net for the unemployed and low wage working poor, as well as healthcare in retirement, and food stamps for those in poverty for whatever reason.

Millions of WWII vets came home and worked forty or more years for one employer and paid into the Social Security Administration for all forty years. Barry Goldwater and Ronald Reagan explained these outcomes only destroyed these dependable wage earners' sense of responsibility; the folks who enjoyed the jobs, wages, security, home ownership, employee healthcare for whites, and earned retirement, only voted Democrat because they had been made intentionally dependent, if you believe the GOP spin.

The forces for change in the GOP in the 1960s wanted to repeal the New Deal. We have been listing these groups and the idea they all began to sell, which they have come to define as economic freedom. John Birch's message on the economy was a form of economic freedom. Bob Jones, head of a leading university training young evangelicals sold religious freedom. William F. Buckley, head of Young Americans for Freedom in the ivy league, sold the idea of intellectual freedom. Strom Thurmond, leader of the Southern Strategy sold political freedom to make Southern segregation acceptable to the GOP and the GOP acceptable to the old conservative wing of the Democratic Party. When Barry Goldwater was nominated as the GOP presidential candidate in the 1964 in his acceptance speech he cited freedom a couple of dozen times as a mantra.

Eisenhower's second term came to an end in 1961. He had accepted Truman's concepts of Soviet Union containment. Truman had to leave the French in control of Vietnam at the end of the war as part of settlement trade offs, and it led to Eisenhower intervening in what became the longest and most deadly hot war during the cold war.

A changing of the guard in 1961 saw Democrat John F. Kennedy defeat Richard Nixon, the outgoing vice president, in a close election. Nixon will return to the national scene eight years later as president in 1969 as our story continues.

President Kennedy at forty-three was the youngest president ever at that time. He was a WWII hero, a Democrat, the first Catholic president, handsome, from a wealthy family; he is still something of icon to many of his generation and mine. He was an inspiration to a generation of young folks but not a significant factor in our story, because he was assassinated halfway into his first term.

Three of his most remembered actions did affect the FDR era, when he faced down Russia over missiles in Cuba, set civil rights in motion by his reaction to police brutality in Alabama, and was the first to cut taxes. His first cut did not cause deficits, as the spin claimed thirty years later excusing deficits.

Police attacks on young black folks, seen for the first time across the nation on TV, triggered Kennedy to set the civil rights agenda. This became the lead in to LBJ's Civil Rights Bill in 1964, the year after Kennedy was shot by an assassin.

Kennedy's showdown with Soviet Nikita Khrushchev's missile ploy in Cuba was the apex of cold war gambits. Lastly, Kennedy reduced the wartime top rate for taxes from ninety percent to seventy percent, but he died before they could be enacted. A slowdown in the economy at the end of the Eisenhower presidency helped Kennedy defeat Richard Nixon in his first run for president. The tax cut ended the slowdown, and caused growth the next year in the economy.

President Kennedy selected his more radical brother, Robert Kennedy as Attorney General, and chose as his running mate perhaps the most effective legislator in American government history, Lyndon B. Johnson of Texas, known as LBJ. In November 1963, LBJ was sworn in as president of the United States following the assassination of Kennedy. The following year he ran for reelection with Hubert Humphrey of Minnesota as his running mate, and won his first full term in his own right.

LBJ took up a number of Kennedy's legislative goals and saw them through to enactment. The first was a tax cut. Taxes were still high (top rate ninety-one percent) when he assumed office, a legacy of fighting WWII and rebuilding (pay as you go) the U.S., Europe, and Japan. Kennedy had looked at the high tax rates and believed that because more taxes were being collected from now well paid labor, and settling the cost of containment that remained expensive, but less so than the cost of war in WWII, that tax rates could finally be eased.

LBJ led Congress to approve, and he signed the Kennedy tax cuts into law soon after being sworn in. He reduced the top rate to seventy percent. Kennedy had increased U.S. debt by twenty-three billion dollars during his time in office; let's remember this the next time taxes are seriously cut in 1981 by Ronald Reagan in Chapter 10.

Kennedy and LBJ both believed in FDR's Keynesian "demand side" economic policy, the theory that the economy grows from demand of consumers with money to spend, and in down times deficit spending by government to prime the pump to reignite the economy is the time to borrow, and when the economy booms it is a time to reduce debt. Over the past eighty-five years, since FDR first bought into these theories, Keynes has been more right than wrong here and in Europe, based on outcomes.

LBJ came of age in rural Texas in the 1930s. His first job was as a rural school teacher in an impoverished school district, and he always remembered that his students came to school hungry every morning. One of his key goals was to end hunger in the United States, especially for families with children; LBJ launched the War on Hunger noted above, as part of what he called the Great Society

It became part of his welfare reform program, and turned the Food Stamp Program (now called the Supplemental Nutrition Assistance Program, or SNAP) into what became a popular program for farmers, the retail food industry, and the poor in every state except Mississippi where they wanted to keep their rural agricultural work force hungry and in debt to the local stores to ensure they remained in debt, dependent, and willing to work spring and fall on the farms, keeping farm profits as high as possible.

LBJ established a national single payer healthcare system for retirees on Social Security (meaning a healthcare system run by the government without insurance companies as middlemen). He proposed and saw through the enactment of Medicare, funded as an additional burden on U.S. payrolls under the Social Security Administration. Like Social Security, this system will become stressed by the president's free trade decision (in Chapter 10).

Medicare is a single payer system. The majority of folks on Medicare who love it protested a trial Medicare type system as an option under Obamacare. The majority of Americans retired on FDR's Social Security and LBJ's Medicare programs now vote Republican and have done so since LBJ left office, in protest to his increasing funding for black children in poverty, on the oft heard objection that their parents are lazy.

Remember how hard it is to change norms once the lie about social insurance being Socialist, Marxist, and anti American, was bought into, and that is what the GOP said not only about Medicaid (welfare) but as they also did about Medicare (social insurance). LBJ's legacy is he extended Social Insurance to include not only white folks, he extended it finally in 1964 to black folks. LBJ's legacy of being a failed president is usually related to his misbegotten never ending escalation of the Vietnam War, and he deserves this critique. His loss of support for his party however relates to his passing the 1964 Civil Rights Act, and he knew it at the time, and said so, which proved to be accurate.

Over the next forty-five years our for-profit (called market-based by the GOP) mix of public and private healthcare systems would become the most expensive single item in America's domestic economic life, and twice as expensive as other government systems on average healthcare cost per citizen (to cover one hundred percent of their citizens, not our eighty or eighty-five percent) in all other developed countries in the world.

We are the only country in the world that funds most of our healthcare as a cost of employment; I call it a burden on U.S. payrolls. Most developed nations deduct healthcare cost in exports. Now that the world has become a global labor market, the impact of this U.S. payroll cost is a factor in the loss of sustainability of positive balance of trade outcomes in America due to mandated labor cost in the U.S. America loses sixty billion dollars in balance of trade each month in the twentieth century.

In spite of this job killing aspect of payroll funding in America, we have never allowed ourselves to seriously consider a government single payer system as a cost benefit for business or government, or as a social benefit for our unskilled and low skilled hourly paid citizens at the federal or the state or regional level.

In 2018 healthcare as a right with a single payer system was a platform pledge in the North Carolina Democratic Party; I was on the state committee representing District 7 and I tried to get a funding factor added; it was defeated primarily by the Bernie Sanders faction. The GOP is happy to allow poor Americans go through life without healthcare coverage beyond stabilization if in critical condition at a hospital emergency room. Democrats support a national fully funded single payer healthcare system, but have not agreed on a plan for its platform. The Democrats have not educated Americans about what single payer really means for a nation's citizens, or how for-profit cost will be reduced. What is needed is an econometric study equal to solving the atomic bomb or moon landing programs.

In fact as the 2020 Democrat primary campaign began, some candidates called for a concept they called "Medicare for all". Other candidates began dissent, arguing that Medicare for all was an assault on private employer funded healthcare that many union members had fought for and had given up pay increases to secure. At this time it is still an open question. No one has explained it is a legacy of Jim Crow, and a discriminatory tax benefit. Why should corporate employees' healthcare be subsidized and not the self employed?

In 2009, President Obama proposed a government option for managing healthcare as an experiment for working Americans not covered by their employer. He could not get it passed even with his own party in control of Congress.

Returning to Kennedy's policy issues that LBJ actually got enacted, it is time to review civil rights in the 1960s time line.

Martin Luther King, the most successful civil rights leader in the history of U.S. race relations, convinced LBJ that the time had come for civil rights in America. LBJ was also pushed by Robert Kennedy (LBJ and Kennedy for the most part hated each other, but managed to get quite a bit done together). Once Americans saw the violence against peaceful demonstrators in the U.S. south protesting against Jim Crow and segregation that erupted on their TV nightly news, LBJ first proposed, then led enactment of the Civil Rights Bill in 1964 and the Voting Rights Act in 1965.

Twenty years later in the 1980s President Ronald Reagan had a similar reaction to Israel's carpet bombing civilian areas of Syria, watching this action play out on evening TV. Watching the killing of children on TV became a restraint on police around the world from casually committing violence against demonstrators, to containment of demonstrators.

Unfortunately we see police violence still today in America even as police now carry body cams and civilians carry cell phones with cameras. We will comment in our summary on the sad situation of police and minority folks too often fearing each other, as lack of progress in getting young minorities employed in many American cities has led to mutual frustration, distrust, and fear. The fear is great enough in 2020 between racial mistrust and millions of guns on the street that it is difficult to hire enough police officers in many cities.

As bad as these situations are, and sometimes the videos themselves escalate violence, televised killing of unarmed kids is a factor in reducing the worst of war, and in controlling police violence for residents. Mosul in Iraq fell to Iraqi forces as we watched on America TV in July of 2017, and saw the heavy toll on children as the newly freed citizens carried out their dead and starving children, the innocent hoping for a better life, the terrorists hoping for what they see as revenge for some, and in answer to a religious demand for too many, and our reserve troops filling in for the too few volunteer military taking the brunt of the mayhem.

In the case of southern police brutality in the U.S. south in the 1960s, TV ended the public display of police on horses and the use of night sticks and attack dogs on young unarmed adults.

A funny aside concerning civil rights for American women. The day before the vote on civil rights a Democratic Virginia Congressman (Howard W. Smith) managed to get a couple of words added to the draft Civil Rights Bill without much notice being taken. These two words changed America forever without a vote in Congress or a hearing by the Supreme Court. He added "and sex" to the citizens new rights to be granted, believing it would kill the bill.
The Civil Rights Bill went through the floor vote process with the added two words unnoticed and the bill passed. These are arguably the most far reaching two words in American legislative history. Today women have rights to their own family planning; they can apply for credit in their own name, they no longer need their husband's permission to obtain birth control options; they can buy a car on credit, or have their union negotiate for a right to return to work after taking maternity leave. None of these were available to

adult U.S. women before 1964. All four of my daughters were born without any of these rights. Today they have all of these rights and have earned their own independence enabling income.

Robert Kennedy was from Boston, the heart of ward (party controlled) politics for the Democratic Party in the north. A ward boss delivered his neighborhood's votes for his party, and the boss delivered the patronage jobs in the police, fire, and other governmental jobs in return. Before uneducated blacks were shipped north by southern politicians, and guns were abundant on city streets, these city jobs were prized.

Other cities such as Chicago, Philadelphia, and even NYC had ward politics, but the Irish and the little they contracted out to the Italians ran the Democratic Party in Boston and Charlestown on the opposite bank of the Charles River. In the 1980s Speaker of the House Tip O'Neill who represented Charlestown in the State House in Massachusetts before representing the Boston District in Congress, epitomized his favorite political adage, "all politics are local". I'd say it is all cultural, and/or economic norms.

The Midwest was different. In my home state of Michigan the UAW (United Auto Workers), and in other industrial areas like Pittsburgh the USW (United Steel Workers) and in Appalachia the UMW (United Mine Workers) dominated an industry, one or more states, and the state and local Democratic Parties. A key national union was the Teamsters who controlled interstate trucking, and until 1968 advised their so called brotherhood to vote the straight Democratic ticket and they did, election cycle after election cycle.

Most of these unions evolved as rough and tough immigrants fought company hired police (seen as goons by refusing to be intimidated by employees) who coerced immigrants who worked mostly in northern state unionized factories. In many ways the early union movement was as much a physical fight at the work site, as it was a legislative or court fight in northern statehouses, or in Washington DC at the federal level. My dad, father-in-law, and uncles, and most of the fathers of my friends were all volunteer organizers between the 1930s and the 1960s.

Perhaps the toughest and most corrupt union leader was Jimmy Hoffa, the head of the Detroit-based Teamsters Union. He controlled the Teamsters' pension fund, which became a slush fund for the mafia in America. In the 1950s a movie "On the Waterfront" was based on a true story which portrayed in full display all the ills inflicted by corrupt unions on their members. The movie was a true representation of the Longshoremen's Union at the ports of New York and New Jersey. Even after a newsman reported and documented all the ills, and a fair election was finally assured by the state, the men reelected the crooks in charge. Was there ever a time in American history when the working poor ever voted for their own best interest?

In the movie noted above the shipping companies' hired goons, the union elected goons, and the city authorities were goons, all in an escalating conflict; it was the union men and especially their families who paid the price. That said, Hoffa raised the wages of drivers and they stuck with him even after he died, and elected his son to replace him; tribal norms just as most other norms die hard.

Industrial and trade unions were not nearly as strong in Massachusetts, which is a financial services and education center. As attorney general Robert Kennedy prosecuted Hoffa and sent him to prison; the union movement got a very black eye. As a result when Nixon ran in 1968 the Teamsters voted for and helped elect the GOP nominee.

Voting norms in the south and in the north among blue collar union movement voters were changing, and in both regional cultures for the same reason. Rights for "others" were seen as a loss of their country. Absolute freedom for their own tribe was never seen as abuse of other American tribes, the ones who also had been promised freedom from abuse.

As we mentioned, LBJ escalated the Vietnam War. In Vietnam, the war took on a life of its own and our young men died, some fifty-six thousand of them. Generals including Commanding General McFarland lied to a Secretary of Defense who managed the war as a numbers game. Robert McNamara as a statistics genius in the U.S. Military during WWII and after at Ford Motor Company, demanded higher enemy kills than loss of America life as the goal.

They convinced LBJ the U.S. was winning the war, based on this simple equation. Mitt Romney's father George Romney dropped out of the 1968 race for president after visiting Vietnam and revealing he believed the generals had brainwashed him. America's civilian leadership seemed to lose sight of the goal (containment) and worried more about selling a positive message of winning, which the soldiers themselves knew was a lie. Intentional blindness happens in both political parities.

LBJ doubled down on the war as the America people lost faith in him. Our sons were dying in a war he could not explain, or why it was worth the loss of life. It was a repeat of the French finally losing faith in Napoleon when his loss of young men did not seem to be leading to French victories; the loss of American lives was not leading to an American victory in the 1960s in Vietnam.

At home, college kids took to the streets, as their bothers, sisters, and friends came home after a year or more in the jungles with a different story than the generals were telling the president through his Defense Secretary. They began to attend anti-war rallies chanting "hey, hey LBJ, how many kids did you kill today".

The GOP saw flag burning demonstrators as anti-American, the WWII vets who had always voted for the Democrats who not only won the war, but rewarded the returning vets with benefits, now saw liberal students on college campuses as being anti-soldiers, and the GOP encouraged that interpretation. I never saw the old timers against the veterans, but the kids who burned draft cards and flags began to see those who accepted being sent to 'Nam as they called it, as compromised. In the end these vets also became Reagan Democrats. The tide was changing, and the Democrats have been at best deer in the headlights too often ever since.

LBJ could not see his way clear to run for reelection. The New Deal years were ending, and FDR's party was out of new initiatives. Still, it would be another twelve years before an American president would attempt to repeal FDR's New Deal.

American labor was sick of war, sick of Washington, and more than sick of welfare. They probably thought their safe banks, mortgages, living wage jobs, healthcare, well funded neighborhood schools, pensions and Social Security, in their segregated towns were in place and were never going away.

American labor never understood the total lack of concern the corporate wing along with the segregationist wing of the GOP, had for hourly wage labor. Thirty-five years later in retirement, they still have not admitted it to themselves, and see relief for unemployed parents as rewarding the lazy. A side benefit has been a demand that the lazy be hired and millions of black citizens are now employed, including millions in the fast food industry. Now they need a living wage.

I think the point is made as I saw it; civil rights polarized blue collar America and they merged with the GOP's southern white supremacists, evangelicals, and held their noses and voted for right-to-work GOP candidates, supporting the Movement Conservative wing of the GOP, even as it opposed all of their middle class enabling rights that FDR, Truman, and LBJ advocated for and saw into law on their behalf before the Democrats ever addressed educational, economic, and personal abuse of black citizens.

The assault on FDR's New Deal continued as this new GOP welcomed Strom Thurmond's southern mix of segregationists and evangelicals moving to the Republicans. Then they were joined by welfare-hating former Democrats still living in FHA funded houses, earning Wagner Act Union wages, whose parents were retired on Medicare and Social Security, while their wives were now free to use their new right to plan their families.

These middle class Democrats had their rights, and they expected to keep them. They just resented unprepared blacks getting what they had not earned, maybe even at their expense, and the GOP was going to stop that in the name of their freedom to enjoy what they had earned.

What could go wrong; men like Ronald Reagan had, and Donald Trump in 2020 has their back, right? They were voting for an ideology, and never knew it, still don't, and worse yet do not know even now after thirty-five years what the ideology of the GOP from Ronald Reagan to Donald Trump actually stands for.

Many blacks continued to accept the status quo out of legacy fear. There was strong, newly recognized resentment awakened for many working class whites, especially northern white union men who saw blacks as lazy, or happy to settle for being dependent on unearned welfare funded out of the union men's hard earned taxes. Many were moved by Reagan's portrayal of the welfare queens, unmarried sex partners of the lazy men, having ever more children, collecting ever more welfare. Their resentment grew an ever angrier political backlash.

The woe begotten former vice president, Hubert Humphrey actually wanted both parties to agree to hire black men; he saw the issue for what it was, economic hopelessness for black men, leading to non traditional black families. Black women did not demand financial responsibility from their men, even as their children went hungry.

Whites did not see this as a social or economic problem; they saw it as a cultural defect among blacks. I base this on the fact I never ever heard a word of understanding of the reality of black poverty, even among those working full time, for minimum wage or less, without benefits of any type, until LBJ addressed hunger. Until then no other politician would address black income disparity, few do now in 2020.

Nixon did try one time for the GOP to help the black man find a place in the economic system and life of the nation, and a way to assume leadership in the black family. Nixon's plan was called "Affirmative Action".

The Detroit firehouse is a good place to explain the concept and the outcome. At the time Detroit was about fifteen percent black, yet had no black firemen. The first answer was, because becoming a fireman was based on testing. If a hundred applied and twenty-five were to be hired, the twenty-five highest scorers were hired. Black schools were segregated in fact if not in law, and provided poor education.

A high percentage of blacks dropped out before graduating. Almost no blacks scored in the top twenty-five percent of the test, meaning none were hired, in spite of no written rule against it. Nixon's idea was to grant enough points to each black until at least fifteen percent were hired, the same as the share of the population, and then to assign them in black neighborhoods. The first few blacks hired under this system outraged those whites who were replaced by the affirmative action hires. This became a focal point of hatred against blacks for white working class voters. This is not a review of the details of the Nixon system but it presents a working understanding of the process and outcome. Today Nixon is not remembered for affirmative action; it is lumped with food stamps as reverse racism, and/or rewarding the lazy.

President Nixon was elected based on his accepting Strom Thurmond's southern strategy, and his pledge to end the Vietnam War. Nixon is something of a tragic figure in American history; to a large extent his wounds were the self-inflicted wounds of a private perhaps even paranoid, complex man. He is seldom recalled as a moderate, and at times his policies were actually liberal; yet he was a man who made his bones as a conservative "commie hunter" in the Senate. In Nixon's eight years as vice president he grew to be a student of international relations which was his strong suit as president.

Nixon's liberal side contributed to the FDR era legacy of progressive solutions to age old political and economic problems. We have already talked about how the limited gold-based monetary systems were under capitalizing America and European countries as they grew many times faster than the gold supply.

The gold standard worked as a back up value for paper money (America printed gold or silver certificates, exchangeable into gold or silver on demand). Nixon saw that the billions of dollars accumulating in Arab and Asian coffers would, if exchanged into the gold promised behind our money, be more than the gold we had. No large industrial nation could have enough gold to meet these new realities. Nixon took America off the gold standard for a second time and for good, ending the gold standard in 1971 as our trade deficit was approaching forty billion dollars a month.

We imported that much more than we exported each month when the price of oil took inflation to new heights. America's "paper money" is still accepted as a preferred currency over forty years later. The price of gold rose from thirty-five dollars an ounce to over a thousand dollars.

It would be good to remember this when we read of GOP proposals to end the Federal Reserve, or to reintroduce the gold standard, as if we were still a mercantile empire of the pre-industrial past! GOP President Trump returned the U.S. to trillion dollar a year deficits. Imagine if that debt had to be repaid in gold.

During the Nixon years the Middle East was supplying our growing energy needs, and Asian countries were offering lower priced (due to lower wages and subsidies from their governments) consumer products with equal or better quality and performance (such as smaller cars in a time of rising fuel prices). As we slowly became a net importer of oil, cars, and then consumer goods, ending our long history as an export nation, Nixon had the same concerns as LBJ for the American economy. LBJ's solution was eighteen percent tariffs which worked to slow the inflow, enough to slow American job losses.

Double digit inflation and interest rates inflicted by the formation of OPEC slowed the whole economy. Nixon finally ended the Vietnam War but had no solutions for either high inflation or the high interest rates.

Jimmy Carter who followed the Nixon years which included Jerry Ford as president when Nixon resigned, appointed the man who solved the inflation and interest runaway problems, Paul Volker. Carter got the blame for the OPEC outcomes, not the solution.

Nixon's second significant (liberal) decision was to index Social Security to the national CPI (Consumer Price Index). At that time unions already had acquired this feature for its members via negotiations; they called it a "cost of living adjustment". As inflation rose, prices rose, and so union wages also rose between contracts each year (cost of living adjustment were reset once a year). This is just a faded memory for old time union guys who became Reagan Democrats.

Most major companies also extended cost of living increases to salaried employees, below a certain cut off point; in my day it was a thousand dollars a month salary. The Social Security COLA (Cost of Living Adjustment as it is called) is something that almost all seniors support. The modern GOP wanted to use a new lower formula; seniors vote GOP, so between the Democrats and the GOPs in Congress in districts with elderly voters it was defeated.

Nixon finally imposed a freeze on prices and wages that included COLA, but it was short lived. Since then, in years of inflation, retirees have received increases. In flat years of falling prices (during the two GOP crashes of the economy) or in the stagnant years of no net inflation in recovery periods like 2015, increases were zero or close to zero.

Wage earners have not had an automatic mechanism to ensure their income keeps up with inflation since free trade all but ended unionization, except in the public sector. This became the norm over the past thirty-five years of GOP economic policy domination.

Moving on to foreign affairs in the Nixon administration, Nixon picked as his Secretary of State a brilliant, mercurial man who saw the world as a place where peace might finally be possible. His name was Henry Kissinger and he called his (standoff) form of peace "detente", and allowed trade to be the basis of cooperation. Henry Kissinger ended the Vietnam War by pretty much withdrawing, leaving the communists in place, as a reunited country. South Vietnam's capital Saigon became Ho Chi Minh City. Today Vietnam is a low cost labor resource for American manufacturers.

Nixon's decision to accept Kissinger's formula for peace left a generation of men in America feeling used by their government. They felt proud of their service in Vietnam, but were distrustful of presidents and government.

Nixon allowed Kissinger to reach detente in the Soviet Union or better said, agreed to a mutual reduction of hostilities for the time being. Nixon and Kissinger also opened China while leaving the one party system in place. Nixon left LBJ's tariffs in place. He did not open American borders to allow China to dump cheap labor; that will be covered in Chapter 10, the Reagan years.

Soviet/American relations improved under Kissinger, lasting more or less until the Soviet invasion of Afghanistan in 1979. The Soviets were supporting a communist overthrow of the pro-west government. This became a ten year war that ended under Mikhail Gorbachev (the last Soviet president), in the first year of the George H W Bush presidency.

To confirm our understanding of the onset of hyperinflation in Nixon's first term, the Saudis raised the price of oil from three dollars a bbl (barrel) to eleven dollars a bbl in 1973, partly as a result of the U.S. continuing to back Israel in the Six Day War, and partly from a worldwide awakening to nationalism regarding natural assets. Much of this new Arab money was then used to rearm themselves after the Six Day War.

This nearly four hundred percent increase in our most strategic and costly import led to hyperinflation. Attempting to control this inflation led to missteps by both Nixon and his appointed replacement Gerald Ford. Nixon and Ford, along with their advisers, did not seem to understand or have a ready economic philosophy that would tame runaway inflation; they kept businessmen at the head of the Federal Reserve. Jimmy Carter finally took the advice of experts and appointed a true profit and loss old time banker to head the Fed, Paul Volker noted above.

Interest rates set by the new Fed Chairman, Paul Volcker, drove down inflation, but not in time to save Carter's reelection plans. Adding to Carter's problems was the Iran hostage crisis. Carter rescued the Shah who had been put in place when the only democratically elected leader of Iran was assassinated by the CIA and the British secret service; this led to Jimmy Carter being only a one term president, then seen as a failed president. I suspect history will provide a more nuanced evaluation of his policies, and the good they accomplished over time.

Nixon's Attorney General, John Mitchell, played hardball in the Attorney General's office. The payoff to Ol' Strom Thurmond delivering the south (meaning getting the south to vote for Nixon) was a standstill on school desegregation. The still liberal courts were not happy, and a judge finally ordered busing in Boston. Boston reacted like it was Selma all over again, and Thurmond gloated. He had proven what he had always said: America in the north was more segregated and as segregationist minded as the south. What was left of loyalty to the Democratic Party among white blue collar males mostly hourly wage laborers, was dead, and remains so as I write.

Nixon was on the brink of impeachment for a cover-up of a petty crime; his first vice president had resigned in shame. To replace Agnew as vice president Nixon chose Jerry Ford, a long time GOP congressman whom everyone liked. The rest of Nixon's second term is unremarkable to our story.

Nixon's issues caused by OPEC continued into President Jimmy Carter's term, so let's get to know this unique man a little better. Jimmy was a southerner, and a nuclear engineer graduate of the U.S. Naval Academy with the intellect and personality the image conveys. Jimmy had as much or more natural decency than most presidents, and almost the least natural political leadership traits of any president. He was a Democrat and former Governor of Georgia, and in 1976 he was elected president. Jimmy was not a fellow most politicians would enjoy a ball game and a couple of beers with, and in Washington DC that matters.

Even more important as Carter came into the White House, never having served in Congress, he ran into a totally new power structure in the U.S. House of Representatives. In 1974 (in the last Congress before Carter) the House made the largest change in their rules since the Civil War, and presidents have been subject to the whims of its members ever since. This was as if one small island was hit at the same time by a volcano eruption, earthquake and a tsunami.

The House ended the seniority system which had kept southern Congressmen as the heads of the twenty-two committees, often for more than twenty years. Before the change in 1974, the southern Congressmen had almost total control of their committees and total control of which bills came to the floor.

At the same time the new regime also established an additional one hundred seventy-two subcommittees in the House of Representatives, each with a chairman and staff. It did not take long for these new chairmen to see the value of televised hearings. The Accounting Committee became the Accountability Committee. One hundred and eighty-eight little kingdoms; Congress has never been a powerhouse since.

With more committee meetings, and going home every weekend thanks to easily available travel by jet, Congress went from being a friendly social place, to a group of individuals more willing to be confrontational with other Congressmen, and now in the twenty-first century almost strangers to each other. This has been seen by many as the end to any compromise as an expectation, and part of why we need to find a new basis for ending gridlock.

The next loss of control followed when the Speaker all but lost influence over the members by ending earmarks (the doling out of "pork" for members to take money back to their districts).

In 2016 the Speaker said that he was almost unable to lead. It is hard to see how a leaderless Congress will ever again get anything done; this does not bode well for a country with a plus twenty trillion dollar debt, and sixty billion dollars a month in trade deficits. In 2020 Nancy Pelosi proved a politically savvy leader can still lead in a time of conflict.

The key factors concerning Carter regarding our story, beyond appointing the man who broke the back of OPEC initiated inflation, was his rescue of America's pro-west leader of Iran during the Cold War, the Shah, when Iran was successfully over taken by the Islamist. In retaliation the Islamist captured seventy-nine Americans and held them hostage until the day and hour Carter left office. The second was the settlement of hostilities between Israel and Egypt.

Carter was defeated after one term by Ronald Reagan, and the Reagan era began. America was one hundred and eighty-nine years old, not at war, and less than one trillion dollars in debt. The Cold War was in its thirty-sixth year, and Reagan had four great goals in mind, roll back the New Deal, cut taxes, balance the budget, and defeat communism.

What almost no one knew at the time other than Paul Volker, the Carter appointed Federal Reserve Chairman, was the devastating effect of inflation on America. Inflation was driving up the cost of goods, Volker was driving up the cost of money, and OPEC had already driven up the cost of energy. In the early 1980s when I ran a business that bought $300,000 machines and I was paying fifteen percent interest; think what that would do to your mortgage payment.

Eric Sevareid, a political commentator on the ABC TV News team, declared that three things had made America great. They were cheap labor, cheap money, and cheap energy; America no longer had any of the three, and no one knew what to do about it. This became my dad's favorite line about American politics for the rest of his life; he passed away in 1998 on the fourth of July, at the age of eighty-seven. By then free trade was providing cheap labor, a gift to corporations and consumers. It also destroyed wages in America.

Nixon, Ford, and Carter had done little to deal with the impact of inflation during their terms even though Carter had set the solution in motion with the Volker appointment.

Returning to the inflation-related malaise caused by the OPEC oil price increases, there was a key but underappreciated impact. This was the effect of inflation on fixed interest rates for long term mortgages for the Savings and Loan banking industry, combined with the limits on the regulated rate of interest they could pay to attract funds.

The GOP was opposed to bank regulations; the crisis was seen less as an economic problem to mitigate, and more as an ideological opportunity to undermine a New Deal program, regulation of mortgage banking including deposit insurance. Bankers wanted access to riskier investments with greater profits, but GOP ideology never considers the impact on the federal budget if insured savings had to be rescued from speculative banking failure. Remember New Deal government insurance of individual savings accounts up to one hundred thousand dollars was in effect in the 1980s.

The effect of inflation on the Savings and Loan industry, and the GOP wish to deregulate banking became a perfect storm that ended in the first collapse of the American economy in over fifty years at the end of the Reagan Presidency. Reagan has never been held accountable for any of his ideology driven policies that failed as we shall review. The GOP trait of not acknowledging harmful outcomes of their policies will be the legacy of the full forty year history of using spin, never taking responsibility for outcome failures, not even twenty-two trillion dollars of tax cuts, or even change course, as the last chapter of our book unfolds.

Chapter 10

Reagan Era 1981 to 2020

The Reagan presidency ended in 1989; the Reagan era endures into 2020.

President Reagan's personal legacy is in the top five in history among U.S. presidents; however, his policy outcome legacy is the opposite. To the extent it is understood it is the most devastatingly costly of any president in American history. The Reagan era view of what our founders intended, is the most distorted and inter-generationally corrupt of any president in history, other than the southern leaders in the run up to the Civil War.

Ronald Reagan's presidency was dedicated to a repeal of the New Deal; while he did not undo the most popular of FDR's many social insurance programs, he was most successful in destroying the living wage legacy of the New Deal, and the safe mortgage banking legacy. He also destroyed the FDR legacy of pay as you go taxation, launching the largest debt of any nation in the history of the world.

It is not that Reagan never did anything worthwhile, or like FDR and all other presidents made mistakes, that is not the focus of this book. Our focus will be on Reagan's main ideological based policy decisions. They were trillion dollar mistakes, including tax cuts, deregulation of mortgage banking, leaving government insurance in place without charging adequate premiums for the new level of risk, and free trade, while leaving employment based healthcare, retirement funding, and other mandated payroll burdens in place. The unaddressed issue is the fact all these decisions placed funding for needed social insurance costs (by income taxes in most countries) in competition with China's slave labor rate wages and cost. These policies also impacted our nation's balance of trade, destroyed jobs and income for the lower half of all wage earners, and reduced to poverty levels towns that lost their factories. That Reagan made all of these decisions without a second thought will be our key insight. We will give President Reagan full credit for his ending the Cold

War. The forty year continuous widening of the wealth and wage gap with no end in sight is the most hopeless fact of all his outcomes.

History will be most laudatory about his willingness to end the cold war without a shot being fired. If I were to sum up his legacy I'd define it as a return to speculative capitalism, which still produces great wealth over time. However, it is a process of boom and bust, with great rewards for the winners, almost always the top twenty percent of Americans, and great pain for the losers, usually the bottom forty percent of Americans, in both wages and in 2020 the wealth gap. And so we begin our final chapter with billionaires and evangelicals in full war cry against secular outcomes of improving outcomes for all Americans, seen as a war on capitalism and Christianity.

In the 1964 presidential race Ronald Reagan was already very familiar to the America public as a movie actor and a TV host for GE Theater, and a GOP political leader. 1964 was not just the year the Civil Rights Bill became law, it was also a presidential election year. Senator Barry Goldwater of Arizona was not a household name in national politics, but he won the GOP primary race as the first candidate of the new majority factions of the GOP who defined themselves as "Movement Conservatives". Reagan gave a speech to introduce Barry Goldwater, his first political speech which is still referred to by Reagan fans as the "A Time for Choosing" speech, and in the process he introduced himself as a new kind of politician, a TV savvy one. We will review Reagan's speech paragraph by paragraph.

It was an eleven page speech and along with introducing Goldwater, it highlighted the intent of the Movement Conservative manifesto, penned by William F. Buckley's brother-in-law as noted earlier. Buckley was a leading intellectual in the GOP, hosting the first successful conservative TV interview show. The manifesto titled *Conscience of a Conservative* is still sold on the internet with Barry Goldwater noted as the author. I keep a copy on my desk along with several other post WWII transitional documents, as well as founding documents including a copy of the U.S. Constitution, the Federalist Papers, and pre-revolution documents including the King James I Bible.

In the middle third of his speech Reagan spelled out his and the Movement's ideas, and where he and Barry Goldwater believed America stood thirty years into FDR's New Deal.

Reagan's first political speech serves as an introduction to blow back not just to the GOP belief in speculative capitalism as a dynamic growth machine, he also longed for a return to pre-regulatory freedoms of the time before the two Roosevelts introduced regulation of economic opportunism and risk taking. Most surprising, he and Goldwater laid out a pristine view of the days when revelation was the authority to govern, and property rights were sacred. Reagan promised a return to the freedoms our founders had actually bequeathed us, which actually looked more like what our founders revolted against. This speech and Goldwater's manifesto amounted to an attack on the Bill of Rights.

Reagan called for repeal and replacement of almost all FDR had introduced, which in fact had relieved and reformed the worst outcomes of GOP speculative capitalism that created the great depression, including a failed unregulated form of capitalism that produced the great wealth that capitalism has become famous for, along with huge crashes that devastated the working class, including their employers and banks, in small towns across the nation every twenty years or so, as America became industrialized.

Our founders gave us Liberty (freedom) and Equality (justice) first announced as an intent in the Declaration of Independence, and enshrined in the Constitution and Bill of Rights from the time of final ratification in 1791. In his speech Reagan introduces the intent of the soon to be new GOP, as an absolute demand that America "chose between Freedom or Security". Based on outcomes it turned out he did intend a single factor of (economic) freedom, the pursuit of dynastic wealth, without the equality of (economic) justice.

In the most undemocratic utterance of any future President of the United States, Reagan dismissed the founders' concept of equality, ending any pretense of democracy. "Government is not the solution, government is the problem"; this is the first of about a dozen folksy quotes I'll cite, that soften the reality of a return to subsistence living for most of the bottom third of Americans, and abject poverty for about ten percent of the citizens of the richest nation in the history of the world. He defined the government as the problem because he was talking about our democratic self government. He meant it as his record regarding outcomes will show.

From 1940 when the Depression ended as America ramped up for WWII until Reagan's election in 1980, every generation of Americans did better than their parents' generation; from Reagan's election until 2020 only half of each generation has done better than their parents.

My breakdown of Reagan's introductory speech and later in this chapter my review of Reagan's presidential diaries will explain why and how implementation of Reagan's policies caused the loss of equality, democracy, justice, and thereby these generational outcome reversals for the hourly living wage middle class, and the working poor citizens of the United States.

I have included Reagan's key thirteen paragraphs, which I have broken down between his thoughts and my comments. I saw his speech not as a new breakthrough, but more as a call for a major fallback to the speculative and thereby disastrous economic times before citizens' rights and a living wage became viable.

Through science and industrialization, citizens were empowered to provide ever increasing value added to the economic output of the United States based on the amount of wealth added per unit of work, combined with the amount of ever increasing knowledge and skill of the work force, part the result of self investment, part tax payer investment, and part employee training.

Combined annual productivity has continued to grow by leaps and bounds, far beyond a fair return on investment for property owners. This has also created ever greater stress and demands on the work force. Remember Lucy in the chocolate factory. This productivity level was never experienced or expected under the Romans' feudal system, nor later during the English feudal system, nor by America's founding generation before the Civil War.

FDR was the first national leader of a modern industrial nation to address this new reality. The GOP still has not accepted that the wage earner is justly entitled to a fair share of the value his labor adds, and that it rightly must be shared partly beyond the owner's fair share with the laborer, and to the nation for the common good and defense for sustainability, the cost of educating our citizens, and building and maintaining our infrastructure. FDR empowered labor with a right to organize and bargain, and the nation to tax at a sustainable level. Reagan and the ideological think tanks of the GOP introduced a concept they quietly defined as public choice solutions, along with for-profit solutions to government investment in the nation's future. My comments are intended to reflect the new reality of FDR's insight, in light of the intent of our founding authority to govern bargain and Reagan era outcomes.

Gridlock in America cannot end until the absolutism introduced during the Reagan Era is understood by the majority of twenty-first century Americans as only protecting property rights, not citizens' rights, and that it goes back to a time of defined religious duties as subjects, without civil (secular rights as citizens) justice.

Remember who wrote the Constitution; it was written by men of property representing the property owners of the individual states at the Constitutional Convention in Philadelphia in 1787. It was written to protect property rights, just as the representatives understood property rights under the English common law they lived under, which continued as the state law after presenting the Declaration of Independence to the world. English common law was supported by the Biblical Christian state church at the time and is still based on revelation as being authorized by the will of God.

Who had to ratify the new Constitution in the thirteen former colonies, now individual sovereign states formed into a Constitutional Republic? Based on the Declaration of Independence the founders announced that the nation would be ruled by the consent of the governed as free men with rights based on the God of nature's creation, assuring equality regarding three basic rights: life, liberty, and the pursuit of happiness.

That meant neither the states nor the property owners were to be the sole interest of the citizens-to-be at the ratification convention even if most represented the property class. The subjects were free to demand ratification based on a bargain whereby they exchanged leaving property rights to be protected by the states, and citizens' individual rights to be entrusted to the national government, in which secular rights are inherent, the gift of a free natural universe the God of creation bequeathed us as our creator.

The government was to be structured under this new document called the Constitution, ratified in 1789 subject to a bill of rights as a republic, to ensure one branch was to represent the interest of the states and their property owners called the Senate with equal representation for each state with two senators each, and another branch to represent the interests of the people (defined as citizens) called the House of Representatives.

Today each representative represents about seven hundred thousand citizens, and each state's number of representatives is based on a census taken every ten years. These two houses made up the Congress of the United States empowered in Article 1. Article 2 empowered the Executive Branch, responsible for the common good and defense of the nation, elected based on both a popular election and an electoral college, and finally a Judiciary to settle Constitutional disputes.

The modern GOP and Reagan's speech to a large extent rely on the intent of the 1787 Constitution, and less so on the 1791 final amendable Constitution including the Bill of Rights. FDR's first speech to a large extent was the first major address by a president based on the outcomes of the new realities of the industrial age, under the original intent of the final ratification of the Constitution in 1791.

Why did the people demand a Bill of Rights? They were agreeing to a bargain exchanging states' rights to protect property owners, for the federal government protecting the citizens of the nation from injustice under the police powers of the state, and from economic injustice under the employment and contracting power of the property owners. They needed assured security that the federal government was empowered to protect their rights. The Bill of Rights protected the people's individual rights. The power to uphold their protection fell to the Supreme Court. In the Reagan era the Supreme Court, under GOP nominating criteria, have arguably failed workers, women, and minorities in favor of property owners and evangelical Christians, as we shall review.

Ronald Reagan's 1964 speech: This was an eleven page address, easily accessed online in its entirety. I'm inserting here a two page summary of Reagan's message. What I left out are the dozens of examples of his objections to what amounts to the government having become too large, too illogical, and too costly, at least for his taxation sensibilities.

I'll give just one of his examples here before the summary. Reagan explained, a judge had told him a young women pregnant with her seventh child came to court for a divorce. The judge questioned the husband who did not want a divorce; however, the husband explained, he made only $250 a month, and his wife was told the welfare payment amount she would get if she divorced him would be $350 and she wanted a raise. Reagan did not see this as a Democrat does, as a lack of living wage issue. Reagan saw the Democrats as do-gooders, denouncing this tolerance as being opposed to humanitarian goals. He ends this with a statement "It seems impossible to legitimately debate their solutions with the assumption that all of us share the desire to help those less fortunate".

In my opinion almost every example misses the point of the purpose of a form of government by, for, and of the people. With President Reagan and the GOP, government is of, by, and for property, profits, and owners. Not a meaningful thought or care is extended to the masses of families who depend on wages, that both the government and the workers invest money, time, and effort to perfect the needed knowledge and skills the nation and its employers depend on, not to mention ever more demand for increased productivity.

This is an example of why Democrats like myself support policies with common good, and establishment of justice outcomes, meaning sustainable rational boundaries concerning profits, wages, taxes, and public aid as part of a just society, and why GOP ideology accepts low wages and taxes for dynastic wealth families and abject childhood poverty for millions of children of working families, as ideology based outcomes without seeing any factor of justice to consider.

There are two or three issues on every page of Reagan's speech that miss the point of more and additional citizens living in poverty as the nation became ever wealthier over the course of the twentieth century. As I read this the first time I thought to myself, the whole concept of the common good, and establishment of justice is lost on this man and his party and its ideology. In the forty years since he came to power, that insight on my part has not changed nor has the ever increasing number of children living in poverty, nor the ever growing wealth of the nation.

"A Time for Choosing"

The Summary: "I am going to talk of controversial things. I make no apology for this. It's time we asked ourselves if we still know the freedoms our founding fathers meant for us. James Madison said, "We base all our experiments on the capacity of mankind for self government".

This idea? That government was beholden to the people, that it had no other source of power is still the newest, most unique idea in all the long history of man's relation to man. This is the issue of this election: Whether we believe in our capacity for self-government or whether we abandon the American Revolution and confess that little intellectual elites in a far-distant capital can plan our lives for us better than we can plan them for ourselves.

You and I are told we must chose between a left or right, but I suggest there is no such thing as a left or right. There is only an up or down. Up to man's age old dream - the maximum individual freedom consistent with order or down to the ant heap of totalitarianism.

Regardless of their sincerity, their humanitarianism motives, those who would sacrifice freedom for security have embarked on this downward path. Plutarch warned, "The real destroyer of the liberties of the people is he who spreads among them bounties, donation and benefits.

The Founding Fathers knew a government cannot control the economy without controlling people. And they knew when a government set out to do that, it must use force and coercion to achieve its purpose. So we have come to a time of choosing.

Public servants say, always with the best of intentions, What greater public service we could render if only we had a little more money and a little more power. But the truth is that outside of its legitimate function, government does nothing as well or as economically as the private sector.

Yet any time you and I question the schemes of the do-gooders, we're denounced as being opposed to their humanitarian goals. It seems impossible to legitimately debate their solutions with the assumption that all of us share the desire to help the less fortunate. They tell us we're always "against" never "for" anything.

We are for a provision that destitution should not follow unemployment by reason of old age, and to that end we have accepted Social Security as a step toward meeting the problem.

We need true tax reform that will at least make a start toward restoring for our children the American Dream that wealth is denied to no one, that each individual has the right to fly as high as his strength and ability will take him....But we can not have such reform while our tax policy is engineered by people who view the tax as a means of achieving changes in our social structure

Have we the courage and the will to face up to the immorality and discrimination of the progressive tax, and demand a return to traditional proportionate taxation? Today in our country the tax collectors share is thirty-seven cents of every dollar earned. Freedom has never been so fragile, so close to slipping from our grasp.

Are you willing to spend time studying the issues, making yourself aware, and then conveying that information to family and friends? Will you resist the temptation to get a government handout for your community? Realize that the doctor's fight against socialized medicine is your fight. We can't socialize the doctors without socializing the patients. Recognize that government invasion of public power is eventually an assault upon your own business. If some among you fear taking a stand because you are afraid of reprisals from customers, clients, or even government, recognize that you are just feeding the crocodile hoping he'll eat you last.

If all of this seems like a great deal of trouble, think what's at stake. We are faced with the most evil enemy mankind has known in his long climb from the swamp to the stars. There can be no security anywhere in the free world if there is no fiscal and economic stability within the United States. Those who ask us to trade our freedom for the soup kitchen of the welfare state are architects of a policy of accommodation."

Author's comment: Read the last paragraph above a second time. President-to-be Reagan is demanding fiscal and economic stability for the United States and then when he became president he cut taxes and doubled military spending, destroying fiscal and economic stability; talk about bait and switch. He actually called those who created the living wage middle class economy of the New Deal who also ended Jim Crow and won WWII against fascism "the most evil enemy mankind has known".

"They say the world has become too complex for simple answers. They are wrong. There are no easy answers, but there are simple answers. We must have the courage to do what we know is morally right. Winston Churchill said that "the destiny of man is not measured by material computation. When great forces are on the move in the world, we learn we are spirits - not animals." And he said, "there is something going on in time and space, and beyond time and space, which, whether we like it or not, spells duty."

You and I have a rendezvous with destiny. We will preserve for our children this, the last best hope of man on earth, or we will sentence them to take the first step into a thousand years of darkness. If we fail, at least let our children and our children's children say of us we justified our brief moment here. We did all that could be done."

President Reagan ended this speech expressing his legacy hopes for our grandchildren. In fact the legacy he has left for them is trillions of dollars of debt, and a nation in as deep a gridlock as in the pre Civil War era. The percentage of voters under thirty-five years old who register GOP is the lowest in fifty years; it is based on Reagan policy outcomes. Half of all voters in this age group's cost of living have more than doubled in their lifetime, while wages have gone up hardly at all.

This speech is considered one of the greatest speeches ever by an American president; not because it was true to our founding principles or because it led to improved outcomes for the American people, it is considered great because one speech catapulted Ronald Reagan to the front of presidential politics.

Goldwater lost in a landslide and Reagan was launched. Reagan became the second GOP president elected using what became known as the Southern Strategy. Richard Nixon had won in 1968 but was too complex to be a change agent; Reagan instituted the ideologies of his "A Time for Choosing" speech beginning in 1981, after he won in 1980.

The ever growing debt, the two market crashes, the loss of jobs and wages to Asia, the end of the union movement, the decline of public education support, the neglect of infrastructure, the rise of voter ID and gerrymandering, the massive military budgets, sixteen years of wars in the Middle East, the end of the draft, and the blind eye to Mexican immigration encouraged and abetted by GOP supporting employers, the contra wars, and now the cultural turning on these immigrants: our children's debt and wage stagnation are all byproducts of this transition, of the GOP backlash against gains for the lower income half of all Americans under the New Deal.

Having gained the role he sought Reagan summed this up in his inauguration speech in 1981 with the following, worth repeating here:

"Government is not the solution to our problems; government is the problem."

Goldwater in his introduction to his manifesto cited a return to revelation as his authority to govern goal. Taking him at his word, he declared an intent to return our American government's authority to govern back to "by the divine right of kings".

America does not have a king or a state church department, so I'm not sure exactly what Goldwater meant. It seems he wished to fix the "mistake" our founders made introducing individual rights, democracy, and judicial review in place of absolute rule for the benefit of property ownership. Perhaps he wished to return absolute control over the families who labor for property owners as granted by divine right, i.e., by the will of God.

What a horrible legacy these Movement Conservative ideology leaders have sold as our founders original intent: Robert Taft, Ronald Reagan, Barry Goldwater, the Koch Brothers, Antonio Scalia, Strom Thurmond, and Dick Cheney who was the dark whisperer in the ears of both Ronald Reagan and George W. Bush. Their ideology produced policies defined as supply side tax cuts, mortgage banking deregulation, free trade that destroyed middle class living wage jobs, and so on. All failed to do more good than harm, and will become Reagan's legacy once the guile and spin of his era is over, when only the truth of his outcomes remain to be repaired and repaid.

Charles Koch makes the list as he has codified the ideology of the GOP by underwriting the institution that developed the economic concept of public choice policies, i.e., outsourcing most traditional U.S. government services to for-profit corporations owned by the wealthy, including as examples jails, schools, healthcare, infrastructure such as roads, and bridges. Note: As a former postal employee it appears the postal service is being starved into a transition to for-profit, supporting absolute corporate control over wages and benefits for employees using state sponsored right-to-work policies. For-profit, public choice employment usually pays much less than the U.S. government, and without healthcare or retirement benefits. The postal service has five hundred thousand employees. These employees would move from the middle class to the working poor, which is typical and the reason the GOP supports this ideology. Typically the for-profit system charges higher prices, which is a double squeeze on the working poor, and the outcome for them is lower wages along with higher cost for basic services like road and bridge tolls.

I have a favorite quote that I heard many years ago from a neighbor regarding the working poor: **"nothing over comes the debilitating effects of poverty like money".** I'd change the word money to a living wage.

Once Reagan was in power he seemed more interested in rolling back history about one hundred years, not all the way back to the days of King James I, just to before the first great depression era of 1907. It seems he wished to go back to a time of low wages, low taxes, and low cost of energy, with little regulation, as if the wealth of industrialism happened without the cost of a successful system of regulation to control speculation, build the huge infrastructure, and the cost of an educated work force suitable for training to operate and repair the mechanized military, or the huge cost in fact of mechanized, electronic, and digitized industry in a now global market.

Had Reagan not read of or even heard about the risk of unfettered speculative capitalism, or did he just rue sharing the rewards of wealth creation with labor, veterans, and a sustainable national government that do most of the heavy lifting?

Let's review how Reagan's dream has worked out so far economically thirty-eight years later. Are investors, the well educated, savers, and dynastic families wealthier? Yes!

Are wage earners more secure with improved wages and benefits including better or fully funded healthcare, and better pensions? No!

Are consumers less in debt, as well as our nation less in debt? No!

Is old age security more secure? Do most of us believe public education has improved? Is America much more secure around the world, and are Americans safer in their workplaces, schools, pews, and entertainment venues? Are the poor less likely to be imprisoned than in pre Reagan days? Have we built and maintained more super highways, airports, railroads, and bridges with less debt than were built in the higher tax days of the New Deal? No to all of these public policy issues!

If not, why are so called Reagan Democrats happy with the outcome of their votes? Did wage earning Reagan Democrats get the benefit of their bargain in believing Reagan's folksy promises? Are they and their children's economic lives more secure in small towns across rural and larger city America? Maybe that's what they meant when they voted for Trump, they wanted their lives to be as great as they were during the days of the New Deal. Today, instead of children following their dads into the factory or mine that supported the town, are they in despair and dying of drug overdoses?

Before we fully move deeper into the policies and outcomes of the Reagan era, let's introduce the man who would be Reagan's main adversary, and the only one left to defend FDR's legacy to the extent it could be saved by what was left of the Democrats' party without union white men and the former segregationist wing of the party, that now called itself the evangelical wing of the GOP. The last man standing as the leader of the Democratic Party was Tip O'Neill.

We've already mentioned Tip in the waning days of the FDR era, so let's re-introduce Tip who was known as the "Man of the House" with an old fashion outlook on politics that hardly looks partisan by today's standards. Tip was an old Boston transactional politician who had long represented Charlestown across the Charles River from Boston Massachusetts; he was the Speaker of the U.S. House of Representatives in the U.S. Congress for all eight years of the Reagan presidency.

Tip was appalled by the president's condemnation of government as the problem that American citizens should intentionally try to starve (Reagan came to call his deficits "starving the beast"). Tip believed the U.S. government had been and should continue to be the solution to almost all that ailed mankind. Tip did not live to see the outcome of Reagan's free trade globalization of the American economy when he opened America's borders to labor rates from China, which Reagan approved by presidential order in September 1985.

President Reagan is the only president I ever heard state that he did not see our Constitutional government as the best solution to protect the citizens of any nation in history. I'm not sure from "the speech" if he had a fully balanced understanding of the checks and balances built into the Constitution, or as importantly, the tension between property rights enshrined in the Constitution and administered by the states, and citizens' rights enshrined in the Bill of Rights including the amendment process, and assurance by the federal government from abuse by a citizen's home state of residence, as a factor of the authority to govern bargain. Remember our federal government governs "by the consent of the governed", meaning the citizens as voters.

As a long time member of the House of Representatives, Tip O'Neil believed that elections had consequences. He believed each president deserved an opportunity to try his hand at accomplishing what he had promised the folks back home his policies would accomplish.

To me this is what democracy means. This is why I did not appreciate to hear in "the speech" that those in the New Deal who rescued capitalism along with the nation in the 1930s were referred to as a small group of elite intellectuals. Like President Reagan they were elected by a majority and deserved to be judged by their outcomes, as Reagan should also.

In Reagan's first year Tip was determined to allow just that, even though he disagreed with almost every issue in the new president's platform. Tip trusted that if Reagan's conservative solutions failed, the media would report the outcomes, and the Congress and the next president could fix the failures.

Tip was wrong. President Reagan ignored the failures, announced it was morning in America, and with a smile sold tax cut debt and a deregulated real estate boom about to bust as had all speculative booms. He called it a miracle even after it went bust, which most of his GOP followers still celebrate thirty-nine years later with twenty plus trillion dollars in debt as the outcome. Just as importantly jobs and wages for the middle class contracted.

Tip told President Reagan that any Democrats who did not want to cooperate and have Reagan's ideology enacted as policy would cooperate if they wanted committee assignments (about the only power left to Speakers of the House by the early 1980s) as long as he was still the Speaker; and they did for most of Reagan's first term until his policies were failing.

The GOP voted against Reagan policy outcomes in a GOP primary for the first time in 2016, but without acknowledging in any way that the Reagan agenda or his policies had contributed to the outcomes Trump exploited. Donald Trump, who ran against the outcomes of free trade and other Reagan policies, repeated the tax cuts as a first legislative step of the Trump presidency, with an expected return to growing debt and deficits, which have ensued.

It is notable that by 1981 when Reagan was sworn in, Strom Thurmond was still a Republican Senator and a leader in the southern faction of the GOP in the Senate. Strom wished to keep as much control as possible in the states and out of the hands of the federal system, especially the federal court system, which could impose and enforce individual rights for minority constituencies that could not be gained through the legislative process, especially in the state Houses. Strom and Reagan had both backed Barry Goldwater for president in 1964. Goldwater was the first candidate for president after WWII who disagreed with Truman about the Cold War, and the first until Trump who openly considered nuclear war as an option as Commander in Chief.

It was a fair question to ask Reagan if he would uphold the Truman Doctrine behind the cold war containment strategy that the past two GOP Presidents Eisenhower and Nixon had upheld. Reagan started out looking like a Goldwater hawk on the cold war but as Gorbachev put out feelers about winding down the cold war, Reagan began to trust Gorby as he was known. He joined Gorby and together they ended the cold war. Ending the cold war was in my mind and in the minds of many Americans, President Ronald Reagan's greatest accomplishment. It was a few more years before the Russian Empire imploded during the presidency of George H. W. Bush and the Soviet Empire ended.

Reagan's personal popularity is well known, but perhaps not so well understood. I see it as a mixture of myth-making by those who deny his failures, the intentional blindness of true believers, and nostalgia for the norms of the good old days, especially concerning cultural norms.

Ronald Reagan in fact had an engaging personality, a sunny disposition, and a charming way about him. It might have been impossible for GOP party advocates to sell their policies if not for the largely true version of Reagan the man as a communicator.

At best the Movement Conservative policies Reagan enacted with Tip

O'Neil's concurrence have done more harm than good; at worst they are as they look when spelled out, disasters that have destroyed the middle class living wage norms of the New Deal era, returned boom and bust speculative capitalism and banking, and created twenty-two trillion dollars of growing and compounding debt on the income tax based general ledger side of the consolidated annual national budget. He also recreated Federalism into the most expensive welfare transfer of wealth from sustainable blue states to dysfunctional unsustainable red states.

Reagan's ideals of unfettered speculative capitalism, unregulated mortgage banking, unfettered free trade, under funding taxes compared to appropriation, and military over spending, in the sense the GOP has refused to tax equal to their appropriations, or their decisions to invade Middle East nations, starting with the Marines in Lebanon thirty-five years ago by President Reagan without a plan, are less a policy and more Reagan's support for a pledge to always vote against tax increases even in time of war, his "Starving the Beast" remedy to perceived New Deal attacks on American capitalism and property rights.

Ronald Reagan was a man bigger than life and as personally humble man as can be found, having a large historical economic impact in American history in his own way, though much less down to earth than Harry Truman, or Jimmy Carter, other modern era personally humble men who became presidents.

In this introduction to Reagan my hope is to help folks who are frustrated by our gridlock and widening wealth gap better understand how people could love Reagan the man, even when his policies failed.   The answer is part Reagan's success as a communicator, part partisan party spin, part the amount of emotion folks put into Reagan's message related to the long ignored legacy of Jim Crow, but in the end,   mostly due to his popularity the Democrats' feared attacking, even the outcomes of Reagan failures. In any case Reagan is still held as a successful president, yet his economic policies cannot be the insight for solutions needed for the remainder of American economic governance in the twenty-first century. That Reagan's tax cut policies are still a key GOP strategy is an ever growing problem.

To ignore Reagan's impact on the past forty years, or to deny his role regarding our current debt, low wages, and our two financial crashes in twenty years, or the current gridlock as not a Reagan legacy is to not allow ourselves to be honest about what has led to the current political gridlock, especially our financial gridlock that has created our ever widening wealth gap that is not sustainable.

While Ronald Reagan joined bedfellows politically in forming a governing majority with the Strom Thurmond and Charles Koch wings of his party, he personally was primarily motivated in reaction to FDR's income tax policies, and his hatred of communism. Both positions were and still are popular with most Americans if not the outcomes. The key factors of the Reagan presidency that have crippled America in a number of ways are based on what I see as secondary ideological issues and while not planned, did in fact destroy the middle class and widen the wage and the wealth gap for the working poor. Also unplanned, Reagan's policies were not reviewed at the time beyond ideological beliefs by anyone other than David Stockman, Reagan's first budget director and then only in the first term until Stockman left the White House.

An interesting thought is to what extent Ronald Reagan's legacy is on trial, if not his fame and love. He remains an idealized leader to millions of folks who are angry with the outcomes of the Reagan era yet still love the man, and have seldom connected any dots between the man, the ideology, the policies, and the outcomes.

In fact the Tea Party makes it a point to spin the cause of the 2007 mortgage boom and bust. They blame Jimmy Carter for ending red lining from before Reagan's Savings and Loan deregulation crash, or blame Barack Obama instead of George W. Bush and Leader McConnell who allowed Freddie and Fannie to deregulate themselves in 2004 while leaving government insurance in place.

In the early twenty-first century there is no president more Americans would like to see added to Mount Rushmore than Ronald Reagan! How worthy is the Reagan legacy compared to the men on that mountain?

Reagan's stated goal was to repeal FDR's programs which he saw as having over regulated and overtaxed Americans, both individuals and businesses. Left unsaid is that he totally ignored the realities of the upside of the New Deal, from safe banking to the consumer economy based on the living wage of union negotiated wages and benefits. That his policies would have a downside to those New Deal improvements is never mentioned in his diary.

In pursuit of this goal the GOP sold Reagan's ideas to America, while claiming that it was the goal of the to make all but the most economically successful Americans dependent on the federal government and the , wholly with a singular intent to garner assured votes from dependents.

I no more believe FDR and New Deal Democrats intentionally kept the poor in poverty for votes, than I believe the GOP ignored the issues of the poor and hungry to intentionally keep them poor and hungry. Both have a higher purpose than intentional poverty to ensure votes. I do however believe one party is way more tolerant (indifferent at the government level) of poverty, and see it as a norm of life in our wealthy nation.

In fact the New Deal made more middle class folks successful, with a lower percent of the population in hunger and with less debt than did the Reagan ideologies of absolutism. Reagan's ideals were a legacy from his years at GE, his support of the belief system his evangelical segregationist supporters Billy Graham and Strom Thurmond brought to the modern GOP, reinserting Nicene Biblical Christian revelation, and the Economic Freedom ideology the Koch Network resurrected from English common law based states' new right-to-work and corporate rights , along with a low education investment, tax, and wage ideology, sold as small government; hardly contained government in fact.

The truth is that Democratic Party policies had moved most wage earners from abject poverty (when the modern era polices were initiated in 1933) to the middle class. It is also true that from 1964 Democratic policies raised both the working poor and the unemployed out of poverty, as well as reducing the number of poor children who were hungry going to bed at night and coming to school in the morning. That women and blacks have progressed since 1964 are also all but obvious to all but the most partisan.

Nearing the third decade of the twenty-first century the number of American children who go to bed hungry has returned, and is now higher than ever, as part of the wealth gap created as an outcome of these policies of cutting taxes, promoting right-to-work laws, freezing minimum wages, and opening American borders for manufactured goods to China's subsistence labor policies, while reducing the budgets for the safety net including SNAP program food access funding.

The GOP refers to FDR and LBJ policies not only as socialist, but also as initiative destroyers that have been inflicted heartlessly (as if they know the hearts of thousands of New Deal legislators) to create a permanent voting block of people who have traded individual freedom for these welfare benefits of FDR and LBJ.

This is their stated belief as spun, that the only purpose of the New Deal and the War on Hunger was to get the vote of poor folks and the working poor blacks and women. It would be logical to expect that poor folks getting a fairer portion in the distribution of national wealth would vote their own best interest.

The spin achieved two objectives: increase the vote of those who came to believe the improvements were unearned and came at the expense of those who already worked hard, and create a sense of shame in those who worked for less than a living wage, keeping them in the dark in fear as they had been kept throughout the history of organized state governance and religion since the founding of the combined Roman church state in the first historical instance of organizing both church and state.

On the other hand FDR Democrats believe the GOP used reduced tax policy to pander to the wealthy and business owners. Since this group of voters is not large enough to elect candidates (at least until they obtained current toleration for dark money as speech) the GOP reached out to other groups. Pandering is not too strong a word for the GOP accepting Strom Thurmond's new southern racial norms that blacks needed to be segregated only because they were not yet ready for a role in government or commerce.

The third major pandering (if that is the appropriate GOP term for programs like LBJ's war on hunger) was at the beginning of the Reagan era. Southern evangelical leaders such as Pat Robertson and Jerry Falwell became active in the GOP; the Reagan team courted their large block of committed conservative voters who saw the outcomes of a number of Supreme Court decisions as the work of "activist jurists". Churches were tax exempt and their pastors defied President Eisenhower, daring him to interfere with their tax exemption. He did not, and they are now fully political and still fully tax exempt, even if a pastor owns several plus twenty million dollar airplanes.

Many evangelical believers had agreed with FDR when he used the argument that the Preamble showed the intent of the founders, and found latent rights for groups of minorities who had been isolated from Constitutional protections because of the dominance of property rights and the old state church laws that had kept the poor, landless, women, and slaves without rights.

Evangelicals often see individual secular rights as government sanctioned sin, which is not what the Constitution intended when the courts were assigned the duty of upholding the secular U.S. Constitution which only means we are a democratic republic with freedom of religion, freeing bishops to full time duties as leaders in the area of salvation for individuals who seek salvation.

The Constitution not only ended the concept of heresy as a crime, it ended the concept of sin as a factor of law making. Sin is a factor of conscience if an individual's path to salvation is based on acts proscribed by the theology of a sect as sins. Evangelicals cannot rid the body politic in the United States of this conflict until and unless they end the use of the word sin in their politicking about secular sin, as if there was such a thing. Secular and sin are mutually exclusive concepts, one regards God, the other Caesar as Jesus states in the Gospels.

Without the concept of sin, the private use, funding, and openly selling birth control equally along with other drugs become a non issue politically. I recognize that the tax free status of birth control pills should accrue to the user, and not to an employer (as a legacy of avoidance of a racial issue in 1951 when the tax exemption on healthcare for employees of corporations was enacted). I do not agree with the GOP jurists who ruled on the issue in the Hobby Lobby decision.

Government promised to never interfere with individual religious beliefs, as long as they do not directly impact the lives of other individual Americans engaged in civil legal activities. Madison's statement that government should not be charged with sorting out heresy still seems wise, considering the number of wars and executions that took place over the centuries for the crime of heresy, until America made Freedom of Religion a secular individual concept and right. Think about it, freedom of religion is not a theological or religious concept. One true religion is more often the concept and demand of organized religion in the world.

The government can only be changed without being subversive, at the ballot box or as an amendment to the Constitution, or by impeachment. In this chapter we will review the Hobby Lobby case in depth, so I'm going to remind my readers that perhaps in John Marshall's most important settled case, Marbury versus Madison, he also established the simple important understanding "every right deserves a remedy", even when it challenges the wishes of a president.

When Marshall's court settled their means of upholding the Constitution they legally changed a fact of governance in America. It was accepted by the president and legislators in the first term of the third president in 1803. Jefferson, Madison, Adams, and Hamilton were all alive and accepted Marshall's settlements of the judicial review issue. As partisans Jefferson and Madison disagreed with Marshall's federalist politics, but accepted the Supreme Court's right to settle the Constitutionality of legal disputes, including the method of settlement in upholding the U.S. Constitution.

Note: Sixty years later in the 1860s Abraham Lincoln's comments on the Dred Scott case I believe best defined the meaning of settled law in the United States. Lincoln stated there were two types of Supreme Court decisions: settled and erroneous. Marbury versus Madison met Lincoln's standard for settled; it was unanimous and it was not based on bias. The Dred Scott case that Lincoln was discussing was neither unanimous nor free of obvious bias, and he defined such cases as erroneous. I suggest we keep Abraham Lincoln's view of Supreme Court settlement in mind as we review Supreme Court decisions in the Reagan era.

In forming the Reagan coalition, a most unlikely component became what was described at the time as Reagan Democrats. FDR era beneficial middle class outcomes were ignored by these often union members, whose families joined the middle class as beneficiaries of FDR's New Deal. The boom and bust history of unregulated banking was ignored. Folks were willing to throw away all they had gained economically because of emotional feelings about a threat to one or more cultural norms the court addressed, be it race, gender, religion, immigration, or wages.

At the time the focus was not on what conservatives would do to labor rights, the goal was to elect conservatives who would vote to stop tax funded food stamps and welfare being extended to folks who were seen as lazy. So-called Reagan Democrats reacting to emotional cultural rather than thoughtful wage issues rejected FDR's New Deal, LBJ's war on poverty, and joined Reagan's war on welfare cheats. Remember Reagan's comment about "welfare queens in their pink Cadillac's" in his 1980 campaign; we cannot remember what that level of bias means often enough.

The red meat fed to this growing political movement was a diet of beliefs sounding like values that left folks open to the reality of money as speech, and governance in the cabinet by industry lobbyists as the gate keepers.

Among those who have been misled by their cultural leaders' siren song of small government have been those who accepted glorification of unattainable self reliance, assuring disaffected voters they could better spend their own money than bureaucrats and politicians (government) who had raised their taxes too high. They ignored the fact that you pay no taxes if you earn too little, while the less you earn the more you need credit, yet most do not understand usury. What could sound more reasonable than our founders had given us a system of limited government, meaning small was better, or was that really what it meant?

Forgotten was the reality that no small rural state that had a devastating catastrophe ever believed that small government was better when seeking federal aid. But most rural states folks bought into the notion, and union folks in industrial states did not question the logic, when the emotion of the idea that their taxes were being spent on food stamps for the lazy was the shiny object they were invited to focus on.

Reagan's stated mistrust of the federal government ever being helpful became a political belief, even a proof of patriotism. He convinced folks that government was an intrusion in employment, healthcare, banking, housing, retirement, education, and welfare relief. He defined it as a threat to every American's individual freedom. While it remains a large but in fact minority belief, small government and self reliance is a fervent belief with a high voter turnout motivating factor. Let one of these voter's children have a devastating disease, or their home be washed away by flood, and listen to the begging for government to respond, adequately, no matter how great the devastation.

The only political solutions to safe and affordable education, banking, thirty year mortgages for home ownership, funded healthcare, and retirement, have been federal solutions only by the New Deal and the politicians in the who have enacted them.

That there has been no successful national market solution to these human needs of us all, or that there was no such solution ever found in America other than government social insurance with regulations since the New Deal, has never needed to be defended.

Now that government solutions have been attacked for almost forty years, is it not time to reconsider the only solutions that have ever worked? Before 1933 and since 1981 the reality of living on hourly wage earnings in blue collar jobs, and/or as domestic, hospitality, or agricultural non skilled jobs which support about thirty-five to forty percent of all families, was and remains barely at or just above subsistence.

In the twenty-first century even when the GOP spent nine years promising to finally fix healthcare access and funding with a market solution for these folks, it still ignored the fact that access and funding for healthcare is a burden on American payrolls in a global economy for sixty percent of all Americans. It is long past time it should be obvious to all that it makes our products more costly to sell overseas, and more competitive for offshore producers here, and this fact is obviously proved by our never ending month after month of sixty billion dollars more imports each month than exports, costing the U.S. a negative exchange of dollars between the U.S. and primarily China.

The key funding and voting blocks of the Reagan era GOP are corporate and evangelical, and both are very good at their core mission. They do not need to attack government or to try to replace it with for-profit solutions as they each worked well in their own sphere, as did government in its sphere on the day Reagan was sworn in. That we were working our way out of the OPEC oil price shock and the Iranian reaction to giving medical aid to the Shah, did not mean the government system that recovered from the depression, won WWII, and recovered was the problem.

The fact is, constitutionally the American government's mission is to lift the boats of all citizens which is in all our common interest. Let's remind ourselves that the core mission of Christianity is salvation. As noted the core mission of capitalism is wealth creation; the core mission of self governance is the common good of all citizens, including the establishment of justice.

A number of founders reminded us that Congress does not meet for the good of property owners, or corporations, or religion, or themselves; they meet for the good of the citizens, which demands a rational balance if the goals are to be met. None of the four should be at war with the good of the citizens.

In the twenty-first century it should be a losing argument to claim that in a nation with a nineteen or twenty trillion dollar economy, affordable access to fully funded healthcare is not a common or achievable good. Fully funded healthcare is common and has been achieved around the world in nations less rich and less indebted to its citizens for their authority.

By the 1970s both the GOP under the leadership of Richard Nixon, and the Democrats under the leadership of Ted Kennedy regarding healthcare, were seriously looking for cost containment solutions. In 1973 Senator Ted Kennedy proposed and Richard Nixon signed a new for-profit model pioneered by Henry Kaiser in the northwest U.S. states called "managed care", that became know as Health Maintenance Organizations (HMOs). The key insight of the Kaiser Organization was a combination of wellness and preventive care for a fixed fee, which appealed to corporate employers. Doctors were no longer fee for service, they became fixed salaried employees; the incentive was that all bonuses were based on keeping enrollees healthy or more pointedly out of the hospital and on the job.

Not all presidents appear to be aware of changes when speaking on healthcare issues, including that enrollees could only choose a doctor in the HMO their employer chose, and that both the doctors and the HMO could change from year to year. Another factor of insurance in general and HMOs for sure was the need to cherry pick enrollees. Pre-existing conditions and corporations employing folks who worked in toxic environments were shunned. Progressive states formed special pooled funds for pre-existing conditions. Right-to-work low wage states permitted annual low price policies. If you became sick your insurance was not renewable.

Ronald Reagan championed for-profit healthcare, believing competition would lead to lower prices. Corporations cut costs and drove non-profits out of business or bought them.

Once for-profits were established, costs soared then prices began to double. The result has become the most expensive healthcare system in the world, with the most uninsured, adding insult to injury. Millions of doctors now are booked as much as six months in advance with the plus one to two thousand enrollees they see routinely each year. I have not found published information regarding the average time primary doctors now spend on dealing with actively sick patients; however, it would seem to be minimal. Billions of dollars are spent on tests and visits just to reestablish that folks with health insurance are not sick. This insight is never mentioned by any of the professional analyses, and I seek out information almost daily. Think about your own doctor visits and the wait when you really need a doctor, and they tell you if it's an emergency to go to an ER; it is recorded on the answering machine of every doctor's office.

In the Reagan era as the emphasis on for-profit market solutions became a GOP mantra, the promise to find a market solution for the ever growing healthcare funding crisis is totally misguided; to expect profit seekers to be the gate keepers of cost control is a fool's errand.

For-profit and healthcare will come to be proven if not acknowledged, as mutually exclusive by their very nature. A motto of consumerism is "buyer beware". If presidents with advisers do not understand the healthcare funding system, and hospitals and doctors do not publicly post fees and charges, and none are required by law to charge all sick folks the same price for the same service, how will we ever have informed and discerning consumers? It is impossible; the system is not designed to provide what GOP politicians say they want for us.

President Obama announced "you can keep your doctor if you want to"; again, this was an example of a president not understanding how doctors are part of insurance groups and how group membership can change, locking consumers out. It is spin and folly. The degree of how uninformed President Trump was with the actual reality of U.S. healthcare systems was almost total, when he said who knew how difficult healthcare is. He promised to fix it without knowing, and yet most folks he promised want to reelect him.

In 2016 the winning argument in the presidential campaign and in both Houses of Congress was a promise to fix America's failure to provide healthcare access and funding for all Americans. The GOP promised to repeal and replace the Democrats' seven year old solution (ACA) and address young healthy folks who went without health insurance, those with pre-existing conditions left out of affordable solutions, and the folks who made too much for welfare solutions and too little to afford the full cost of market insurance.

No one talks about the lost revenue to the healthcare funding system pool that occurred when Reagan introduced free trade, opening America's borders to China's slave labor rates. This not only destroyed living wage jobs, but also reduced the flow of funding the employers had provided as part of their employees' benefit package. We will address the full results of free trade on the common good and established justice in Reagan's second term.

As much as race has been a continuing issue since our founding, neither the GOP (which is racially whiter than the Democratic Party based on registered voters) nor the Democratic Party are known as a racial party. The GOP is known as a party advocating state and property rights, leaving individuals with both greater opportunity and risk, while Democrats are known as a party of individuals joining to advocate social insurance or mutual security solutions for issues working families cannot provide for themselves without government assured regulation or insurance. Large or small government is a debating point, but it is another folly; America is big, its population, economy, and footprint across the nation and the world are large, and of necessity it's government is very large.

Most of us know in fact there are areas of life where we like to be allowed to make our own choices: whom we marry, how we raise our children, our religion or not, where we live, and our line of work. Some of us disappoint ourselves but most accept the outcome. Most of us cannot afford to buy a house, educate or tend to a seriously ill child, provide one hundred percent on our own for retirement, or rebuild after a horrendous act of nature, and we blame the government at least partially for the outcome if we or our children are left out in the cold. Can we agree government is us and is not the problem?

Yet we often allow folks with an agenda to convince us to believe otherwise. Remember that the outcome of a policy promoted by a small group with an agenda can make things worse, yet even if the outcome is worse than before the new idea was tried, we are more sold on the new reality, because we have a new mindset about it.

That being said, unless we are willing to acknowledge the children of the non-competitive live in hunger and sickness, which is not sellable when so stated, even most conservative voters want to believe healthcare, basic nutrition, and housing are funded beyond what each poor low wage or unemployed family can provide. We are shocked when we hear of families living in cars, yet I volunteered at a food bank at my local Catholic Church in NC, and heard folks often say "no meat please, I live in my car and I cannot cook it".

FDR recognized this and the Democrats used both social insurance and welfare as a mixed solution beyond the tax breaks granted to working individuals and families. In 2018 the GOP did attempt to find a market solution to fund healthcare for the poor; of course it cannot be done, and they failed. Ronald Reagan believed absolutely in for-profit solutions within the market economy. In the end the final plan the GOP brought to the table some thirty-seven years after Reagan stated his healthcare solution preferences, the GOP's best efforts for a solution for funding the poor could not even garner a majority vote in spite of the GOP holding a majority in the legislature. Healthcare for the poor will always be part of any nation's safety net tax expense.

In late 2018 the Democrats took back the House of Representatives largely by emphasizing the failure of the GOP's market solution to healthcare funding. The biggest GOP failure in selling their solution was their inability to assure folks with pre-existing conditions of continued healthcare access and affordability.

Without a national healthcare system, for-profit healthcare is an insurance issue that leaves at least the poorest of citizens almost fully at risk. The reason for insurance is that no one in the bottom two thirds of the wage gap earns enough money to be self reliant. It is that simple.

All buyer beware debit type high deductible, uncancelable insurance cheater's game is unjust insurance, supported only in low pay right-to-work states. All of us are at risk for huge medical bills at some time in life; if we have insurance and we are diagnosed, we are covered; if we are not at risk, we did not lose money, we had gained earned access meaning peace of mind. Peace of mind, assured access, and affordability are the real payoffs, obviously for the sick, and in fact also for those who do not get sick.

As for the GOP and healthcare legislation, at this point in our history if you accept that your political party does not allow Medicare to negotiate pharmaceutical prices, then you agree it is obvious the GOP protects profits over the healthcare needs of citizens as consumers.

I do not suggest you change parties, but I do suggest you threaten to withhold your vote if your Congressman or Congresswoman will not free up Medicare to negotiate drug prices as a first move away from an absolute pure for-profit market solution to healthcare in America.

Economic free market supporting economists like Milton Friedman who mentored Ronald Reagan, Paul Ryan, and Alan Greenspan, have all reinforced each other's goal of conservative market solutions to social issues without a single working program in place after thirty-seven years. This is the reality of policies based on ideology, such as a belief that the market can solve all cost problems in society and ignore outcomes.

I agree there is a moral dilemma providing aid to folks who do not work (not as costly as bailing out speculative bankers), but it is still a moral hazard to guard against. However, the outcome is hardly random for about seventeen million children of the working poor, going to bed hungry every night; the GOP intentionally works to increase that number, not lower it. They have been arguing since the end of slavery "if you feed them, they will not work"; they do not offer employment at a wage above base subsistence. Any disruption such as sickness or a layoff, the children are not just hungry they are starved. The future adult lives of children raised in such unmitigated poverty is much more expensive to our nation in lost opportunity than the cost of providing a less debilitating living experience in childhood; I'm referring to police and prisons cost, and the repeat costs of inter-generational poverty.

Many Reagan supporters saw themselves as advocates of smaller less costly and/or intrusive government based on three Cs of conservative principle, as I heard their intent: Christian faith, Capitalistic solutions, and Conservative government.

The funding and idea producing factors of Reagan's coalition concentrated less on openly selling these ideas, and more on building a new cultural and economic argument of good and evil. We will see an evangelical wing of the new GOP at war with secularism and court legalization of sin (birth control, abortion, same sex marriage, and enforcement of public schools free of Christian proselytizing), corporate and dynastic family wealth at war with taxes, and an end to union rights, coupled with a boost in law and order policing.

Among the factors of these campaign ideas we see the sunny TV side of Reagan's messaging, coupled with young dirty tricksters Roger Stone and Paul Manafort the behind the scenes, and the their partner Lee Atwater who passed away at a young age. We were exposed to a relentless blitz of what came to be known as dark money supplied by corporations and dynastic families of wealth, selling innocent sounding theories of "public choice" and "economic freedom" allied under dozens of patriotic sounding tax free education foundations undermining what are often the best interests of families that labor for wages.

If that's the ideal it is no more realistic than a liberal belief would be if Democrats promised they could solve poverty with welfare. Neither capitalism nor welfare has a mission to end poverty.

However, thirty years into public choice and economic freedom the GOP still has not explained to American voters what these ideologies actually mean regarding wages, benefits, and earned rights in retirement any more than which version of Biblical Christianity will become America's governing Christianity, or how national infrastructure and/or military strength will be funded or successful if the central government ever in fact becomes a small government in a dangerous world.

None of the leaders of any of the three groups noted above, the cultural leaders, the economic leaders, or the political leaders of the modern GOP discuss the first forty years of negative outcomes for the bottom half of U.S. citizens, since they first gained control in 1981 other than spin, and conservative media follows suit.

So let's review President Reagan's policies one by one and see if I can back up my assessment of the Reagan legacy among the major wings of the GOP. Let's start with tax cuts as that was the new president's first priority, confirmed in the two most honest assessments of his record I have read. The first assessment is his first year budget director David Stockman's book *The Triumph of Politics*, and the second is Reagan's diaries updated nightly during his White House years, published after he left office.

They are in agreement on policy the first two years, less so on outcomes. David pointed out the facts to his boss, and the diaries record Reagan's comments about David's advice. Reagan advises "I had to take David to the woodshed, I explained to him he was wrong, we do not cause deficits, the Democrats do that".

Reagan was wrong about the outcome even after David pointed out he was wrong about the Democrats; he made no bones about the fact he became a conservative because the Democrats tax and spend. This is the most obvious example of how Reagan would spin a truth even when the first truth was to disagree with his own Director of the Office of Management and Budget, and his second "truth" was to explain how he denied his own team's variance report. David reported the planned outcomes variances, an everyday occurrence in millions of organizations' financial departments, every month in modern America. Simply put, Reagan rejected David's report and then spun the facts to suit his need. Once again what I call intentional blindness.

Most anti-tax citizens of wealth see any demand on their wealth as confiscation and any tax-based sharing of common good not addressed in the price wage profit triangle as "re-distribution", they dismiss the idea from the Preamble of the goal to establish justice for the citizens of the nation.

I hope to see, but do not ever expect to, that the two parties can agree on what the term "distribution" as used by FDR during the New Deal actually means. "Re" as a prefix to distribution should be dismissed from the American political economic lexicon as a pejorative. We can never have an equitable distribution system in America until there is agreement on the need for a return to a living wage for the middle class, and sustainable taxation as part of the nations budgeting, ensured by those who enable all of the wealth in our capitalist system, the owner class. Notice I did not say create all the wealth. That common description of their role is too broad. Creating wealth in America is a mutual effort of owners, labor, and government.

Owners create one hundred percent of the selling prices in America at each level of the selling system with markups at each level, yet none take into account an earned and just laborer value added wage, meaning a return on the wage earners' investment in his skills that added value. Cost of labor is always at the lowest the market will bear, and provision for taxes is always at the lowest the accountants can achieve. Sustainability of the nation and its citizens are not an abiding concern of America's systems of governance or commerce.

The value added by for-wage labor, and the cost of government that has produced the American economy, are not addressed at the costing stage of pricing as an American business practice; only the lowest possible cost of goods sold in what we have noted before is arrived at via mutual opportunism.

This must be fixed if we are ever to end the nightmare of labor rights versus corporate rights gridlock, or the folly of tax cutting below the actual appropriated cost of government. I do not believe we will address the actual income and spending variance of the federal government's budget based on income taxation enacted by the legislature and the president, and the actual spending budget of the same until we end the folly of unitary budget reporting.

The GOP guile is always the same regarding deficits; they are all for reducing spending and they mean it even if it destroys the common good and established justice of the nation; however, any cost cuts for the common good get appropriated for either defense or low tax state welfare federalism block grant increases, and impacts established justice.

Once sworn in, President Reagan announced at least six key initial issues he wished to address as listed below. Over the rest of his eight year term, to a large extent the timing to introduce these policies was based primarily on issues that arose and were treated as a reaction based on his and the Movement Conservative GOP ideology, once they were finally addressed, usually without open hearings or deliberations.

The first issues to be subject to the Reagan Revolution agenda were:

1-   Reduce tax rates across the board, making them less progressive in the interest of growth enacted in 1981.

2-   Deregulate all federal departments, as FDR had over regulated both business and corporations from the start.

3-   Rebuild the military to drive communism into bankruptcy, doubled in 1981 along with the tax cuts.

4-   Support Paul Volcker's tight money supply to defeat inflation, seen through to success, actually a policy begun by Jimmy Carter.

5-   Reduce bloated federal spending as much as possible, never even tried.

6-   Institute Free Trade, in the best interest of consumers and growth, established in 1985 as a Presidential Order.

Like all new presidents the Reagan administration began to develop its own first budget shortly after taking office, led by David Stockman, Reagan's Budget Manager.

We start our analysis of Reagan's tax policies acknowledging the Democratic Party did support high tax rate policies to fund recovery from the depression, win WWII, rebuild the nation thereafter, and fund the containment of Russia.

Reagan called FDR's tax rates "tax and spend", then forgot how low the total debt of the nation was on the day he was sworn in, nine hundred and seven billion dollars, or how easily it could spin out of control if taxes were not assessed honestly, based on appropriations which create spending.

David Stockman tried hard to help Reagan understand how the federal budget system worked, but left frustrated that Reagan never grasped it, or refused to acknowledge it if he did. Per Stockman's book Reagan was totally deaf to reality; further, all of Reagan's other advisers except Stockman supported Reagan's convenient blindness and still do thirty-nine years later.

Reagan's rants about the Democrats became "they had been the party of huge deficits", which they were not. Only one charge was true: they taxed high, high enough to address the national spending they appropriated.

Reagan accepted his budget director's input in drafting his first budget, and Stockman enthusiastically embraced Reagan's argument that taxes were too high, cutting them from a top rate of seventy percent to fifty percent. Reagan had announced he wanted a balanced budget, meaning he wanted Congress to appropriate no more than he taxed; he did not want to have to borrow to fund his budget. Remember only the U.S. House of Representative can create the spending rate (appropriations) which then must be reconciled and approved by the Senate and signed by the president.

So we need to asked how did Reagan, a reasonably knowledgeable new president we can assume based on having already served as governor of California, with oversight of a huge budget process similar to the national system, expect to cut funding by almost thirty percent and not cause billions of dollars in deficits as he raised defense spending?

Reagan did understand this question as Stockman did; he had an answer. Stockman recommended cutting the two biggest costs in the consolidated federal budget at the time. They were defense spending and Social Security. Of the two only the Defense Department was funded by income taxes, and that was one hundred percent of Carter's deficit of seventy-nine billion dollars which Reagan inherited for the 1980-1981 budget. Remember presidents are elected in November and are sworn in in January. Federal budget years are from October 1 to September 30. Reagan's first budget began on October 1, 1981 and ran to September 30, 1982.

Social Security is funded by a payroll deduction, with a fifty percent tax deductible contribution by each beneficiary, matched by the employer. The SSA system cannot borrow by law, is in surplus by about 2.8 trillion dollars in 2020, and acts in the consolidated budget numbers to lower the income tax cuts deficit by the amount of the Social Security surplus.

The third largest cost of government became Federalism once President Reagan changed this founding concept for help building roads, ports, and canal across the nation. He expanded and converted it to provide block grants of redistributed welfare to the poor states who chose low taxes, low wages, and low education expenses as their states' economic choice. These funds are redistributed from progressive states to right-to-work states.

The federal government now only collects net income dollars from twenty high tax, wage, and education spending states, and redistributes it to the thirty states that tax, educate, and legislate low wage policies, all as GOP public choice policy.

Public choice policy is a GOP funded and advocated economic theory that won a Nobel Prize for economics. In practice it never produces a modern living wage economy outcome for hourly wage labor, or a balanced budget for government. If you have not heard of it, it is because the GOP not only spins it with falsehoods, it also spins by omission, not fully explaining policies they know informed voters will reject.

President Reagan asked his cabinet and financial advisers for a policy that would address the new debt his tax cuts were going to create, since he was cutting income taxes and the budget was already in deficit. Remember, Reagan was promising he would balance the budget, a GOP long time policy goal they condemned the Democrats for not maintaining in spite of high tax rates, thus the accusation of tax and spend Reagan campaigned against.

In effect, now that he was president, Reagan understood his promises, and seems to have known that he needed a silver bullet to make the new pending reality balance.

It is time to introduce the Laffer curve, and professor Arthur Laffer's theory of supply side economics. As a side note, as I final edit in January 2020, President Trump has recently awarded the Medal of Freedom to Professor Laffer for his economic contributions to the United States. President Trump just used the Laffer theory to cut U.S. taxes weighted to favor the wealthy for the third time in the Reagan

Era, and already the theory has doubled deficits again for the third time.

So to restate, in 1981 President Reagan who had a limited knowledge himself regarding federal budgeting, advised his team he wished to cut taxes and still make the budget balance. This was before any analysis of what his department heads had assessed regarding what they would need or wished to recommend for their departments' 1981-82 budgets to begin on October first 1981.

Reagan promised to cut taxes and balance the budget. You would think like FDR in 1933 a president making big promises to change the course of the nation would have advisers and plans ready to go; well, not so much. This is the big difference between the modern FDR Democrats and the modern Reagan Republicans. FDR wanted workable policies with rational boundaries regarding goals, cost, and funding. Remember before FDR began any new federal spending programs he cut federal pay and pensions, generating freed up cash to spend on relief.

Reagan and the modern GOP have developed an ideology of beliefs, closer to how wishes work than how plans based on analysis and discipline work relative to outcomes that are subject to oversight and variance reconciliation corrections year to year based on outcomes.

Luckily for Reagan his team had a theory on which to base the whole economy of the United States that had never been tested, and they dove in head first.

The surprising answer came from a retired professional football quarterback, and low seniority U.S. Congressman named Jack Kemp, who was also a pal of David Stockman. Kemp had a reputation of being interested in a more progressive form of conservatism as I remember it. He wanted to cut the cost of government and balance the budget, and do it without cutting benefits the American public liked. President Reagan himself was comfortable to propose cuts to New Deal programs including Social Security. Kemp was a little more temperate but he and Stockman did believe even Social Security could be trimmed if it was part of a larger overall plan to cut taxes and balance the budget.

Dick Cheney was an adviser to the president, and heard from Jack Kemp and his Harvard economics grad friend and fellow believer in a new economic theory they thought would meet the president's wish list, called supply side economics. It was economist Arthur Laffer who was proposing this phenomenon on which he based his theory called the Laffer curve. Laffer's belief was the more income taxes are reduced, the more economic growth the economy will experience, based on more investment and greater output meaning growth, leading to more consumption. In the end the new activity and profits even at a lower tax rate would actually pay for themselves and generate more net total tax revenue than was lost by the cut. What could possibly go wrong?

Dick Cheney who would remain a GOP presidential adviser, and even later a GOP vice president, would be wrong about almost every idea he ever put forward judged by outcome. He loved the Laffer curve theory and immediately took it to President Reagan, who also loved it.

Without further analysis it was adopted and accepted as a keystone belief of Reagan revolution dogma by the majority Movement Conservative wing of the party. Reagan's economic adviser who helped convince the president of the merits of supply side, Larry Kudlow, is now President Trump's chief economic adviser thirty-eight years later, and he has spent most of the time between Reagan and Trump spinning a false reality about supply side outcomes and the national debt on TV talking head shows, mostly on conservative stations.

You cannot make up the staying power of false spin when it is a belief system of millions of people who want it to be true as an absolutist ideology. Another true believer in supply side economics as a cure all magic solution was a gadfly named Steven Moore; he has remained for thirty-nine years along with Kudlow touting a false narrative about supply side, tax cuts, and debt, and was nominated in 2019 by President Trump to serve on the Federal Reserve Board. Moore was okay with Trump, but Wall Street raised enough fuss that Steven finally withdrew. Thirty-nine years of failure, and even when Trump ran against Reagan outcomes without mentioning his name, he repeats the worst sins of the old master, and has now infested the government again with Reagan's retreads.

David Stockman was raised as the grandson of a depression era farmer who was the epitome of a frugal old school Republican even if he supported FDR's crop support system of farm social insurance welfare. As a brilliant student David made his own way to Harvard. He had become a budget policy wonk, and not only loved Laffer's product, he advised President Reagan it could work **"if"** enough discipline was applied to government spending.

Ronald Reagan was very happy to agree with Stockman on both points. Reagan was far removed from the reality of America's middle class life it seems, let alone distanced from the working poor. He seemed to believe that most working class Americans agreed with him about cutting Social Security, which he acknowledged was needed but he thought it was too generous!

When David Stockman released President Reagan's "Economic Recovery Act of 1981" it included a twenty-five percent cut in federal taxes over three years. Stockman calculated the cuts the department heads would have to accept in developing their budgets, and advised each of the Cabinet heads to pass them on to their career budget heads within their portfolio planning for the 1981-82 budget year spending plan. Stockman believed they would all comply, and was totally convinced any who did not would be overruled by his president.

Shortly thereafter President Reagan had his first budget proposal from Stockman for his department heads to review. It cut taxes and spending and actually showed a surplus, and all the Movement Conservative believers working in the White House like Larry Kudlow were on board, except Reagan's fellow anticommunist and Californian he had appointed as his Secretary of Defense, Caspar Weinburger, whom Reagan fondly always called Cap.

I don't know what they truly believed, but from the first day in 1981 until the 2018 Trump tax cuts (the third major cut by a GOP president in thirty-eight years) were introduced, not one GOP leader has ever even hinted that supply side tax cut policy failed. The current status of the less than one half trillion dollars of deficit Trump inherited in Obama's last budget, now in 2020 is set to cost more than one trillion dollars of debt for President Trump's last full year budget.

President Trump's 2020 budget also projects another ten trillion dollars of debt by 2028. The Democrats again predicted that this third supply side tax cut would again trigger trillion dollar a year debt accumulation; the GOP once again promised Trump's tax cut would pay for itself. Now that the only growth is in the deficit the GOP is again mute.

The second thing to remember about President Reagan as we assess his impact on our nation's economic well being was his strong support for the military and his hatred of communism. Reagan's Secretary of Defense objected to the Stockman budget and requested the defense budget not be cut, in fact demanded it be doubled, and **Reagan approved the change.**

The outcome of cutting taxes while increasing spending was predicted by Tip O'Neill, the Democratic Party Speaker of the House as soon as the original Stockman budget was presented, as he did not believe Reagan would really cut the defense budget based on his campaign promises about more than containing communism; he was committed to defeating it.

As we shall see, other than the value we place on ending the Cold War which Reagan did achieve as his greatest success, he was happy to suggest his spending drove Russia into this outcome. In fact, economically the outcome was more debt accumulated in Reagan's first year than was accrued in the entire first two hundred year history of the United States.

How and why, thirty-seven years later, a third GOP president once again cut taxes and increased military spending with the debt now at more than twenty-two trillion dollars is unimaginable to me, but it seems of little importance to my family and friends who vote GOP.

Going back to David Stockman, he suggested a cut in the minimum Social Security payment and a repeal of the Social Security annual cost of living adjustment. Who knew that the elderly who had paid in all their lives definitely vote, and love the Social Security check they earned and depend on each month. Reagan rejected the SSI savings and let it go away also; the deficits began, and the debt climbed instead of being paid down.

The GOP and its voters have allowed themselves the same false beliefs Reagan defended. We will make no progress in reducing gridlock in America until we have a national come to reality moment on the facts and truth about the cause and effect of GOP tax cuts that are primarily for the wealthy, and the cuts to common good programs to fund this wealth transfer, which also lessens the established justice afforded citizens of the nation. All to benefit the few who also claim title to all profits beyond the least the market will bear in a share of profits from the only economic system the nation supports, and the one I support, namely capitalism.

How can the GOP ever square the circle of their past forty years as the dominant political party if they do not understand and admit their outcome failures, and the cost of their absolute belief in an ideology that backfired in so many ways for the majority of citizens without correction?

Voting for chaos in hopes of a reset is as ill informed as the long blindness to the GOP policies that created and sustained what they now refer to as the swamp. In 2016 Donald Trump actually campaigned against Reagan's policies to the disheartened old Reagan Democrats without advising them, or them recognizing it was the outcomes of the Reagan economics they now rue blindly.

The next issue Reagan dealt with was the mess the OPEC oil price increase of the 1970s had inflicted on the Savings and Loan Industry by introducing a decade of inflation. Jimmy Carter moved back from the mistake Nixon made putting Arthur Burns in charge of the Federal Reserve. After Arthur Burns, Carter appointed Paul Volker to head the Federal Reserve and Reagan reappointed him and he did solve the inflation issue.

In 1983 Reagan deregulated the Savings and Loan Industry. He allowed bankers to increase risk, while he kept FDR's deposit insurance in place. Once again Reagan used his folksy charm to sell a bad idea with a simple comment **"Bankers know better how to invest money than bureaucrats".** Of course the question was not who knew what, but what was the level of risk taken with other people's money, and who was stuck with the bill when speculative banking was allowed to again put the nations economy at risk. What followed was four years of economic boom, followed by seven years of economic bust. The GOP brags of the boom and ignores the bust.

A side issue to tax cuts. Tax credits for investing in real estate did grow the economy for three years as a separate policy from the supply side cuts as Reagan was also a big believer that growth of the economy was the market solution to all economic problems. They worked so well the economy overheated and these tax credits were repealed three years later. Without the tax credits the Savings and Loan Real Estate boom busted, triggering the overlooked mortgage insurance on Savings and Loan deposit accounts that had been left in place, costing an extra one hundred and fifty billion dollars of additional unbudgeted deficits, causing an extra one hundred and fifty billion dollars to be borrowed beyond the tax cut and military spending debt that accrued.

As interest rates rose in the 1970s new deposits eventually required more in interest than Savings and Loans low down payment thirty year mortgages were yielding. These banks were operating at a loss. They were in every town and every Congressman was concerned as well as the banking, home building and real estate markets. It was a true dilemma and called for the most careful handling. Reagan's advisers saw it as an opportunity for speculative greed to be sold as a market solution.

It is understandable that the president addressed this as a crisis. That the reason Reagan signed the bill was not to save the banks so much as it was an unfettered free market experiment is less understandable, except that he based his beliefs on ideology not analysis.

The whole Reagan team loved deregulation; they ended the cap on interest rates the S&L could pay for deposits as well as the rates that could be charged, ending New Deal limits on "usury" (unsustainable or unaffordable interest rates). Today's four hundred percent interest on payday loans are a direct result, crushing poor folks in areas like

West Virginia when the coal industry is in deep decline.

Along with the change in interest rates, Reagan lowered underwriting standards, so the old income requirements and equity down payments were lowered. All except one GOP banking chairmen in Congress from then until now have championed deregulation of banking, finance, and mortgage lending. Senator Chuck Hagel was Senate Banking Committee Chair in 2004, when he attempted to limit Freddie and Fannie's subprime goals. Senator McConnell refused to bring the bill to the floor, and President George W Bush kept it in his pocket, thus allowing F&F to set their own disastrous goal at sixty-five percent, but once again I'm getting a little ahead of our time line, although it is applicable.

If that was President Reagan's only ideological mistake, then the S&L would have made a lot of short term money and gone bankrupt when the failures started in the first contraction of the economy in 1987. The mind boggling mistake that I see as intentional blindness in the whole greed scheme not only failing, but also crashing the nation's economy and costing hundreds of millions of dollars to bail out, was the fact that Reagan and the Democratic Congress left FDR's government savings insurance guarantees in place while deregulating risk. It was mindless and unconscionable yet Cheney, McConnell and Bush repeated it with Freddie and Fannie in 2004, and the taxpayers were again stuck with the bill because they left the government insurance in place as the mortgage banks were allowed to increase their risk.

In the end much greater risk was still insured without increased premiums, and the tax payers were still on the hook. Reagan's S&L crash was a one hundred and fifty billion dollar disaster to bail out, not including the plus trillion dollars individuals lost as the economy went bust.

This Reagan speculative boom and bust re-introduced the GOP's twenty year cycles of unregulated speculative banking, after more than fifty years of safe regulated banking once FDR created depositor insurance with regulated underwriting standards as part of his FDIC insured deposits for commercial banks program in 1933. So as the whole industry collapsed and millions of folks lost their homes, and over a thousand towns lost their mortgage banks, the loss of hundreds of billions in dollars of deflation in real estate occurred and the taxpayers were on the hook. To this day I have never heard a single GOP TV talking head admit in any way that their ideology or President Reagan was in any way at fault.

What I've called intentional blindness is exhibited here. It might have been an oversight regarding the Savings and Loans and not leaving the insurance in place as regulations ended, but it should not have been for people at economists Friedman's and Greenspan's level of knowledge, both Reagan advisers, unless it was intentional so that savers would not withdraw the key funding source for S&L liquidity. The only success story of this whole mess was that the GOP managed to protect President Reagan and the GOP policies from the blame.

The S&L industry did not wind down until George H.W. Bush was president. Deregulation of the S&Ls in 1983 by President Reagan caused them to collapse as an outcome when the bankers reverted to speculative lending similar to GOP speculative lending in 1907 and 1929. There is no question this speculative deregulation was Reagan's policy and bore his signature, and after a three year burst of lending and growth the bubble burst and the Reagan policy failed.

It took three years until 1991 for the speculative projects the banks funded to go bankrupt. By then George W Bush was president. The GOP applauds Reagan's three years of growth almost as genius, and never blame him for his bank deregulation debacle. The chief cheerleader for Reagan and his policies was Larry Kudlow, President Trump's chief economic adviser thirty-three years later.

The final collapse and bailout (remember Reagan left the government guarantee of the S&Ls in place as he deregulated the risk side for these banks) of the S&L industry took place on George H. W. Bush's watch. The first Bush president was a one term president when the collapse caused a falloff in tax receipts and he had to pass an emergency tax increase after campaigning as a Reagan Republican saying, "read my lips, no new taxes".

Bill Clinton was a southern Democrat from Arkansas, not a New Dealer, and he was not going to criticize a popular president, and never did. America seems to have never learned a thing from these two major policy failures; both supply side tax cuts and bank deregulation policies failed more than once, yet they remain GOP ideologies, and the voters do not seem to care, forty years later.

I find it difficult to see how we can return to any form of sanity until we allow ourselves to understand these experiments did not work, and acknowledge the ones that did. In the end I always say policy matters, and it's best to judge presidents according to a sober analysis, asking did they do more good than harm. FDR introduced regulation of banking risk, and taxation equal to the needs of the nation based on Congressional appropriations. These policies worked to better all classes in the nation. Reagan deregulated banking and cut taxes below appropriation even in times of war (cold or hot), and ran up debt. These policies have worked well for the two upper classes in America, but they have been a disaster for the three lower classes. I define for this book the upper classes as the dynastic rich and the very well off, and the three lower classes as the working middle class, the working poor, and the unemployed for whatever reason.

The GOP has never admitted that deregulation of mortgage banking caused a return to old GOP speculative boom and bust economic crashes, or that having left deposit insurance in place during an intentionally triggered speculative boom during a period of deregulation caused all this additional debt and misery for the tens of millions of Americans affected, who lost their homes and/or small businesses once they lost their hometown banks.

Insuring the common good and protecting established justice is part of the Preamble to the U.S. Constitution, a stated intent of our founders; federalism is the only form of insuring the common good, even though I'll advise we should end Reagan's overhaul of federalism, as he turned it into block grants to the states, including the thirty states that do not pay net federal income taxes at all which has destroyed the concept of established justice , unless the GOP ends its fight against taxes and a living wage needed to fund a sustainable nation, as well as the state level.

Reagan's tax cuts had a secondary goal; he announced his intent to cut government domestic spending as a percentage of GDP. The president did reduce education and welfare programs, assuring Americans that this combination of tax cuts and cuts in social programs would lead to his promised balanced budget.

Reagan's Conservative Party partners accepted the southern wing's anti-union, anti-public school, and anti-welfare policies based on southern state Jim Crow laws during the New Deal, and on a new theory that the U.S. Constitution did not allow groups such as unions, civil rights groups, or school integration agitators to interfere with state laws. The Koch Network called such organizations collectives, as in Russian worker groups.

Patrick Henry, John Calhoun, and Strom Thurmond each made a stand for states' rights; Henry in the eighteenth century, Calhoun in the nineteenth, and Thurmond in the twentieth. Henry's debate was with Marshall at our founding during the Constitution Ratification convention in Virginia. Calhoun's was the most dramatic, leading South Carolina to initiate the Civil War over the issue he defined as a state's right to nullify any federal law it disagreed with. The third fight was the battle to maintain separate but equal segregation in the south, which led to the busing issue north and south in the 1970s as the states defied the Supreme Court's school desegregation order, Topeka School Board v. Brown.

Based on a stated belief that federal regulations were a drag on the economy, Reagan promised to grow the economy by reducing government regulation, first in mortgage banking, second for business, while expanding world trade based on unfettered free trade policies. He addressed finance (taxes and deregulation) in his first term creating massive deficits, and free trade in his second term which ended America's status as a net lender nation among our trade partners. After his re-election America became a net debtor nation for the first time since the founders paid off the new states' war debts from the Revolutionary War.

An ideology of the GOP during the run up to the Reagan era was the concept of free trade. President Reagan did not make a serious move to implement free trade as a policy in his first term. However in 1968 LBJ had implemented a tariff that also allowed industries impacted by unfair trade practices to make a case for relief, usually including a cease and desist order or a stronger rebuke, noted in the last chapter.

Free trade was the fourth Reagan economic change reversing FDR era economic philosophy and was the most devastating economically to the well being of the United States economy, especially to living wage earning union labor.

The fallout from Ronald Reagan's GOP ideological based ending of LBJ's fair trade policy impacted the largest source of funding for family living wage income and fully funded healthcare insurance in America. Before Reagan, more than sixty percent of Americans depended on one hundred percent employer funded tax exempt healthcare. Of all the policy failures of the Reagan presidency this was the most damaging and costly. This singularly was the most destructive economic decision ever made by any president in American history.

On the first Saturday in September 1985, President Reagan was weekending at his beloved ranch in California. Traditionally presidents give a five minute radio address on Saturday mornings, as Reagan did on this morning. I listened as he casually announced he had decided to not re-extend the fair trade standards from 1968 even as Asian markets were already making inroads into American markets with their government's help by dumping products such as high gas mileage cars and low priced shoes. So without consulting Congress, Ronald Reagan destroyed the manufacturing and family living wage with family healthcare base, as well as the sustainability of the American economy, especially in small towns with a factory or two.

Did the genial and lovable President Reagan make another folksy inane statement as he proudly announced his latest great idea? Yep. He said,

"If Asian nations want to wear out their people making good quality consumer products for low cost, I will not prevent millions of consumers from enjoying these savings, to save a few thousand jobs of shoe makers in Maine."

Over the past thirty-five years since Reagan made this executive decision without thought, not knowing what he did not know, America's balance of trade has been about sixty billion dollars negative every month. This has funded China's becoming the most financially liquid and successful manufacturing country with the largest balance of trade surplus; they are now using these funds to capture our America business empires. When Trump criticized American trade policy he was hard on Clinton and Mexico, but he was less so on Reagan even as he attacked China's policies.

Like all Movement Conservative Reagan policy approvals, unfettered free trade was supported based on ideology with little analysis. With the OPEC rise in gas prices in the 1970s Japan was exporting high quality compact automobiles that got about twenty to twenty-five miles per gallon versus American autos that were only getting about twelve to fifteen mpg at the time.

To his credit Reagan did allow quota setting to limit Japan's auto imports to help the American auto manufacturers in his first term, as the true believers were yelling for him to open America to free trade which was at the time just another GOP ideology.

Japan did agree to a three year voluntary restraint agreement (VRA), setting the first year limits on export cars in America to one million eight hundred sixty thousand, which in the end became the total exported in each of the first three years. At the time America's auto sales were ten million six hundred thousand per year.

LBJ had passed fair trade laws in the late sixties, along with quota setting, and tariffs. One was a ban on dumping. Taiwan had been dumping shoes and there were three or four small shoe manufacturers in the state of Maine who filed suit requesting a desist order stopping these illegal imports; the shoemakers from the state of Maine won their suit. This was in 1985, the same year that tariffs were set to expire.

The final step in a fair trade lawsuit was left to the U.S. president to end the tariff or enforce the judge's decision. As a result, on September 1, 1985 President Reagan no longer had to take action to introduce free trade, he just announced his decision on the tariffs, and announced he would let them die. No hearings, or vote in Congress, just let them die without any knowledge of what the fallout would be. Ideology like revealed knowledge of the pope of old is not to be questioned, it is believed to be absolutely true by the faithful. This is what in 2019 Attorney General Barr demanded for Donald Trump based on the GOP ideological belief in what they call the unitary president. This means his decisions are never to be questioned, as is demanded in Article One of the U.S. Constitution. This is why I reject modern GOP ideology; it demands an end to the U.S. Constitution, and I call this a form of domestic treason.

Over the next few years the few thousand lost jobs became millions of lost jobs. Reagan's reelection was advertised as "morning in America". Today the outcomes of Reaganomics have become our darkest hours in American history for former middle class families.

The outcome of president Reagan's five policy outcomes reviewed above (tax cuts lower than appropriations, deregulation of the Savings and Loan Industry, ending usury interest rates in America, deregulation of executive branch oversight, and introducing unfettered free trade while leaving payroll mandates and tax incentives in place) were at the heart of the anger and disappointment of America's 2016 GOP voters who elected President Trump, who promised a resurrection of American manufacturing to the millions of hourly wage earners adversely affected without any mention that they were in fact the results of Reagan GOP ideological decisions.

Reagan's acolytes, especially George W. Bush in the twenty-first century ushered in nation building, the exporting of democracy, and regime change as key foreign policies goals, sold as aspects of American Exceptionalism. All this as Movement Conservatism was doing all it could to stifle democracy at home, seemed lost on the G. W. Bush wing of the GOP.

These G. W. Bush policies were not key Reagan objectives. Bush did continue to promote fiscally irresponsible competing goals of what by then was routinely called supply side Reaganomics, regarding his treasury department's tax budgets and defense department spending objectives.

Reagan and George W. Bush, and now Donald Trump are the only three presidents in history to set such disparate goals for their administration's department heads. By disparate I mean his budgets intentionally increased spending, while his treasury budgets cut taxes. All were based on an ideology as hopeful and unsuccessful as a gold promising alchemist in the Middle Ages.

As a result the Reagan Democrats voted casually, based more on how they felt emotionally about his message than on how well they understood the changes they voted for, and just as casually the president established these ideological decisions with little thought to any downside to his visionary beliefs.

As a result the past two generations that have come of age in America and almost for sure the next have been subjected to hourly wages and benefits that have caused almost all non-college educated children and grandchildren to be less well off than their parents were. The now long retired Reagan Democrats know it has happened, yet are still voting for Reagan's unreformed GOP, and still do not know who to blame, who to trust, and who to vote for with any confidence. Playing to their fears still captures their votes, as much or more than any policy outcome reality.

This is the reality I foresaw on day one as the only possible ensuing outcome when I heard President Reagan introduce free trade on his regular Saturday morning radio show in September 1985. That was the day as a politically uninvolved factory owner, I became an activist to inform the dormant Democrats of what they were allowing the GOP to inflict on not only my factory's loss of the U.S. market to China with nothing to replace it, but also to the destruction of my employees' lives.

Everything that had been created for the middle class under FDR's new deal was losing its funding due to the squeeze from importation of China's slave wage labor rates buried in the import price of these low wage, no benefit hours embedded in imported goods. Goodbye living wages with fully funded healthcare, secure mortgages, supported by millions of factories across the nation; hello Wal-Mart wages, without benefits, the only offset being Wal-Mart prices in return.

This is the Reagan revolution that has endured through two GOP President Bushes, as well as two Democrat presidents somewhat removed from the FDR era, with debt rising, wages stagnant, and the wealth gap growing as taxes were cut. The debt grew a little faster under Republicans, and a little slower under the Democrats. The deregulated mortgage banking President Reagan introduced and President George W Bush repeated led to two collapses in real estate speculation that crashed the total economy, which the Democrats helped rebuild, but otherwise the domestic landscape has reflected Reagan, not FDR since 1980.

Until further notice it will be Donald Trump who continues this mindless increase in the wealth gap as his first major legislative victory was the third GOP major tax cut since 1981. It is easy to see that President Trump does not have a thought out living wage restoration agenda based on any meaningful policy idea; just more spin and more social media outbursts.

No one knows the tipping point that will significantly overwhelm the federal budget, causing massive increases in interest payments due to inflation and/or the premiums that will be required to finance these trillions of GOP tax cuts, causing general fund shortfall deficits.

In 2020 with three years of watching the tolerance level of Donald Trump and the GOP including the main funding source, the dynastic billionaire families of the Koch network, and the main source of votes among the GOP base of evangelicals and their pastors, and of white working class folks who "just want their country back", all of whom have supported Trump as he has embraced the Putin post cold war model for replacing communism with a form of autocracy supported by the oligarchs and the Russian Church, I now believe there is a movement across the West to replace liberal democratic republics with the Putin model.

The "I just want my country back" crowd do not define a replacement but they openly state the whole thing has to be blown up before it can be fixed. This seems to be the tolerance they display for the Trump actions to date.

I was very happy when Reagan's diaries were published about ten years ago, as noted above. They are well worth reading and contain almost no myths or spin other than the intentional blindness we each hide from ourselves. Reagan daily reassured himself of the correctness of his personal opinion of himself and his policies even in the minds of his opponents; if they would only listen to his message and hopes for America they would understand, he mused nightly the whole eight years in keeping this diary.

By the time in 1981 when Reagan became president, the Soviet Union was already changing, more so than was known in the West. Containment in Europe (NATO) as a block on Stalin era occupation of Eastern Europe was still in effect, as well as Stalin's ugly wall across Berlin as the face of the standoff.

Reagan's best line of his presidency was in front of Stalin's wall, when he said "Mr. Gorbachev, tear down this wall". Mike Deaver, President Reagan's promoter and producer, of course filmed and distributed this photo op across the world.

In the 2016 election Donald Trump and Bernie Sanders campaigned on the problems of free trade for the American middle class, one co-opting the anger of older voters, the other the hopes of younger voters with large college loans and few living wage job prospects; neither candidate had a meaningful idea or plan including a sellable solution to fund or fix it.

Neither Sanders nor Trump have mentioned once and may not even know how or when fair trade was sanctioned, or when and how it ended in America, or could tell you off the top of their head how free trade was enabled. If they do, they have never explained it to the older or younger generations. No analysis of the cause, or defining the fix, just a lament for their tribe's hopefuls.

I've never met a GOP voter who believed how simply Reagan just let fair trade die, when told the story of how Reagan ended fair trade one Saturday morning by deciding to not renew LBJ's tariffs, just like the GOP wanted to repeal Obamacare, without a workable market solution. The GOP did know twenty million folks losing healthcare would be an election issue. So they promised to replace it; they still do not know how to fund it within their ideology, any more than

Bernie knows how to fund free healthcare and college educations for all within his belief system.

Reagan, if his guys knew it, never tod there was any downside to unfettered free trade, any more than they acknowledged there was any downside risk to keeping deposit insurance as they deregulated the lending side of mortgage banking and left the taxpayer insurance in place.

Containment of communism in Asia was pretty much settled by the time Reagan took office. Vietnam had its own version of communism combined with nationalism and adopted the mercantile form of capitalism pioneered by China for its new wealth, based on abundant cheap labor, and the same combination of nationalism and mercantilism in Russia based on abundant cheap oil and gas wealth sold via pipe line to Europe.

China adopted and perfected a limited mercantile form of capitalism that has been in place for plus thirty-five years while remaining a one party communist country, phenomenally successful at the expense of American wage earners and taxpayers; while their leader functions as an autocrat.

Ownership of property in these countries has risen, while labor has remained coerced, and the state party is both nationalistic and autocratic. America still supports Asia's form of slave labor, at least when it is disguised as cheap labor hours shipped under an unfettered form of free trade, imposed on a whim by President Reagan on an otherwise typical Saturday morning at the small broadcast booth his team had set up at his ranch.

By the 1980s the key areas of communism containment contention were in Central and South America (including the Caribbean), and the Middle East. On the first page of *The Reagan Diaries*, he notes his concern about El Salvador and the Contras next door in Nicaragua.

More than jobs, wages, healthcare funding, education, housing, infrastructure, and hunger combined, more than all of America's domestic issues, Reagan was obsessed in his diaries by the Contra issue. Two small undeveloped countries with less than ten million citizens, and it concerned him in every meeting of his presidency with every world leader he met. I found an amazing insight into President Reagan's mind as I read his diaries, and I began to tally this obsession, trying to understand the motivation for such an overwhelming diversion from growing economic realities going so wrong at home.

There are more entries concerning these small Central American countries than any other single issue Reagan mentions in his diaries over his eight years in office, forty-eight for El Salvador and sixty-seven mentions for El Salvador's arch enemy the Contras of Nicaragua. There is more reminiscing each evening about these two small poor Central American countries than taxes, deregulation of mortgage banking, and free trade concerns combined over the full eight years.

Things were going well, ending the cold war, and lowering the number of ballistic missiles, but from 1987 onward the economy was slipping. No key adviser or other world leader ever showed much concern about this Central American spat between some rich Creole land owners protecting their wealth, and nationalists whose Native American leaders wished improved lives for their poverty stricken followers. I personally doubt that ten percent of El Salvadoran rebels called Sandinistas could explain the difference between capitalism and communism; they were landless peasants and wanted to end hunger for their children.

In President Reagan's 1980s Central America, the rich were seen as freedom fighters and the poor were seen as terrorists. Labor coercion and property abuse problems were never discussed more seriously than to define the dispute as class warfare, at least not in my reading, and I read a lot and have visited most of Central America and seen the poverty firsthand.

If any place still fits Hamilton's comment about the few and the many regarding the two levels of society in poor agricultural societies, it is the Hispanic societies where we see land ownership as the only form of wealth still in the hands of a few old families, at least in the Americas where the United States had demanded to be the guardian since the Monroe presidency.

No week went by without oval office discussions of the Contra issue. No state visit occurred over the eight years without a diary note about Reagan letting his fellow national leaders from all around the world know the importance of the these two small countries. Reagan's concerns regarding these two small nations are a greater obsession than any other single concern of any other president whose diary or biography I've read, and I've read the lives of more than half of all our presidents (with the exception of Abe Lincoln and Jeff Davis who obsessed daily over the Civil War). Over one million El Salvadoran's now being deported by Donald Trump's ICE agents were given "sanctuary" in the United States in the 1980s by Ronald Reagan, and who knew much if anything of this then or now?

As a personal aside per the diaries, almost every week one or more of the Reagan children dined with the president, and almost as often Nancy was out of town, and he often mentions being lonely. This is somewhat at odds with the myths about his poor family life with his kids. In reading the diaries Ronald Reagan seemed closer to his children than the media had led me to believe.

Reagan enjoyed his job, and appreciated when the staff allowed a six hour work day in the Oval Office. Reagan also enjoyed his weekends at Camp David and vacations at the ranch in California with Nancy that included a swim, a horseback ride, and the almost nightly showing of an old movie from his era in Hollywood, for the whole eight years.

The Reagans had three or four couples who were old friends they saw often and spent holidays with, including their children. It was a close, upscale, warm, and seemingly happy life, as President Reagan relates in his diary. President Reagan comes across as a relentless campaigner for his programs and his party. I was amazed at the amount of travel he undertook in support of both at his age.

Concerning his mindset, it is obvious that once he believed something, no amount of bad news or failure had much effect on his opinion or his continued belief in his vision. The truth is he seemed to be always an optimistic if myopic man and president. To the extent I'd be critical of him personally I'd only add that his diary confirms my earlier comment about intentional blindness in the process of political myth making in both parties, but especially with this president. He was as good a friend as he was a poor problem solver. He never really saw a problem unless it is was obvious such as a kid in a wheelchair, or that offended a norm of his social group.

He was very sympathetic to anyone in distress and personally wanted to help. On the other hand, he seemed almost devoid of comprehension of the mass of people who were afflicted by any issue, or the role government could play funding the National Institute of Health (NIH) to alleviate issues that affect hundreds of thousands or even millions of folks in our wealthy country.

A few years ago when there was an Ebola virus scare, the NIH had both a serum and a plan and did control the outbreak and prevented it from becoming an epidemic; just a little more forward thinking than was typical for a good if limited man. This type of policy analysis is not on display as a personal concern at any point in his eight years of up dating his diaries; when he became afflicted with Alzheimer's, only then did he and Nancy seem to understand why stem cell research was needed. Private for-profit drug companies do not invest in cures for uncommon or rare illnesses. We need the government to fund a pool of money and design and enforce a reward system, such as research grants and patent laws.

We needed LBJ's funding tax on the payroll FICA Social Security system to fund and run the Medicare system, which provides a funded retirement onset healthcare system, and created a source of funding for old age maladies that have extended life for most of us.

Did Reagan know that it was a woman Secretary of Labor that made both programs possible? It was his ideology that caused him to oppose all taxes, with little support for targeted user funded programs such as the gas tax for roads, or FICA for safe banking regulations to work.

His seeming inability to process facts that do not confirm his beliefs was perhaps even more limited than for most folks. His ability to acknowledge, let alone hear anyone else's truth was almost nonexistent; he seemed very disappointed by anyone who did not see him as he saw himself. What I call Mike Deaver's myth making, he saw as his greatest asset. Likewise, if he believed something about a person or a situation, no facts seemed to dissuade him in any way. He rejected missteps of those he admired, and saw only bad motives for those he did not see as allies.

President Reagan made a number of entries in his diary, which many if not most of us would see as public policy comments, and many or most would likewise see as institutional racism, if not personal racism. Reagan seemed to see surface issues and not the institutional downside for victims, such as poor children going to school hungry. He had an easy, in some ways even a lucky life in spite of his father's alcoholism having caused insecure finances; reading his diaries he seemed content.

The following example from *The Reagan Diaries* illuminated to me President Reagan's limited ability to see a full picture of almost any situation once his mind was set based to a large extent on the institutional values of his political parties ideology.

Reagan openly discussed apartheid, the system of laws designed to keep whites and blacks separate and unequal in South Africa, as did many other DC policy makers, and confirmed this in his diary using conservative spin comments, like George Will's Washington Post op-ed quote that had become an often stated GOP talking point; "If four million white South Africans who control the economy and the government were to be governed by twenty-eight million uneducated inexperienced blacks, if democracy was to come to South Africa, it would be one man, one vote, one time, with both the economy and the government in ruin". The common add on was, and the whites as well as the blacks would all be worse off.

Reagan did not see this as a racist view and he explained it to the first black Jurist on the U.S. Supreme Court, Thurgood Marshall. Marshall had mentioned in an interview that he considered Reagan's description of his opposition to ending apartheid to be racist. Reagan was "hurt" by this per his diary and news reports, and he invited the judge to lunch at the White House. They explained themselves to each other. His diary note that night expressed his satisfaction that he was sure he had set the judge right, and that Marshall now understood the black man had no better friend than himself.

Once again, to my mind Reagan for all of his good qualities, this incident confirms his lack of self awareness of any validity to a differing opinion from his own well meaning and therefore moral (it is safe to assume) beliefs.

I'll give just two more examples. There are many, on many subjects, but a typical one was with Tip O'Neill regarding Reagan's fast growing budget deficits. Reagan insisted these deficits did not exist each time the Speaker brought up the subject, and further insisted that the Democrats had run up untold inconceivable deficits forever. They had not. Reagan's first year deficit was double the total debt in the federal books from the past one hundred and ninety-three years combined by all previous thirty-nine presidents. The Democrats taxed at higher rates to pay for WWII, cold war containment, and social policies among all other costs. Reagan stopped claiming his tax cuts would pay for themselves, he just came up with a folksy saying to express his new pleasure that his deficits were **"starving the beast"**. Even so Reagan continued to deny the debt was a result of tax cut programs.

Reagan had not sold supply side tax cuts as intended to starve the U.S. government; he sold them as self funding, and then could never bring himself to equate the horrible outcomes to his policy.

Reagan resented high taxes and ignored the result of the FDR tax policy which produced sustainable moderate deficits even in time of war. If Reagan ever understood the two sides of these tensions he never admitted it, as he ignored the negative effect of his own failing tax cuts along with his military ramp up, which caused the deficit to increase by over half a trillion dollars a year for his entire presidency, a plus four hundred percent increase in eight years, the largest increase of any president in history

On the other hand, Reaganomics policy led to raising payroll taxes to build a surplus of Social Security receipts based solely on his FICA tax hike for wage earners. The deficits in the combined budget at four trillion dollars negative over eight years would have been almost double this net debt report if the Social Security surplus was not being borrowed by the federal government and then reported as the net debt in a consolidated report.

Reagan left office convinced he had lowered the deficit and the debt having stopped the Democrats' deficit spending, although he did admit otherwise once. This is not stated in his diary. The one time he mentioned it was his farewell speech as he was leaving office in January of 1989. The speech was pure Reagan for the first ninety percent; he focused on 1982, citing how he instituted the Reagan Revolution, and the American Miracle, all the new jobs, all the growth in jobs and wealth. He never mentioned final outcomes, only the positive side of the onset of his cutting taxes and reducing regulations. Only at the end did he murmur (the speech was televised) he had one regret, it was the deficits.

He did not mention he had changed his promise of self funded wealth improvement for all. Without saying why he had already changed his promise, saying tax cuts were meant to starve the beast; yet he was elected to govern for the common good. His only outcome was to have failed the only duty he swore to accomplish when he swore to uphold the Constitution. Ronald Reagan in the end set up as an outcome decades of a widening wealth gap, little trickle down, and a return to governing based on fear instead of hope, and never ending deficits.

It is arguable that not a dollar of this debt has ever been paid down to this day and American taxpayers have continued to pay the interest on it. Clinton did cut taxes with GOP help (Kasich of Ohio) and for four years we had a surplus; however, the surplus never actually reduced the net debt in the end. The accumulated compounded interest has now added an additional amount of debt more than equal to Reagan's original debt.

This is similar to what happens if a private individual makes only a minimum payment each month on their credit card balance. Thankfully so far the U.S. still has a good credit rating, but it has nothing to do with GOP policies; it is one hundred percent based on the credit rating of those twenty large high tax, high wage, well educated, mostly blue states.

One last example of mis-remembering (a form of ignoring reality) noted in the diaries regards President Reagan's wife Nancy and her use of an astrologer. When Reagan's first Secretary of the Treasury Don Regan (a former Wall Street banker) resigned, he wrote a book. In it he mentioned that a California astrologer visited the White House often, and Mrs. Reagan consulted with her on planning her husband's activities; I also read this story in the New York Times. On the night Reagan heard about this revelation, he rants in the diary about how untrue it is. In fact it did turn out to be true, and he knew it to be true, but he had a need or a quirk and we all have some, that did not allow him to acknowledge what he did not see as the image he had of himself and his wife, or so it seems. All the stories I've reviewed here that I read in the diaries I had already read in newspapers or seen on TV. What I've noted is a sense of how comfortable he seemed about his ideas that I saw as out of touch.

While ignoring facts and realities are hardly more than a source of eye rolling when an elderly uncle engages in them, it is far different in a national leader. When you read the diaries or remembrances of former aides, they saw time and time again during serious discussions about national policy, that the facts were not accepted by President Reagan if different than the perception he held.

From tax cuts to military spending to arms sales to Iran, nothing else in Reagan's everyday performance explains these unforced errors (to use a sports term) in policy disasters. The Reagan era had its share of disasters which had no effect on his popularity. The myth making that denies the reality has led to repeats in later GOP presidencies.

I'm aware I'm focused on the nature of Reagan the man at this point in our narrative more than his policies as I've addressed his diaries. In relation to FDR, LBJ, Washington and Hamilton policies, I believe the man and the myth is the real story of the whole Reagan era. These four great leaders saw problems and conceived solutions, or found solutions they could adapt to the American situation at the time. Reagan felt the sting of high taxes even if it was war time, and even more so once the war was over.

I find he was a good man who meant well and trusted easily if he liked you. He heard the siren song of low taxes and bought into an ideology. I do not believe he ever fully understood the full game plan, and therefore he could not anticipate the outcome or trust any one who told him the ideal had down sides; that is my best read of both the man and the myth. This does not excuse those behind the myth who knew and know better; the outcome suits their game plan to a tee.

The defining facts about major change agent presidents is the fact they are all famous and seen as great presidents no matter what errors they made, such as LBJ and Vietnam. Until Reagan, their own ideas changed the American experience for definable better policy outcomes for the many.

Reagan is the only president that a majority of Americans today consider a great change agent president, whose policies were based not on his own ideas, but on an absolute ideology. And he is the only president to date whose outcomes have arguably created more harm than good for the many.

Reagan's ideological mess will not be fixed until history takes a true look at the actual outcomes of his policies in the light of day. It's like having an alcoholic in the family; there will not be much progress until the alcoholic family member and the family all admit to the facts. It is the absolutism, money, adherence to an evangelical, segregationist, and pre-revolution preference for property rights over citizen's rights in our democracy, that has put and kept a minority ideology in control of a great nation where positive outcomes for the many have stagnated. The final assessment can only be that Reagan's changes were a disaster for the many and a gift to the minority even if many more than the few Hamilton warned about.

So let's move on from the effects of Movement Conservative ideology on the citizens, to Reagan's decisions concerning federalism. He defined his federalism as New Federalism, which differed from Hamilton's or Nixon's or Carter's federalism which was the government using federal strengths for the common good of all.

Reagan's federalism was based on an old concept from the days of slavery, which looks back to the big question of states rights versus federal rights, referred to as Dual Federalism, a theory of federalism that only existed from 1789 to 1791 at the time of our founding. It was a time when authority to govern at the state level still depended on

English common law and the will of God, before the Bill of Rights was exchanged for America's authority to govern. This authority was granted by the people of the nation voting in each of their states of residence as "by consent of the governed"; this ended the concept "by the will of God" but it is still alive in many states; the concept of established justice is ignored.

The ideology of the modern GOP has not fully accepted democracy or the idea of the majority as the intent of the Constitution beyond the Senate and electoral college compromises we have acknowledged throughout this book, nor all the citizens as sovereign. They still govern as if the state is sovereign over the people and over the federal government, and with God's will from Biblical Christianity as a governing factor regarding property rights to be seen as the key natural right, as if that is not only what revelation mandated, but also the inalienable rights from the God of nature.

The Center for the Study of Federalism is one of many so-called think tanks supported primarily by sixteen families (last I heard), who control dynastic billionaire family accumulated wealth foundations such as the Koch Network, and who have supported the ideology behind this anti-American idea, ignoring the changes made in the lives of U.S. citizens by ratification of the Bill of Rights in 1791, including an end to abuse by states and by the property owners the states enable, regarding the U.S. citizens they hire.

This federalism center was founded in 1992; its members proclaim that from 1789 to 1901 the Supreme Court viewed the Constitution in terms of the concept of Dual Federalism. You can follow their arguments on their web site from Jefferson to Madison and Jackson, on to Teddy Roosevelt and his trust busting, into FDR's New Deal, and finally to Ronald Reagan. Reagan bought into the Koch view of Dual Federalism when Goldwater was a key member of the John Birch Society along with the heirs of the Coors family, the Bradley Foundation, the current Koch brothers' father, and their leader at the time, the leader of the Welch family fortune, and others including members of the Gulf Oil and Mellon Bank fortunes.

The Federalism Center uses 1789, as that was when the U.S. Constitution was ratified, but before the Bill of Rights was ratified in

1791. In 1789 the citizens of the new United States were seen as dual citizens of both the new nation and the new states, but the national government had very limited concern for the citizens of the states. The national government also had no authority to govern. Each state also still had a state church, with no defined authority for secular government police powers, but all citizens had to pay taxes to fund the state churchmen's salaries even if a nonbeliever or of another creed.

Once the Bill of Rights was ratified the authority to govern was established, and the establishment clause ended the idea of a state church in America. It took another forty years to fully phase out its role, yet its theology is still a major ideological conflict for members of the former southern states evangelical form of protestant beliefs including the laws regarding slavery and the treatment of black citizens.

After ratification the whole concept of dual federalism ended, as citizens were now protected from abuse of their individual rights to justice by the federal government, even abuse from the states, as they were a citizen of the nation first, regardless of the state of residence. The Fourteenth Amendment to the Constitution settled this matter after the Civil War, and the eleven southern states ratified it.

Remember my discussion of how long it took the south, until after the Civil War, to be dragged into adherence to the Bill of Rights in clearly mandated language, and how hard the GOP has fought this understanding, catering to the wishes of their corporate, evangelical, and dynastic families of wealth wings of the party's base voters, many of whom overlap with the nationalist wing, as we enter the third decade of the twenty-first century.

President Reagan's plan on behalf of the controlling ideology of the GOP at the time was to separate the federal government's effect on citizens of the red states from any role in the states other than funding. Of course it backfired on both sides. The southern congressional folks wanted the money for their states but refused to accept federal oversight as required by the Constitution. So the blue states are now stuck with funding nearly all of the red states' social programs and are doing so without any cooperation, thus gridlock.

Ronald Reagan redistributed the wealth of the approximately twenty successful states to the approximately thirty intentionally poor states as a form of interstate welfare, as he restructured the American federalism system, both ideologically and functionally. If the thirty poor states chose that because of a belief in small government as the best outcome, then it is past time for the northern states to stop funding the southern states and let the citizens who support this ideology live with the outcome.

I remember when Reagan called Democratic food stamps socialism, and accused the Democrats of pandering for votes. Reagan rewarded his voters with a form of socialism never acknowledged, and claimed to do so because the governors knew better how to help their own people. These are the governors who use the GOP economic system called Public Choice to ensure more wealth for the property owners of their states, by ensuring low spending on education, establishing policies that ensure low wages for those who perform physical labor for a living, and always without healthcare access funding by the local employer or the state taxing system(s) based on small government ideology.

The GOP has spent thirty-five years continuing Reagan's form of federalism, ignoring that wage laborers in the poor states have remained poorly educated, poorly paid, and poorly cared for within their state's government managed social systems. All federalism does at this point is to allow them to cut taxes even more in their states, and dump more of the social cost of low wages on the unsuspecting taxpayers in the wealthier states.

No system of ensuring the common good has been proven in world history to be more effective than American federalism as instituted at our founding and maintained until President Reagan changed the intent of this formerly "common good" legacy of our founding era.

We may remember reading in Chapter 6 that in 1806 Thomas Jefferson suggested it would be in the nation's interest for the federal government to enhance interstate transport including canal, bridge, and road building. Jefferson was not the first American founder to consider this question. Washington had advised his fellow founders that when he was a young surveyor and later as a military commander during the war he had seen the possibility of such future infrastructure needs.

He was concerned as this was not spelled out as a federal power in the Constitution. However, Madison had solved the problem in the Constitution with the powers granted to Congress to legislate. Both Jefferson and Madison had opposed Hamilton's concept of a federal bank and the use of federal credit based on the ability to tax, operate a national bank, and fund projects with federal credit using federal bonds. But Hamilton's suggestion was proposed by Washington and approved by Congress. This allowed the federal government to create a self funding nation respected as an economic peer among the nations to this day.

Infrastructure has been funded since WWII with a gas tax which is now and has remained at eighteen cents per gallon since the 1990s. In the meantime the miles per gallon of gas for American cars has almost tripled from about ten miles per gallon to thirty miles per gallon, while infrastructure construction costs have at least doubled per mile. That means every mile an American drove twenty-five years ago produced almost .02 cents towards maintenance based on 1994 labor rates. Today every mile an American drives produces .007 cents for maintenance, and the cost is .0035, meaning we have to drive six miles before we fund a full penny towards maintenance of our roads and bridges. It is mindless. The GOP for-profit system would allow all the new investors to charge both the full cost of maintenance, as well as whatever overhead cost they would add, and return on investment interest, and enough to build a reserve fund they do not pay tax on but can invest and earn the interest on, plus a management fee, and finally a profit for the owners, just as for-profit healthcare, prisons and schools have done.

The GOP will not let we the people fund our own road system at cost, but they will allow their PAC funding supporters to charge many times the $1.08 cents per gallon a funded government system would cost today, for an increase of $0.90 cents a gallon. This is unjust for low income wage earners if minimum wage is not adjusted accordingly.

It is time to raise the gas tax, yet Reagan left another legacy when he endorsed another snake oil salesman pitch regarding income taxes, a bi-annual GOP pledge that limits each GOP member of Congress who pledges to uphold the U.S. Constitution from keeping the Constitution sustainable economically. We will address this "no new taxes ever, not even in time of war" pledge Reagan endorsed shortly. For now the pledge means the gas tax budget gap is left unaddressed.

The snake oil salesman's name is Grover Norquist. He was a partner with Reagan in the campaign to "starve the beast", the beast being our own government that keeps us safe and creates the economy our economic system of capitalism has thrived in.

Are the terms "established justice" and "the common good" a Constitutional intent, or a scheme to trap the poor in dependency in exchange for their vote? Remember the Barry Goldwater rant against taking Arizona's money to help New Jersey or Louisiana recover from storm damage; he must have forgotten it was New Jersey money that helped build the dam that made living possible in Phoenix heat, and helped his family's merchant fortune and his wife's mining family fortunes.

It was President Polk who had forced Mexico to relinquish the hill of copper that Goldwater's wife's trust fund depended on. That is the same federal government and early states and their sons who died in the western wars that Goldwater held in contempt, believing the pioneers did it all themselves and owed the U.S. government and its citizens nothing in return.

We may also remember from Chapter 5 that Thomas Jefferson proposed to establish government funded free education to ensure the common man would be ready to make improvements in the domestic economy of the nation, as well as in his own family's standard of living, and to ensure elections were decided by an informed electorate.

Democrats address the common good by supporting a concept called social insurance. Those of us who vote in favor of social insurance policies hope a majority agree, not as a bribe but as good policy, perhaps the best family planning any family can invest in. As an example Social Security is the most popular social insurance system in American history and has been since 1935.

President Reagan really believed that if he could separate the states from the federal government, and wind up with smaller, or less as he saw it, intrusive government at both ends, (that the majority of Americans depended on, not understood by Reagan), that the majority of citizens would be happier. He sold the dream, but not the outcome, and they are unhappy and do not know where the blame lies as they listen to GOP spin.

This reality is another rung on the ladder of Reagan's failures that have created more debt, more gridlock, and made his GOP into a deceptive minority party that can only hold office with dark money, gerrymandering, voter suppression tactics, and spin.

The most amazing thing to me about the spin machine Reagan created in his first year under the direction of his public relations guru Mike Deaver, was the fact that Reagan blamed the Democrats for his new debt. David Stockman reported that when he showed Reagan the new debt and told him it was GOP debt, Reagan said "Now David that's not true, we do not create debt, that's what the Democrats do." Reagan also noted the conversation in his diaries as was mentioned earlier. The voice of a man with an iron will, a fixed mind, and a simple friendly personality.

Let's discuss the image part of President Reagan's legacy. Myth became a campaign strategy under Mike Deaver, who was a full time television and movie producer before he came to work for President Reagan. In the Reagan campaign and again during his presidency, Deaver was first and foremost an ad man providing video promotions over the full term of the Reagan presidency. As a lifetime natural performer (played the lead in his high schools annual plays), photogenic and adept on camera as a former radio, TV, and movie star, performer Reagan and ad man promoter Deaver were an ideal pairing. Reagan's continuing personal popularity throughout his time in office and after created an opportunity for the GOP to convert much of that good will into popular myth on behalf of the party.

To explain my use of the term myth, I'll note that President Reagan was the first president in U.S. history to my knowledge who had as a key adviser a great video publicist to go along with the typical speech writers and press agents of all modern presidents. What we saw was a naturally likable president who was also a trained spokesperson and actor, who was presented as professionally as any Madison Avenue ad agency would present a mass-market consumer product. As a result, a majority of Americans saw and still see President Reagan as a spokesman for the American dream. He and Deaver used the campaign slogan "Morning in America" during his campaign for his second term and folks felt it and loved it, even as deficits and debt grew out of all proportion to any previous time in U.S. history.

The more worrisome part of the myth is the continuing disconnect between the stated goals of Reagan's economic policies, and the actual outcomes for the middle class. Middle class people believed in, loved, and voted for President Reagan twice. They have continued to love him even though his policies reduced their and their children's standard of living over the following forty years as most of his key policies have remained in place, just as FDR's key policies did after his final term in office.

President Reagan and the GOP as part of his legacy did and do fall back on the concept of absolutism, to avoid compromise of contested issues between the political parties. Absolutism was practiced at GE Corporation from 1947 until at least the end of the Jack Welch era there. It was based on a public relations concept to enhance the image of the company in the eyes of consumers and employees. The board of directors authorized a new vice president level department and hired Lemual Boulware as head of the department.

One of the public relations methods was sponsorship of GE theater on television which Ronald Reagan was eventually hired to host. When Reagan was hired his job was to advise both the employees and the customers that the company saw GE investors and managers in a mutually beneficial and satisfying partnership, all in the best interest of three groups, including customers, employees, and even their suppliers.

This project was intended to improve relations and became known as

Boulwarism as it morphed primarily into a labor management tool. President Reagan worked indirectly under Lemuel Boulware from 1954 to 1960. Lem as he was called introduced single offer negotiating; any request to negotiate would cause instant gridlock in a union negotiation. It meant the plant would be shut down, sold, or moved if the first and only offer from the company was not accepted.

Eventually this led to so many closings of union factories by GE that the CEO, Jack Welch became known as Neutron Jack. The gag was, the buildings were still standing but all the employee had evaporated. This was also a key factor in the concept of outsourcing as a cost cutting, union busting, evasion of healthcare and other benefits. By the end of the process the whole concept of defined benefit retirement pensions ended, and were replaced by the defined contribution 401k tax exempt savings that has enriched millions of mid level employees. Those who are successful combined thrift, earning a living wage that allows for some discretionary income, and working for an employer who established such a program. In the post Reagan era most low and modest income retirees, and those who have experienced business or health setback without adequate insurance have only Social Security to rely on.

Lem even wrote a book about this absolutist method of negotiating that is still in print called *The Truth about Boulwarism*. Tea Party politicians such as Senator Ted Cruz and the Freedom Caucus in the U.S. House of Representatives use this tool every day, even if they are not aware of it. President Trump may not have heard of it, but he is a master of the method if he is a master of anything, other than tax avoidance, which he brags about.

Lem wrote his book seventeen years after he retired. His job description outlined that with the professional staff he was to establish, the new vice president was to develop an understanding of what customers thought of GE and its products, and what employees thought of GE. The job of the new department was to establish a baseline using satisfaction surveys of what customers thought of the company, and how satisfied they were with the products. Second was a survey of how satisfied the employees were with the company and what their employment meant to them. The outcome was GE had some work to do with customers, but for the most part GE was thought of as a good company. There was shock regarding the low level of satisfaction among union employees, less so expressed by salary employees, understandably.

If you read the book, and if you have also read the John Birch Society's manifesto (ghost written by William F Buckley's partner and published over Barry Goldwater's name as author), you will see much the same absolutist ideology on every page. It was pretty much just as revealed by the first Roman Pope in 325 AD, when he established that the Roman economic system, feudalism granted the king **absolute** authority over all of the property and all of the subjects of each kingdom controlled by the Republic of Rome across Europe.

Future president Reagan's GE assignment was to visit hundreds of factories and explain in his folksy way how much hourly workers on the shop floor were partners with management and their foremen in this great enterprise, helping them to accept this viewpoint and realize they would not need a union; nor would they feel depressed about work if they allowed themselves to better understand and help management create this feeling across the whole company. As Monty Python put the question "do you believe it is all for the best", only Reagan's job was to tell them that it was their duty to believe it was all for the best. Reagan transitioned from B level movies, to hosting a t show, to putting a happy face on absolutism at the hands of corporate goals.

In the boardroom and the GOP the absolutist belief about corporations was that they were entitled to all of the profits beyond the least the market would bear, and what they could buy using guile and mutual opportunism, paying the lowest taxes they could spend money on lobbyists to ensure, and engage in practices not based on how safe they were, but on cost price analysis. Meaning at Ford Motor Company, this practice at its worst meant once Ford knew that a few Pintos would explode in flames in a rear end collision based on the design and placement of the gas tank, they calculated the cost to replace millions of them on the road, or to pay the settlements of a calculated number of deaths they could settle monetarily for less than the cost of replacement. Look it up, that was an actual corporate board decision. Welch rode Lem's theory for many years of growth and profits; today the outcome of the process is a company that is just a shell of what it was; bad outcomes led to disaster.

I submit this is true of Reagan and the GOP twenty years into the twenty-first century. The bad outcomes are coming home to roost and troubles lie ahead if America does not improve outcomes for the bottom half of our citizens who have been hurt by these outcomes. They already outnumber Republicans, they just do not vote at the same high level as the better educated Republicans.

I will not dwell on exceptionalism as a core GOP value, but it has become a code word that key factions of the GOP use to represent the Reagan legacy, as it is seen by those sustaining the myth without question or candor in addressing to what if any extent his policies fell short, especially his economic policies.

The five themes of Reagan's American ideals are personal freedom, free trade, personal responsibility, capitalism, and Christianity. His focus on ideals allowed him to gloss over any downsides or blame for negative outcomes.

Reagan's southern strategy wing of Movement Conservatism loved this aspect of the Reagan myth, just as they have lost patience with stagnation of jobs and wages, endless terrorism and limited wars, and the opiate drug issue that is especially prevalent in the small towns that lost their key employers. A top book a few years ago was *Hillbilly Elegy*, a story of a young man who made it out of the coal belt then the rust belt, what was left behind, and his less than sureness of who to blame.

As noted, the export of democracy to countries not advanced enough to sustain it was not a core value for Reagan. However, the ideals of freedom, capitalism, and Christianity in former colonies that had not become free, capitalistic, or Christian since the end of colonialism under Britain, France, Spain, or the Netherlands, were Reagan's goals, especially in Central America. For many Americans it was hard to be against these values, although at the time of our revolution our founders revolted against the idea of an absolute state church, as well as the colonial business model of rigged trade policies.

Domestically, I submit Reagan believed in an opportunity-based society, as former Speaker of the House Newt Gingrich called Reagan's policies. He wanted to eliminate what he saw as the business stifling and personal dependence producing effects of FDR's security-based social insurance society, as his party's think tanks spun the New Deal outcomes.

Did Reagan have an understanding of or concern for a living wage for labor? Did he understand that wage earners had become the engine of the consumer economy which was created by FDR's New Deal? Reagan never to my knowledge mentioned let alone discussed support for the living wage concept or its importance.

If Reagan had any ideological belief in what made the American economy work I believe it was in his discussion of trickle down in a growth economy. His casual folksy comment to explain what he meant was **"a rising tide lifts all boats"**.

I doubt he really thought about the fact that consumers dealing with banks, hourly wage earners dealing with corporate employers, and minorities dealing with lingering societal norms were struggling with overwhelming latent and legacy odds all day every day that manifested as abuse to the communities kept in poverty by the freedom the GOP courts extended to banks, corporations, and employers, regarding what the GOP voters mean when they say they want their country back.

My lament of the wealth gap and the loss of the living wage middle class is not the full story of the last forty years in America. Today in my family four of our seven daughters are nearing retirement, two are retired and one is disabled since birth. Three of our four oldest grandchildren have graduated from collage, four more are in college, and one has graduated from medical school.

Our family is not that unusual in modern America, at least for the top half of the wealth gap who are more educated and are able to keep more of what they earn. Most have more savings than credit card debt, most have meaningful 401k savings. I celebrate how hard they all worked to achieve these outcomes. However, in my family we have members who are not academically adept; as in times past, they work for hourly wages. Their lives are as difficult today as lives were for folks who lived before FDR's New Deal.

Ronald Reagan casually, without any policy review or consideration of how much middle America depended on payroll mandates for their high standard of living, caused the near total destruction of an hourly living wage economy for nearly half of all American families, concerning free trade which he addressed the first year of his second term as we discussed earlier.

To a large extent GOP discussions over the past forty years of the Reagan era have revolved around personal responsibility, self reliance, and various concepts of self esteem related to freedom. And who would be critical of or deny they care about these self images that most of us were taught and teach our children?

So the message can be defined as benign at worst, or as a worthy goal at best. If the GOP openly proposed to limit veterans' benefits, or Social Security, or a family healthcare plan that covers dad's heart attack, mom's breast cancer, or a child with a rare disease, they would lose. So what is absolutism in pursuit of? A reduced standard of living for the middle class and the working poor to ensure a fuller return of all profit improvements accruing exclusively to the investor class? The legal term for this in salesmanship is legally known as guile, and is employed as political spin. Yep, putting the best spin on things by corporations, pastors, doctors, and politicians are all protected in law, and are not treated as fraud. Guile is a legal defense for fraud. I saw a fifty million dollar case against a vendor thrown out of court on a simple guile defense.

The GOP still supports the idea that tax cuts drive job growth and thereby increase total tax revenue. Conversely they seem to believe that sustainable living wages destroy jobs. Henry Ford among others proved a hundred years ago that higher wage employees spend more, thus increasing growth and driving great wealth building, available to distribute however the nation decides the economy will be designed to work in the most just outcome, based on contribution first, and a minimum level of societal cohesiveness.

Ford did not introduce a theory or an ideological based philosophy, he just doubled working men's hourly wage from $2.50 a day to $5.00, made more cars, added more jobs to meet the growing demand, and he made more money. The following year it repeated, and so it grew. I doubt he ever used the term sustainability, but he in fact defined it. Even before FDR and unions Ford proved the value of demand side growth as an on the job experiment.

The only promised byproduct of supply side was a "trickle down" economic improvement for millions of low earning and under employed Americans. At the same time the GOP still argued daily in the healthcare debates in 2018 in favor of letting markets solve the healthcare dilemma for the poor, who are poor because of a market solution to employer labor cost the GOP implemented thirty-five years ago.

Remember Reagan's casual folksy bromide for supply side economics (and he had one, as we have seen, for every new policy he introduced) that a rising tide lifts all boats. No one ever said more benign asides or produced more disastrous outcomes in the economic history of American national economic policy than Ronald Reagan. I refer to supply side and free trade as casual ideas.

These were the Reagan era "policy goals". It seemed the Holy Grail or the mother of all policies had been found, truly something of a eureka moment for all Americans. Actually it was a tragedy sold as a dream.

In 1986 Reagan approved a tax increase to slow the expanding bubble but it was too little too late. It also included repeal of the real estate tax credit, which led to the final collapse of the Savings and Loan banks and the failure of the construction industry, which spilled over into the total economy, further reducing tax receipts. Failed policies have economic consequences; to repeat my favorite saying, policy matters.

This is the time to explain the terms consolidated budget and year end reports. Like all such reporting, the budget is the expected income and expenses, and the report is the actual outcome at the end of the year. Governments do not report profit or loss, they only report deficits or surplus.

There are two main tax systems for funding what today is called the consolidated federal budget. One half of the consolidated budget is the general fund budget based on congressional spending and funded by the income tax system managed by the IRS. The other half is the U.S. retirement system funded with mandatory FICA taxes on employer and employee payrolls over each future recipient's working life, managed by an independent agency called the Social Security Trust Fund.

Until about fifty years ago the federal annual report only covered the annual budgeted tax income and the actual expenses. The net outcome was reported for the federal government as the federal budget year end report. The goal was a balanced budget; taxes and expenses were kept pretty much in line or elections would have consequences.

This reporting system was ended by President Lyndon B. Johnson during the Vietnam War. He consolidated the federal income tax system budget with the FICA budget and it seems to have blurred the ability to see what was being spent on the unpopular Vietnam War LBG inherited and made worse.

It was a bad idea for voters when the Democrats did it, and it is now abused for the same reason by the GOP and has been since the Reagan administration. Today it is used to hide the actual results of the federal budget, leaving politicians free to spin the blurred cause of tax cut debt as they wish.

If the federal budget was reported separately it would be almost twenty-five trillion dollars in debt.

The Social Security Trust Fund manages FICA, which is made up of payroll taxes paid half by wage earners and half by their employers. There are two parts to this tax fund. The first is to fund Social Security, the second is to fund Medicare. These are respectively the old age retirement funding and the old age healthcare funding systems. Both systems are managed and operated by the Social Security Trust Fund, and in 2020 it is 2.8 trillion dollars in surplus.

By law the FICA system cannot borrow, and makes no promise that current rates are guaranteed. It does report each year on how long the current system can pay today's rate of retirement and healthcare benefits unless Congress changes the rates. As baby boomers retire Congress must replace borrowed FICA dollars with newly borrowed federal debt or increase income taxes to pay back the FICA surplus the Congress had required baby boomers to pre fund for just this anticipated reality.

In 2020 the GOP spins this borrowing to redeem FICA bonds Congress borrowed to cover GOP tax cuts during the war on terrorism, and entitlement caused debt. This more than spin, this is a bald faced lie. Never let the GOP claim paying back FICA over charges since Reagan signed the surplus rate into law, as if they are borrowing to pay to fund Social Security and use that as a reason to cut Social Security.

One of my key suggestions at the end of the book for improved outcomes over the remainder of the twenty-first century to improve the factors that lead to gridlock and impede compromise is a return to the former method of federal budgeting with separate reporting of the general income tax based budget and the Social Security payroll contribution budget, making the actual balance of each easier for all tax payers to read and understand, and harder for guileful politicians to misrepresent.

When discussing debt, Republicans always fail to mention that the Social Security Trust Fund is still two point eight trillion dollars in the black, and is increasing its treasury bond reserves some plus four hundred billion dollars a year. Who created this surplus, and why and how was it created?

As is only fair, it was created by today's (baby boomers) retirees. Reagan's advisers saw debt looming ahead for the Social Security Trust Fund due to the inflation of the 1970s, stemming from the OPEC four hundred percent increase in the world price of oil.

However over that decade, from Nixon to Ford then Carter and finally Reagan, Social Security payments were raised by the inflation rate each year as the price of oil continued to rise as OPEC (mostly Middle East oil producing nations) reduced production causing the cost of oil to soar higher each year. This was an increase in future cost for the nation that was never anticipated and oddly is still left out of policy debates by both parties. Social Security monthly retirement payments were nearly doubled over this decade.

In the twenty-first century young employees now contend with funding this higher cost of oil, the inflated value of homes, and inflated FICA tax, even as the GOP has frozen minimum wages and destroyed the bargaining power of hourly wage workers, with their right-to-work ideology.

This is what the party of capitalism has dealt young working families. It is not surprising they fail to see that socialism is not the answer. What is called for is a more fair distribution of America's huge national economy that FDR created and Reagan deconstructed, not a call to destroy productive corporations as some young folks on the left seem to want, as the last gasp of a prosperous United States.

Back to the mid 1980s. The GOP led by President Reagan and the Democrats led by House Speaker Tip O'Neill jointly appointed the Greenspan Commission to raise the FICA tax to assure Social Security would be funded at the newly inflated cost (the OPEC oil price inflation we've mentioned) for the rest of the current retired generation at the time.

Additionally, the increase in FICA tax was needed to fund the unanticipated larger number of retirees, the result of much larger numbers of the baby boom generation born after WWII (the largest generation in U.S. History born between 1946 and 1964) who began to retire in 2011. Those numbers will begin to wane in 2029 when the last of them finally retire. With the mass introduction of the birth control pill in the mid 1960s, the American birth rate began to fall and the projected demands on the Social Security Fund also began to come down.

However, President Reagan had also introduced free trade as America's trade policy. No one anticipated China would capitalize so quickly and become the low cost supplier to the world. By the time I visited China ten years later, they were already running a sixty billion dollar a month surplus of U.S. dollars into their economy filling the shelves of Wal-Mart and most retailers in America.

When will a GOP president finally say it is time to feed the beast again, if they want our current nation to survive? Is it possible they do not want us to survive, or just not as a nation of citizens who share in the wealth of the nation, a return to a nation of aristocrats and servants perhaps? Most of us can still vote; it is up to us.

Meaning some GOP Senators and Congressmen who represent large constituencies of working folks have already stated they would let America default on its debt, claiming this would be without consequences. Good luck with that when the doo-doo hits the fan, as President George H.W. Bush called such results. The cost of interest on our debt will go up so fast and so high it will devour America's wealth, and if it bad enough the debt they buy will cost us even more than high interest, it will cost us a new Constitution without or with a very limited bill of rights.

I do realize a majority of elderly white males still seem to hate welfare more than they care about a living wage for their children, or passing on huge debt to their grandchildren. Perhaps they will not wake up until their own Social Security is cut. Remember the Social Security Trust Fund cannot borrow. There is no set guaranteed future minimum payment promised for Social Security, so if the fund does not take in enough after the surplus is used up or Congress lets America default and does not increase the funding source, the cuts will be automatic.

This means if you now receive twelve hundred dollars a month, and some day there is not enough to pay that, it will not be cut to zero dollars, but if there is only enough being paid in to fund nine hundred dollars a month for your earned benefit that will be your new rate. So all the bugaboo about running out of money is just that, a form of spin; it is not how Social Security works.

The Libertarian Wing of the GOP does have a plan, called Economic Freedom, but it is only paid lip service in Congress; in the light of day they do not yet fully support it. This is what happens if general revenue shortfalls cause insolvency, other than the printing press at the U.S. mint, which drives inflation through the roof. Insolvency means federal bonds can no longer be sold, or can be sold only at a destructive interest rate.

Reagan Democrats do not seem to mind shutting down the government when it is time to raise the debt limit to allow the Treasury to continue funding the tax cut binge for the wealthy. Perhaps one day it will take a missed Social Security check to clear the fog!

The GOP does not attack Social Security per se, they just use projected shortfalls as a problem, undermining the hopes of young folks for the future, and thus their willingness to fund it. The favorite undermining tactic against Social Security is to point out that when it was founded in 1935 the demographics showed six workers for each retiree, and now there are only three. They fail to mention that the modern day three workers produce about five hundred times the wealth as six did then due to continued improvements in productivity, and that productivity will continue to increase in the future.

Today the three workers produce one hundred eighty thousand dollars of GDP or sixty thousand dollars of wealth for every one of the three hundred twenty million folks who live in America, meaning a GDP in America in 2017 of over eighteen trillion dollars. That is the last year I had actual numbers for. I'm sure in 2020 the GDP is at or near twenty trillion dollars.

The real problem under the current GOP starve the beast pledge that Reagan approved and is still re-pledged by nearly all GOP legislators every two years when they are sworn in, is the fact that even as productivity increases, wages (upon which Social Security is funded) are stagnant.

If wages increased, tax revenue into Social Security and the general fund would increase, as the wealthy currently pay less than one percent into Social Security and Medicare, leaving the FICA tax capped at one hundred twenty-eight thousand dollars of income per year. A twenty year cap on the federal minimum wage has also been a twenty year cap on increasing the funding of Social Security, while the GOP has left the Social Security cost of living adjustment in place. We will see how long that can remain if Trump's economic growth increases inflation a lot faster than wages.

As an example of the effect of elderly voting percentages, minimum wage is not cost of living indexed, but Social Security is. Seniors have had a Social Security raise in thirty of the past thirty-five years. Folks earning the federal minimum wage have not had a raise in years. This is not sustainable, equitable, nor family friendly. We need to reinstate a cost of living raise annually for federal minimum wages for the young or end cost of living for the elderly.

So supply side did not work as advertised, and the Reagan tax cuts led to deficits. Were any other supply side ideas enacted, one might ask, and if so how did they work out? Maybe we should first add that the supply side guys also loved the Chicago School of Economics at the University of Chicago, and the teachings of its leader Milton Friedman. Friedman, affectionately referred to as Uncle Milty, was a guru to Paul Ryan and Federal Reserve Chairman Alan Greenspan. Today the GOP gurus are more often employed by Koch Network alumnae of the economics department at James Mason University that is also funded by the Koch Network dynastic billionaires.

More than any other twentieth century American economist, Milton Friedman was a conservative believer in smaller government, lower taxes, and less regulation, especially of business and finance, and a foe of the New Deal. His ideas have not carried over into the twenty-first century as strongly as the economic ideas of another Chicago school alumni and Nobel Prize winner, James McGill Buchanan.

Friedman would accept an end to social insurance (Social Security and Medicare) in return for smaller government and for individuals providing their own families' education, healthcare, and retirement costs. I never read how he expected the folks who do most of the dirty and menial jobs would fund these needs of the nation, if employers continue to have absolute rights and power to set wages based on the market. To me Milton Friedman was a dreamer who seems to have forgotten the reality of life when his idealized view of economic governance was not the condition most Americans lived in, meaning in poverty and fear of loss of their income and their whole life's savings before the New Deal.

Milton Friedman was a less involved and James McGill Buchanan was a more involved adviser in post colonial nationalist Chile. It is a fine example of a modern divide between property rights and feudal limits and Chile remains a near feudal society for millions.

Reagan agreed with Friedman, as we will see by his statements as he continued his efforts to repeal, reduce, and free business and citizens from government intrusion as he and Friedman saw it. We have already reviewed how President Reagan deregulated the Savings and Loan mortgage banks. Milton Friedman was the key economist in America who wrote in favor of bank deregulation as part of his intellectual dissection of the New Deal.

So what does a free market loan center in small town America look like for wage earners living under Reaganomics trickle down wage levels forty years later? Instead of Savings and Loan banks in every city in America, we now have payday loan, car title loan, and pawn loan shops in every city in America. These all but unregulated loan shops legally charge as much as plus five hundred percent APR interest. Reagan's repeal of usury laws has proven again that deregulated usury rates are more a crippling trap than a benefit for the working poor.

Today in the face of this turnabout in the cities of most GOP members of the U.S. Congress, they still vote against any protection for individual consumers and have restricted bankruptcy laws to ensure a speedy cleanup of unsustainable corporate debt, while re-writing individual bankruptcy laws to allow high interest loans to folks unable to compete for wages in the marketplace, so that they have access to loans they cannot afford and reduced legal rights to escape from loan companies designed to keep them in debt for life.

Almost all GOP Congressional members oppose the Consumer Protection Agency, refuse to fund it, even claiming it is not Constitutional. As if they are the review court lawyers themselves with a highly tuned sense of justice regarding a natural need for loan sharks, in our below poverty level market wage system for millions of low wage American families since the GOP opened our borders to Asian wage rates and froze the minimum wage.

The Tea Party came to power on this type of debt, denouncing the victims, not the perpetrators. In founding the Tea Party Rick Santelli ranted about deadbeats tricking banks into giving them loans they did not deserve and lied to obtain, demanding President Obama not bail out these cheats. Rick is still on CNBC TV promoting Trump's tax cuts; either he never understand the subprime mortgage market or his whole successful rant was just spin. If you agree with Rick that the poor outsmarted the banks to obtain the loans that destroyed their credit, you do not understand who engaged in fraud (guile), and who were the victims.

If Tea Party beliefs about the U.S. Constitution were true, we would need a Constitutional reset to define how a modern wealthy continental democracy of plus three hundred million folks could ever work. If the GOP continues to ignore supply side policies that increased government spending while cutting taxes, left government insured savings at risk while deregulating underwriting standards for mortgage banks, and worst of all continues to leave healthcare to be funded on domestic payrolls for most families in the free trade global economy, the solvent nations of the world holding U.S. debt will act, led by China to force a reckoning of our debt.

As for the Supreme Court, if settlement of dissent is limited to only what was known in 1789 we would have no idea on what a right to charge five hundred percent interest would be based. The Tea Party and Freedom Caucus, supported by Evangelical Christians, claim the Constitution should be interpreted on what the founders meant in the Constitution with no consideration of any societal changes over our first two hundred years. Jesus ousted the money changers for usury, as did kings; it is so destructive it even drove Christian Germans to vote for Hitler.

What would the founders have believed about five hundred percent interest rates? I believe they would have revolted against such pure confiscation as abuse of authority. So should we, for those people who do not qualify for traditional banking due to the GOP's minimum wage and unsustainable right-to-work laws. The early right-to-work states remain the worst examples of states living off block grant federalism.

There are Congressional Democrats who vote with the bank lobby, but on the whole the Democratic caucus enabled and continues to support the Consumer Protection Agency's policies and regulations.

Only a family that would set up a business like Amway, where plus ninety percent would be small business investors who become independent Amway sales contractors fail, would accept that high failure rate is a reasonable risk for those induced to believe in Amway as a safe investment, and continue to entice new recruits with the hyped spin of focusing on the income of the top one percent of salesmen, also known in more regulated times as pyramid selling, another form of guile.

Betsy DeVos now sells that same level of honesty as the GOP head of the U.S. Department of Education in President Trump's Cabinet. DeVos is selling economic freedom (a Koch ideology (Betsy is a member of the Network) to millions of students who are destined to fail, to protect opportunity for the two percent, as well as to protect her accumulated personal wealth from paying taxes that are required to fund universal public education, a former GOP core value that is now being deconstructed.

Economists call these policies unsustainable. Without sustainable tax rates the government does not collect enough taxes to cover appropriated spending, and without sustainable underwriting banks do not earn enough profit to be sustainable. The same holds true for a family if wages are not sustainable.

GOP think tanks are mostly funded as tax free educational organizations and there are a lot of them, such as the Heritage Foundation and so on. They seem to not be troubled about the millions of folks living in poverty. They seem to see poverty as a natural state for the bottom third to half of all U.S. citizens, they even admit it among themselves.

In an unguarded moment in his quest for the U.S. presidency against President Obama, Mitt Romney suggested the percentage of American voters not worth caring about was forty-seven percent. He went on to say he based that on the fact that forty-seven percent are not going to vote for him, a Republican, no matter what. It too often seems the common good is not part of modern GOP leaders' interest, in spite of the fact that it was seen by our founders as the purpose of self government.

If the Republicans know that forty-seven percent of voters vote Democrat, and over three percent of Independents vote Democrat, why, since the end of WWII and forty years into the Reagan era, would key GOP leaders including Strom Thurmond, Billy Graham, Barry Goldwater, Charles Koch, Milton Friedman, William F. Buckley Jr., Ronald Reagan, Dick Cheney, Alan Greenspan, Pat Robertson, Paul Ryan, Tea Party politicians, Donald Trump, and now in the U.S. House in the Freedom Caucus, commit to absolute gridlock, rather than even one percent of compromise?

The absolutist GOP ideology is always spun as freedom and opportunity or support of faith, patriotism, and responsibility. They do not accept for a minute that the other plus fifty percent of voters have rights and reason behind their votes. They argue that the Democrats have intentionally destroyed plus fifty percent of American voters' liberty because welfare, Social Security, and Medicare are all only offered to voters to trap them in dependency in exchange for their vote.

Life, Liberty, and the Pursuit of Happiness make up the key stated purpose of our form of self government. Do GOP policies improve the lives of the lower fifty-one percent of Americans? Does living in poverty improve anyone's sense of freedom, and finally, how does the absence of hope enhance happiness?

Meanwhile, access to recourse in the courts for debtors unable to pay due to entrapment, mediation, or adversity has been reduced at the request of the high interest lenders' lobby. Government has become the enabler of abuse of low income voters in debt; what a twist on the founder's intent as well as Jesus' lesson of what he thought about abusive money lenders!

At the time of the Constitution ratification and the Bill of Rights, absolute abuse had been at the hands of the king's sheriff and the absolute authority of Roman Catholic bishops during the Inquisition, and carried out by their jailers or torture chamber attendants; that was how punishment was meted out upon the working poor in the days of a cashless society. Today the high interest debt industry and the rigged court system amount to modern abuse for millions of folks, all fostered under an ideology of "freedom" yet as coercive psychologically as the king's torturers' rack was physically.

In fact the victims are disparaged as the opportunistic or irresponsible half of this game that the high interest lobby invented for ignorant borrowers, counting on their naivety, meaning they should have seen the trap and avoided it. They demand a buyer beware legal standard for folks who have never been aware of almost any of the traps of the mutually opportunistic free market as it has been distorted under a legal standard that protects guile as a sellers' norm available to professional market practitioners.

The practitioners in the Reagan era have included the peddlers of education products and loans, the peddlers of mortgages and mortgage loans, the sellers of dare to be great get rich quick using my techniques and the enabling loans, corporate purchasing agents enticing vendors to fund corporate capital investment in special purpose tools and equipment without an equal offsetting defined mutual benefit, and of course Amway would-be self employed dealers.

Note: Before assuming the office after winning the presidency in 2016, Trump paid a twenty-five million dollar judgment in settlement of his now defunct Trump University education scam that cost students thirty-five thousand dollars each with no marketable improvement in the students' earning ability.

Congress and the courts allow these traps for the same folks the GOP insist do not deserve to earn more than seven dollars and twenty-five cents per hour, based on their low level of skills, knowledge, and abilities. Economic freedom as a governing ideology is a reintroduction of abuse, as the promise of America is being deconstructed along with our government.

I am eighty years old; in my lifetime I have never once heard a U.S. president say America should do something about the pain young children of the poor endure from something as easy to cure as a toothache. Why can folks like me not sell these ideas to those earning seven dollars and twenty-five cents an hour as a reason to vote for politicians who will require those who earn billions of dollars to ensure their underpaid employees' children never again have to live in hunger or pain?

The working poor do not understand what causes their poverty or how to improve their wages, debt, healthcare, or standard of living. It is obvious to me that those who are unprepared, for whatever reason, to compete in the marketplace should be protected by their government from the unrelenting opportunism they do not comprehend, if the right to govern is based on a promise to protect the electorate from economic abuse by the few as a minimum standard of justice.

The working poor are not able to understand how and why they should vote a self interest if not for themselves at least for their children, as they are tired and unaware of how they will find the time, travel, and knowledge to vote, let alone vote in their own best interest. That there is a popular political movement to keep folks poor and kids in pain, in a wealthy, educated, Christian majority (take your pick) nation, is shameful, and none more so than evangelical pastors.

This low level ability to understand and thrive occurs among one or more members of most families from time to time. Why do we not require our government to protect them from the worst of the free market guile that produces all of the wealth as well as most of the abuse? Elizabeth Warren created just such a entity in the government under Barack Obama; the GOP has for the most part refused to fund it.

In his budgets Reagan proposed to end subsidies for Amtrak, Small Business Administration loans, and the Export/Import Bank, to name a few. All three are still on the books, as Congress and the American people who elect their local representatives to Congress disagreed. Actually the EXI Bank receives no subsidies, quite the opposite.

In 2016 the self-named Freedom Caucus (young Congressmen who are more conservative than the Tea Party) failed to renew the Export-Import Bank because, they said, "they were sent to Congress to repeal (these) unpopular laws". They allowed the authorizing legislation to die in committee, so the enabling laws could not be voted on by the full House of Representatives.

The outcry was so loud across the country that about half of the GOP joined all of the Democrats and reinstated the bank, with over seventy percent of Congress voting yes. This decision by the seventy percent was based on economic and business reality. The small group of true believers in the so-called Freedom Caucus has again vowed to repeal it as soon as possible; it seems they just need more gerrymandering to get the representation for this minority opinion to stick. Note: In the 2018 midterm election the GOP lost the majority in the U.S. House of Representatives in spite of gerrymandering.

Neither the Civil War nor the Reagan revolution won the Constitutional battle for states' rights over individual rights that had also been fought in the ratification process at our founding, but the Freedom Caucus is offering a new battle plan based on stripping the executive branch of its Constitutional power to manage the government. This was in their reelection promises for the 2016 Congressional election which they won by gerrymandering. To their surprise the GOP won the 2016 presidency also. So far they have been less vocal about pushing executive power to the point they claim the president's decisions must be subject to congressional review. Both claims were and are unconstitutional. As part of the madness of where the U.S. electorate is today, President Trump and his aides are claiming he is not to be subject to review. This same GOP acted shocked that the 2019 Democratic majority in Congress impeached President Trump for refusing to be subject to review, after they had made it a platform promise in case Hillary won.

The Freedom Caucus folks have become as absolutist on the role of government, as the evangelical wing of the GOP on social issues, or the Progressives on latent individual rights, and the Libertarians on taxes, labor rights, and the use of gerrymandering.

A couple of major departments of government were slated for elimination by Goldwater and again by Reagan, and by several GOP presidential candidates since. Among them were the Energy and Education Departments. They are still part of the federal government some fifty five years later. Instead of eliminating departments,

Reagan added Veterans Affairs to his cabinet as a federal cabinet department.

In effect China has used President Reagan's casual enactment of a bad idea on ideology alone to make America their junior partner in some ways in a mercantile trade relationship. This is as bad for industrial modern America as warm weather crop mercantile trading was for the southern plantation economy in pre-revolutionary times.

Apple is a perfect example. Apple took advantage of China's low labor rate, and over time hired more than five hundred thousand employees in China. Between the cost in China and sales in the U.S., about five hundred dollars per device, Apple took most of the profit in Asia, not in the United States. Apple now has more cash than the U.S. government on any given day, on deposit, untaxed in Asia, and is paying only pennies on the profits taken by the U.S. marketing end of the Apple empire.

When President Trump comments on how stupid America has been regarding Asia, I wonder if he or his supporters ever realize President Reagan's starring role in what President Trump understandably defines as stupidity. Reagan's concern for risk assessment was casual, if not intentional; he defended it as a gift to American consumers. It was a gift as harmful as the Trojan horse.

Trump's solution to bringing manufacturing jobs back to America was to re-impose tariffs beginning with steel and aluminum. As we have seen with Trump's decisions on immigration, he has a habit of implementing his policies without hearings or Congressional review, and without pre negotiations with our allies and our trading partners around the world. Tariffs are another example of this preemptive mindset.

So far the reaction to Trump's tariffs has been led by General Motors who announced the closing of five plants and the layoff of fourteen thousand employees. Trump paid subsidies to farmers whose contracts for agricultural goods were canceled by the Chinese in retaliation for the tariffs.

Trump said his predecessors negotiated bad trade deals. He did not mention that the worst bargain of all was not a deal, it was a gift to China and American corporations, triggered one day as a nice man's idea he believed was true but was not, that free trade was in fact a naturally good idea. I take it he believed it was in America's best interest. As Mark Twain said "What gets us into trouble is not what we don't know. It's what we know for sure that just ain't so".

The negotiated deal Trump was talking about was NAFTA, negotiated by Bill Clinton who too often thought more like Reagan than FDR. Trump was wrong about Canada. We enjoy a twelve billion trade surplus in our trade with Canada that predated NAFTA and survived under NAFTA, because of a settlement made long ago for a policy of free trade based on an open border between our countries, provided that Canada would not develop their own auto manufacturing industry if U.S. manufacturers set up employment and sales arrangements mutually beneficial to both countries. I was raised in Detroit Michigan and often used the Ambassador Bridge from Detroit to Windsor Ontario Canada. There were always trucks headed both ways carrying both U.S. auto manufactured components and assembled autos in fulfillment of this relationship. In 2020 America, Canada, and Mexico have a new agreement; let us hope it is of mutual benefit; that would mean it was negotiated with rational boundaries.

Once President Reagan's free trade ideological beliefs kicked in after September 1985, he enabled free trade between Asia and America much as Trump too often acts on his ideas. Both GOP presidents have acted without further review or due diligence; Reagan just abruptly announced decisions, as does Trump. Neither ever looked back at their outcomes, a practice in keeping with GOP legislators alike. Reagan and Trump policies often have unintended consequences which are left unattended. The Democrats may also be reluctant to look back, but they have always been diligent about hearings and professional input beyond lobbyists in drafting and enacting their policies.

In trying to sell GOP ideas about cutting Social Security, President Reagan advised younger laborers that if they did not support his lowering of the minimum payments and the cuts in the annual increases at the start of his first term, Social Security would not be there for them later. Many young people spent the last forty years believing they would never collect a retirement from the FICA payroll taxes they were paying, between this Reagan sales pitch and the GOP blaming their tax cut U.S. debt on entitlements. The Social Security scare was a lie.

Continuing wealth creation due to continuing improvements in productivity should be taken into consideration. We should not arbitrarily limit the rich getting richer, but if Adam Smith, and Alexander Hamilton are right, then a portion of that wealth must be shared with labor and government to keep the nation, its economy, and its families sustainable.

If the GOP continues to win the debates over minimum wage (no increases), unions (against living wages for workers as well as not having the right to collective bargaining, in favor of state right-to-work legislation), and off shoring jobs in the decades ahead (free trade), America will return to a pure rich/poor country of only the few and the many with no meaningful middle class. This is how it was before the New Deal created a meaningful American middle class that included millions of living wage earning families, but only after the war, and then only for about fifty years.

The Strom Thurmond/Ronald Reagan legacy lives on in the Tea Party, the Freedom Caucus in the U.S. House, Liberty University, and Koch Network educational enterprises, as examples which continue hoping to eventually fully kill the FDR New Deal.

We have talked about inflation and its effect on the national economy regarding OPEC oil price increases. However we have not talked much about deflation, even though it took place in 1907, and 1929, and again at the end of the 1980s with the bust of the Savings and Loan industry. America has suffered through policy-caused deflation twice in the Reagan era, the second time in 2007.

Deflation is another word for going bust due to insolvency caused by unsold inventory, and/or selling assets at liquidation prices or that have to be written down (a paper loss which can put bank debt in default). This can wipe out companies' net worth, forcing insolvency, leading to liquidation with huge write offs and losses of money, taxes, and jobs for the owners, the community, and if widespread enough, the nation.

When companies as large as General Motors were forced to be in technical insolvency due to a lost ability to borrow after writing off the book value of twelve million leased vehicles still with leases paid on time, GM had to mark down the book value of cars that still had functioning leases but lower projected future buyout values, in what had become a depressed economy. Only President Obama's decision to make the U.S. government the lender of last resort saved the U.S. auto industry.

GM did not lose a single real dollar on that day, but did have a sixty billion dollar write down of projected possible loss that put the company out of business and seven hundred thousand union rate wage employees out of work. This deflation of the economic risk was again not considered, as W's economic supply side brain trust decided to shut Lehman Brothers and go broke, for what ever personal reason Wall Street had a need to punish an arrogant banker.

The GM finance division was sold at a deflated price to a business in which former Vice President Dan Quayle (under George H.W. Bush) and former Treasury Secretary John Snow (under George W. Bush) were partners. They bought the GM finance division at the deflated (net present) value, continued to collect the revenue, and at the end of the lease periods had made for themselves most of the billions of dollars General Motors had been forced to give up. Today that business continues as one of the largest auto finance banks in the world; U.S. consumers see ads for Ally Bank on TV almost daily.

When presidents Bush and Obama bailed out Wall Street, the price of autos rebounded, creating billions in windfall profits for the opportunistic Cerberus Hedge Fund (Ally Bank owners) that paid only fifteen percent taxes on the GM profits. So as millions of wage earning American lost their jobs, homes, and savings, Cerberus partners made $60,000,000,000 and paid only $9,000,000,000 in taxes, and continued in business as Ally Bank.

It is undeniable that every side of supply side economics enacted in the Reagan era, however they were structured or promised, backfired against wage earners. Reagan's free trade policies, union busting

407

right-to-work policies, and ignoring increasing shortfalls in healthcare funding, all hurt the country's taxpayers, but they hit hourly wage earners hardest. Now their children are graduating from college in debt into an economy without enough living wage jobs, while their grandfathers think Donald Trump and an all GOP Congress will Make America Great Again with a third round of debt creating tax cuts.

West Virginia's current outrage from the pulpit is largely directed at abortions, guns, welfare, same sex marriage, immigrants, the press, and a war on God fearing Christians by secular folks accused of destroying the Constitution. However in 1924 the U.S. Supreme Court upheld Virginia's Racial Integrity Act, in a case called Buck v. Bell. It is a case worth reading to understand the level of bias against the mixing of the races, and the length the men of the southern states would go to, to limit first mixed raced children, as well as so called feeble minded white children, but also an idea that led to state supported abortions, and sterilization of young black women and even chemical castration of black men, once the population of blacks in the south outgrew the need for field hands as the nation industrialized. Basically the issue was an immoral false science called eugenics.

The south used it for racial reasons, and the numbers were never reported. The numbers we do have indicate it was used on at least tens of thousands of black women. This is the same "science" Germany sited as it sterilized hundreds of thousands of "undesirable" folks, including using this Supreme Court case to justify at the war trials after WWII that what they engaged in was not a war crime by American standards.

One of the most enduring success stories of the GOP myth making machine is the "Reagan Recovery", the so-called largest and fastest economic recovery in history after any recession. For the eight years of Obama steadily working our way out of the 2007 collapse of the deregulation of subprime mortgages, his progress was sold by the GOP as a poor performance compared to Reagan's. Actually Obama's recovery has continued, while Reagan's led to another recession and bailout that impacted his successor's single term -- the collapse of his Savings and Loan deregulated banks.

The problem is, the GOP completely ignores the boom and bust reality of the twelve years of Reagan's two terms and his vice president's single term. Yes, we had those three great years of supply side growth after the tax cuts, tax credits, and real estate trust incentives, but when it busted they woke up to a terrible debt and the cost to clean up the crashed housing market; they blamed it on Jimmy Carter and his unrelated ending of Jim Crow red lining, and credited Reagan with the manufactured boom.

I actually heard two young men discussing Reagan's and W's crashes on Fox News one day, and they cited it as if it was the only fact in history, stating that America had a long history of economic corrections following periods of twenty years of growth. They ignored that it had been proven that the reality was due to unregulated speculation, and the New Deal fix had worked to end this recurring nightmare for working folks and small net worth savers, in cities both large and small.

The GOP does remember and likes to remind us that in 1937 FDR did not claim a recovery, only relief as his initial program for out of work labor was called. Relief was the first of FDR's promised three R's (reform and recovery were the other two). Safe banks were the first reform. When his relief effort was cut back in 1937, the U.S. returned to a near recession level of activity. However, that the reformed banks and stock market kept the economy from slipping back into depression goes unacknowledged.

Only later did FDR turn from his first two programs, relief and long term reform, when at the beginning of WWII in Europe his Lend-Lease aid to Britain put the factories back to work at full levels. All sides agree the depression did not fully end until WWII returned America to full employment.

Regulated and insured banks are safe banks. This is not in question in any other major industrial nation in the world. Neither is the concept that current spending in excess of current taxing is debt financing, so further tax cutting is moronic; the GOP has intentionally inflicted a national madness on our population.

Take away the veneer of myth, and a fair assessment of the Reagan presidency would fail him on economics, job creation, bank deregulation, and trade, along with a D at best on civil rights, the Middle East, and South America. It would give him a very high grade on his Russian policy, party building, reductions in the nuclear arms race, and his restoration of American pride.

On how he made Americans feel about themselves and their country he would get an A. So far that has been enough to sustain the myth; it may not be enough for history to sustain the myth, which will assess his presidency, especially his economic policies, quite harshly I'm very sure.

In spite of Reagan's stated goal to repeal the New Deal, he had hardly any lasting effect on the FDR legacy more negatively profound than labor rights, yet labor voted for him and against their own interest, so it is hard to grade him as far as these voters are concerned. The AFC/CIO rank and file members voluntarily abandoned their own blue collar political norms as they became Reagan Democrats.

They voted both terms for Reagan and to this day vote for his anti living wage GOP party. Reagan believed in a wealthy nation that tolerates a third of all working families living in poverty based on his ideology of small government, which was the thinking behind his statement "The government is not the solution, the government is the problem".

One issue that Reagan inherited and endorsed that did not come home to roost until George W's presidency was finalizing the ending of the draft and creating a so-called "all volunteer military". Vietnam had been unpopular. Ending the draft was politically popular.

When George W sent the U.S. military to war, first in Afghanistan against abettors of terrorists, and later in Iraq preemptively for the first time in U.S. history, he did so without re-instituting a draft. The key problem has been there have not been enough volunteers in total in two wars for over fifteen years. There especially have not been enough volunteers of the caliber required to man the modern military, just as Ike found even in WWII, when he created the federal education department.

President George W. Bush used the National Guard as the key solution to manning his two wars on terror. In the past nineteen years of continuous wars military reservists were sent to war zone tours of duty for up to ten tours. The reserves were never designed to be America's regular army. They were designed to be the emergency force, the first ready force as a defense until draftees could be trained and brought up to speed in case of foreign wars, and as a first line of defense if the homeland was invaded.

This created as many or more problems than Reagan hoped to cure when he made the all volunteer military permanent. This decision could not be graded at the time; today I'd give it an F for the same lack of foresight or rethinking what the decision would mean over time.

Reagan had a casual conversation at the time with his economic guru Milton Friedman who recommended a "professional" army because as he said "you want your doctor to be a professional, why would you want anything less in your soldiers?".

We have military academies for our "professional" soldiers, but we do not require six to eight years of training for our infantry. We still do not have adequate consensus about why we are sending our soldiers into combat; we have reduced dissent about combat deaths, I hope not because it is no longer "our" sons and daughters dying.

So began a new chapter in American history, with former presidents becoming wealthy on speaking fees paid by old beneficiaries of their policies. Harry Truman must have rolled over in his grave. No president so far has been found to have traded policy for fees, but earning huge speaking fees after the presidency is not seen as healthy or right by a lot of folks in either party. Bill Clinton turned this process into a nine figure fortune. Remember Truman said "I will not accept speaking fees; the presidency is not for sale". That was then; today, Harry would be appalled.

President Reagan's Vice President George H. W. Bush, was elected as the forty-first president in 1989. In January of 1990 he was sworn in, and was the last WWII veteran to be elected president. Bush, like

Carter, is now seen as the very decent human being he was. H.W. had perhaps the best eye for picking foreign affairs advisers of any president with the possible exception of Truman after the war ended in 1945, but neither were seen as dominant leaders in their time. One exception in H.W.'s cabinet was his selection of Dick Cheney as his Secretary of Defense.

President Bush had held enough varied jobs in the federal government to know how the system worked, and how to make sure his policies were compatible with American norms. He was the last president to be serious about America's policy needs for the global realities at the end of the twentieth century.

By the time Soviet Leader Mikhail Gorbachev came to power, almost no one trusted the USSR. But Gorbachev was not formed in Stalin's mold nor even Khrushchev's. To Reagan's credit he came to trust Gorbachev, who was deconstructing the USSR himself because it was not working economically internally for Russian citizens, especially consumers.

At first Reagan rejected Gorbachev's disarmament proposals. Reagan pursued a defensive missile shield, but eventually they did agree to the largest destruction of stockpiled warheads and missiles of war in the history of the world.

By the time Iraq attacked Kuwait (former territory of Iraq) in the first Bush administration in 1990, Gorbachev had joined in backing President George H.W. Bush's UN resolution to declare war on Iraq. Under the first President Bush, at least for a moment the U.S. and the Soviet Union were allies. Communism finally collapsed in Russia in the George H. W. Bush administration, a combined triumph of Truman and every president until the USSR collapse, i.e., they were all dedicated to Truman's containment policy. This collapse without a nuclear war is the only way to assess without despair the loss of over one hundred thousand American warriors who held communism in check without a nuclear war during the containment wars in Korea and Vietnam.

The USSR collapsed in 1989 with the fall of the Berlin Wall and freedom in Eastern Europe; even East and West Germany reunited.

Containment policies and the success of capitalism as an economic engine defeated communism without the U.S. or Europe firing a shot, let alone the two nations going to war and it could have meant a nuclear war as Barry Goldwater had advocated only thirty years earlier. H. W. Bush managed to invade Iraq without upsetting the Middle East oil monarchs, or getting bogged down in a quagmire. This reinforced my opinion of how special his judgment of horseflesh was in the foreign policy arena.

H.W. Bush was determined not to bogged down in the Israel versus Palestine mess either, and like Obama later he met all of the security needs of the Israelis without becoming involved in their all but self destructive disputes with neighbors on both sides. I know they are the ones on defense, yet the only methods they are now engaged in is leading to apartheid, not a path to peace or world acceptance.

If H.W. Bush had a weakness in the Middle East, it was his tolerance for the Saudis, who allowed the radical Wahhabi form of orthodox jihad beliefs about Islam to flourish in their country. They funded or tolerated their citizens' funding radical Islamic extremism across the Middle East into the schools they invested in, and in the process re-introducing the sword as the Islamic solution to their clerics' judgments on the modern world.

In 2017 we saw a schizoid performance during President Donald Trump's first overseas trip. He spent the first few days in Saudi Arabia condemning the fruit of Wahhabi theocracy while dancing with the leaders, and selling them another one hundred billion dollars of munitions, with little or no oversight of where these weapons would wind up. The Bush family is invested with the House of Saud amounting to billions of dollars, another mitigating factor in this relationship.

The Bush family has been a key beneficiary of the Carlyle Group since its inception by former President George H.W. Bush's inner circle of advisers. Carlyle is a unique hedge fund type investing option, something of an alternative type of finance management firm, combining relationships, politics, opportunism, and wealth accumulation. Every president since Lyndon Johnson has managed to make millions of dollars off their presidency with the possible exception of Jimmy Carter; I do not know how much he has made in speaking or book fees. It has now trickled down even to Congressional leaders and committee chairs.

The Carlyle Group is now the largest stockholder in U.S. defense industry stocks. A serious read about this entity is eye opening. Like all U.S. presidents since Truman, Bush kept a close eye on the powerful Saudi lobby, and its large cast of supporters in the U.S. Capital. The best read I've found on this whole murky mess is a book titled *Secrets of the Kingdom* by Gerald L. Posner.

Vice President and later President Bush had a more realistic understanding of the Middle East than any other American president in the twentieth century in the GOP, in spite of what I related above, much like Joe Biden in the Democratic Party, even if their viewpoints differ. Neither was ideologically committed to a single view or approach to international problems. Like Truman they knew the history, and considered that long history critical to understanding the hatreds that fueled the continuing tensions. President George H.W. Bush better understood the diplomatic, political, and financial relationships of the region than his son George W. Bush, the forty-third president of the United States. H.W. Bush also was a great judge of national security, military and diplomatic talent, and his son was not. I'm referring to the people Bush Jr. used as advisers who assured him the Iraqis were ready for democracy, meaning "regime changing by force". Ideological Neocon Middle East military preemptive strike activists advised his total mess making in Iraq.

On taxes, H.W. Bush forty-one lost his base when he said "read my lips, no new taxes". Then, being a rational man as deficits rose he raised taxes, thus tacitly acknowledging the failure of the Reagan tax cuts based on supply side theory. He was the only major GOP politician to raise taxes since the Reagan collapse, which was the onset of overwhelming deficits and debt. In fact, George H.W. Bush's initial view of supply side tax cuts paying for themselves was called "voodoo economics", as good a nickname as the more often cited Reaganomics, supply side, or trickle down.

Bush forty-one became a single term president; no other GOP politician has suggested increasing taxes again in the past thirty-six years even as debt has climbed to twenty plus trillion dollars. Raising taxes as a Republican was a "mistake" H.W. Bush's son did not repeat eight years later, and he was re-elected for a second term in the middle of a total military and economic fueled boom leading to a bust in both.

Because the lowered tax rate did not support George W. Bush's ongoing wars, he added more than five trillion dollars of additional national debt during his two terms. The five trillion was based on the tax cut and wars. W's economic bust only impacted his last year in office, but it left a one point five trillion dollar deficit going forward. The extra one trillion dollars a year for the first few years of the Obama administration was the cost of cleaning up the Wall Street mortgage bond fiasco.

George W. Bush left ongoing yearly deficits of more than a trillion and a half dollars a year that took the next president, Barack Obama, almost five years to reduce to under half a trillion dollars a year, adding another ten trillion dollars of debt based on bad policy and inadequate taxing during war, as well as another boom and bust deregulation of mortgages to work out on Obama's watch, even though not due to Obama's policies.

So George W. Bush left office with economic collapse in progress, two ongoing wars in progress, plus trillion dollars of debt, and half trillion dollar deficits as far as the eye can see.

A short introduction to the Obama presidency is actually an introduction to absolute gridlock and dilemmas that are yet unresolved. The GOP has been all too happy to frame both the Wall Street recession and the ongoing debt as Obama's legacy, and to frame the longest recovery in U.S. history only as too slow.

The eight year GOP blame game is continuing monthly on President Trump's watch. One of the first claims of the new president was "I was left a real mess here" as if the deficits, debt, and wars without a draft were all the result of Obama policies.

Neither had a meaningful impact on either the FDR or the Reagan era legacies, which remain the key competing economic legacies

415

conflicting America from the twentieth century into the third president of our third century as a nation ruled under the authority of "by the consent of the governed". Lincoln called this authority "of, by, and for the people"; at least it was the GOP orthodoxy of their first president, but hardly the belief of today's Freedom Caucus that has replaced the voice of the Tea Party in the U.S. House.

Both of these far right GOP Congressional caucus groups vote closer to Strom Thurmond's 1948 politics that opposed FDR's New Deal policies, including restraints on voting rights, cuts in social insurance benefits known as welfare, elimination of unions, a freeze on minimum wage increases designed to keep pace with inflation, restriction of women's family planning and equal pay rights, opposition to equal access to affordable and safe mortgages, and opposition to affordable limits on usury (interest rates).

Being from the south was about the only thing about Bill Clinton that was in keeping with the policies and concerns of FDR and both LBJ and Carter I refer to Bill Clinton as Reagan-like, as Reagan had successfully spun his programs by ignoring the outcome. Clinton was not about to take on popular myth; he was more concerned with election and reelection than sustainable policies.

Clinton was the son of an alcoholic father; he rose from modest means on academic aptitude, personal charm, and never-ending drive. He lacked ideology, set values, and simple sincerity as he maintained his personal popularity and became a near billionaire.

In 2016, his wife Hillary was the Democratic standard bearer for the U.S. presidency on the Democratic ticket. She was a more serious policy wonk than her husband, but less blessed with the charm of a natural politician.

A short note on Hillary. As a bright lawyer she is cautious to a fault and she has always worked her own agenda (carefully). It has made her an easy target. The GOP and Fox News have painted her as dishonest, and Trump voters want her in jail, even though she has never been indicted let alone convicted of any crime. Many women love her, but Trump has painted her lawyerly answers as deceptive to his great benefit, an odd outcome for a man more than loose with facts.

Bill Clinton loved being president almost as much as FDR and Reagan. He was also a man of personal excesses that impacted but did not destroy his presidency or his legacy. The GOP portrays him as morally failed; the Democrats then and now somewhat excuse him as being merely a rascal, similar to the way the GOP does with Trump now. The evangelical leadership has recently given Trump a "mulligan" regarding a romp with a porn star he paid hush money to.

The policies from the FDR era (1933-1981) that Clinton compromised on with the GOP were mostly Kennedy or LBJ policies enacted after FDR's death in the 1960s. Clinton understood Reagan's popularity, so he seldom disparaged Reagan missteps other than on tax cuts, and stayed close to Reagan on welfare and work as well as prison building and Wall Street's bidding, which paid off personally for him in retirement.

Clinton is hardly worth much mention in my book, other than to say he neither made any FDR policy worse nor any Reagan policy better, except for debt as noted below. He was lucky due to a high tech boom on his watch so the economy grew.

Clinton doubled down on the GOP's wish to reduce welfare cost as explained above, partly due to his trade off to get a tax increase; in return he and the GOP also allowed financial institutions to continue to invent less safe products with less oversight. This led to the dilemma for Freddie and Fannie and W's ill fated decision to let Freddie and Fannie set their own subprime and Alt A goals which Wall Street used to bail themselves out, at least the smart ones who saw the handwriting on the wall. The tax increases Clinton got in return gave America the only balanced budget (for five years) in our whole Reagan supply side economic era.

For the first time in history by a Democratic president, Clinton also negotiated and signed into law a bill that advocated in favor of GOP free trade policy. Clinton added NAFTA, the free trade agreement that included the U.S., Canada, and Mexico. As a son of the south Clinton was no more committed to unions than the GOP, with the possible exception of the teachers' union.

Donald Trump promised the old Reagan Democrats who hated the outcome of free trade that he would repeal or renegotiate NAFTA and bring the jobs back; he said he would do this by setting up a border tax on imports from Mexico. President Trump did renegotiate a replacement trade deal with Canada and Mexico at the beginning of 2020.

Only in tax policy did Clinton revert to FDR's pay as you go tax rates. Clinton did address healthcare reform, turning it over to his wife as her project. No healthcare bill was ever sent to Congress as a result of Hillary's efforts. I testified before a committee established by Hillary to listen to assorted folks concerned about healthcare funding impacting small businesses of between fifty and five hundred employees. I represented my trade association, the Precision Metal Forming Association, along with my friend Dick Wilkey of Milwaukee. Hillary never developed a healthcare bill the legislature seriously considered.

Bill Clinton did return the budget to the black for his last five years in a row, by working with the GOP, leaving his successor George W. Bush a surplus of two hundred billion dollars a year.

It is good to be lucky, and Clinton did enjoy the high tech boom in the 1990s, while George W. Bush inherited a high tech bust in 2001; but high tech has little to do with either president's legacy. High tech is a phenomenon unto itself it seems, and is second only to free trade in its effect on job creation or better said deconstruction. It is the key to automation, and therefore a huge contributor to loss of non professional and hourly employment in America. Both the number of jobs and wage levels offered have been cut due to automation, a factor often overlooked by both parties when discussing the American economy, and it is the largest threat to family funding in the twenty-first century as far ahead as we can see in 2020.

Clinton understood the appeal of welfare reform and the GOP get tough sentencing policies to Reagan's white male blue collar voters, and was willing to go along with the GOP policies to get his tax increases and balance the budget as noted above. In doing so he hurt the black community that has been the democrats most loyal backers if one of the lowest voting percentage factions in America.

Law and order have been GOP code words for reducing fear of crime as a byproduct of black neighborhood education, employment, and family dysfunction issues of long standing, and another area where neither party has made much progress other than improving nutrition for some at great cost, and with much offsetting protests of these unpopular programs.

In the 1990s the Republicans were again demanding relaxation of bank regulations. This led to repeal of a Congressional policy from the pre FDR era, namely the Glass-Steagall Act. Very few FDR era policies have been repealed. Simply stated, this one ended the separation of Wall Street banks from Main Street banking. Wall Street is for professional investors; they do not accept consumer pass book savings, the life blood of Main Street consumer banking that only became sustainable once government oversight and insurance were implemented early in the New Deal. Glass-Steagall separated Wall Street at-risk private money investment banking from consumer (retail) insured savings banking with regulated underwriting standards to maintain minimized risk, meaning typical unsophisticated consumer banking such as savings accounts and mortgages were insured and regulated, balancing safety and risk including government oversight. Needed capital formation commercial banking for economically sophisticated investors was regulated to allow speculation only within rational boundaries. Oversight of these boundaries was intended to limit investor fraud and risk to the total U.S. economic system.

The legislative bill for the repeal of Glass-Steagall was created and sponsored by the chairman of the Senate Banking Committee, Phil Gramm of Texas, and Clinton signed it as an almost final act in 2000. Who knows why, unless it related to his retirement project, the Clinton Foundation funding, fueled by Wall Street as well as international contributors.

Eight years after George H.W. Bush left office having served one term, his son George W. Bush returned the Bush name to the oval office as the forty-third president of the United States. We have already seen how Clinton continued Reagan's policies from the 1980s by working with the GOP Congress he could have treated as an opposition Congress but did not.

We have seen, even before we introduce the election of George W. Bush (also called "W" or "43") as the next GOP president, Clinton set the stage for W to resurrect and double down on Reagan's supply side, free trade, trickle down, brand of economics his dad had called voodoo economics for good cause.

On the day George W. Bush was sworn in, the budget was balanced with surpluses forecast for years to come. The deficit was falling, the country was at peace, and the total debt of the United States stood at five point eight trillion dollars, sixty-five percent of which accrued under Reagan, twenty percent under H. W. Bush, and fifteen percent left from the first thirty-nine presidents.

That means W cost the United States about eight hundred billion dollars a year, the loss of the Clinton surplus, plus five trillion dollars on his watch, plus another three trillion dollars more that spilled over into Obama in his first two years until he started to get W's budget policies headed in the right direction again.

From Reagan to Obama the hold Reagan's policies had on all of them makes the era more interwoven than almost any other time in American history. This is much like the era of the Virginia presidents in the first thirty-five years of our founding, other than four years of John Adams of Massachusetts, or the FDR era we reviewed in Chapter 9 for the Democrats.

W emulated Reagan, calling him his political hero, re-instituting Reagan's economic policies, as well as Reagan's approach to the defense budget. W again doubled U.S. military funding, this time for a whole new issue in American history, a preemptive war in Iraq. For the first time in modern history he financed a war primarily with debt instead of taxes.

Surprisingly W's vice president was Dick Cheney, a former Congressman from Wyoming who became a presidential adviser in the Gerald Ford White House, and then became a key adviser to President Reagan which we have discussed above.

Among all of the post WWII presidents W did not look forward so much as he looked backward twenty years to the Reagan era for his governing values and priorities. Other presidents have continued in place policies, but few had looked backward as W did.

I'm inserting a small insight at this point that only became fully understood in the Trump administration. In the same year 2000, President Putin was also elected president of Russia in the seventh year of the collapse of the Soviet Union, with the Russian economy in total collapse and chaos, and the East Bloc nations of the old USSR in flight into the arms of the European Union and NATO.

There was little for President Putin to look back on that was helpful for his desire to resurrect the power and glory of the Russia he longed to redeem. However, Putin was able to look forward and formulate plans because in his first year in office the economic outlook for Russia changed dramatically. Russia, although broke, held massive reserves of natural resources including oil which was selling at less than ten dollars a barrel. Within his first year the world price of oil increased to over ninety dollars a barrel.

Europe as well as the U.S. saw Russia and Putin as an ex KBG operative with a nuclear arsenal, and a dangerous foe. Putin was pretty much blocked out of the world economy and the free world banking system by both the U.S. and Europe.

Putin was the former manager of privatization of Russia's natural resources. As president he quickly gained control of the oligarchs he had helped create, as he parceled out Russia's extraction wealth in his previous assignment. The oligarchs had already formed an association with the Jewish Russian mafia who had found a means to launder money out of Russia through Cyprus into real estate in the U.S. which was not regulated by the Federal Reserve, the U.S. Treasury, or the IRS.

There was and is a large Russian Jewish immigrant population in NYC, among whom there are a number of lawyers who belonged to the so called Russian mafia who had found ways to circumvent both Russian and American law. Putin and the oligarchs were only too happy to invite the Russian Jews to become part of the new Russian tolerance for deal making under the new order after the fall of communism.

The Russian mafia had found a financially troubled builder in NYC with a luxury brand in need of construction financing, and the oligarchs needed high dollar assets they could buy without oversight in the U.S. to facilitate laundering Russian wealth into American dollars in American banks.

The Russians moved their money into Trump organization properties setting up an LLC to own the properties registered offshore, and personally bought condos in the Trump-named properties. The money flowed through the escrow accounts of Russian Jewish lawyers in NYC, and then into a Trump Organization account. I am unaware of any proof of this flow legally; this is the system that Paul Manafort, Wilbur Ross, and Michael Cohen all engaged in as members of Trump's inner circle as reported in the NY Times, and has been spelled out in a popular book, *House of Trump, House of Putin* by Craig Unger. This money laundering scheme suited President Putin, and would remain a quiet situation until Mr. Trump became president.

During his campaign Trump allowed a fellow traveler dealing in tax evasion and money laundering, Paul Manafort, to become his campaign manager. Manafort had laundered his own sixty million dollars of fees earned in support of the Russian-backed president of Ukraine, and had not paid taxes under the Russian mafia's real estate money laundering scheme. Manafort was prosecuted for these crimes and is now serving time in a U.S. prison.

The Russian mafia scheme came to light when Manafort came under the scrutiny of the FBI and U.S. Justice Department, due to Russia's support of Trump's campaign. This inquiry was called a witch hunt by President Trump; it is really more of a spider web hunt. Manafort laundered his money into eight properties. It has been asserted Trump enabled Putin's partners to launder trillions of dollars into thousands upon thousands of condominiums. Prosecutor Mueller sent President Trump associates to jail on money laundering and tax issues, while the probe of Russian interference in the U.S. 2016 election inquiry continued.

Worth noting and again reported in a number of publications, Putin allowed a place for religion to return to Russian life which matched the hopes of the Russian people. Putin made a deal with the Orthodox Church to protect believers at the Russian Naval operation in Syria, in return for support of his presidency by Russian church leaders, again reported in a number of news stories over the course of Russian support of the Syrian government.

Putin also developed a pipeline to sell gas to European countries. Eventually Putin made his contempt known for former USSR eastern European countries seeking membership in the European Union, the Euro Zone, and NATO. Paul Manafort was an adviser to one of the Russian-backed political leaders of the Ukrainian government.

Lastly Putin acted to reassert control over Ukraine and Georgia before they were swallowed up into NATO. Ukraine was the breadbasket for Russia, and Georgia controlled the warm water ports that gave Russia access to the Black Sea and thereby the Atlantic Ocean from the south.

Putin's actions complicated relations with Russia for Europe and the United States. As a result, first W then Obama tried to work out a tough stand regarding Putin's initiatives without re-igniting the Cold War. They had little success other than they did not ignite any acts of war of any type, until 2016 when Russia launched a cyber attack against the U.S., defined by the U.S. Military and Intelligence leaders as an act of war.

That action is now at the root of the investigation into Putin's old money laundering friends. Donald Trump became president, unwilling to accept the fact that the cyber attack came from Putin's Russia. Instead, Trump attacked his own intelligence institutions as well as U.S. relations with the European Union and NATO.

The famous Mueller report was completed in April of 2019 The political game is no longer the story of what actually happened, but rather did President Trump commit an impeachable offense in battling the inquiry. The report did find Russia guilty of interference and it also found that the president and his campaign did not collude with Russia in their crime. A number of Trump campaign insiders did meet and talk to Russians during the campaign and when the FBI became aware of this and interviewed the staffers, they lied about their contacts. The enduring feature of this episode is an argument over who acted improperly: Russia, Trump and his aides, or the federal police powers who secretly discovered and pursued an understanding of what was really going on between Putin and Trump, and associates of each. The Democrats see chargeable offenses, the GOP sees over zealous distrust of a partisan president the Democrats disliked, and thereby criminal intent to prosecute. Fishing to find a crime as it were. The GOP has no interest in punishing Russia for it's cyber war attack on the U.S., so far.

The true relationship between president Trump and his campaign supporting friends in the U.S., and Putin's friends in Russia only became knowable to the American public upon the conviction of Trump's one time campaign manager Paul Manafort. But it only reflected on Manafort's proven money laundering; the question is, did all of the Russian-owned Trump property purchases that are known to have taken place get funded with clean after tax money or not? That is the billion dollar question, and the only one that I believe remains a terminal threat to President Trump if fully exposed.

Many investigative reporters were connecting the dots, such as NY Times Op-Ed contributor Seth Hettena and others regarding how Russian oligarchs laundered money into Cyprus banks, and then used the money to buy condos in the U.S. without tax consequences. That Manafort and Michael Cohen had access to this process convinces me Trump did too, and I believe the details will emerge before the 2020 election cycle plays out, or we will have a constitutional crisis.

Back to our story line. The key issue in W's first year that complicated costs and created friction for him was the September 11, 2001 attack on the World Trade Center in New York City. The American Intelligence Agency quickly determined that a new terrorist group called al Qaeda led by Osama bin Laden of Saudi Arabia had assembled and trained in Afghanistan. The attack led to George W. Bush's decision (which Putin did not oppose) to invade Afghanistan; seventeen years later America is still entangled in what is now an

Afghan civil war.

Within two years for whatever reason other than Vice President Dick Cheney's one percent theory of war (explained below), W then invaded Iraq preemptively. As the Iraq war waned the deposed political party that led Iraq re-emerged in Syria in the Obama era. Both Iran wars were opposed by Putin, leading him to protect the Syrian leader who protected his naval base and the Orthodox Christian Russians living there.

The twenty-first century up to the beginning of 2020 needs to be viewed from what is now known about Putin and Trump. If they did not personally collude to establish a coordinated relationship, they have both taken advantage of the relationship behind the backs of the U.S. government and the public and continue to do so at each meeting they attend.

So even though Bill Clinton ran surpluses in his last five annual budgets, the first budget that W submitted himself was for 2002. By then W had submitted his tax cuts bill and the GOP controlled Congress had approved it. The 2002 budget returned the U.S. to deficit spending, and the debt returned to climbing, supply side continued to produce debt not balanced budgets, and the GOP continued to spin the results.

To tie September 11th back to our first comments about the budget Bill Clinton left, the main reason for W's massive increase in spending can be traced to that single day in 2011 when the Saudi dissident Osama bin Laden sent his Wahhabi Sunni jihads flying hijacked planes into the Twin Towers in New York City, and another into the Pentagon. A fourth plane crashed in a field in Pennsylvania after the terrorists were overcome by ordinary American passengers who rose up and forced the terrorists to crash the plane. In the process, they saved hundreds or thousands of ordinary folks' lives at whatever next targets the terrorists were headed for. Arab Muslim terror became a new American defense issue. Non-state terrorism became a new form of war.

Bin Laden, son of a Saudi near billionaire, grew up in Saudi Arabia, home of Wahhabi Muslim teaching, the most repressive form of Islam in the world today as supported by Saudi religious leaders, with the sanction of the Saudi Royal family. The Saudi kings are allied with the Wahhabi clerics and have allowed the clerics to preach their Wahhabi ideas of jihad while enjoying a share of Saudi oil money in return for church support of the Saud family as masters of the Saudi State and its oil reserves. This is not unlike how the Irish saw their Irish priests and British overlords during the famine, or how Constantine established the relationship between his Biblical bishops and his feudal kings as we saw in Chapter 1.

Under the current Saudi system there is no judicial review, meaning the king can make any laws and he is never subject to review or court ordering but he must do it in the name of God, as only God can make law in Muslim nations. Only the Wahhabi clerics can approve a Saudi king's proclamations as being in keeping with the will of Allah.

Likewise the Saudis have no elected House of Congress with oversight or impeachment rights, or to appropriate government spending. There is no right of appeal and no individual rights for Saudi citizens. The recent (2018) state sanctioned murder of an Arab reporter living in America is an example of the Saudi king's absolute authority.

This Arab joining of an imam and a civil king have left the Saudi citizens in about the same dilemma that our founders revolted against some two hundred and forty years ago. So far the Saudi government is buying off the populous with a small percentage of the oil money in return for civil peace.

The Iraq war idea was sold on what has proven to be faulty beliefs in W's White House about supposed Iraqi "weapons of mass destruction". These same ideas led to so much pressure on the intelligence community that W went to war on not only scant, but false evidence that was spun, spun, spun. When no weapons of mass destruction were found, Vice President Cheney then advanced what he called his one percent solution. The Iraq misadventure had huge and tragic consequences for forty thousand young Americans in the "all volunteer" military, as reservists had to carry much of the day-to-day load in Iraq when the all volunteer military found that sustainable recruiting of qualified trainees was impossible as the war dragged on.

Cheney's one percent solution is described as, if there is even a one percent chance of weapons of mass destruction in a rival nation, America should take preemptive military action. President Obama reeled that doctrine back in. President Trump has expressed doubt about the reliability of the U.S. Intelligent Agencies citing the weapons of mass destruction snafu, and if it was advanced by the CIA and not the other way around, yet he has shown a reluctance to put U.S. boots on the ground.

What is maddeningly difficult to understand about W's funding scheme is the fact that it was openly based on borrowed money as he went to war while keeping his then recent tax cuts in place. W actually advised Americans to go shopping, as he sent our under-manned so called professional army to war. The most unique thing about W's manning of the Iraq and Afghan wars is how many men and women died who were parents due to the older average age of guardsmen and women who were sent on repetitive tours.

Of note was Vice President Cheney's reminder to W that Reagan had "proved deficits did not matter". Cheney was the wonder boy who brought Reagan the theory of supply side and never learned anything from the debt, and re-sold it to W along with the Iraq war. If there is any politician of the twenty-first century that we should chant "lock him up" and who belongs in jail it is Dick Cheney.

A short recap tying the Trump cabinet to the failed Freddie and Fannie scheme that was as noted several times left with government insurance guarantees in place. Many made a fortune on the bailouts and cleanups, once the taxpayers absorbed Freddie and Fannie losses. Among the many speculative greed investors was Steve Mnuchin, now Trump's Secretary of the Treasury. Steve and his investors bought out the remains of a Savings and Loan called Indymac and renamed it One West Bank. Wall Street referred to Steve's bank as a foreclosure machine. Once the smoke cleared Steve sold the bank for a billion and a half dollars profit. Personally I am not sure how Trump expects Steve to apply such skills to aid the folks who voted for him.

So far Mnuchin has helped Trump pass a tax cut that allows Mnuchin himself to keep more of the profits he's making on his plus billion dollars windfall the taxpayers funded, and now he is helping Trump put off releasing tax records that could highlight how much of the president's income was shielded from taxes even before Trump cut his own family's taxes for the future.

Reagan's political heirs, George W Bush and his VP Dick Cheney who recommended supply side tax cuts to both presidents, repeated Reagan's policies and achieved the same economic outcomes: higher national debt, a higher share of U.S. wealth in the hands of the few, a decrease in living wage jobs across the United States, a second mortgage deregulation boom and bust of the economy with the crash again insured at a cost to the nation, and a windfall for several years for Wall Street investors who gleaned the deflated wreckage.

Meanwhile in 2018 the GOP Congress set tax rates one more time insufficient to fund Congressional appropriations. Not taxing enough for the continuing wars meant another year the wars were funded with debt. All this is good it seems for the true believers as the debt is seen as another installment towards the final starvation of either the beast or entitlements.

The debt ceiling was not raised only into 2020 in 2019. In 2019 the debt ceiling was handled as a kicking the can down the alley exercise. The debt ceiling will be reached, where it is at, about twenty-two trillion dollars, on March 2nd 2020.

Vice president Cheney was just as wrong on the Middle East when he listened to an Iraqi expat named Ahmed Chalabi in advising George W. Bush on Iraq policy, as he had been about Arthur Laffer and his deviant curve. If ever two presidents listened to a cement head it was Dick Cheney who echoed whatever they wanted to hear.

As Speaker of the House in 2018 Paul Ryan still believed in supply side economics as his time in Congress came to an end. The GOP never lost faith in Ryan as their economic guru. He cut taxes, and in return the beneficiaries of that tax cut over the next few years will make Ryan a multi-millionaire for life. He didn't run for Congress again.

Alan Greenspan was President Reagan's and President George W. Bush's economic guru. Greenspan and Ryan were both fans of Milton Friedman, and even more unbelievable, the novelist Ayn Rand. If you read political economic history books such as *Dark Money* and *Democracy in Chains*, you will find a history of dozens of these economic freedom soothsayers. They are to families' living wage outcomes what elixir peddlers were to those who were sick or in pain before modern medicine.

Make no mistake, the anger and/or revenge driving the crowds to Donald Trump and Bernie Sanders in 2016 were reacting to their disappointment of these GOP policies selling feel good rationales that actually resulted in loss of family income, and/or wealth. They included normal sounding ideas such as mortgage deregulation, tax cuts, and free trade . In practice they were a death warrant for the living wage concept in America for middle class hourly wage earners, in favor of dynastic wealth holding families.

The biggest threat to Trump's first budget which began October 1, 2017, was his stated goal of a four percent growth rate (if achieved) to the cost of inflating interest rates that would be imposed to fund the U.S. debt. The economy heating up that fast would have led the Federal Reserve to rightly raise interest rates, thus raising the cost of funding the interest on the national debt by additional trillions of dollars over the next ten years; no worries, four percent was just a casual Trump promise; it never happened.

At the end of 2018 the Federal Reserve began the process of increasing interest rates and President Trump then condemned the Federal Reserve almost daily, as it was projected by the U.S. Office of Management and Budget that President Trump's first budget based on his tax cuts would nearly double President Obama's deficit in his final year in office.

Trump's fiscal year 2018 deficit was projected to end at more than eight hundred billion dollars of debt and his second year deficit in 2019 was projected to end at 1.1 trillion dollars of newly added debt. The 2018 prediction was on target, while 2019 is not reported at the time of this book's publication.

President Trump cut taxes as he had promised by five hundred billion dollars a year, and interest rates so far have only gone up one percent. This is why the annual deficit is projected to be over one trillion dollars a year. These new interest rates will be enough to return deficits to over one trillion dollars a year, making it the single largest item in the budget.

It's even larger than the Defense Department's military budget or the block federalism budget that sends welfare money to low tax states who refuse to tax themselves, and use the small state bargain from the founding to cheat the high tax states who fund the whole government.

So far President Trump has not yet eliminated any cabinet positions. However, he has downgraded the ambassador to the United Nations and since 2019 they are no longer a member of the cabinet.

For the most part President Trump has appointed secretaries to his Cabinet whose ideology reflects the GOP wish to reduce the mission of among others the Education Department, the EPA, the Energy Department, the Interior Department, the Housing Department, the Labor Department, and the Health and Human Services Department. These are the very departments that were established to cope with the fallout of those states that refuse to assess sustainable taxes, or fund their hourly work force and their children with living wages or funded healthcare.

One last Dick Cheney story before moving on. A fellow named Paul Wolfowitz was the head of the Johns Hopkins graduate program in foreign affairs when Cheney was looking for a theory for his young president to put a plan in place "to rescue democratic seeking Iraq dissidents, who would be welcomed by the Iraq people, seeing the United States military as liberators". Through Wolfowitz, Cheney found someone with a solution to recommend to W as a winning strategy to both promote the war at home, and assure a winnable war in the Middle East.

True of most Movement Conservative policies this one was based on unquestioned ideology typical in the Reagan era; the upside was misrepresented, and the downside risk was ignored intentionally.

Just as when Reagan was looking for someone to promote tax cuts and Cheney found Arthur Laffer's supply side economic theory, Paul Wolfowitz had what W needed, and Cheney brought him to W.

Wolfowitz had found an Iraqi in exile we mentioned earlier named Ahmed Chalabi. Chalabi was a guest lecturer who would visit Johns Hopkins from Paris. Paul Wolfowitz was only too happy to recommend Chalabi to Cheney and W as a man who not only wanted to overthrow Saddam, but also predicted a quick and easy overthrow; Chalabi said American invaders would be greeted with rose petals in the streets.

Wolfowitz was a former GOP adviser dating back to the Reagan era in what was called the Neo Con wing of the GOP. Some have nicknamed Neo Cons "chicken hawks", political partisans anxious to send other people's sons and daughters to war, to make America look strong to the American voter.

Once again, Cheney introduced a plan that was destructive. This time the victims were members of the U.S. military, mostly U.S. Army reservists, and the citizens of the Middle East, not to mention U.S. taxpayers someday, for now they use debt, as you may remember.

I say someday, as Cheney like Reagan saw debt as win-win; he could keep taxes low, and starve the beast so some day even Democrats would have to agree to a reduction in, if not the ending of, Medicare and Social Security as the general income tax based economy becomes insolvent due to interest on the debt.

Cheney's advice about Chalabi fell short by the same magnitude as Cheney's supply side plan for the American economy. Both have been total disasters, yet unmentioned as being so, or acknowledged as a huge source of our debt.

Chalabi's story for W included information that Saddam had weapons of mass destruction, was hated by the Iraqis who would greet Americans as liberators, and that he (Chalabi) was ready to be the new leader of Iraq, and was a great friend to Israel and the U.S. All pipe dreams as it turned out, and known to the CIA.

The CIA warned W that Chalabi was allied with Israel's enemy Iran, was a shady banker, and was not to be trusted. Cheney disdained the CIA's advice as Trump has again almost twenty years later, and W backed Chalabi. Later when Cheney's rosy scenario failed, he blamed bad intelligence on the CIA and got away with it. Since his election Trump has used Cheney's misuse of the CIA as part of his excuse for not trusting the CIA and other intelligence groups.

The CIA was correct in all they had to say about Chalabi, but to this day W, Cheney, the Neo Cons, and the GOP hold the CIA responsible for the "bad" intelligence that led W astray.

Early in 2020 President Trump is all but at war with almost all of the U.S. Intelligence Services, at the same time he faced an impeachment trial in the U.S. Senate. It is yet to be seen how this will play out for the nation, or Trump's presidency. No doubt Iran, China, North Korea and Russia love the mess this president has made of U.S. intelligence agencies. What is surprising are the GOP Senators on the Intelligence Committee who allow this abuse to continue.

So America invaded Iraq, and won the invasion phase in just a few weeks. The slow loss of Iraq to total civil war chaos took ten years. It has cost a few trillion borrowed dollars, forty thousand maimed or killed young Americans, and the Middle East is in deeper trouble than ever, while Saddam's defeated army was allowed to go home with their weapons and lay low, only to rise again ten years later as ISIS, backed by Iran.

Obama confronted Isis in Syria and Iraq, yet drew a Red Line, then flinched. President Trump gave the U.S. more targets, the situation improved, and then President Trump withdrew, leaving Russia to manage Syria and it's beleaguered dictator. However, new hot spots have flared under President Trump in Mali and Yemen.

Iraq had a good idea about how things would work for them after the 2008 election. George W. Bush had tried to negotiate an exit strategy that would include U.S. boots on the ground to insure success for the government he had put in place. W's handpicked compromise leader for Prime Minister, Nouri al Malaki, was recommended by Chalabi when he failed to win enough support in Iraq for himself. Malaki refused W, then again refused Obama's offer of boots on the ground for backup as we withdrew from active patrolling of Iraq roads. Patrolling roads in the Middle East is so dangerous that the U.S. Army pays a forty thousand dollar bonus to soldiers if they volunteer to become truck drivers, attracting recruits from poor families, another burden of low wages.

W inherited Alan Greenspan as the Federal Reserve Chairman, who was appointed as chairman more than a dozen years earlier by President Reagan. Greenspan was still chairman and had kept interest rates low from the George H. W. Bush presidency into the George W. Bush presidency. This accomplished two things that W loved. One, the U.S. could borrow at very low rates to fund the GOP starve the beast debts. W's tax cuts were retained as he went to war and the budget was spinning out of control, so low interest rates remained helpful. W actually advised Americans not to worry and to go shopping.

The second was its affect on home prices. As prices soared on easily available cheap credit interest rates, a housing bubble developed again which led to bubble type financing and sales schemes. This greater fool theory we've mentioned before blew up under Reagan twenty years earlier, which holds that in a time of inflating prices, each fool can buy for a higher price in the knowledge he can sell later to a greater fool.

The only non-foolish leader in the GOP during W's eight years regarding both Iraq and the subprime fiasco turned out to be Chuck Hagel, now seen as a pariah by the GOP. Greenspan admitted he "truly believed that investors cared about their own best interest"; later he said "I was surprised that exuberant greed overcame my belief".

A good movie to catch the drift of this phenomenon is *The Big Short*. My wife and I did not short the housing market, but we did sell our two appreciated condos, parked our tax free profits after living in each for two years before we sold, first in 2003 then the second in 2005, and rented for a couple of years. It was part luck and part seeing the handwriting on the wall, which tells me the men on Wall Street who knew more than I did also saw the crash that I saw coming from 2005 until it happened.

We bought back into the housing market in the Boston area in 2007 as prices were bottoming out, our bid of one hundred twenty-five thousand dollars under asking price was countered with an offer of one hundred thousand dollars under and we bought back in.

The crash was totally due to supply side (increase the supply of homes in the hope a growing supply would produce a growing demand) which worked as long as the credit standards were lowered, and money was cheap and plentiful; all this after fifty years of FDR safe banking regulation that had worked under GOP deregulation based on ideology, and still no recriminations, or rethinking in the GOP or its base about the mindlessness of deregulation of mortgage underwriting standards.

Who did the GOP leadership, the conservative media, and the GOP faithful all blame for the cause of the second largest economic crash in American history? The answer once again was Jimmy Carter, again with a kicker that Bill Clinton had supposedly made Carter's policy on mortgages in black neighborhoods even worse.

As we have already reviewed, Carter never lowered underwriting standards for mortgage credit, meaning his policy did not address subprime borrowers' loans, underwriting, or usury, it just ended abuse of credit worthy black citizens, ending red lining that allowed federally insured banks to refuse to grant insured loans in black neighborhoods even if financially qualified.

These assertions were made again recently in my hometown newspaper in a letter to the editor by a writer who was advancing this GOP spin. The writer made his claim based on a Fox News talking head who falsely blamed Carter and the editor printed his bogus claim even though I had sent the editor a copy of the Federal Reserve report that refuted any connection between subprime and CRA. It seems there is little interest in American journalism in tackling complex partisan issues to an understandable depth so as to meaningfully inform average readers as citizens and voters.

This is a failure of the press. If they continue to print false claims once the editor knows it is false, he or she is hardly offering a community service or an information service. The assertions were refuted the following week in another letter to the editor by a retired banker who had worked under Carter's Community Reinvestment Act (CRA) rules for thirty years.

To restate the truth (the lie has been told so many times that the truth deserves an airing once in a while) the Community Reinvestment Act (CRA) is a program created by President Carter; it was actually a civil rights bill. It required credit worthy minorities who live in low income areas could not be denied credit by federally insured banks. It was not a cause of the subprime mortgage crisis; as the Act clearly states, the loans are to be made "consistent with safe and sound operation". It was just addressing another of the many successful segregation containment policies and legacies that survived the 1964 civil rights bill unaddressed.

Since then community banks have made loans to qualified borrowers in minority communities without lowering any of the underwriting rules. These banks borrow from the Federal Reserve and enjoy stable deposits from savers due to FDIC, the FDR safe banking social insurance program from 1933. FDIC to this day insures savers' deposits in regulated banks; the U.S. government collects a small fee, and provides oversight of the banks, including underwriting and usury limits that insure safe banking up to two hundred and fifty thousand dollars. This system is popular and successful; the GOP has not tried to deregulated it, they know it is popular.

Subprime has never been allowed as a significant percentage of the mortgage portfolio of these banks. The CRA program did not change that status, and FDIC community banks have never crashed as an industry or required a government bailout of the system.

To this day you will still hear GOP talking heads mention Carter and/or Clinton as having caused the real estate crash of 2007-2009. By 2007-2008, W was bailing out Wall Street, and his deficits were running annually at a rate of negative one point seven trillion dollars per budget year. This was the annual deficit rate Obama inherited in 2009 . When he left eight years later he had reduced the annual deficit to under half a million dollars. President Trump once again, for no good reason he explained, has again cut taxes, and the annual deficit is back at plus one trillion dollars a year for fiscal year 2020 the last year of his first term.

A trillion dollars a year deficit seems to be a GOP threshold they strive to achieve in their quest to starve the U.S. Government into having to agree to destroy Social Security and Medicare.

Folks are for the most part mute about W, and the GOP still maintains the myths about Reagan. The closest they come to discussing W is to give him credit for keeping us safe; they do not even add, after September 11. They give Obama no credit for keeping us safe for the next eight years, or anything else, not even saving the domestic auto industry and the millions of jobs in that supply chain.

Vice President Cheney has also been barely touched as the problem causer supreme he was, twice in the 1980s and again in the 2000s. Cheney remained stubbornly defensive as Obama's second term wound down. In 2018 a pretty good movie was made that rightly portrayed Cheney as the cement head dark whisperer he was.

In 2019 William Barr, a fellow believer along with Cheney in the unitary president idea, giving the President absolute ruling power instead of co-equal branch power, wish to make GOP presidents imperial, meaning not subject to oversight. Barr made his GOP bones protecting Reagan from the Iran Contra fallout, and again he is acting the partisan and not the defender of the U.S. Constitution he is sworn to uphold. In Papa Bush's authorized biography in late 2015 he called Cheney old iron ass! Note: We did not address the Iran Contra in this book; as bad as it was it did not impact the governance issues that are our focus in this book.

Barack Obama became president in 2009, and submitted his first budget based on the outcomes of taxes, the deep recession, and the wars, all part and parcel of W's policies over his two terms, all but two years of those terms with a GOP majority Congress.

So the first black man to become president of the United States of America, Barack Obama, was faced with cleaning up huge policy messes both militarily and economically that were sponsored by W, and enacted by the GOP majority. From day one Obama was scapegoated as the problem because he fixed the GOP crash, and ended the GOP war and body bags from a war of choice too slowly, as the GOP has spun the Obama legacy..

How was Obama greeted by returning GOP Congressional leadership in January of 2009? Mitch McConnell bragged that they would do everything they could to block anything Obama proposed, to ensure he would be a one term president, and they did vote to block everything; yet they failed on that promise and Obama was reelected. McConnell did manage to steal a Democratic nomination to the Supreme Court over the last year of Obama's Presidency after Justice Scalia passed away.

Instead of helping clean up the mess they and W created, the GOP made things more difficult, more expensive and worse for Obama and the American taxpayers, sticking to McConnell's absolutist no compromise promise to ensure absolute gridlock during Democratic Presidents' terms.

The signature accomplishment that Obama is remembered for, was his addressing the millions of Americans without healthcare, especially those with pre-existing conditions, a Reagan legacy of for-profit medicine which allowed for-profit insurers to in effect refuse to ensure folks with pre-existing conditions. Some progressive states set up expensive pooled insurance for such folks.

The GOP and all of the red state governors prefer a "cheap" insurance plan that demonstrates just how callous they are towards preexisting conditions. These plans (outlawed in most states with rational boundary common good theories of government) are not renewable if the enrolled patient is diagnosed with an expensive ailment that is then rated as pre-existing. This again ignores established justice.

This literally dumps the hapless sick person into no man's land of denials and/or catastrophic cost, and an early death or long term suffering with an inability to be employed. If that person is lucky enough to qualify for welfare, the GOP has long had a policy of denigrating those on welfare, and cutting funding for these so called lazy deadbeats.

It is the most often cited reason my friends and family give me for why they vote against liberals. They site this until it impacts one of their own. I've had this happen to two of my elderly friends who are outspoken supporters of the GOP. In both cases they blamed Obama when it turned out their adult child was seriously ill, out of work, and yet did not qualify for Medicaid or a SNAP card.

Obama's new program outlawed this form of insurers' cherry picking less expensive healthy folks that left the most at risk Americans without access to affordable healthcare when they need it most.

The Democratic Congress under Nancy Pelosi's leadership as Speaker of the U.S. House of Representatives enacted without a single GOP vote a new fifth government form of support for healthcare funding in America. It was called the ACA, the Affordable Care Act; it was almost immediately re-branded by the GOP as Obamacare.

The four healthcare programs already in place included veterans, discriminating tax breaks for those employed by corporations or unions (usually called private pay healthcare that does include self pay), Medicare for those who paid into payroll FICA (which is a burden on payrolls, employment and wages in the global economy), and Medicaid which many GOP governors withheld (at least for some who qualify) as was federally allowed by a five-four vote of the GOP majority Supreme Court. Along with Medicaid which is subject to GOP funding cuts almost every budget fight, Medicare is falsely scapegoated as the cause of their tax cut debt that is now pushing twenty-two trillion dollars, as redemption of surplus FICA bonds are retired to fund baby boomers as anticipated in the 1980s on a bipartisan basis noted above.

The GOP Public Choice policies on funded healthcare are not in the best interest of the voters or their retired parents or children. The actions noted in the two paragraphs above would discourage GOP votes in America from anyone in the bottom seventy or eighty percent of the income and wealth gaps.

The new ACA healthcare program had huge political consequences. It added millions of folks to the block grant federalism Medicaid program in most states. The Medicaid portion of the program as enacted was overturned by the Supreme Court, even as ACA itself was approved by the Court by one GOP vote, by Chief Justice John Roberts. The court made Obamacare available under Medicaid only in states where the governor approved it. All Democrat governors made this option available for poor folks with pre-existing conditions; most GOP governors did not, at least at first.

The ACA proved again that presidents seldom know what citizens live with regarding healthcare access and funding when Obama announced "if you like your doctor you can keep your doctor". Of course this was not true. Insurance companies, employers, and private practitioners all make decisions on which insurances they will accept or not.

These GOP Public Choices sold as economic freedom mean insurance companies need to charge less for healthy people who will not use insurance much in each price set year, and more for sick people who will, as the government during GOP majority rule allows profit to be the first principle concern of these plans. The GOP sees this market solution as an ideology. The Democrats believe the best basic healthcare plan the nation can afford that covers all persons is the intent and right, if the purpose of the authority to govern granted to state property rights and federal citizens' rights (with citizens' rights out ranking states' rights) is the Constitutional intent of the established justice and common good theories, per the Preamble, as a guarantee of justice for all. Whew!

You might ask, what is the difference between a citizen and a person in Constitutional law (for a fuller understanding read a short history of the Fourteenth Amendment) It is a fiction used in situations of partisan gridlock. The GOP uses it to claim corporations are persons with special rights such as money as speech based on the First Amendment. The Democrats use it in the census or to ensure an immigrant visiting in America legally or not, cannot be denied service by any public hospital.

The GOP states it believes competition in the market place is the best chance for healthcare to be affordable for all. They never admit that profit is the first goal of corporations, not low cost for consumers.

What makes capitalism so good at its first intent makes it all but impossible to solve expensive social issues.

The surest path to profit is to avoid high cost unknown risk, and/or allow the market to set different prices for different market reasons across America and around the world, even if that is injurious to millions upon millions of Americans, who were promised in 1791 that the federal government would ensure an absence of abuse of any U.S. citizen regardless of state of domicile, defined as justice. Ignored in the south, it was made a mandate on all states after the Civil War.

The purpose of insurance is to spread the total risk of a pool of folks, even three hundred and thirty million folks, funding the lowest cost to protect them all, while the cost is sustainability. The Democrats believe that is the meaning of "the common good". The lowest cost insurance is a public program funded by a tax or fee on all users, as the public model does not pay executive overhead, a fee for cost of money (return on investment), nor fund a profit to distribute to stockholders, nor pay taxes. The term for such a financial structure is a utility. This describes the most common mechanism of common good outcomes of secular government. Remember what the Preamble defined as the common welfare, the founders referred to as "the common good".

Finally, a public model insurance can negotiate the lowest rates, as it has the largest possible pool of folks for whom to negotiate prices, for use of goods supplied by the market, such as prescription drugs and medical equipment. Medicare enjoys a lower cost in each of these categories compared to all private health insurance in America, except drugs, as the GOP ideology does not allow Medicare to negotiate drug prices, and too many Democrats like Republicans are in effect bought off.

At present these profit centers spend billions of dollars as free speech, making sure you elect folks to Congress that represent their profit interest and not your individual common good best interest. This surely ignores the intent of established justice. That is what the GOP calls Public Choice policy and economic freedom ideology.

The Democrats prefer social insurance mandates where all pay, and all earn access. I outline how this could work in my suggestions at the end of the book. The GOP calls my plan socialist and anti-capitalism; it is neither, it is another category from these two mechanisms all together.

You have read that I fully endorse capitalism for what it does best, create wealth. I just do not believe pre-existing conditions are best served by markets, let alone speculative capitalism. Remember as this debate continues that government services based on taxes are delivered at cost.

Capitalism is based on a return on invested capital and a profit on top of that, as well as a management fee for operations. It is wonderful for creating wealth; it has no incentive to make it affordable for all, even those too sick to work and earn access. Under Truman's 1951 solution when the U.S. Government under the New Deal Democrats first acknowledged that healthcare should be a right for persons in a wealthy nation, white mostly Christian southerners refused any solution to healthcare funding that provided healthcare for black persons they still considered less than equal citizens, even those who fought in WWII.

Obama was reelected in 2012, and for the next four years the GOP campaigned against Obamacare, with a promise to repeal it and replace it with a market solution to ensure lower cost healthcare for all. When that failed, the GOP rolled out the old for-profit scam that was the lowest cost with the most profit that Obama had ended in 2009 with the introduction of ACA. That was low monthly fee, high deductible, healthcare insurance that the companies were free to not renew for anyone who was diagnosed with a condition during the year the insurance was in force that would become a pre-existing condition the following year.

In the 2016 presidential election the GOP's number one promise was to repeal and replace Obamacare if a GOP candidate won. Based on GOP's failure to deliver in 2017, the Democrats retook the U.S. House in 2018 in spite of severe GOP gerrymandering across the country.

The GOP failed to deliver their own healthcare plan in Congress by one vote, even though they controlled not only the presidency but also the House and the Senate. GOP Senator John McCain was not running for re-election; he protected his Arizona constituents with pre-existing conditions by voting against his party president and Senate leader. Both showed their contempt for those with pre-existing conditions. If President Trump had chosen to express this contempt as he express his contempt of McCain, he would have said I prefer citizens who do not get pre-existing conditions.

President Trump, having denigrated McCain's service earlier, treated McCain, a Viet Nam war hero, as a rat ever since, as if voting one's conscience in Congress is a disgrace. When Senator McCain died, Trump continued the disdain. The GOP demands absolute party loyalty over the Constitution, over the needs of any senator's state, or the needs of any Americans living in his or her state.

The GOP replacement bill did not fund pre-existing conditions, and across the nation for the first time a majority of voters finally understood what a threat this was for tens of millions of people. Some even finally understand that it could happen to them, or their family and that is the purpose of having insurance. Not enough understand it yet, but it was a good start to a rational outcome for the future.

In Barack Obama's second term with a GOP Congress, he cut military spending and accomplished one small tax increase. This reduced the deficit to under five hundred billion dollars a year with just enough new borrowing to fund the interest on the thirty-five year accumulation of federal compounding debt under the continuing Reagan era starve the beast supply side economic tax cut policy shortfalls.

Over the course of eight years with House Speaker Boehner's help, Obama cut W's deficits from one point seven trillion dollars a year coming out of the major economic crash, to four hundred eighty billion dollars a year. The GOP pronouncement was that all of Obama's successes were too slow to be worthy of acknowledgement.

Late in President Obama's second term he and GOP Speaker of the House Boehner agreed to a "grand bargain". Obama would give two dollars of spending cuts for every dollar of tax increase that Speaker

Boehner would agree to. Speaker Boehner brought his and Obama's tentative agreement to his GOP caucus. The GOP caucus rejected the proposal and their speaker. They drove Boehner out, and disparaged Obama again for having the slowest recovery in history. Boehner did not run for re-election.

Going back to the beginning of Obama's first term, conservative media began a long process of discrediting the new president. He was condemned as a socialist for saving the banks and the auto industry; actually he recapitalized the banks and the auto companies, acting as lender of last resort. He did not let the auto companies die (as unfettered GOP capitalism called for) because he cared as the Democrats always do about the six hundred thousand jobs the industry directly funded. Nor did he nationalize the banks, as a number of European nations did, which was pure socialism Most European nations nationalize their banks as the bust became global, in the globalized economy of the twenty-first century.

Both of President Obama's decisions worked, without a single GOP vote. The domestic auto industries and the associated jobs were saved, and the government loans were all paid back at a profit, based on the shares taken as collateral. Once again the credit of the nation based on the power to tax the large wealthy well educated states as envisioned at our founding by Alexander Hamilton and accepted by George Washington, worked much better than the fully socialist, and fully conservative models of the various nations of Europe.

The GOP kept up the drumbeat of negativity about the character, politics, religion, even the nationality of the new president attempting to right their ship. I heard it all from my friends and family every day for those eight plus years, and still do.

Obama ran for president on a promise to end the wars and bring the troops home, stabilize the economy, reduce the deficit, and fund healthcare for the poor. He accomplished or made great progress on all he promised. However, the GOP still opposes his policies and castigates him daily as a liar or worse, and a disgrace to America they were ashamed of.

I rate Obama's outcomes as having done more good than harm.

The collapsing Gorge W. Bush economy Obama inherited put eight million folks out of work. It took seven years to put them back to work, for the most part without a raise even to account for inflation over the past twenty or more years for those earning less than a living wage in a minimum wage base held hostage economy. As union membership fell, and right-to-work expanded the wage stagnation, an ever hotter anger flamed for those who had supported all of the GOP policies that led to such an outcome.

This intentional blindness will continue as long as the value system of the GOP not only tolerates white nationalism in its many forms from near benign to full Charlottesville.

The GOP campaigned on claims that Obama's economy caused more folks to be out of work and on food stamps than ever before, as if W's eight million job destroying crash never happened, or never had an impact on the families' needs of those who lost their jobs. These are all examples of political spin in support of a myth that denies accountability for outcomes and prolongs the gridlock.

I rate W's policy outcomes as having done more harm than good.

Look it up, read the history. This is a pretty fair account of the FDR era, the Reagan era, as well as the story of western world governance from the Romans and feudalism to the Freedom Caucus in Congress that champions the theory of economic freedom and for-profit public choice even for healthcare victims with pre-existing conditions in their families, and most families do have one or more.

I started this book sympathizing with a typical female GOP voter who was dismayed that her party was not supportive of equal pay legislation, but voted with the GOP because she hated the 's stance on abortion. On the other hand there was the typical female Democrat voter who appreciated her union living wage and fully funded healthcare yet voted for right-to-work anti-union GOP candidates because she resented the 's support of welfare for the working poor and those who do not work for whatever reason, as she sees too many of them as lazy.

Politicians have passed convoluted statutes as we have reviewed; it was the GOP wing of the Supreme Court that truly under-served women's best interests and in the process drove an ever bigger wedge between property rights and individual rights, as well as widening the wealth gap. The GOP court that gave us school busing and abortion rights are vilified by the Reagan era GOP as activist judges.

Earlier we reviewed contentious modern Supreme Court decisions, the Lily Ledbetter, Hobby Lobby, and Citizens United cases.

My argument was the Court should have sent these cases back to the Legislature, as it was civil law that had been allowed to be in conflict regarding two equal competing rights, the company's privacy, and the women's right to equal pay in the Lily Ledbetter case. Luckily Obama did ask the Legislature to address this conflict in law, and hopefully resolved or at worst improved this conflict for female employees in the future.

The second case was Hobby Lobby versus Obamacare. In the second decade of the twenty-first century, some folks in America have access to healthcare with a tax break if an employer provides healthcare as a benefit, while others do not have the same access or tax break if they are self employed or work for a small business that cannot afford to access the potential benefit.

The payroll tax break for healthcare for employees of corporations was introduced due to the legislature's inability to deal with Jim Crow issues after WWII, and has continued as an abusive legacy of racial inequality in America ever since, surviving the civil rights era. When the Civil Rights Bill ended Jim Crow in 1964, the legislature did not go back and address the structural norms that had made segregation part of both races' day-to-day life. No mechanism of governance has ever rectified any of these Jim Crow legacy issues. As an example millions of black American men still work as day laborers without any of the benefits afforded long term payroll employment as mandated by government. At what point in our history will the GOP ever come to grips with the Constitutional concept of established justice!

Women did not have family planning rights in the U.S. until the same

Civil Rights Bill in 1964. A right was never established for an employer who owned a corporation to refuse an employee's access to the tax break based on the owner's religious beliefs. However, the GOP jurists agreed to hear such a religious objection for the Hobby Lobby owner. The court allowed it, again by a five-four partisan margin to rule in favor of the religious owner under the same latent rights ideology they used for the gun rights decision as noted earlier.

No consideration was given to the rights of several thousands of women's civil, labor, family planning, privacy, or taxpayer rights. An even more uncomfortable factor of tying a tax break to employment, this also applied to an order of nuns who ran a non-profit business with female employees to support their convent, and felt the same objection that the Hobby Lobby owner did. I could go on with how many conflicts this decision ignored.

Anyone with an open mind on either side can see the abuse of the rights of the injured women inherent in the outcome of this decision. Without a further thought the five male jurists severed these women's tax exemption access rights without recourse.

The final case I've offered for consideration was the Consumers United case. Again by a five to four partisan vote the GOP jurists under the Fourteenth Amendment allowed defining political spending on voter education by tax exempt corporations as free speech, in undisclosed and unlimited amounts.

The Fourteenth Amendment intent defined citizenship rights for black Americans. The federal court granted state chartered corporations personhood as a federal right, and therefore entitled them to the same Constitutional rights originally granted to citizens in recognition of the authority to govern bargain that ratified the Constitution, and added the clause that settled the mandate that states are subject to the Bill of Rights.

One last issue relating to the court about the privacy issue. Abortion rights were settled in 1973, in a convoluted manner as is too often true in America. The legislature had never made abortion a legal right in America; instead, legislators had passed laws making abortions criminally illegal, but not murder. In 1973 what is now referred to as a right was actually decriminalization of abortions. The Roe v Wade decision does not guarantee women the right to an abortion. Roe only outlawed state laws prohibiting abortion in the first trimester of pregnancy, based on a right to plan family creation decisions in private.

The Court found that a state has a compelling interest in protecting the health of pregnant women and the potential life of a fetus, but that during the first trimester, when a fetus is not viable, that right is outweighed by a woman's fundamental right to privacy implicit in the fourteenth amendment: "...nor shall any state deprive any person of life liberty, or property, without due process of law". The decision allows states to address regulation of abortion in the second trimester.

If a GOP Supreme Court reverses Roe v Wade, it will not, of itself, make abortion legal or illegal or define the level of criminal or civil offense a state may enact. The holding would only weaken the fundamental right to privacy guaranteed by the Fourteenth Amendment, and leave states free to prohibit abortion in the first trimester.

What I suggest is the establishment of a true right to privacy, meaning it needs to be a criminal offense to expose private consenting abortion activity between doctors and women. Until there is a meaningful majority that is willing to elect legislators committed to either extreme, that is, willing to vote to enact a legal right to abortion, or enact as a criminal charge an attempted murder statute for any woman seeking, and a murder charge for any woman obtaining an abortion, the nation will remain in gridlock on this issue.

Some states want to criminalize all reproductive rights including birth control. In all such states GOP voters also support the GOP ideology of economic freedom, meaning they also want to grant full economic freedom regarding corporations even if they do not know what the GOP ideology is. A brief description includes property owners rights to set wages, determine working conditions, and end federal funding for welfare, and make all public schools private and for-profit with no tax funding at the federal level.

My antidote is to end federalism. The citizens of such states would soon discover they cannot fund their state or maintain civil society under such a regimen. I favor letting the few states where a majority would vote in favor of such economic and social political policies do so.

I also believe the politicians elected on these policies would be voted out of office based on their policy outcomes. Within a very few years so governed states would lose most industries that require an educated workforce. I favor this experiment in a few heavily evangelical politically driven states, before they bankrupt the whole nation based on the national electoral college and the impact on gerrymandered outcomes, as such states threaten to cause eventually.

These economic freedom ideas are in fact the policies of the Trump administration's self described "deconstruction of the deep state" intended as their future solution for twenty-first century America with no defined replacement, as they wish to end an income tax funded role for the government in providing most citizens' common good needs and established justice rights.

An example of the outcome of a politician's economic freedom policy all but bankrupting his state is former Kansas GOP Governor Sam Brownback who cut his state's income taxes based on a campaign promise, leaving them insufficient funds to cover the state legislature's appropriations. The governor did this intentionally to get money for his state by taking advantage of block grant federalism Reagan established in the 1980s that subsidizes low tax states. Federalism bailed out Governor Brownback's foolishly imposing GOP tax cut ideology on Kansas. Kansas voters continue to believe they are conservative and remain reliable GOP voters, who accepted the tax break believing the GOP could accommodate this without any negative consequence. How does block grant redistribution of progressive income tax submissions relate to established justice?

Their gerrymandered congressional representatives bring home this stolen bacon, buried in President Reagan's redesign of federalism into thousands of block grants. What he did in the dark but with full intent, was redistribute wealth from states that sustainably tax the top half of income earners to ensure adequate nutrition, education, healthcare, and shelter for their working poor and to fund one hundred percent of the net income of the United States. The outcome is a wealth transfer to opportunistic states that under tax, stagnate minimum wage laws, and enforce right-to-work laws. Meanwhile, those in successful states bail out fiscally failed states as poor state welfare.

Without federal(ism) transfer payments, no governor could do what Brownback did, and have his party and its ideology remain in office and continue to control the state and spin the outcome. If you are not aware of this GOP ideology endgame, it is because of the GOP's success spinning their policies and their outcomes.

The whole GOP Reagan era reminds me of two W.C. Fields' quotes I remember from his movies: **"Anything worth having is worth cheating for"**. The other when he was asked while playing cards, is this a game of chance? He responded: **"Not the way I play it."**

No one reading this book should believe I want to end judicial review. I assure you there is no such thing as a conservative judge who was proving his/her respect for the "founders' intent, or the meaning of any word in 1791", who voted for Citizens United. The five GOP jurists blatantly voted for corporate money interests over individual citizens' rights promised in the Declaration of Independence, regarding authority to govern based on consent of the governed, ignoring both the common good and established justice goals. In plain English this means the court's first duty is to the citizen, not to a state created entity, i.e., a corporation.

The five jurists in the three cases I reviewed in this book voted based only on the founders' first intent in the 1789 Constitution, without consideration of the founders' final intent when the Bill of Rights was ratified in 1791 with defined rights for citizens, and a clause allowing the Constitution to be amended. This made all terms of the 1789 Constitution ratification final, subject to the additional terms of the Bill of Rights which ended any state right to abuse U.S. citizens' right to justice under law. Liberty and justice were key factors in the expressed goals in the U.S. Constitution ratified in 1789, but not due process and other assurances of what established justice meant to citizens; thus the demand for a Bill of Rights. Establishing justice had been a key goal of the founders as defined in the Preamble of the

Constitution in 1789. The Bill of Rights established court ordering priorities at the federal level, never accepted in practice to this day by those who claim original intent of court ordering priority only from 1789 when it remained the same as common law in the states it was feared, where property rights and the state church were the first court ordering priorities.

The Bill of Rights added assured justice for citizens as the first court ordering priority to the Constitution once ratified in 1791. It took fifteen years for the founders to go from announcing their goal for the future, to enacting the full intent of their new form of government based on consent of the governed for governing a society of free men.

Liberty, often referred to as freedom, is the key factor in the ideology of the modern GOP. Assured justice for the citizen is not an intent in the judicial philosophy (dual federalism) of the modern GOP. As often noted in this book, the modern GOP does not spell out its true intent in the party's platform every four years, because in 2020 it is an established ideology with absolutist demands for belonging, as failure to conform means a form of shunning. The beliefs of this ideology have been formulated and refined by the GOP Koch Network funded Federalist Society relating to court settlement doctrine referred to as original intent; meaning retention of common law property and state church priorities in practice after ratification in the southern states. This manifests as a first court ordering intent in states rights states, which did not accept the full concept of citizens' rights, before or after the Civil War. The key insight consistent since our founding is the issue of race regarding justice.

Judging as by outcomes, absolutism lives on in the land of self governed freemen, under the God of revelation, and not nature's God as was the intent. Blackstone's solution for England in the 1740s addressed in our introduction on page three, seems a bedfellow to Bill Barr in 2020. So I ask, is original intent referring to Constantine and his approved Bible, or the English language James I Bible, or Blackstone's commentaries on common law, or the founding documents of the United States of America, or the Southern Manifesto of Strom Thurmond's intent, or a bastardized ideology clarified for the members satisfactory to Charles Koch?

Modern GOP jurists use a bastardized interpretation of the Koch Network Constitutional theory called dual federalism that goes back before the Bill of Rights Amendment was added. It was bastardized deliberately, as a new intent was sneaked into the Fourteenth Amendment after the Civil War era, for the same reason the Fourteenth Amendment was used in Roe v Wade. It is the only place in our founding documents where citizens are referred to as "people" or "persons" instead of citizens. States constructed corporations, and refer to them as having the state rights of a person or persons, based on the fact that people own corporations. However, that does not make the construct (a corporation) a citizen of the United States, which I believe means a corporation has no standing before the Supreme Court to argue a dissent.

We have many bastardized legacies of the racial bias behind the original intent of slavery that remain unaddressed. Once slavery was outlawed segregation began, culminating in a legal right to separate but equal until this was struck down in 1954. Since then the GOP has pursued a willful effort to eliminate equality as an American right for women and their bodies, racial minorities, and laborers, as well as to eliminate equal justice, a right to fully negotiate wages, and perhaps most egregious, any right of folks who are entitled to these rights to equal representation in Congress. Additionally, the GOP partisan jurists so far have refused to settle the abuse of gerrymandering, and have returned it to the states that are the abusers of one man one vote rights as equal justice.

When advocates for women, racial minorities, and labor win control of the U.S. House as they did in 2018, they are not treated equally by the GOP as Representatives. The GOP has evolved into a stonewalling political mob in contempt of these Representatives and their constituents. Compare the Tea Party to the new Social Democrats; one has been seen as extreme, but for traditional norms. The women and minorities are treated with contempt as if they are not Americans citizens yet.

In the 1860s when the Fourteenth Amendment was ratified the drafters did not want to refer to black citizens as possessing equality even if they were free of slavery, thus the mischief that has ensued as the court has intentionally misused equal justice and the freedom intended for freed former slaves.

If corrupt intent is protected as free speech for corporations as "people" or "persons", we have a bastardized theory in need of review, not a reason to call for an end to judicial review. Today's GOP jurists actually always treat corporations as citizens of the United States regarding judicial review, but not always blacks if the dissenter is a black woman and the defendant is a U.S. corporation as in the Lily Ledbetter decision.

Let's review the Hugo Black theory of corporations' money as speech in politics, and original intent. Hugo Black was a Supreme Court Justice and former KKK member from South Carolina, who introduced spin as racial mischief to cover up a double standard of justice for blacks. He was proud of how his southern states had perfected this trick in writing the Fourteenth Amendment after the Civil War. Citizens of any state have Supreme Court standing as citizens of the United States. I do not know how corporations which are constructs under state law and are not citizens of the United States can have standing before the Supreme Court. Do we need to modify the law so the owners of corporations are sued in federal courts?

The Supreme Court does not deal in policies, but they do deal in outcomes. In the Reagan era I rate their outcomes as having done more harm to the many than good.

I believe the 2016 campaign portended a weakening if not the end of the current GOP Movement Conservative's Southern Strategy coalition. This would include the economic coalition of Wall Street corporate free traders, the Chambers of Commerce Main Street small business interests, and Neo Con military hawks. The only faction that is still more adamant are GOP nationalists, especially those who project the "rights" of white nationalists, and the evangelical wing that evolved from segregationist into faith based under a theory called the Southern Strategy. Under this strategy southern evangelical pastors became political activists, while daring any politician to take their tax exemption away; none have.

The American political divide is no longer purely a racial bias. It is more complex than that. This bias includes poor black folks, poor white folks, poor other folks, and anyone who advocates equality as an ideal. The GOP often refers to well off advocates for equality and justice for poor and working poor citizens as elites who support equality, but live as isolated from poverty as any segregationist did in the past. The term they often use is "limousine liberals", as if you can't be well off and have political values. The GOP as well as evangelicals to a large extent have made being well off an expectation of voting as conservatives.

Nationalists and conservatives advise rejecting any political policies that look like socialism. They also reject or at a minimum resent voting rights for non contributors to society, and support anti-immigration policies, while flirting with providing cover for racists. This branch of conservatism will continue to be a large and troublesome minority in what will amount to a separate branch of the GOP, just as the Dixiecrats were of the old Democratic Party of Strom Thurmond, or as the Tea Party continues to look more like every day in the twenty-first century.

Hopefully it may prove to be a short lived branch of the GOP that did not understand the 2008 crash or bailout, but found it easy to hate and blame poor folks who bought houses they could not afford from folks much smarter than them, who personally enriched themselves with every subprime variable rate mortgage they peddled with glee and glib and guile, and paid the politicians to leave taxpayer insurance in place.

At this point young evangelicals seem dismayed with both parties. I believe they are available to be recruited back into the Democratic Party if resolution of Supreme Court social issues can be found. Young evangelicals were seven percent less conservative in 2018 than evangelicals over thirty-five.

There is no way poor minimum wage folks without access to healthcare can believe, with an informed opinion, that the GOP with their corporate first concerns can or will be an advocate for the needs of the poor.

Today's trickle down is not much more than U.S. pre-revolution era gleaners' rights, as in the days of the divine right of kings. After the harvest peasants living at near starvation subsistence levels were allowed to enter the masters' harvested fields, and any stray grains lying among the chaff were available to be gleaned by the laborers for personal use.

The Democratic Party at the present time is well versed in the issues of discontent of folks who should be their natural voters. However, they have been as tin eared as their party's leader Debbie Wasserman Shultz was in 2016. In 2020 the Democrats still do not have a candidate or a message that is adequate to the opportunity of the outcomes of the Reagan era. For now the GOP pope seems to be William Barr. He and Senate Leader McConnell are upholding not the U.S. Constitution and not Donald Trump, they are upholding the ideology. If the GOP does not come to its senses or the Democrats do not find their soul again, our fate will be the same as Jefferson Davis's for the same reasons.

After thirty-five years of Reagan policy failures, the Democrats still have no better policy solution for the middle class on the economy than the GOP has on healthcare. The only things the two parties agree on at this point is remaining in gridlock, and using mutually agitated fear and hate to raise money.

The first Democrat to come along with an understanding of and the ability to define how and why working poor Hispanic folks feel they have been left out of the economy the Reagan era for-profit folks subjected them to, is Alexandria Ocasio-Cortez. AOC, as she is known to her plus eight million social media followers, is a young mixed race Hispanic woman bartender from the Bronx who graduated cum laude on scholarship from Boston University. Her first major piece of legislation is called The New Green Deal. It is a fourteen page condemnation of the Reagan agenda outcomes, tied loosely to the risks and opportunities of the real but as yet not fully agreed, climate mess impacted by fossil fuels. So far climate change is in gridlock, with the GOP denying the science in support of the fossil fuel industry, and the Democrats supporting clean water, air, and energy.

Even less well known is a Harvard and Oxford grad and young

former mayor of South Bend Indiana, who can actually articulate the problems the Reagan era left, as well as handle with balance questions about how to move on policy-wise from where we are. His name is Pete Buttigieg, candidate for president of the United States. Mayor Pete's fund raising indicates the level of his political skills. As the former mayor of his hometown, which is a majority black ex-industrial town in the Midwest, policing problems and his homosexuality seem to be the only impediments to national office from a conservative state, as the 2020 presidential campaign heats up.

Donald Trump won the United States presidency with a populist, nationalist message and a promise to drain the swamp, which my friends who voted for him interpreted to mean a wholesale house cleaning and overthrow of the whole Washington mess, which seems to mean the professionals who operate the government policies our Representatives vote for each congressional term and each annual budget cycle.

What Trump called draining the swamp, his first Chief Strategist Steve Bannon called the deep state, and promised to deconstruct it across the federal government. This squared with what my most rabid anti Obama and Trump happy friends called the need to blow the whole government up and start over.

This policy as a chief goal was not a campaign promise, and has not been debated legislatively or argued in the Supreme Court. In practice it has been impetuous, rash, ill-conceived, and often vindictive, from ignoring staffing, to immigrant children in cages, to tariffs doing more harm than good. Steve Bannon left the administration and his assistant Steven Miller became his replacement. Steven is if anything more brash and brutal than Bannon, which seems to suit Trump and his base to a tee.

In his first two years Trump attempted to put policies in place that confront the rule of law. It seems the swamp often had competent people enforcing legislated as well as administrative law. Trump seems as frustrated as his base; for sure he is not a skilled or patient legislator. Will his demand for disregard of the law in pursuit of expediency actually work, or will he fail and in the end be undone by the law? So far he has been more adept at choosing aides willing to flout the law, than he has been at finding staff who can convert his instincts into functional outcomes. At the end of his third fiscal year, two Supreme Court nominees who owe more to Mitch McConnell's sharp elbows than Donald Trump's presidential skills, and a tax cut engineered by Paul Ryan are about all he has accomplished that cannot be undone by the next president's pen.

Chief Strategist Steve Bannon was a self described economic nationalist reacting to the now globalized world economy. His three key areas for new policy making were promised to be:

1- Disengagement from Asian partnerships as unfair, such as accepting China's mercantile business model, a rejection of TTP (the Trans Pacific Partnership) specifically, and bilateral alliances, especially NAFTA in the Americas. At the onset of 2020 TTP and NAFTA have been abandoned.

2- Application of America first to sovereignty issues, including but not limited to borders, immigration, and access to our secrets: personal, corporate, and governmental. The Paris Climate Accords have been abandoned, as well as the Iran Nuclear Treaty.

3- Deconstruction of the administrative state. Trump and his supporters wanted to accomplish as much reduction as fast as possible without foot dragging. The plan has been implemented; the outcome has created chaos as a byproduct.

At CPAC (a GOP idea meeting each year) in February 2017, Bannon boasted that the Trump administration had placed uninformed unqualified secretaries in charge of domestic executive departments. He did not want experts fighting for more authority, he wanted leaders willing to deconstruct these departments who would agree to and carry out drastic reductions in funding and manning, if not total deconstruction. It reminds me of Goldwater's answer to the question about his new legislative goals: "I don't have new legislative goals, I have goals to cancel and reduce many legislated programs now on the books". This has created an odd intersection between the Trump base and the Charles Koch minions. Koch hates Trump personally, but loves the economic results of his anti regulations, and anti administrative state policies.

Bannon's wholesale number of cuts took place in the first six months simply by under staffing executive departments such as EPA and the State Department. Domestic policy ideas that are less than fully thought through are being implemented by Executive Order. The fallout is being spun, and chaos has become the norm. My friends who vote GOP admit they do not know the full extent of what if any damage is being done, but they still support their man.

Regarding national security it was noted by the FBI that many Trump advisers met with Russians in secret and when questioned lied about it. When confronted with proof (legal wire taps of Russian officials), at least four key advisers admitted they lied. No one has given any explanation of why they met with Russians and lied; based on Trump activities over the years it has been speculated he asked them not to mention it, as it would be taken the wrong way.

The lies led to appointment of a special Prosecutor named Robert Muller. Regarding the question of obstruction by the president's not allowing his aides to testify, the special prosecutor reported two facts that only Congress can resolve.

These facts in the final report are (1) the president cannot be indicted under current Justice Department rules, and (2) based on the facts found by the special prosecutor's investigation, the Mueller team is likewise unable to exonerate the president. Criminally the president deserves to be prosecuted and tried. There were up to eleven prosecution violations of the law, yet the solution cannot be accomplished by the executive branch or the Justice Department. Mueller told us that unless the Congress acts, the president broke the law, without consequence.

With 2020 an election year both parties seemed to be treating this as a political dilemma, more than a legal or rule of law issue. And then President Trump invited a new president of Ukraine to interfere in the 2020 election, and Trump was indicted, and impeached in the U.S. House; the trial was in the Senate in 2020, where the GOP holds a majority, and the Senate voted on party lines to acquit the president.

So at the end of our saga, most of the FDR/Truman/LBJ legacies are still in place, but the current Democratic Party does not take or get credit for that fact. They do not seem to even be able to explain what are Democratic values when discussing policy on TV.

President Reagan is still seen as the amiable and steadfast man he was, more than the unsuccessful policies president he also was, based on outcomes including national debt increases and middle class jobs and income losses. This tends to give us a one sided view of him as a hero, while the actual outcomes of his policies mostly go unmentioned or are blurred in spin.

I wish President Trump the same luck I wish a plane pilot. I hope a safe flight for us both, as my safe flight is dependent on his successful flight plan. That said I do not anticipate President Trump's policies will be sustainable. I understand from his book that those who have done business with him found him to be a mutual opportunity deal maker. He was very adept in the opportunity game of grabbing the winnings and walking away from the losses. I see him governing the country the same way, allowing the few the economic freedom to grab the winnings for his class, and leave the losses for the nation's many to absorb without a concern once again for economic justice for the losers.

In my mind, betting on Trump is like betting with a bookie who fixes the game to ensure he is always on the right side of the point spread, and believing his wishing you good luck is a sincere expression of his concerns.

In the end I find it an amazing feat for a national minority political party (about forty-three percent or less) to destroy what was a growing middle class, and burden the nation with more that twenty-two trillion dollars of debt, and yet hold itself blameless for nearing forty years, and spin it so well it has worked.

So far being the important message!

Summary

First, to end gridlock we as a nation must agree to fight to ultimate victory by one political side or the other, or agree to accept the wisdom of compromise and incremental progress.

As for the economy it comes down to either all profits above subsistence wages go only to the owners of wealth, or we develop a society where the price of goods and services include a cost equal to a living wage, attainable for most, along with sustainable taxes for government that are assessed equitably, with a trade policy that does not allow the balance of trade to soar out of control. The domestic economy must fund our government and our citizens as well as our corporations.

A living wage, perhaps with a minimum supplement as automation produces more and more wealth, with less and less labor. The living wage concept must provide access to all the basic necessities of modern life useful to the citizen and the nation, including but not limited to education, healthcare, retirement, safe mortgages and banking, clean air and water, safe food and drugs, and access to heat in the winter, cooling in the summer, all now as underfunded as our annual budget. Which means we must stop routinely intentionally cutting taxes less than required for Congressional appropriations, while looking to the safety net as the first place to cut spending. As dynastic owners of corporations retain more and more of the wealth, the ever increasing military budget cannot be funded by earned income taxes alone if the chief concern of foreign policy is not the safety and security of the citizens, but the wealth of corporations and dynastic wealth.

Pending equality of economic justice in America we must limit money as political free speech. We must require judicial review cases with rights in dispute to be returned to the national legislature for resolution of those questions of citizens' federal rights in conflict under existing law. In the end all abused rights must have a remedy.

Gridlock between civil secular law rights and religious beliefs has to be recognized for what it is, a threat to both religious freedom and individual rights. If the above issues are fought to the end and one side "wins" leaving the other side's rights abused, we will have destroyed the intent of the Bill of Rights.

The following suggestions are made with balanced outcomes in mind.

My last thought regarding understanding rights. In 1954 one of the most resisted court decisions in our history was Brown v Board of Education. All the court did was declare "separate but equal" unconstitutional, overturning a Supreme Court ruling from the 1890s. The real issue was segregation based on what was often called white supremacy. Equality of life, liberty, and pursuit of happiness defined the intent of the court's only jurisdiction in the dissent the NAACP brought to the court. Fifty states each reacted in their own way.

With this thought in mind I hope you will read and consider the following suggestions for working towards new better laws in compromise over the remainder of the twenty-first century.

My Twenty-first Century Policy Suggestions
(not in any order)

1. Immigration

Immigration has arguably been escalated into our number one factor of gridlock by President Donald Trump since 2015, yet I did not make it a major part of the book. The reason is we have a better solution in place than I can come up with. It passed the Senate in 2013 with more than sixty bipartisan votes. It was written by what became known as the Gang of Eight, four GOP Senators, and four Democrat Senators. It never came to a vote in the House, as the freedom caucus reminded leadership of the Hatch Act, and held Speaker Boehner in fear of ouster if he violated this internal GOP guideline, i.e. never bring a bill to the floor unless it favored by a majority of GOP members.

This ended the age old reality that sometimes a majority of one party and a minority of the other represents a majority of the citizens the total House represents. President Obama advised he would sign the bill into law if passed. I'm sure President Trump would not sign it into law if it was brought to the floor today, even if it passed both Houses this time. The Bill did not become law because of the Hatch Amendment, named for a disgraced former GOP Speaker of the House. My first proposal for the twenty-first century is, the next time we have a rational president, Senate, and U.S. House, we should reintroduce the same 2013 Bill known as the Border Security, Economic Opportunity, and Immigration Modernization Act of 2013.

It may need a little tweaking in conference, but it is ready to go; all it takes is a return to non absolutist compromise, and a return to a workable level of tolerance.

2. Gun Rights

Each individual citizen has a Second Amendment Right to gun ownership for protection of the citizen's home and self. This is not **an** absolute right. Each individual citizen has, per the Preamble to the Constitution, a right as an intent of the Constitution to expect justice, to be assured of domestic tranquility, and a promise the government will promote the general welfare, and common good for all citizens.

The modern GOP holds as an absolute partisan ideology that Second Amendment rights are or are nearly absolute. The modern holds a partisan ideology that the intent of both the Preamble to the U.S. Constitution and the amendment clause in the Bill of Rights supports equal justice for all in the pursuit of happiness as a latent right and a definable equality of justice in case(s) of conflicting rights.

In this second gridlock issue, I see a definable right in conflict with a definable expectation of what justice must acknowledge as an abuse. In court settlement of conflicting rights, there can never be a hierarchy of two Constitutional citizens' rights. As Marshall stated, "each right deserves a remedy".

Therefore my second suggestion is a request that we end the gridlocked Second Amendment conflict between those who correctly support gun rights in protection of their homes, persons, and families, as well as sporting, and range uses, and those who equally correctly advocate for children, parishioners, and citizens, students attending school, church services, or public events, to quietly pursue their education, salvation, or entertainment in venues free of assault by high capacity, rapid fire military style weapons, too often in the hands of under-vetted, unregistered, uninsured, careless gun owners or wielders.

American legislation and judicial review have a duty to settle this gridlock in a way that ensures both group's rights are brought into balance between assured freedom as well as assured justice, between the rights of individual gun owners to defend themselves, etc., and citizens' rights to protection from abuse, now addressed less than equally by their government in Congress or in the Courts.

At a minimum I recommend mandated requirements including as a burden for legal gun ownership, a lockable gun safe and/or trigger safety device on guns in the home, on their person, or in their car. I further suggest liability insurance should be a required purchase, issued only to state licensed owners, as the best and most common form of regulation regarding many legal devices that have both a useful purpose as well as a fatally dangerous downside if misused.

Before the modern era Seneca commented that "any good that could be used for a bad purpose is not an absolute right" and several of our founders' writings indicate they agreed. This is the government's just and police power basis for a right to regulate a good, that is also and has been ripe for misuse.

3. Labor Rights

Citizens who labor for wages have the same interest in the sale of their investment in skill and knowledge, as well as a return on their physical toil, as property owners have in a return on their debt or equity investment in profit or rent seeking property.

This includes workers' right to associate democratically, assess dues on all beneficiaries, elect officers to manage the affairs of their association, and the use of dues income to purchase legal representation in negotiation of the sale of the members' labor, and to fund all messaging and/or lobbying efforts on behalf of the members, as was granted as a Constitutional right by the Wagner Act in 1935.

The Wagner Act was weakened by the enactment of the 1947 Taft-Hartley Bill that ended certain Wagner Act federal rights of individual citizens who join labor unions. The Wagner Act empowered the states to enact right-to-work legislation banning all such actions in their state that were formerly allowed under Clause 7 of the Wagner Act.

The modern Republican Party promotes an ideology that property rights are absolute regarding employment terms including wages and conditions of all citizens they employ in domestic employment at the work site in the individual state of such employment.

Note: Right-to-work is a state law, and it prohibits each discrete union within their state borders from being part of any national union, or national contract with a national employer with sites in more than one state.

The modern   supports the right to associate, the right to representation, the right to negotiate using professional negotiators, the right to assess and collect dues, the right to negotiate wages, benefits, working and safety conditions, work rules, and for a closed shop with check off, and access to the federal courts equal to the rights of corporations as persons. They support this as a basic right for any U.S. citizen regardless of the state they live in. The U.S. Supreme Court should uphold this for all employees whose labor involves interstate commerce.

Court settlements must not only protect the rights of owners to manage their businesses and earn a return on their investment, the court must also assure that employees as citizens of the United Stares are assured non-abusive earnings rights equal to investment in the skills and/or toil needed to produce the owners' return as well as the citizens' cost of living, recognizing the fact that owners make all pricing decisions.

Therefore, the government or a collective bargaining agreement must ensure labor costs are adequately addressed within that pricing decision for labor involved in interstate commerce. Employers cite return on investment rights, labor must have equal rights to a return on their investment needed equal to the value they add to the employers' investment return.

Only the federal government can protect the balance of rights of all parties to each exchange between unionized employees and property owners, including government mandated labor costs such as healthcare, minimum wage, unemployment, and workers compensation.

As an honest broker the Court must accept the need for balance that ensures equality in resolving disputes between competing labor and employer rights.

In this historical review we have noted the overreach of labor unions at times, such as the Teamsters creating national shutdowns even in wartime for nothing more than a quick pay raise. We have noted the overreach of corporations such as GE refusing to bargain in good faith (Boulwarism) destroying jobs, families, small towns, even impacting the taxes required to defend the market that made the stock owners' wealth possible.

We have also reviewed the outcome of courts taking sides in settling modern complex cases such as Hobby Lobby where many rights were in conflict and the Court's choosing to establish a hierarchy of rights rather than returning the legislative hodgepodge back for legislators to sort out.

The Hobby Lobby 5-4 majority court decision was both abusive and unjust. In fact this settlement severed connection between the Bill of Rights and America's authority to govern by consent.

The five GOP Jurists voted against women's rights including an expectation of equality regarding tax law, equal pay rights, a right to privacy in making their reproductive decisions, all in conflict with the owner's newly defined latent religious right as an employer, which I agree was due for recognition.

Nowhere in any of the factors of the Hobby Lobby case was there mention of the legacy behind Obama's use of the payroll tax deduction. It was a racial abuse legacy in need of correction since 1951 when the payroll tax deduction for healthcare was enacted to exclude blacks under Jim Crow laws at the time.

Adam Smith and John Locke as well as Thomas Jefferson and Alexander Hamilton all agreed that wage labor absolutely at the will of the employer is tantamount to wage slavery.

I believe President Reagan's free trade decision in 1985 to open our consumer markets to China's wages without any Congressional hearings was in fact an abuse of labor rights in America, when he made the free trade decision without considering all mandated government labor costs that would be affected negatively, impacting millions of citizens who labor for wages. My suggestion below on a solution to healthcare funding in America would go a long way toward righting the impact of this GOP free trade policy made without due process in the legislature or the courts.

Note: the Koch Heritage Foundation has stated that their objection to food stamps is they do not help promote self reliance. More than two thirds of the folks on food stamps work full time for capitalist employers. I love the wealth capitalism creates, but there is no mechanism in it to allow employees to become fiscally self reliant no matter how hard or long they work at poverty level jobs. Two sides of the same coin that is controlled in absolutism by the employers at this time.

Two quick examples for understanding the "value added" factor in the production of wealth that provides the non controversial idea of the owners' and investors' "return on investment". First lets look at investors building and equipping a for-profit hospital. No one would consider making such an investment without also expecting to hire doctors, nurses, and support staff. Employees' contributions to this enterprise founded with a goal to make a return on investment, is what economists call value added. All of the staff have an investment in the knowledge, skill, and effort they bring as input that creates billable outcome, no less so the skill to drive a 50,000 pound eighteen wheel truck five hundred miles a day safely, and economically. The investment is skill and toil, different than a doctor, so is the pay. Professionals have power, semiskilled and common laborers do not. Less than a living wage is abuse.

Congress does not limit doctors' professional associations' ability to collect fees, spend money on lobbying, and so on. However, if the nurses join a union, Congress has severally limited their rights to bargain for a return on their value added. Second if a construction company buys a forty dollar shovel and hires an uneducated man with a strong back to be the value added component, Congress has all but stripped the union representing laborers from insuring a fair return for that man to be able to support a family however hard he works, as the Courts do not address less than a living wage that leaves a child in hunger as abuse.

In the 2020 Democratic presidential primary debates a new comer to presidential politics was Andrew Yang. He is notable as he has introduced a new concern for the living wage dilemma. The new factor is the loss of jobs to technology, including computers, programmable controllers, robots, sensors of many type, and so on. In fact automation in all its forms in the long term may even be a bigger living wage for all issue than the global economy has been to date. Yang's insight has become my new concern worth passing on: an annual income for all Americans similar to what the Saudi's with their oil wealth, as does Alaska. Candidate Yang is proposing a thousand dollars a month for every citizen; I'm not sure of the correctness of the number, but I believe the time has come to consider free education through college, free healthcare, and a supplemental income as an American birthright. This also means more pay for less work, if we are going to get all the work done in the future that will continue to be required. If our economy now produces plus twenty trillion dollars a year with less than full employment, then we need to address what that means to each new citizen from birth. The best gook I've found that explains what is happening is *A World without Work* by Allen Lane.

4.   Consolidated Federal Fiscal Year Budgeting Reports, and Year End Outcome Reporting.

The U.S. Federal Government has two primary tax systems. The first is the income tax funded general budget. Each individual's contribution is based on type of income, amount of income, and legal deductions; these taxes are used to fund all general expenditures of the federal government as appropriated by the U.S. House of Representatives and approved by the Senate and the president.

The federal general fund payments can be funded with income tax proceeds, or the federal government can borrow to fund any deficits between the tax rate set by Congress and the amount Congress appropriates each year for federal government expenditures primarily by the executive departments, and to fund the appropriated contracts once they are settled and due for payment.

The second tax system is the FICA tax budget and year end report. This tax funds the two programs that make up the U.S. old age and disability retirement social insurance (Social Security) and healthcare programs (Medicare). These are social insurance **programs meaning** entitlement is earned, as opposed to welfare programs that are not earned and are funded out of the income tax general fund.

The FICA tax is a mandatory payroll tax program funded half by American employee earnings up to a defined maximum, and half by their employer (this is another mandatory payroll cost in the United States that President Reagan ignored when he unilaterally granted China access to export their slave labor content merchandise to compete against citizens' retirement funding base).

The Social Security Trust Fund trustees manage these two programs. By law they cannot borrow money; the trustees advise Congress each year of the status of the surplus available for the coming year(s). Congress sets the tax rate and the rules of eligibility for these programs. The trustees cannot raise this tax, only Congress and the president can. The look ahead informs the number of years the current income and savings will be able to meet the current payment rate. If income does not meet outflow, the program does not go bust or end, it continues at the funding rate the tax supports at that time. This system plays no role in the debt of the interest bearing loans that were loaned against the future taxation on the income of citizens and corporations in America. The bonds sold to fund these loans on the faith and credit of the United States is a promise each generation makes to tax itself or obligate future generations to fund. The GOP, as an ongoing policy for forty years, has chosen to fund these loans as an obligation on future generations of America as a selfish opportunistic, and obscene theft of their descendants' future

The U.S. federal government's year end report is published by the Treasury as a "consolidated fiscal year end report". At the end of 2018 the FICA tax fund was in surplus by nearly three trillion dollars, and its operating budget was in surplus by nearly four hundred billion dollars.

The 2018 federal general ledger report funded by income taxes or federal borrowing was in debt by nearly twenty-one trillion dollars; the 2019 operating budget deficit was over eight hundred billion dollars in deficit. Yes, you read that correctly, the Social Security fund is in surplus, and one hundred percent of the total current federal debt is due to tax cuts, enacted to produce less income than appropriations approved by the Congress and Republican presidents since 1981 in all but five years of a Democrat president. The GOP has cut taxes on purpose three times; each time caused deficits of at least half a trillion dollars for ten years since overspending less than one trillion dollars has occurred up to 1990. From 1981 to 2020 GOP policy has cost plus twenty trillion dollars of new debt.

The GOP spins the debt issue in the Social Security Trust Fund use report, which is required to report the actuarial status of the fund based on current factors, meaning the fund builds up surpluses, and uses current cash flow as well as the surplus to project the long term viability of the fund at current payouts.

The GOP could make this point clearly if they chose to, but they mix the two reports, ignore the actual debt their current policies create, and bash the possible debt in the future the Social Security Trust fund will face if Congress does not act at some time, if cash flow becomes less than the then current payout rates.

However, if they fail to act, it will not create debt, it will create a political hazard for any future politician who does not address the cuts that inaction will require at that time. By law if the Trust has less cash available than the then in place payments due it cannot borrow, it must cut the payments proportional to the shortfall. The GOP already mis-states redemption of Social Security surpluses loaned to the government to fund income tax cut shortfalls. The GOP calls new loans to reopen the Social Security bonds entitlement caused debt, an absolute lie.

The U.S. has been engaged in wars the GOP declared for over seventeen years as I write. During that time the GOP enacted a tax cut only two years before going to war in Afghanistan. That tax cut is still in place, and the GOP cut taxes a second time fourteen years later. This has required both GOP presidents and a Democrat president to borrow to fund the wars.

Of the seventeen years of war, the GOP has controlled both the U.S. House and Senate fourteen years and has never once in all those years proposed a rethink of borrowing to fund the wars. The GOP increased military spending refusing to tax to protect the nation. The wealthy establishment families support this future debt while funding political messages to avoid their duty. More unpatriotic in my mind than avoiding the draft.

Consolidated reporting distorts and hides the true status of each tax system, as well as the health of the retirement system, and the true nature of the federal debt reality. Budget sanity will not return until the two tax systems are once again returned to separate reporting as they were before the Vietnam War funding cover up under LBJ that ended separate reports.

I recommend a return to the U.S. Treasury preparing and reporting separate budget and final fiscal year income tax based general revenue reports each year, and separate Social Security Administration trustees year end reports.

This will allow the concerns and the fixes to be analyzed, based on who pays and who collects within the two tax systems. Since Ronald Reagan was elected in 1980 the Social Security tax has increased as salaries have stagnated, while the income tax rate has been lowered as the productivity and profits of the corporate world have risen. Thus one is over funded and borrowed from, as the other is under funded, both in the dark and both subject to more heat than light in political debate.

5. Federalism

Federalism is in my opinion the least well understood of any of the federal programs. I'm suggesting we re-think, change, and greatly reduce the free ride that certain low tax, low education investment, and low wage states have chosen to inflict on the rest of the nation which the GOP has chosen to fund in the dark in exchange for the votes of these intentional state welfare cheats.

Federalism was a founding concept used to build post roads and ports. The program did grow over the years; however it was reinvented by President Reagan to funnel hundreds of billions of dollars a year into block grants from economically successful states who over fund a fair share of the federal budget year after year

470

relative to their own state's basic needs, as a form of welfare transfer payments. The two intents of block grants was to end oversight, and blur the amount, the recipients, and how it is distributed. It has succeeded to meet Reagan's intention perfectly.

To help readers understand this gross unfairness consider Donald Trump's attack on the funding of NATO. He has been exactly right about the unfairness of the USA's share of the burden. The Federalism program is as unfair to the twenty states who fund the United Sates budget and credit worthiness, and as undeserved by the small government opportunists in the thirty states that do not contribute a single net dollar to the sustainability of the large states who do.

Let's start by fully explaining what block grant federalism does, and why it is such a large federal budget buster. Federalism as it now exists is a set of more than six hundred billion dollars of annual spending programs that redistribute income tax revenue from the twenty states that fund all U.S. government spending each year. These twenty mostly blue states actually provide one hundred percent of America's cash flow, as it is the credit rating of these twenty prosperous states that provide the total credit worthiness of the United States.

This will remain true as long as the GOP pledge to never raise taxes for any reason which they've been supporting for over thirty five years. The pledge for no new taxes remains in effect and is still taken by nearly all GOP legislators every two years. Besides the wealth created by the twenty most prosperous states, America's ability to raise taxes is still a factor, but without the will to tax citizens and corporations more than we do now there is an impact on American credit worthiness, so for now all the taxes we spend as well as all the interest we spend on the GOP debt is funded based on the fiduciary steadfastness of the twenty prosperous states.

That the GOP has shut down the nation more than once and refuses to tax sustainably is destructive to the future options of the young and unborn who will inherit this end game funding of these disastrous policies.

In the system our founders revolted against the only concern for sustainability was of the dynastic inheritors of property. In the U.S. Constitution of our democratic republic, sustainability is the goal for each citizen as well as the nation, but not of the property owners. Our system allows for personal risk taking and loss. Donald Trump spent his whole life pursuing this right. Our founders did not offer him the same rights once he opted to become the chief fiduciary of the American experiment.

None of the thirty intentionally poor states contribute a single net dollar to the federal treasury each year, and most have not since the income tax was created over one hundred years ago. Not only do they not fund the federal government, not even a dime goes towards the military budget; they do not and cannot fund basic subsistence standards for the bottom forty percent of the U.S. citizens who reside in each of these states, who can mostly be defined as the working poor.

These intentionally poorer states could not borrow a dime of the money their representatives vote to require the federal government to borrow each year, based solely on the tax flow and credit ratings of the high tax and wage states.

The Senators from each of these states however relish shouting their disdain for redistribution of wealth when it comes to welfare in America, a term they claim to hate as rugged self responsible folks. However in the dark of the cloak closet they somehow enrich their friends back home, and themselves it seems over time.

But when it comes to feathering their own nests and those of their sponsors, created on the backs of their own intentionally low educated and paid citizens, these mostly GOP politicians know no shame. In my mind this is a form of abuse the Bill of Rights was enacted to prevent. In fact the Bill of Rights was intended to protect citizens from any form of abuse, by any level of government in America. It is long past time this intentional abuse of poor folks across America ended.

States with a tradition of low wage and low tax ideology tend to support GOP policies, at least as they are defined using partisan spin.

There are a number of primarily red, right-to-work states that do not support and will not tax to fund Medicaid for the working poor and unemployed citizens, or to adequately educate children in low income districts, at least adequate to the needs of a modern economy, or to subsidize the nutrition, housing, transportation, or warmth in winter for their under educated and under employed citizens and their children
.

In fact they argue this is not a proper function of government. Men of the modern GOP such as Barry Goldwater, and former Arkansas Governor Mike Huckabee claim this is based not on the U.S. Constitution, but on the Christian Bible revelation of divine rights, dismissing our Bill of Rights that are based on the God of Nature as defined in our Declaration of Independence which was based on the philosophy of natural rights, replacing divine rights in our national Constitution. Remember the founding generation left divine right assumptions in state common law unaddressed. It is long past time to sort this out, and correct the record once and for all.

In these low wage, low tax, right-to-work state systems, the unmet costs of subsistence level education, healthcare, housing, nutrition, and transportation are subsidized via the income taxes of the states that do have political systems that support sustainable tax investments in their citizens. Many corporations have as a business model dependence on millions of low income employees subsidized by the tax payers in the same twenty prosperous states, none more that Wal-Mart and McDonald's.

This is intentional opportunism. It is time to end it and force reality on those states that operate this way. These same states intentionally limit ballot box access, and gerrymander to ensure lopped-sided representation by the minority of citizens who prosper from this system.

The federal government can and does set minimum standards of sustainability and rights that make up the promise of life, liberty, and the pursuit of happiness in our nation. There have always been states that cannot or do not consent to provide these minimally acceptable standards of American life. Over the years the federal government developed programs to fund these social tragedies and oversee them in these so-called poor states. The factors of poverty in each state receiving subsidy is to a significant degree dependent on the political policy outcome of low taxes, low cost education, and low wage employment. A high poverty level state over a long number of years is a political decision, what the GOP calls public choice policy making, only practiced at the state level instead of the federal level.

Reagan's Block Grant Federalism program also reduced federal oversight, allowing these subsidized states to enjoy the economic and political benefits of a safety net, while not having to tax their own citizens, while scolding that welfare is socialism. This was Reagan's most successful domestic program; however it is a time bomb waiting to explode.

These states enact right-to-work laws loved by corporations that do not consider a living wage concept in setting prices nor give employees the right and means to negotiate for a living wage including healthcare, as the Democrats' empowered hourly wage folks had at the time to form unions with negotiating rights. The Democrats also enacted employer provided healthcare as a tax free benefit in 1951 (a de-facto right for whites only at that time), if their union or business employer chose, or it negotiated to provide it.

Food stamp cards, Medicaid, and subsidized housing among other programs make up the intent of these subsidized states' welfare transfer block grants. I do not expect to see an end to the Senate system (two from each state regardless of population that also skews the presidential electoral college). I do expect to see an end to gross misuse of federalism that unjustly supports low wage and low tax states' policies, as well as adding to unending debt at the federal level, while blaming Social Security as the cause of GOP tax cut debt. That debt is actually caused by over funding military spending, creating interest on their debt, and subsidizing profit for corporations taking advantage of poverty level wages via block grant federalism, while cutting taxes.

Like the consolidated budget, these costs become blurred between who pays and who benefits. The Reagan argument spin was that states know better what their citizens need, perhaps the biggest partisan spin of all, as that is not how it is allocated by the poverty tolerant states.

State politicians who campaign on a promise of small government should not be able to vote for low taxes, and then expect their federal representation to redistribute block grants from successful large states with sustainable higher taxes, wages, healthcare support, and education costs, that generate high income tax receipts. States' wealth or poverty outcomes are based on those intentional ideological public choice policies. In the subsidized states not all citizens live in poverty; employers, well paid professionals, and well funded retirees enjoy the savings.

In the twenty-first century Reagan's federalism block grant resets have played out since the 1980s when he instituted this blue state wealth redistribution that ever more states have adopted, even if they are not traditional poverty states such as Kansas and Michigan.

The does support federalism, both monetary and other. The difficulty will be to divide the assistance actually received by the poor with how GOP governors use federalism without oversight.

The federal government will have to replace these block grants with vouchers or some other form of funding directly to the recipient or the healthcare provider, or school, or social service provider directly, with oversight.

Note: In Europe federalism was a key factor in for England in Brexit. There are four net contributor countries among the givers who call themselves the frugal four, that resent the takers and may also wish to leave the EU ; however, the reason behind the friction is different than in the U.S., not a matter for additional discussion in this book.

6. Universal Healthcare

Universal healthcare means providing healthcare services for all U.S. citizens, as well as safe emergency care for all persons found to be sick or injured with assured privacy for all involved in such care. Affordable fully funded access to healthcare is the most serious economic and social crisis in twenty-first century America.

Our current for-profit healthcare system that typically only partially insures most Americans but not all, is at least fifty percent higher and as high as double the cost per citizen served than any social insurance system currently in use among all of our large nation trading partners, yet it leaves some ten to fifteen percent of citizens totally uninsured, and another forty or more percent under insured, especially in families with a member who has a preexisting condition.

Converting our under regulated, and out of control expensive for-profit system offers the largest single cost savings available that our nation can institute in the twenty-first century; yet it remains the single most fraught issue with racial baggage and misinformation of all other political issues in America.

Aversion to a universal single payer healthcare system, or for that matter any role for the federal government in healthcare access or funding, except the employer tax break, is absolute and dead on arrival in today's GOP.

This GOP aversion is the majority position of voters in at least twenty-four states that claim to favor low taxes and self reliance. They blindly disregard the cost and desperation of healthcare until faced with a health emergency themselves. This false belief in an ideal of self reliance, negating support for a universal common good this nation can afford, is the most irrational voting pattern I'm aware of among my own family members. Even when faced with such a situation and rushing themselves or a sick child to the emergency room, a service they will never pay, they still vote what is taught by their local conservative Christian politician and/or pastor.

The GOP loves to lionize state government and demonize the federal government, so let's see if they are ready to move basic healthcare funding and administration to the states, as they will almost for sure have to if Block Grant Federalism is ever totally eliminated.

Social insurance using government's ability to set the maximum funding to be paid for all families with less than six figure incomes has proven to be successful in industrialized large population nations around the world, who are providing free basic healthcare for all citizens, and emergency healthcare access for immigrants who are always legal if employed, as the employers can get work permits, where refugees are treated humanly.

High wage individuals are still able to purchase supplemental, catastrophic, or boutique healthcare services. The GOP calls such affordable and workable systems "socialism", as if any government role is the same as a government owned and operated total economic system without recourse, which is a true socialist government.

The current GOP ideology called public choice (rarely discussed publicly) has a core principle in support of for-profit healthcare only, based only on an absolute market based ideology, ignoring all of the negative outcomes.

In 2017 the GOP proved it was unable to define a market solution to the full cost of health insurance for all if it included full coverage without a large premium for pre-existing conditions including high end pharmaceuticals, compounded by over investment in facilities, equipment, and physicians in high income cities, while rural and/or low income areas' healthcare needs remain under served.

Note: the GOP solution left the administrative cost of their preferred for-profit health insurance industry unaddressed, a key source of campaign funding for politicians of both parties. In the end the GOP disregarded the extra cost of administration, advertising, and lobbying.

Over three quarters of all Americans are partially insured, and a small minority are fully insured under an employment tax break that was granted to white employees of corporations in 1951 to avoid funding healthcare for blacks in the Jim Crow era, as noted above. Remember, Jim Crow ended in 1964, but the healthcare legacy effect on black folks' healthcare was left unaddressed then as now. Another item I've noted often, for a reason; it needs to be fully understood by all Americans.

Few Americans even know how healthcare employment based tax breaks in today's global economy started in the first place. In America it is a legacy of southern state segregation after WWII. Blacks did not become fully employable by corporations and unions until 1964, and parity in pay and benefits is still disparate.

Also in 1964 a new payroll based system was instituted to ensure healthcare access for retired Americans who qualified for Social Security. This, like the payroll funded tax break for employees of corporations, was discriminatory, but it worked for those it covered until 1985 when President Reagan instituted free trade access without tariffs for goods and services earmarked for social programs that work in other countries under VAT tax systems, among favored nation trade partners.

This access was granted without considering America's payroll funding realities. This was possible because President Reagan did it not as a request to the legislature which would have led to hearings, but as a presidential prerogative by executive order, without a second thought by the GOP about the outcomes, then or now. At this point in time not even the Democrats remember their history of common good social insurance outcomes.

It is manifestly true that low paying service corporations have no appetite to fund healthcare for their employees, such as McDonald's, Wal-Mart, and other such large employers with a business plan based on low paid hourly workers often employed by franchise owners in these very large corporations.

McDonald Corporation loves to advertise they are the best first job; however if you eat at McDonald's during the day or late at night you will notice that most of the employees are not teenagers, or first job young adult folks. They are either low paid career employees, or low paid working age folks who work part time at two or more jobs. Many are heads of families without funded healthcare access, dependent on welfare, despised by even those who receive it, and more so by those who misunderstand the reality of forty years of Reaganomics and who believe welfare funds an easy free life style to those too lazy to work.

The fast food corporate model depends on millionaire owners owning multiple units if they are good operators, meaning they can manage thousands of low paid employees, subsidized by the high cost of federalism funded education, Medicaid and food stamp cards in poor states (as addressed above in suggestion 5. Federalism), and state tax funded welfare in large prosperous states, all as much a subsidy to corporations as to the poor overworked, underpaid, career employee, subject to daily misinformed outrage.

In 2018 more than twelve percent of all families remained totally uninsured, other than to be made stable in emergency rooms and then released, in spite of the success of the ACA (Obamacare) program in constraining the historical rate of annual increase in the cost of for-profit healthcare in America. Annually the cost of healthcare in America advances at least double the inflation rate, while minimum wage rates have remained stagnant for more than two decades.

Another factor of free trade that is almost never mentioned is the reality that the labor content of imported manufactured goods pays nothing into America's payroll related taxes including hourly based income taxes as well as funded healthcare, FICA, and state programs that cover the cost of unemployment insurance and worker's compensation.

The GOP mantra extolling the idea of self reliance rings hollow in such an economy. The solution has to be some form of shared cost where all pay in, and all earn access according to ability to pay, which is what the defines as social insurance, and collects on a pro rata basis.

Despite not having a policy maker as capable as Frances Perkins since the New Deal era, the has not established a think tank where the focus is to work out the econometrics of such an outcomes.

So what's left as a way to fund affordable healthcare in America?

I suggest we choose a dedicated consumption tax, either a national sales tax or VAT tax. Everyone is a consumer in one way or another with money they earned or that is spent on their behalf. So all pay, and all earn a right to access healthcare, funded by federal sales tax on all goods and services of domestic origin or from the global economy.

Who should collect this dedicated sales tax? I believe it should be the states. If we want our basic healthcare system for all to cost no more than the most expensive among our trading partners where ever in the world, each state needs to enact a twelve percent sales tax on everything purchased in that state, regardless of country of origin and whether it is purchased in a store or on the internet.

We have two requirements for such a system I believe. First, it must be the same rate in every state, so states with lower incomes based on labor rights and employment costs will have lower gross sales because those citizens have lower incomes, meaning everyone in such a state will also have less healthcare dollars available, which will open their eyes to the reality of what low taxes, poor education, and low wages really cost.

The gross revenue per citizen will be different state to state, but it will not be due to an offset for wealthy folks. There will be no tax savings in poor states if all states must collect twelve percent; buying big ticket items such as airplanes and yachts in low tax states will not be like regular sales taxes, instead this twelve percent will be earmarked for healthcare funding only, and must be paid to the state the luxury asset is domiciled in.

Second, because low income folks in all states will be impacted by the regressive effect inherent by sales tax, the impact must be factored in with a voucher system to address this disparity, issued directly to the lowest income folks with refunds for a portion of their taxes, or via some form of a supplement, or a card that allows it not to be charged at the cash register as an exemption. There must be a retinal scan or other biometric authentication to use the card.

My preferred solution to funding would be to base the buying power in each state on the twelve percent dedicated sales tax whatever the total economy of each state, divided by the number of citizens. This will determine the voucher amount for each citizen as their share of the funds, to be used to buy either a market insurance plan approved by the issuing state, or a regional or national plan licensed to offer a plan in the citizen's state.

The only other federal role would be to set the minimum requirements for healthcare insurance to be offered to each and every American citizen regardless of their state of residence. The federal government would subsidize the cost of each voucher in any state too poor to fund the minimum health plan if twelve percent of a poor state's economy will not fund the cost between the state revenue and the cost of a basic plan in that state. This transfer payment would be in support of citizens, not the state of residence, and unlike today's federalism block grants would be issued direct to the citizen.

I have chosen not to address abortion as a discrete suggestion item in spite of its level of contribution to national gridlock. If healthcare reverts to the states, abortion healthcare questions will also revert to the states. The federal civil right that currently grants women a right to seek abortion is based on a woman's latent constitutional right to privacy regarding family planning issues. This right to privacy must remain a federal right. Some states will not fund abortion and they may even find a way to outlaw it. However, it will be difficult to prosecute if none of the doctor-patient relationship is open to questioning even by subpoena under federal privacy rights.

The offset for the new tax to be paid by all consumers on all goods and services regardless of origin within the global economy will be the reduced cost to employers and government taxing entities no longer funding healthcare related costs for employees, pensioners and current low income beneficiaries within the federalism system. All employment based healthcare funding in America will end for corporations, for private employers, for states, counties, cities, and the federal government.

No federal or state income tax or property tax would be required to fund healthcare in the future, except for the modest cost of any shortfall should any state's economy be too small to meet a basic plan cost. All of the above listed tax systems would be reduced accordingly.

A portion of these reduced costs must become increased take home pay for employees, lower property taxes for homeowners, and lower rent for those who live in apartments, based on newly lowered landlord property taxes, regarding an end to both active and retired employees' healthcare costs, and city, county, or states for teachers, police, firefighters, and all other public employees.

Ensuring that the newly reduced cost of healthcare for employers, both public and private, is shared with employees to address the reality of now having a higher cost of twelve percent on all goods and services, will take some mandated input either in each state and/or nationally through the introductory years.

The hodgepodge of payroll, FICA, pension, and low income program spending for healthcare currently absorbs eighteen percent of GDP. As these funding sources are phased out, the new consumer funding source in each state would be freed up for other distribution channels such as wages, profits, education at the state level, and hopefully even debt reduction at the federal level. Tax revenues on employees' increased incomes would offset any cost of subsidy in low wage states.

This would all but end true for-profit healthcare in America. The insurance options for each state would include a federal option, most likely the Obamacare exchanges or the Medicare administration. States could create their own state rules on insurance, granting access within the twelve percent tax, and the minimum national standard program.

It means the healthcare industry would have to tighten its belt by six percent over the transition phase. This is a lesser contraction for the healthcare industry to absorb than the impact of free trade effected costs for the rest of the economy since the 1980s, both non-healthcare industry, and hourly wage family income.

The current inequities between generations of retirees, families raising children, and young adults funding the cost of education and dealing with wage stagnation are all addressed in this suggestion. All children in low wage families would finally have healthcare.

Insurers would operate as for-profit competitors within the budgets of the states they do business in, or operate as non-profits, allowing the industry to remain market based at some levels. The healthcare profession would be required to work out their new relationships and funding options from the current bloated cost over an agreed phase out/phase in number of years.

The cost of too many drug stores, and too many medical buildings filled with corporate employed doctors seeing up to two thousand patients a year, many of them more than once a year for fifteen minutes each, will subside; appointments would be available with your primary care doctor, instead of waiting six months if you are actually sick, or being referred to the emergency room. Rural hospitals will be able to pay an income equal to the cost to attract candidates to rural areas.

Large wealthy states such as New York, California, and Texas may choose single state systems. I can see perhaps between eight and fifteen regional systems, if not fifty.

The U.S. tax base is depressed a bit by the more than seven hundred billion dollars the U.S. imports versus what is exported each year. I believe that the sales tax on these imports sold in the U.S. will help resolve some of the trade-off issues. Everyone will be paying in, even those now living in the under the table cash economy. As a trade off, U.S. exports will be lower cost, which should improve all aspects of the trade balance equation.

Note: For-profit healthcare is a legacy of deregulation (HMOs), and not a presidential order. However, President Reagan's ideology all but ended anti-trust concern in America, driven particularly by the heirs of the Wal-Mart fortune who funded the legal battles to defang antitrust enforcement in the 1970s and 1980s. This fit the Koch Network's public policy ideology (public choice) that was first adopted by President Reagan.

Non-profit healthcare faded, and the rate of cost increases doubled over the past thirty-five years versus pre Reagan rate hikes. Under this system every doctor's office and every hospital would be required to publish a menu of services and their costs, based on full average final pricing as established by each state, (not each item such as pill, x-ray, and so on within the service); these costs would be negotiated, and in the end settled by the states, as other insurance product rates are regulated as a common good.

For instance, once the state rate is established, this will be the set rate for every knee replacement in each hospital, and will not vary from place to place. This will greatly level healthcare cost inequities, as well as duplication of investments in large cities; this will also create a more just system of clinics and public medical transport to regional hospitals for visits with specialty doctors or for expensive treatments.

The best market idea the GOP ever had about healthcare costs was the HMO system; it helped for about twenty years after Richard Nixon signed it into law, until Bill Clinton signed the Balanced Budget Act in 1997. The outcome was to let the HMOs cherry pick who to insure; hospitals were hurt, and millions of non-profit hospitals sold out to for-profit systems, who as independents could set up cherry picked options for employers, while running tight budgeted levels of Medicare and Medicaid if they so wished .

Note: I do not know if it was intended or not, but HMO's destroyed non-profit hospitals in America as thousands of non-profit hospitals closed or bought by for-profit systems. This ended the Catholic, Baptist, Lutheran, etc. hospital systems and replaced them with Wall Street funded corporations.

7. Education Spending

The only truly critical federal educational needs at the public school level K-12 are science and math including digital based systems courses, and/or tech training for students with mechanical aptitude who are headed for enlistment in the voluntary military, or hoping to become skilled in a trade. This is usually funded by the employing industry or the federal government in other competing industrial global economy nations.

As noted previously, President Eisenhower, as the Allied Commander in Europe during WWII, was fighting a highly mechanized war with Germany and Japan and found his troops' education was lacking. American high school graduates did not have the basic education needed to be ready for complex mechanical and electrical training. Both Germany and Japan were very science oriented and had no offsetting concerns about religion based on revelation being in conflict with science education. In the U.S. today the tensions between secular and religious belief systems in America are often fought at the local school board level.

Many young persons choose the military for a career, as poorer school district graduates usually have fewer college and/or career options than wealthier districts. As an option addressing a number of issues encompassed in this suggestion, I propose the following.

I suggest the federal Education Department be eliminated, except for a technical education department as required by the U.S. Military, to be established within the Defense Department as Ike originally suggested. Education would continue at the local district level as originally proposed at our founding by Thomas Jefferson; at that time there was no educational role established for the national government.

All high schools in the nation would be required to participate in the new elective technical education program. The Defense Department would determine where this program would be provided based on the size of the district and the number of volunteer applicants with test based aptitudes to meet the cost benefit ratio developed by the U.S. military.

The U.S. military has long used aptitude testing to qualify recruits for Military Occupational Skill training with great success. I personally took these tests my first week in the army and like many friends over the years my own career was greatly influenced and enhanced by this early training.

The courses would include practical technical level mechanic courses designed by the Department of Defense, as well as academic science and math courses. This would be a four year plan; enrollment would be by application, testing and acceptance by the Department of Defense, beginning at the high school freshman year, or as determined by the Defense Department.

Teachers and/or military specialists would be part of the local school system as the needs of the service dictated. Any military teacher would be subject to the local school administrator's oversight regarding use of facilities. The school districts would be compensated for all costs including a fair share of capital and operating budgets affected by the military's needs.

Such classes would count for credit depending on content. In addition to funding the schools and teachers, those students who chose to enter this program would also receive a meaningful stipend, and thereby owe the U.S. Military a standard enlistment into the military specialty they studied to qualify for. These courses could also be offered as adult education courses if the military and local school boards agreed. No student under eighteen years old could enter this program without parental consent. If a parent declined to consent, the student when eighteen would be allowed to apply at the community college level.

I believe this would be a win-win for the Defense Department, the graduates' post service careers, and the private employment sector once these knowledgeable and skilled veterans complete their technical military enlistment duties. Some would enter the private sector after serving a basic enlistment, and some would choose a career in the military; all of these trained technicians would be of value to the nation for their entire working career, and would provide their families enhanced opportunities for living wages.

As the only cultural portion of the training would involve the norms of the discipline the student trains for, and of the U.S. Military, the social conflicts should be minimal. Both public schools and private schools would be eligible. All supplies including labs, books, computer hard and software would be supplied by the program. The only government oversight would be by regional military staff assigned to the program.

All other concerns of the federal Education Departments including legal and economic issues if seen to require continuance would be transferred to the Justice, Treasury, or other Executive Departments applicable to the concern.

8. Civilian Service Corps

A similar training program to the Department of Defense program could be established to fund education for services in rural and poor under served localities. I recommend the Labor Department to develop an education and training experience for non academic students, to prepare them for semiskilled employment needed by all rural communities at the city and county level. This education and training could include farm and forestry skills as well as road, sewer, water quality, and storm sewerage maintenance. Healthcare technicians and service jobs could be part of this program including elder and preschool care.

Labor Department funding of these training programs would interface with local high school curriculum development related to education and gaining experience, as well as providing needed services in rural communities, and also providing first work experience in under served areas of the nation. These trades and services would be made available to America's non college or military bound high school teens in poor school districts in low tax and wage states that have high school dropout rates.

If skills training were available it would provide an incentive for students to stay in school in those school districts too poor to offer vocational training. If the program included a stipend for students willing to accept a four year commitment in rural services after graduation, the program could again be a win-win for the communities and the students as teens, as well as adults later in life.

Shop, mechanical, agriculture, building, maintenance trades, as well as licensed or permitted grooming, home care, and medical specialties, etc. can all be taught, with a stipend for not much more money than is now wasted on non academic but capable students who become costly due to dependence on social services, the cost of prisons and parole, or the cost of the opiate crisis. Graduates would owe a number of years of living wage service in under served communities, especially in health departments and city services; then they would move on with experience added to their training while still in their mid twenties, just as the outdoor skill set would, as addressed above.

Staffing shelters, rehab facilities, day care centers and home confinement are all areas of possible employment for young folks who demonstrate empathy for and interest in such areas of care giving. Building exterior maintenance, grounds and equipment maintenance and facilities, as well as driving and vehicle and equipment repair, clerical and data entry support, and institutional food preparation are all examples of traditional employment opportunities that have lost funding as public choice taxing has eliminated such job opportunities at the city, county, and state level in much of rural state America. Savings at the federal level from reduction of federalism and welfare healthcare costs can be re-directed to these seeming make-work but in fact needed services across the nation that do not have a current source of funding.

9. Social Security

This suggestion is to keep the Social Security System currently in place, and allow the Trustees to raise the amount subject to FICA every five years to assure sustainability in line with changes in national productivity and cost of living. Social Security can only remain viable if the cost of living increase mandate now in place also becomes a mandate for Congress to assure the Trustees are able to meet the additional cost of this mandated funding, from wage laborers who no longer enjoy cost of living adjustments, or a rise periodically in the minimum wage base pay, or have a right to join a union with authority to operate in a manner competitive with corporate boards. I believe raising the upper income funding level to $250,000 per year will seriously address the wealth and income gap that has been widening for forty years.

10. Environmental Protection Agency

I suggest all major polluters of any type, defined as a business that pollutes and generates over one hundred million dollars a year in revenue must meet minimum federal standards to continue in business. Failure to comply for three annual sample periods in any ten year period would cause loss of their license to do business, without appeal upon the third failure to comply. This would include officers and board members. Businesses would be fined at least ten percent of the market value before the fine, and they would be required to sell to the highest bidder less the cost of a reserve to remediate the damage.

11. Voter Rights

My eleventh suggestion regards fair and just individual representation in the U.S. House of Representatives. I have just two things to say about voting rights; gerrymandering is not justice, and absence of justice is abuse. The second I address below, but it is not for the legislature. It is my only suggestion for a new amendment to the Constitution. It addresses voting as a right.

Regarding gerrymandering, it must stop or we are no longer a democracy nor a just nation. If you oppose democracy in the name of economic freedom, you are an enemy of the Constitution, which is a term dating to the Greeks in the time of Pluto meaning justice. There is a name and a consequence of that already; as so many say about immigration and guns, "it's time to apply the laws already on the books".

12. Sustainable Taxation

Since 1981 under the theory of economic freedom, an ideology of low taxes (as opposed to sustainable or adequate taxes, equal to appropriations), the GOP has budgeted and taxed based on their ideology, without consideration of the needs, size, sustainability, or wealth of the nation, or regard for the amount of national debt relative to the size of the economy, or the fairness to future generations.

A rule of thumb in evaluating unsustainable debt among nations is a ratio of one-to-one. In 2018 America ended the year with a nineteen trillion dollar economy and a twenty-one trillion dollar debt. We are at the threshold of unsustainable debt, without serious threat of high inflation. The true number is actually hidden in the consolidated year-end reporting I addressed in Suggestion 4.

At a minimum GOP policies have led to under funding infrastructure, debt repayment, education of the lower third of all school districts, the safety net for poor families especially with hungry children, and affordable higher education. I'm sure readers could add to this list.

A good example of ideology impacting a basic need is infrastructure, the building and maintaining of federal roads and bridges, grids, and so on. The first federal gas tax earmarked for roads and bridges was enacted in 1932, for .01 cents a gallon. It was last raised in 1993 to 18.4 cents a gallon; it is not indexed for inflation. The inflation between 1993 and 2018 in the United States was equal to more than sixty-five percent.

In 1993 American automobiles averaged less than fifteen miles per gallon. Today they average more than twenty-eight miles per gallon; the tax is still frozen at 18.4 cents a gallon. The average hourly wage of a road builder when the tax was last set was under fifteen dollars an hour; today it is over twenty five dollars an hour. The net funds per mile of road available for new and rebuilt roads has been cut by nearly seventy percent over the past twenty-five years; the outcome is obvious to all drivers.

We see this outcome in inadequate roads and unsafe bridges. The current GOP idea is private for-profit road construction and , a more costly solution as a travel solution for those who work for less than a living wage. For-profit roads are another example of the GOP's economic freedom public ideology called public choice. This ideology calls for for-profit solutions for public needs, instead of common good government utility solutions. The object is to increase the wealth of the few in America, without regard for the loss of wealth for the many. This is exactly the opposite of the goal set by our founders when they stated a key goal of the federal government was to provide for the common good and established justice.

The simple idea that taxes as a concept are always bad needs to be realigned with the true cost of governing a mobile transcontinental society. The ideas of debt financing and privatization have created more cost problems than they have solved as well as service to the citizens in prisons, hospitals, schools, and so on, and needs to be a factor in budgeting for the next seventy-five years.

13. Judicial Review

Regarding the Supreme Court, any dissent accepted for adjudication that impacts more than two conflicting individual rights and/or property rights must be returned to the legislature for mandatory resolution of the conflicting rights, if a remedy for both is not possible in the Court.

An example cited in this book is the Hobby Lobby case. This case is a perfect example of the United States' long legacy of conflicting laws, masking cultural solutions that in the process denied justice. In 1948 Harry Truman attempted to pass a universal single payer healthcare bill. It was voted down along cultural (Jim Crow) lines. Truman vetoed their decision and the legislature overturned his veto.

In 1951 without a vote the IRS granted corporations and unions with hiring halls a tax exemption for employer provided healthcare insurance (in 1951 corporations and unions did not usually employ blacks or sustain employment for women who became pregnant).

In the early 1960s the birth control pill was invented and declared safe by the Food and Drug Administration for women's use. For the first time in history women had a safe and assured method they could use to legally plan their families; it was a medical solution and it was a healthcare and health insurance issue. Truman made it an employment issue for white middle class women when the pill was approved, without any notion of such an outcome being possible a dozen years after his decision to tie health insurance tax relief to corporate employees.

Most women were not covered by health insurance for this cost. In 1964 women and blacks both gained full civil rights equality; it required employers to hire blacks and women gender and racially blind. It also gave women a constitutional right to plan their families in private with their doctor. The Civil Rights Bill further required women to be treated the same as men regarding pay and benefits including funding prescriptions; birth control pills were dispensed by prescription only.

Note: Access to these rights was still less than fully equal for all.

Employers still retained the right to decide which doctors were included in their plans, and what procedures and prescriptions were covered. The employer did not have to fund birth control pills yet, but the women would buy them without a tax break. Even in 2020 the uninsured face a higher price for private pay prescriptions than insured corporate employees, an outcome I still view as abusive legislative discrimination.

The Robinson-Patman Act disallowed higher prices for one class of consumer over another from 1936, another FDR policy. This Act became moot when President Reagan lowered regulatory pressure. It has not been repealed, and it did not always apply to individuals; it remains another discriminatory outcome of healthcare law.

In 2010 President Obama enacted the ACA healthcare bill which mandated employers of a certain size to fund healthcare for employees. It is still the law, and still does not provide regulated prescription pricing for all Americans.

Hobby Lobby is a crafts and home goods private corporate retail business grossing plus four billion dollars of sales a year, with more than thirty thousand employees. The corporation was required to provide healthcare for employees under President Obama's ACA legislation. This case has been noted twice earlier. In 2014 in a five-four partisan decision the GOP Court ruled in favor of granting the corporation an exemption under the religious freedom statute.

Thousands of women lost not only the funding they qualified for as employees, they also lost access to the discount employment insurance they were entitled to, and the tax exempt portion of the out of pocket money they spent. A level of denial of equal rights that was equal to abuse.

As noted earlier this case involved Constitutional law, labor law, medical law, freedom of religious exemption from having to commit a sin, individual privacy rights, price discrimination law as drug companies in the U.S. are allowed to charge lower prices to group buyers of drugs than to individual buyers. It also sanctioned tax law inequality. The court ruled only on the owner's religious freedom to the neglect of all other factors of abuse incidental to their decision.

The tax break the owner family derives from being incorporated when it comes to shareholder returns remains in place, as do all other personal protections for being an individual private owner of the business. The ruling was based on a new twenty-first century Constitutional partisan decision that corporations are persons, I assume as corporations got the tax break, not the owner who has the religious freedom, not the corporation. This was not an original intent of the founders, as corporations are a state not a federal jurisdiction. No consideration was granted to the abused woman for her Bill of Rights assurance of justice (a remedy) from government inflicted abuse.

The court did not find for the owners' religious beliefs; they had to find for the corporation's religious beliefs as the tax exemption was only granted to the corporation, not the owner it seems. Corporations do not have an individual vote yet, so they do not grant authority to govern at the federal level, yet five learned men voted to grant authority to abuse female citizens to a corporation to allow government abuse of a citizen, to prevent a religious man from sinning who considered the corporate action would be his sin by God. I'm pretty sure the intent of religion is not tax exemption, it is salvation. I am also pretty sure that God does not judge the sins of corporations, but it might be a more just world if He did.

There are two or three Constitutional issues here, as well as a few legislated laws in conflict. The president and/or the legislature, i.e. the United States government, should not create such mishmashes without considering the consequences and whose ox is being gored. But under gerrymandered laws the GOP jurists currently feel free to create these civil unjust outcomes.

This level of gridlock in America is hostile to the intent of established constitutional justice. This level of neglect of individual rights in conflict are casually ignored. We are mired in quicksand: moral, cultural, legal, and ethical, affecting our avowed love of freedom and justice. We can do better, and it is time!

GOP evangelicals have launched a defensive war in America without having been attacked, and the Supreme Court has gone along with it.

493

It seems to me the Court must establish under which concept of God in America they adjudicate: the God of revelation authority to govern we rebelled against, or the God of nature we avowed to govern by authority in our Declaration of revolt.

In all of our founding documents from the Declaration of Independence which is the only one that mentions God, to our Bill of Rights granting natural rights that flow from the nature of the universe God created, as understood after the reformation and the enlightenment found the authors of revelation to have been fallible. This was the understanding our founders intended when they founded a secular form of government.

How does the Supreme Court adjudicate in favor of an employer's belief in sin based on revelation which is his personal right, and how does the employer have a greater claim than the Constitutional right of the women who are granted a secular right in a commercial relationship concerning in effect a tax on a commercial establishment licensed to do business in interstate commerce? The enterprise being taxed is an institution created by the state, is it not? Does the Bill of Rights not prevent a state licensed entity from abusing the right of a citizen of the United States, over an employee(s)?

If our natural right to liberty in America was granted as an understanding of the limited role the God of creation extended to His creatures, and not the state church revealed law of the Roman's Biblical Christian God, how was the shielded owner's right to believe in sin of greater standing than the employee's right to a secular tax exemption?

The Godly slogan on our coins does not define one distinct belief system regarding God in America, other than nature's God who represents secular natural right, with no defined taboos, memorialized by bishops as sin.

American law both civil and criminal is a police power of the secular state in our Constitution is it not, and not a enforceable religious doctrine accommodating intolerance of any other American's differing belief system relative to sin?

The religious freedom act used the Biblical Christian concept of God, as well as revealed sin over the natural freedom due the free women of America who do believe in contraceptives, as allowed by the God of creation. If there is a dissent worthy of adjudication it is how the religious freedom act was legislated and judged. We have not settled the dispute between common law advocates and judge based law, ever.

Our nation's commitment to justice is part and parcel of God having granted humans liberty to be free. That is the understanding of the U.S. Constitution, and the authority to govern bargain the GOP seems to deny or ignore. The Democrats have chosen not to fully protect U.S. citizens, as we remain in cultural gridlock, and are not advocating for labor, birth control and tax exemption justice. I mentioned in the introduction the friction inherent between state common law and federal statute law, in settlement by the judges of the Supreme Court. Judges proposed by the GOP in the twenty-first century adhere to common law beliefs that pre date the Constitution since the ratification, enactment, and adjudication of the Bill of Rights. It is time this mess was settled.

It is time we settled the question: what concept of God was our nation founded under Constitutionally? Was it Biblical Christianity or nature's God the founders cited in our Declaration of Independence? If anyone would argue they are legally the same God, how does religion established at Nicaea have standing before the U.S. Supreme Court over the secular rights of the Hobby Lobby women denied their tax break? One government granted absolute authority over subjects to a crowned autocrat, the other established justice for free citizens.

It is time our federal court ruled on Constitutional law, not state corporate rights, or Biblical Christian revelation based on pre-founding concepts of sin, or the Christian God's authority as absolute.

14. Speculative Banking Using Depositor Funds

We must end speculative banking using insured bank deposits, and uninsured operating funds overnight (so called repos) to fund any form of bank capitalization, or any form of deposit insurance. We must end government guarantees on all forms of mortgage banking unless the insurance is tied to adequate regulation and oversight (underwriting regulations).

This nation should never use any credit instrument not regulated by the U.S. federal government, and no dollars should ever be used as repo overnight capitalization reporting, for any bank or any form of lending more risky than a treasury bond.

Since 2000 I have seen so called repos being used each night to report capitalization of risk instruments for another day in the global economy, then repeated nightly for years. I used to buy overnight six figure repos through my local commercial bank using my working capital back in the 1980s and 90s. By the mid 2000s the world needed working capital to open for business each morning that was in fact loaned out at risk in support of a bit higher return for the so called Masters of the Universe.

In 1983 President Reagan assured us that bankers knew better how to lend money than bureaucrats when he deregulated the risk side of the Savings and Loan industry while leaving deposit insurance in place. W did this again in the Fannie and Freddie deregulation collapse. This placed Wall Street bank employees, money market customers, and investing customers all at risk without oversight, without a share in the upside for the American taxpayer, yet at risk for all the loss on the downside. We covered both the debacle of the Savings and Loan and the Freddie and Fannie bailouts all funded by U.S. taxpayers as GOP policy in Chapters 9 and 10.

At a minimum there should be a heavy social insurance premium on each transaction (like FDIC insurance on bank deposits in the U.S.), equal to the cost of the 2007-2012 collapse. This would be so costly it would put an end to risking the liquidity of the global economy for the benefit of the opportunistic few, using other peoples' money.

I suggest no division of a non American bank outside the U.S., and no American bank inside the U.S. could use repo dollars to capitalize a risk outside of the U.S. No non U.S. bank could use repo dollars that originate inside the U.S. or from a U.S. corporation or bank inside or offshore to capitalize any lending anywhere in the world more risky than a U.S. government bond.

This must be legislated, compliant with the regulatory departments of the executive branch of the U.S. government, and enforced with all of the tools made available to the U.S. Federal Reserve in all of its dealings with the international banking settlement regimens that the United States is a party to. Working capital must never again be the funding source of U.S. speculative capitalization of high risk bonds. I do not see that clearly assured under the Dodd-Frank Act.

My intent is to ensure that American families, home owners, small businesses, as well as all federal and state chartered bank depositors are protected from the downside of any investment risk greater than FDIC underwriting standards. No speculative scheme can ever again in the United States expose the FDIC insured sector of the economy without a stake in the rewards. The GOP went crazy when Obama allowed the U.S. to act as lender of last resort to save jobs, and to allow taxpayers a return if the jobs were saved. They were and it did, but the GOP is still scapegoating the success of Obama's effort.

No speculative risk investment in the U.S. must ever again expose any citizen with a cash net worth of less than two hundred and fifty thousand dollars to any uninsured risk, subject to being made whole as the punishment for creating such a lending instrument that arises in the dark, as it did in credit default swaps, repos, and derivatives beginning unregulated in 2000, all becoming capitalization for Alt A and subprime mortgage bonds, yet subject to government guarantees via Freddie and Fannie and other such Government Sponsored Enterprises (GSE).

The George W. Bush crash was many times more costly than the hundreds of direct dollars the Reagan crash cost the American taxpayers, and the reduction in net worth to tens of millions of ordinary American savers, home owners, and small businesses and small business owners.

15. Religious Freedom

This may sound similar to the Hobby Lobby discussion but it approaches this very gridlock prone contention from another direction.

I'm suggesting that we reestablish Madison's insight that led to religious freedom in America, which replaced what was at that time in America a limited form of tolerance based on the diverse ways each colony had been established. Only by making freedom of belief a right would citizens be assured of their rights regarding religion; even non-belief was to be free of abuse, as established in Virginia by James Madison before he became the Father of the U.S. Constitution and its first ten Amendments, known as the Bill of Rights. Intolerance must replace hate as a definition of crimes based on identity abuse or disregard for secular intolerance. Love and hate are extreme emotions; tolerance is the duty level of the Constitution's secular rights intent; it should be so designated.

16. Constitutional Right to Vote

My final suggestion is my only suggestion for a Constitutional Amendment. As a nation with authority to govern based on the philosophy of "By the Consent of the Governed" in our democratic republic a right to vote should be a foundational right.

Our next amendment to the Constitution should establish the right to vote as an inalienable right for every American citizen eighteen years or older without limitation except for treason.

Last words

At home: Reagan's most famous speech was "A Time for Choosing". It's now time to choose FDR versus Reagan's outcome goals, or find a new set of goals for a new era, and then find the policies to defend, based more on the goals and less on absolute belief systems or ideologies that disregard established justice or common good and established justice outcomes.

Internationally: As this book goes to print in early 2020 America has 60,000 human targets in uniforms stationed in the Middle East as President Trump plays chicken with Iran and neither side has any good options. Thirteen hundred years ago Mohamed died, and Islam divided the peoples of the Middle East between Shia and Sunni sects. One hundred years ago England and France, with America's agreement, redrew the borders of the nations of the Ottoman Empire without regard for the thirteen years of animosity between the sects, and the various other peoples of the region. Only the interest of the three victorious allied nations mattered. They were first and foremost for all three the oil they all needed for their navies. Second was England's wish to control the Suez Canal for access to India. Third was a settlement solution for the Jews of Europe. Unsaid was England and Frances idea of colonialism. President Wilson had a 14 point plan that did not become a major part of the outcome.

It is time to let the peoples of the Middle East redraw the map of the Middle East. Two things related to the settlement of the Jews must be the only insistence of the United States, and that is the factors Harry Truman insisted on as his price for settling the lingering Israeli question from WWII; a two state solution to the Israeli vs. the Palestinian impasse, and it must be agreed to by all. Israel keeps its 2020 borders, and the fake nation of Jordan created by England and France with a ninety-five percent Palestinian population and a Hashemite ruler must become the independent nation of Palestine, with an elected government.

It is time for a new generation, and they must find their leaders and their rational boundary goals, and compromise to find policies to build on, only if the outcomes accomplish more good than harm in each era. Harmful outcomes must be acknowledged and addressed.

Coming out of the twentieth century, the century of FDR and Reagan, it is time for the future leaders of America to chose which philosophy of governance to build on between the blue v. red values on our title page.

Tom McGrath; January 2020, in my eightieth year.

Email address: AmericanGridlock2020@gmail.com

Dedications

Tillie Fischer McGrath, my Jewish mom who always insisted her kids could do anything if they stuck to it; we mostly proved her point.

John Francis McGrath who taught labor must demand their trade union bargaining unit representatives negotiate a living wage; just as stock holders must demand their Board of Directors negotiate a return on investment equal to insuring sustainable new investment.

My wife: Carol, who like most wives suffers from SSF (spousal storytelling fatigue), who walked me through about five rewrites, a dozen introductions, and several edits before it finally felt like my story. In fact I could not have written this book in a manner that would have been understood by anyone but a policy wonk if not for Carol's patience and wisdom.

My daughter: Nora Robbins, an Evangelical Christian author. Critiquing these tales from her point of view helped me understand the difficulty honoring secular rights if the activity allowed is seen as a sin against God; she and I debated the alternative in a nation with too many of each to ignore the dilemma, and key issues of gridlock easier to debate than resolve. I make the case there will be no peace in America if the pastors do not find a solution; civil politics cannot solve or accept intolerance as a civil constitutional norm.

My step daughter, Sheryl Smith. First an editor, also a fellow believer that improving tolerance and compromise is essential. Sheryl, more than anyone over the past three and a half years, has been the creative editor . From the font, to the flow, to the look and style of the book I owe it all to Sheryl. I never knew how many details there were to turn ideas and stories into a book. I have no idea how many hours Carol (my wife) and I have put into writing the book, and doing the final editing of content, spelling and grammar. Sheryl has put in almost as many. In the end, the single most important help from Sheryl was pushing me to keep it readable. All the errors that remain, I claim as my own. It is hard to get an author to freeze his creation, and make the end the end.

My daughter-in-law Sandee Kurtz, who created the front, back, and spinal cover designs and helped launch the book.

My grandchildren and great grandchildren, those here and those to come, who might read their great great-grandpa's view of his world late in life, and marvel at both how much things change and how little people change.

Lastly, voters who believe they "just want their country back" without realizing what the impact would be on all of us.

Made in the USA
Columbia, SC
21 February 2020

88175085R00280